W9-ALL-726

Fodor's 2008

15d
pb

CHICAGO

WITHDRAWN

Where to Stay and Eat
for All Budgets

Must-See Sights
and Local Secrets

Ratings You Can Trust

EAU CLAIRE DISTRICT LIBRARY

Fodor's Travel Publications   New York, Toronto, London, Sydney, Auckland
www.fodors.com

FODOR'S CHICAGO 2008

Editors: Heidi Leigh Johansen, Sarah Sper, Adam Taplin, Erica Duecy, Stephen Heyman

Editorial Production: Bethany Beckerlegge
Editorial Contributors: Kelly Aiglon, Jay Cheshes, Elaine Glusac, Wendy Kasper, Roberta Sotonoff, Judy Sutton Taylor, Jessica Volpe
Maps & Illustrations: Bob Blake and Rebecca Baer, *map editors*. David Lindroth, *cartographer*; William Wu; Adam Cohen, Earth Data Solutions. Additional cartography provided by Henry Colomb, Mark Stroud, and Ali Baird, Moon Street Cartography
Design: Fabrizio LaRocca, *creative director*; Guido Caroti, Siobhan O'Hare, *art directors*; Tina Malaney, Chie Ushio, Ann McBride, *designers*; Melanie Marin, *senior picture editor*; Moon Sun Kim, *cover designer*
Cover Photo (Millenium Park): Kim Karpeles
Production/Manufacturing: Angela McLean

COPYRIGHT

ISBN 978-1-4000-1795-9

ISSN 0743–9326

SPECIAL SALES

This book is available at special discounts for bulk purchases for sales promotions or premiums. Special editions, including personalized covers, excerpts of existing books, and corporate imprints, can be created in large quantities for special needs. For more information, write to Special Markets/Premium Sales, 1745 Broadway, MD 6-2, New York, New York 10019, or e-mail specialmarkets@randomhouse.com.

AN IMPORTANT TIP & AN INVITATION

Although all prices, opening times, and other details in this book are based on information supplied to us at press time, changes occur all the time in the travel world, and Fodor's cannot accept responsibility for facts that become outdated or for inadvertent errors or omissions. So **always confirm information when it matters,** especially if you're making a detour to visit a specific place. Your experiences—positive and negative—matter to us. If we have missed or misstated something, **please write to us.** We follow up on all suggestions. Contact the Chicago editor at editors@fodors.com or c/o Fodor's at 1745 Broadway, New York, NY 10019.

PRINTED IN THE UNITED STATES OF AMERICA
10 9 8 7 6 5 4 3 2 1

Be a Fodor's Correspondent

Your opinion matters. It matters to us. It matters to your fellow Fodor's travelers, too. And we'd like to hear it. In fact, we need to hear it.

When you share your experiences and opinions, you become an active member of the Fodor's community. That means we'll not only use your feedback to make our books better, but we'll publish your names and comments whenever possible. Throughout our guides, look for "Word of Mouth," excerpts of your unvarnished feedback.

Here's how you can help improve Fodor's for all of us.

Tell us when we're right. We rely on local writers to give you an insider's perspective. But our writers and staff editors—who are the best in the business—depend on you. Your positive feedback is a vote to renew our recommendations for the next edition.

Tell us when we're wrong. We're proud that we update most of our guides every year. But we're not perfect. Things change. Hotels cut services. Museums change hours. Charming cafés lose charm. If our writer didn't quite capture the essence of a place, tell us how you'd do it differently. If any of our descriptions are inaccurate or inadequate, we'll incorporate your changes in the next edition and will correct factual errors at fodors.com immediately.

Tell us what to include. You probably have had fantastic travel experiences that aren't yet in Fodor's. Why not share them with a community of like-minded travelers? Maybe you chanced upon a beach or bistro or B&B that you don't want to keep to yourself. Tell us why we should include it. And share your discoveries and experiences with everyone directly at fodors.com. Your input may lead us to add a new listing or highlight a place we cover with a "Highly Recommended" star or with our highest rating, "Fodor's Choice."

Give us your opinion instantly at our feedback center at www.fodors.com/feedback. You may also e-mail editors@fodors.com with the subject line "Chicago Editor." Or send your nominations, comments, and complaints by mail to Chicago Editor, Fodor's, 1745 Broadway, New York, NY 10019.

You and travelers like you are the heart of the Fodor's community. Make our community richer by sharing your experiences. Be a Fodor's correspondent.

Tim Jarrell, Publisher

CONTENTS

ABOUT THIS BOOK

Our Ratings

Sometimes you find terrific travel experiences and sometimes they just find you. But usually the burden is on you to select the right combination of experiences. That's where our ratings come in. As travelers we've all discovered a place so wonderful that its worthiness is obvious. And sometimes that place is so unique that superlatives don't do it justice: you just have to be there to know. These sights, properties, and experiences get our highest rating, **Fodor's Choice**, indicated by orange stars throughout this book.

Black stars highlight sights and properties we deem **Highly Recommended**, places that our writers, editors, and readers praise again and again for consistency and excellence.

By default, there's another category: any place we include in this book is by definition worth your time, unless we say otherwise. And we will.

Disagree with any of our choices? Care to nominate a place or suggest that we rate one more highly? Visit our feedback center at ⊕www. fodors.com/feedback.

Budget Well

Hotel and restaurant price categories from ¢ to $$$$ are defined in the opening pages of each chapter. For attractions, we always give standard adult admission fees; reductions are usually available for children, students, and senior citizens. Want to pay with plastic? **AE, D, DC, MC, V** following restaurant and hotel listings indicate whether American Express, Discover, Diners Club, MasterCard, and Visa are accepted.

Restaurants

Unless we state otherwise, restaurants are open for lunch and dinner daily. We mention dress only when there's a specific requirement and reservations only when they're essential or not accepted—it's always best to book ahead.

Hotels

Hotels have private bath, phone, TV, and air-conditioning and operate on the European Plan (aka EP, meaning without meals), unless we specify that they use the Continental Plan (CP, with a Continental breakfast), Breakfast Plan (BP, with a full breakfast), or Modified American Plan (MAP, with breakfast and dinner) or are all-inclusive (including all meals and most activities). We

always list facilities but not whether you'll be charged an extra fee to use them, so when pricing accommodations, find out what's included.

Many Listings	
★	Fodor's Choice
★	Highly recommended
⊠	Physical address
✦	Directions
⌂	Mailing address
☎	Telephone
🖷	Fax
⊕	On the Web
✉	E-mail
💷	Admission fee
☉	Open/closed times
Ⓜ	Metro stations
☐	Credit cards

Hotels & Restaurants	
🏠	Hotel
🛏	Number of rooms
☐	Facilities
⍣○⍣	Meal plans
✕	Restaurant
✎	Reservations
⟍	Smoking
💷	BYOB
✕🏠	Hotel with restaurant that warrants a visit

Outdoors	
🏌	Golf
⛺	Camping

Other	
🅒	Family-friendly
⇨	See also
⊠	Branch address
☞	Take note

Experience Chicago

WORD OF MOUTH

"There are so many things to do in Chicago that it would take weeks to choose my top picks. Architectural tours, museums, zoos, nightlife, theater, dancing. . . ."

—JJ5

"I highly recommend a walking tour with Chicago Architecture Foundation. Check out www.architecture.org."

—Scout12

CHICAGO PLANNER

The Second City?

New Yorkers will tell you theirs is the greatest city in the world. But Chicagoans beg to differ. Chicago's charm is indisputable—the impeccably clean streets; the Midwestern-friendly vibe; the alluring mixture of lush parks, Lake Michigan, and slick skyscrapers. It's what keeps the debate going (log onto the Fodors.com "Talk" forum and check out one of the "favorite city" debates!), and what keeps everyone coming back.

Word of Mouth

"Chicago is fabulous! The architecture is positively amazing. The people are friendly. We found the city very clean and beautifully landscaped. Prices are more moderate than New York City. Though streets were busy and full of people, there weren't the mobs of New York." —djkbooks

"While I love New York City, Chicago is amazing, especially around the holidays. Spend your time visiting the neighborhoods. If you want to include some great shopping, you must visit the Wicker Park neighborhood and Lincoln Park boutiques." —allure

Getting Around

Chicago has an excellent network of buses as well as trains, which are collectively called the El (for "elevated," which many of them are). The combination should bring you within ¼ mile of any place you'd like to go. Those with city smarts will find it safe to take any train, any time. Others may want to take extra caution after 11 PM. Buses are almost always safe; there are several express buses running from downtown to destinations like the Museum of Science and Industry.

As of this writing, the fare for any bus or train is $1.75 and a transfer is 25¢, or $2 if you're paying cash. Travelers may want to get a Visitor Pass at their hotel, the airport CTA stations, or any visitor center. These passes allow unlimited rides for a small fee and are worth it as long as you take three trips a day.

For directions to specific places via public transportation, for public transportation maps, and for locations to buy transit passes, see ⊕ www.transitchicago.com.

Three free trolley lines (Navy Pier, Water Tower Park, Museum Campus) circulate downtown attractions. Originating at both Ogilvy and Union Metra stations, with a transfer point on State Street near Macy's, they run every 20 minutes from 10 AM to 6 PM daily. Service begins on Memorial Day and runs through Labor Day. More information is at ⊕ www.cityofchicago.org/transportation/trolleys.

If you drive downtown, park in one of the giant city-owned parking lots underneath Millennium Park or by the Museum Campus, which charge a flat fee. Private lots usually cost double.

A Few of Our Favorite Things

What do Fodor's editors do when they head to Chicago? Here are a few of our personal picks. We love walking along the Chicago River and watching the boats ply the water, then strolling down State Street to the old Carson Pirie Scott building, just to admire the iron scrollwork outside. We gallery-hop in River North, and duck into cute boutiques along Oak Street. We head to Hyde Park to gawk at the colorful, noisy monk parrots. We never leave without indulging in deep-dish pizza. We won't tell you which baseball team we cheer for, but we do love going to the games. And at night? You can find us catching the blues at B.L.U.E.S., going to an outdoor concert (we've seen great ones at Grant Park), howling at Second City improvers, or having drinks at the Signature Room at the John Hancock.

Visitor Centers

Chicago Cultural Center (✉ 77 E. Randolph St., at Michigan Ave. ☎ 312/744–2400 or 877/244–2246 ⊕ www.877chicago.com or www.choosechicago.com ⊘ Weekdays 10–6, Sat. 10–5, Sun. 11–5).

Chicago Water Works (✉ 163 E. Pearson St., at Michigan Ave. ☎ 877/244–2246 ⊕ www.877chicago.com ⊘ Daily 7:30–7).

Millennium Park Welcome Center (✉ 201 E. Randolph St., in the Northwest Exelon Pavilion ☎ 312/742–1168 ⊕ www.millenniumpark.org ⊘ Apr. 1–Oct. 1, daily 9–7; Oct. 2– Mar. 31, daily 10–4).

When to Go

June, September, and October are mild and sunny. November through March ranges from crisp to bitter, April and May can fluctuate between cold/soggy and bright/warm, and July and August can be either perfect or the deadly combo of high heat–high humidity. That said, the only thing certain about Chicago's weather, according to locals, is that it will change. If you head to Chicago in warmer months, you'll be able to catch some of the fantastic outdoor festivals; during the holiday season, the city's decked out in lights.

Local Know-How

Most businesses in Chicago are open 10 to 6. Some shops stay open as late as 9. Restaurants can be closed on Monday and usually stop serving around 10 PM on weeknights, 11 PM on weekends. There are a few 24-hour diners, but they are more rare than you might expect. Bars close at 2 AM or 4 AM.

You can avoid the long lines at Chicago museums by buying tickets online at least a day in advance. The most popular architecture tour, led by the Chicago Architecture Foundation, always sells out—be sure to buy tickets in advance.

TOP CHICAGO ATTRACTIONS

Sears Tower Skydeck

(A) Take the ear-popping ride to the 103rd-floor observatory, where, on a clear day, you can see to Michigan, Wisconsin, and Indiana. At the top, interactive exhibits tell about Chicago's dreamers, schemers, architects, musicians, writers, and sports stars. Kids love Knee-High Chicago, a 4-foot-high exhibit that has cutouts of Chicago sports, history, and cultural icons at a child's eye-level. Security is very tight, so figure in a little extra time for your visit to the Skydeck.

John Hancock Center Observatory

(B) The third-tallest building in Chicago has the most impressive panoramic views of the lake and surrounding skyline—it's high enough to see the tops of neighboring buildings in vivid 3-D, but not so remote that you feel like you're looking out from a plane. Our tip? Skip the observatory and head to the bar that adjoins the Signature Room restaurant on the 95th floor—you'll spend your money on an exorbitantly priced cocktail instead of the entrance fee and enjoy the same view. Women, head to the 95th floor ladies' room for the best view in the whole building.

Shopping on the Magnificent Mile

(C) Exclusive shops, department stores, and boutiques line the northern half of swanky Michigan Avenue. Even better, the concentration of prestigious stores in vertical malls means you can get a lot of shopping done in winter without venturing into the bluster outside.

The Blues Scene

(D) Explore jumping North Side clubs, like Kingston Mines, or South Side venues, like the Checkerboard or Lee's Unleaded Blues (where greats like Muddy Waters and Buddy Guy first honed their talent), for the sound Chicago gave birth to—the

scintillating electric blues. If you're here in June, don't miss the Chicago Blues Festival, which packs in fans every summer.

Navy Pier

(E) Yes, it's a little schlocky, but Navy Pier is fun, especially for families. Everyone can fan out to shop in the mall, play minigolf in the Crystal Ballroom in winter, see a movie at the IMAX Theater, or explore the Chicago Children's Museum. Plus, there's a stained-glass museum, a maze, and a 3-D ride that whizzes through scenes of Chicago. Meet up later at the Ferris wheel for a photo op or just settle on the pier with a drink and enjoy the view.

Art Institute of Chicago

(F) This Chicago cultural gem has the country's best collection of impressionist and post-impressionist art. It's also a great place to see all those paintings you've only seen on postcards, like *American Gothic* and *Nighthawks*.

Adler Planetarium & Astronomy Museum

(G) How can you not enjoy the snazzy 3-D sky shows at the country's oldest planetarium? Older children and physics fanatics get geeked about the interactive science exhibits and the high-tech Sky Pavilion, while younger visitors get a kick out of the cultural exhibits.

Field Museum

(H) Say hello to Sue, the Field's beloved gigantic T. rex, before immersing yourself in this extraordinary museum's collection of anthropological and paleontological artifacts and animal dioramas. The dinosaurs are the thing here, but surprising collections of items like Tibetan Buddhist alters, mummies, and the re-creation of famous gems may entice you to linger for hours.

Museum of Science & Industry

(I) Travel down an elevator to a "working" coal mine, walk down the cobblestone streets of old Chicago, explore the caves of a human heart, or watch quietly as a baby chick pecks its way out of its shell at this unusual museum.

Shedd Aquarium

(J) We find the experience of watching entire universities—not just schools—of fantastically colored fish, as well as dolphins and whales, completely mesmerizing. Don't miss the Wild Reef exhibit, where stingrays slide quietly under the Plexiglas at your feet.

Frank Lloyd Wright Architecture

(K) Frank Lloyd Wright's Prairie School captured the flat, expansive Midwestern plains he saw around him. Oak Park, a Chicago suburb, has many fine examples, though one of the best is Robie House in Hyde Park, which is open for tours.

Millennium Park

(cover) Make a beeline for Frank Gehry's **Jay Pritzker Pavilion,** where an incredible sound system allows audiences to enjoy concert-hall sound in the great outdoors. The *Bean* is a luminous polished-steel sculpture that plays tricks with the reflection of Chicago's skyline.

SOAKING IT ALL IN: RIVER & LAKE TOURS

Coursing through the heart of the Windy City is the majestic Chicago River, lined with some of the city's finest architecture and dotted with river walks and restaurants. Hop in a boat, kayak, canoe, or gondola and sail down for some of the prettiest views of the city. Some tours even head out to the lake for a skyscraper-studded panorama.

Best Tour Companies

The **ArchiCenter of the Chicago Architecture Foundation** (⊠ *224 S. Michigan Ave., Loop* ☎ *312/922–3432* ⊕ *www.architecture. org* ⊙ *Sun.–Fri. 9:30–6, Sat. 9–6*) conducts excellent, docent-led boat tours of the Loop. Our favorites are the "Early Skyscrapers" tour and the "Modern and Beyond" tour. The ArchiCenter also has walking and bus tours and hosts exhibitions, lectures, and discussions.

Watch the panoply of Chicago's magnificent skyline slide by from the decks of *Chicago's First Lady* or *Chicago's Little Lady,* the fleet of the **Chicago Architecture Foundation River Cruise.** Make reservations in advance for the popular 90-minute tours. **Ticketmaster** (☎ *312/902–1500* ⊕ *www.ticketmaster.com/illinois*) sells tickets by phone, online, and at the Hot Tix booth in the Chicago Water Works Visitor Center. Ticketmaster fees apply at these outlets. You can also purchase tickets at the *Chicago's First Lady* ticket window or at the Chicago ArchiCenter (224 S. Michigan Avenue). ⊠ *Southeast corner of Michigan Ave. Bridge* ☎ *847/358–1330* ⊕ *www.cruisechicago.com* ✉ *$26 Mon.– Thurs., $28 Fri.–Sun.* ⊙ *May–Oct., daily; Nov., weekends.*

TOUR ALTERNATIVES

■ Pinching pennies? Hop on a Shoreline water taxi and cruise down the river. You won't get running narration, but it's affordable (tickets are $6 one way weekdays, $7 weekends) and not crowded.

■ For a more adventurous spin down the river, rent a canoe or a kayak. Just beware of large boats and crew shells. **Chicago Canoe and Kayak** (⊠ *3400 N. Rockwell St.* ☎ *773/704–2663* ⊕ *www.chicagoriverpaddle.com*). **Chicagoland Canoe Base** (⊠ *4019 N. Narragansett Ave.* ☎ *773/777–1489* ⊕ *www.chicagolandcanoebase.com*). **Wateriders** (⊠ *900 N. Kingsbury Ave.* ☎ *312/953–9287* ⊕ *www.wateriders.com*).

Other Recommended Companies

Shoreline Sightseeing. Shoreline's been plying these waters since 1939 and has tours of both the river and Lake Michigan. ⊠ *West end of Navy Pier* ☎ *312/222–9328* ⊕ *www.shorelinesightseeing.com* ⊙ *May– Oct., daily; Apr. and Nov., weekends.*

Wendella Sightseeing. See the city just as the sun sets on the Chicago at Sunset tour. There's also a river architecture tour and a combined river and lake tour. ⊠ *400 N. Michigan Ave.* ☎ *312/337–1446* ⊕ *www. wendellaboats.com* ⊙ *Apr.–Nov., daily.*

Mercury Cruises. Mercury does quirky tours, including Canine Cruises, where dogs are welcome, and Pirate Cruises for kids. ⊠ *112 E. Wacker Dr.* ☎ *312/332– 1353* ⊕ *www.mercuryskylinecruiseline. com* ⊙ *Schedule varies with season.*

CITY ITINERARIES

Two Hours in Town

If you've only got a bit of time, go to a museum. Although you could spend days in any of the city's major museums, two hours will give you a quick taste of Chicago's cultural riches. Take a brisk walk around the **Art Institute** to see Grant Wood's *American Gothic,* Edward Hopper's *Nighthawks,* and one of the finest impressionist collections in the country. Or check out the major dinosaur collection or the gorgeous Native American regalia at the **Field Museum.** Take a close look at the sharks at the **Shedd Aquarium.** If the weather's nice, stroll along the lakefront outside the **Adler Planetarium**— you'll see one of the nicest skyline views in the city. Wander down State Street, the Magnificent Mile, or around Millennium Park. If you're hungry, indulge in one of Chicago's three famous culinary treats—deep-dish pizza (head to **Pizzeria Due** to avoid the lines at **Giordano's, Gino's,** and **Pizzeria Uno**); garden-style hot dogs; or Italian beef sandwiches. After dark? Hear some music at a local club. Catch some blues at **Blue Chicago** to get a taste of authentic Chicago.

■TIP➔ Remember that many museums are closed on Monday.

A Perfect Afternoon

Do the zoo. Spend some time at the free **Lincoln Park Zoo and Conservatory** (the tropical plants will warm you up in winter), take a ride on the exotic animal-themed carousel, and then spend a couple hours at the nearby **Chicago History Museum** for a quirky look at the city's past. If you'd like to stay in the Lincoln Park neighborhood a bit longer, have dinner at one of many great local restaurants and then head to **The Second City,** the sketch comedy troupe that was the precursor to *Saturday Night Live.*

■TIP➔ The Second City offers free improvisation following the last performance every night but Friday.

Sightseeing in the Loop

State Street, that Great Street, is home to the old **Marshall Fields,** which has been reborn as Macy's; Louis Sullivan's ornate iron entrance to the former department store **Carson Pirie Scott;** a nascent theater district; as well as great people-watching. Start at Harold Washington Library at Van Buren Street and State Street and walk north, venturing a block east to the beautiful **Chicago Cultural Center** when you hit Randolph Street. Grab lunch at the Museum of Contemporary Art's serene Wolfgang Puck café, **Puck's at the MCA,** and then spend a couple hours with in-your-face art. Go for steak at Morton's or the Palm before a night of Chicago theater. Broadway touring shows are on Randolph Street at the Oriental or the Ford, or head elsewhere downtown for excellent local theater—the Goodman, Steppenwolf, Lookingglass, and Chicago Shakespeare will each give you a night to remember.

Get Outdoors

Begin with a long walk (or run) along the lakefront, or rent a bike or inline skates and watch the waves on wheels. Then catch an El train north to **Wrigley Field** for Cubs baseball; grab a dog at the seventh-inning stretch and sing your heart out to "Take Me Out to the Ball Game." Afterward, soak up a little beer and atmosphere on the patio at one of the local sports bars. Finish up with an outdoor concert in **Grant or Millennium parks.**

Family Time

Start at **Navy Pier**—or heck, spend all day there. The **Chicago Children's Museum** is a main attraction, but there's also an IMAX Theater, a Ferris wheel, a swing ride, a fun house, a stained-glass museum, and in winter, Chicago-themed miniature golf in a sunny atrium. If the crowds at the Pier get to be too much, walk or take the free trolley to **Millennium Park,** where kids of all ages can ice-skate in winter and play in the fountain in summer, and where giant digital portraits of Chicagoans spit streams of water to help cool you off. Whatever the weather, make sure to get your picture taken in the mirrored center of the *Bean*—the sculpture that's formally known as *Cloud Gate*. At night in summertime, take a stroll by Buckingham Fountain, where the dancing sprays jump to music and are lit by computer-controlled color lights, or take a turn on the dance floor during Chicago's nightly SummerDance celebration.

■ TIP➔ Fireworks explode near Navy Pier every Wednesday and Saturday night at 9 PM, Memorial Day through Labor Day.

Cityscapes

Start at the top. Hit the heights of the **John Hancock Center** or the **Sears Tower Skydeck** for a grand view of the city and the lake. Then take a walking tour of downtown with a well-read docent from the **Chicago Architecture Foundation.** In the afternoon, wander north to the **Michigan Avenue Bridge,** where you can take an informative boat tour of the Chicago River. Enjoy the architecture as you float by, resting your weary feet.

Shop Chicago

Grab your bankroll and stroll the **Magnificent Mile** in search of great buys and souvenirs. Walking north from around the Michigan Avenue Bridge, window-shop your way along the many upscale stores. Hang a left on **Oak Street** for the most elite boutiques. **Accent Chicago** (875 North Michigan Ave.) or **City of Chicago Store** at the Chicago Waterworks Visitors Center are where serious souvenir hunters spent their cash. Dedicated shoppers will want to detour a little farther south to **State Street** in the Loop for a walk through the landmark Marshall Fields building, now Macy's. For a culture buzz, check out the **Museum of Contemporary Art** (closed Monday). After making a tough restaurant choice (Prime rib at Smith & Wollensky's or Lawry's? or deep-dish pizza at Giordano's?), consider a nightcap at the **Signature Room** at the 95th floor bar on top of the John Hancock Center—the city will be spread beneath your feet.

GETTING OUTSIDE: PARKS & ZOOS

Chicago may not be the country's biggest city, but it's arguably the prettiest. Architect Daniel Burnham designed the city to have plenty of green space so city dwellers could relax, and even the tiniest green outpost usually has some sort of public art. With winter never too far from thought, Chicagoans pour into the city's parks and zoos at the first hint of summer, or take to conservatories when the weather's less than ideal. The following are our favorite city parks and zoos.

Parks

Garfield Park Conservatory. One of the most exotic places to visit in winter has Victorian glass rooms of tropical palms, spiny cacti, turtle-filled ponds, and a children's garden with a slide that winds through trees. The Sweet House nurtures chocolate, sugar cane, pineapple, figs, and other plants that sate the sweet tooth. ⊠ *300 N. Central Park Ave., Garfield Park.*

★ Fodor's Choice | **Grant Park & Buckingham Fountain.** Two of Chicago's greatest treasures reside in Grant Park—the Art Institute and Buckingham Fountain. Bordered by Lake Michigan to the east and a spectacular skyline to the west, the ever-popular Grant Park hosts many of the city's outdoor events, including the annual Taste of Chicago, a vast picnic featuring foods from more than 70 restaurants. The event precedes a fireworks show around July Fourth. The fountain is a wonderful place to people-watch.

The centerpiece of Grant Park is the gorgeous, tiered **Buckingham Fountain** (⊠ *Between Columbus and Lake Shore Drs. east of Congress Plaza*), which has intricate designs of pink-marble seashells, water-spouting fish, and bronze sculptures of sea horses. It was patterned after a fountain at Versailles but is about twice as large as its model. See it in all its glory between May 1 and October 1, when it's elaborately illuminated at night and sprays colorfully lighted waters. ⊠ *South Loop* ☎ *312/747–1534.*

Lincoln Park Conservatory. Green grows on green in the lush tropical main room of this refreshing city greenhouse. Stroll through permanent displays of orchids, palms, and ferns, or catch one of the special shows, like the fragrant Easter Lily show in March or April and the festive Chrysanthemum Show in November. The peacefulness and lush greenery inside the 1892 conservatory is a refreshing respite in the heart of this bustling neighborhood. ⊠ *2400 N. Stockton Dr., Lincoln Park* ☎ *312/742–7736* ⊡ *Free* ⊙ *Daily 9–5.*

★ **Millennium Park.** The Bean, the fountains, the Disney-esque music pavilion— all the pieces of this new park quickly stole the hearts of Chicagoans and visitors alike. This is one of our favorite places to spend a sunny day.

The showstopper here is Frank Gehry's stunning **Jay Pritzker Pavilion.** Dramatic ribbons of stainless steel stretching 40 feet into the sky look like petals wrapping the music stage. The sound system, suspended by a trellis that spans the great lawn, gives concert-hall sound outside. So what can you see on this beautiful stage? Take your pick. There's the Grant Park Music Festival—a free classical-music series—as well as the city's popular free summer concerts, including the jam-packed Chicago Blues and Chicago Jazz festivals.

Hot town? Summer in the city? Cool off by letting George W. spit on you. Okay, it's just a giant image of him and a bunch of

other faces rotating through on two huge (read: 50-foot-high) glass block–tower fountains. The genius behind the **Crown Fountain,** Spanish sculptor Jaume Plensa, made an opening where the mouths are on the photos, and water comes shooting out at random intervals. Kids love it, and we feel like kids watching it. It's at the southwest corner of the park.

You've seen the pictures. Now go, take your own. The **Cloud Gate sculpture,** otherwise known as "the Bean," awaits your delighted *ooohs* and *aaahs* as you stand beneath its gleaming seamless polished steel. It's between Washington and Madison streets. Go on, get camera happy.

If you're feeling artsy, you can find out if there's a show playing at the indoor, underground **Harris Theater for Music and Dance,** behind the Jay Pritzker Pavilion.

In summer, the carefully manicured plantings in the **Lurie Garden** bloom; in winter, the **McCormick Tribune Ice Rink** is open for public skating. ✉ *Bounded by Michigan Ave., Columbus Dr., Randolph Dr., and Monroe St., Loop* ⊕ *www.millenniumpark.org* 🎫 *Free* 🕐 *Daily 6 AM–11 PM.*

Zoos

★ **Brookfield Zoo.** Spend the day among nearly 3,000 animals at this gigantic zoo. The highlights? First, there's the popular **Tropic World,** a simulated tropical rain forest where monkeys, otters, birds, and other rain-forest fauna cavort in a carefully constructed setting of rocks, trees, shrubs, pools, and waterfalls. Next, test your "flying strength" in the **Be a Bird House** by flapping your "wings" on a machine that decides what kind of bird you would be, based on how you flap. We also like the **Living Coast,** where you can venture through huge glassed-in pas-

sageways to see sharks, rays, jellyfish, and turtles swimming by. Daily dolphin shows are a favorite even for adults. Walruses, seals, and sea lions inhabit a rocky seascape exhibit. Don't worry if you don't want to trek around the grounds—you can hop aboard a motorized safari tram in warm weather ($2.50) or the heated *Snowball Express* tram in the cold (free).

The two best educational exhibits are Habitat Africa and Swamp. In **Habitat Africa,** you can explore two very different environments. See such tiny animals as klipspringer antelope, which are only 22 inches tall, and rock hyraxes, which resemble prairie dogs, in the savannah exhibit, which also has a water hole, rock formations characteristic of the African savannah, and termite mounds. If you look closely in the dense forest exhibit, you might be able to find animals like the okapi. The **Swamp** is about as realistic as you would want an exhibit on swamps to be, with a springy floor, push-button alligator bellows, and open habitats with low-flying birds vividly demonstrating the complex ecosystems of both southern and Illinois wetlands.

For hands-on family activities, check out the **Hamill Family Play Zoo** (🎫 *$3.50, children $2.50*), where kids can learn to care for nature by playing zookeeper, gar-

Fodor's Choice | **Lincoln Park Zoo.** Lions, gorillas, and bears, oh my! At this urban zoo, you can face-off with lions (separated by a window, of course) outside the Lion House, watch 24 gorillas go ape in the Great Ape House, or watch some rare and endangered species of bears, such as the spectacle bear (named for the eyeglasslike markings around its eyes).

dener, or veterinarian. The **Children's Zoo** ($1, *children 50¢*) includes a petting farm, excellent animal shows, and the Big Barn with its daily milking demonstrations. Watch the dolphins show off and act silly at the **Seven Seas Dolphin Show** (*adults $3, children $2.50*). ⊠ *1st Ave. and 31st St.* ☎ *708/485–0263 or 800/201–0784* ⊕ *www.brookfield-zoo.org* Zoo $10 ($6 children), free on Tues. and Thurs. Oct.–Feb.; dolphin show $2.50; parking $8* ⊘ *Oct.–Mar., daily 10–5; Apr. and Sept., weekdays 10–5, weekends 10–6; May–Aug., daily 9:30–6; Oct.–Dec., daily 10–5.*

Animals both slithery (pythons) and cuddly (koalas) reside in the glass-dome Regenstein Small Mammal and Reptile House; if you're looking for the big guys (elephants, giraffes, black rhinos), they're in the large-mammal house. For youngsters, there are the children's zoo, the Farm in the Zoo (farm animals and a learning center with films and demonstrations), and the Conservation Station, with hands-on activities.

⊠ *2200 N. Cannon Dr., Lincoln Park* ☎ *312/742–2000* ⊕ *www.lpzoo.com* Free ⊘ *Daily 9–5.*

AUTHENTIC CHICAGO

So you've done the Art Institute and the Sears Tower—now it's time to put away your tourist hat and make like a local. Luckily, it's not hard to figure out what Chicagoans like to do in their spare time. Here's how to follow in their footsteps.

Visit an Ethnic Neighborhood

Chicago is a city of neighborhoods, and in many of them you can see traces of each successive immigrant group. Each neighborhood in the city has its own flavor, reflected in its architecture, public art, restaurants, and businesses, and most have their own summer or holiday festivals. Here are a few stand-out 'hoods.

Little Italy. Though most Italians moved to the West Side a couple of generations ago, Little Italy's Italian restaurants and lemonade stands still draw them back.

Andersonville. The charming diversity of the Swedish/Middle Eastern/gay mecca of Andersonville means you can have lingonberry pancakes for breakfast, hummus for lunch, and go to a club after dinner.

Chinatown. The Chinese New Year dragon parade is just one reason to visit Chinatown, which has dozens of restaurants and shops and a quiet riverfront park.

Devon Avenue. Devon Avenue turns from Indian to Pakistani to Russian Orthodox Jewish within a few blocks. Try on a sari, buy a bagel or electronics, or just people-watch—it's an excellent place to spend the afternoon.

Pilsen/Little Village. The best Mexican restaurants are alongside Pilsen's famous murals. Be sure to stop into the National Museum of Mexican Art, which will give you an even deeper appreciation of the culture.

Bronzeville. Bronzeville's famous local historic figures include Ida B. Wells—a women's rights and African-American civil-rights crusader—the trumpeter Louis Armstrong, and Bessie Coleman, the first African-American woman pilot. The area has nine landmark buildings and is rapidly gentrifying.

Enjoy the Lake

San Diego and LA may have the ocean, and New York its Central Park, but Chicago has the peaceful waters of Lake Michigan at its doorstep. Bikers, dog walkers, boaters, and runners crowd the lakefront paths on warm days; in winter the lake is equally beautiful, with icy towers formed from frozen sheets of water.

BIKE ALONG THE LAKESHORE

★ To bike any part of the gentle dips and swells of Chicago's 20 mi **lakefront bicycle path** is to see the city: the skyline, the people, the water. The breeze from the lake mixes with the sounds of the city at play as you zoom by, carefree, whiling away an afternoon.

The **Chicago Park District** (✆312/742–7529 ⊕www.chicagoparkdistrict.com) is a good source for bike maps.

For information on biking in the city, contact the **Chicagoland Bicycle Federation** (✉9 W. Hubbard St., South Loop ✆312/427–3325 ⊕www.chibikefed.org).

Bike Chicago (✉600 E. Grand Ave., Near North ✆312/595–9600 or 773/327–2706 ⊕www.bikechicago.com/home.asp) can deliver a bike to your hotel and pick it up after your ride. Fees start at $8.75 per hour and $34 a day. It also runs a free three-hour lakefront bike tour daily, weather permitting.

You can rent a bike for the day or by the hour from **On the Route** (✉3146 N. Lincoln Ave., Lake View ✆773/477–5066 ⊕www.ontheroute.com), which stocks a large inventory of bicycles, including

Beaches

Osterman Beach

Foster Beach

Montrose Beach

North Avenue Beach

Oak Street Beach

12th Street Beach

Jackson Beach Central

South Shore Country Club

children's bikes. They also supply helmets and other safety equipment.

BOATING

Nothing beats the view of the Chicago skyline from the water, especially when the sun sets behind the sparkling skyscrapers. Plenty of boats are available to rent or charter, though you might want to leave the skippering to others if you're not familiar with Great Lakes navigation.

Sailboat lessons and rentals are available from the **Chicago Sailing Club** (✉*Belmont Harbor, Lake View* ☎*773/871–7245* ⊕*www.chicagosailingclub.com*). The Chicago Sailing Club focuses on sailing instruction for all levels and includes a program on keeping your boat in tip-top shape.

Sailboats, Inc. (✉*Monroe Harbor, Loop* ☎*312/861–1757 or 800/826–7010* ⊕*www.sailboats-inc.com*), one of the oldest charter-certification schools in the country, prepares its students to charter any type of boat.

For a more placid water outing, try the paddleboats at **Lincoln Park Lagoon** (✉*2021 N. Stockton Dr., Lincoln Park* ☎*312/742–2038*), just north of Farm-in-the-Zoo.

BEACHES

One of the greatest surprises in the city is the miles of sandy beaches that Chicagoans flock to in summer. The water becomes warm enough to swim in toward the end of June, though the brave will take an icy dip through the end of October. Chicago has about 30 mi of shoreline, most of it sand or rock beach. Beaches are open to the public daily from 9 AM to 9:30 PM, Memorial Day through Labor Day, and many beaches have changing facilities.

BEACHES	Block	Best For	Bathrooms	Changing Facilities	Showers	Lifeguard
Far North Side						
Foster Beach	5200 N	Families	yes	no	no	yes
Montrose Beach	4400 N	Learning to sail	yes	no	yes	yes
Osterman Beach	5800 N	Quiet conversations	yes	no	yes	yes
Hyde Park						
South Shore Country Club	7100 S	Quieter beach	yes	yes	yes	yes
Jackson Beach Central	5700–5900 S	Beach trip after the Museum of Science and Industry	yes	no	no	yes
Lincoln Park						
North Avenue Beach	1600–2400 N	Margaritas at the upstairs concession	yes	yes	yes	yes
Near North						
Oak Street Beach	600–1600 N	Singles scene	yes	no	no	yes
South Loop						
12th Street Beach	1200 S at 900 E	Post museum-hopping break	yes	no	yes	yes

The **Chicago Park District** (☎ *312/742–7529* ⊕*www.chicagoparkdistrict.com*) provides lifeguard protection during daylight hours throughout the swimming season.

All references to north and south in beach listings refer to how far north or south of the Loop each beach is. In other words, 1600 to 2400 north means the beach begins 16 blocks north of the Loop (at Madison Street, which is the 100 block) and extends for eight blocks.

⚠ **Along the lakefront you'll see plenty of broken-rock breakwaters with signs that warn NO SWIMMING OR DIVING. Although Chicagoans frequently ignore these signs, you shouldn't. The boulders below the water are slippery with seaweed and may hide sharp, rusty scraps of metal, and the water beyond is very deep. It can be dangerous even if you know the territory.**

Brave the Cold

The city's brutal windy winters are infamous, but that doesn't keep Chicagoans from making the best out of the long cold months. Throw on lots of layers, lace up your ice skates, and show those city dwellers what you're made of.

★The rink at **Millennium Park** (⊠*55 N. Michigan Ave., Loop* ☎*312/742–1168* ⊕*www.millenniumpark.org*) has free skating seven days a week and a lustrous view of the Chicago skyline. Skate rentals are $7 a session.

On snowiest days, some hardy souls **cross-country ski** and snowshoe on the lakeshore—bring your own equipment.

Loosen up by playing outdoor paddle tennis at **Midtown Tennis Club** (⊠*2020 W. Fullerton Ave.* ☎*773/235–2300* ⊕*www.midtowntennisclub.com*). If it's snowing, they turn on the heated floors.

Holiday-walk Chicago's windows during the **Magnificent Mile Lights Festival,** in November, the Saturday before Thanksgiving. The celebration includes music, ice-carving contests, and stage shows, and ends in a parade and the illumination of more than one million lights.

FREE THINGS TO DO

It's easy to spend money in the big city: think shopping, museum-entrance fees, restaurants, theater. But if you'd like to put your wallet away for a while, here are some of our favorite options.

Free Art

■ Chicago has some of the most famous public art in the country, including a **Picasso** piece in Daley Plaza, **Alexander Calder's** *Flamingo* in Federal Plaza, and the *Cloud Gate* sculpture in Millennium Park. For a fairly comprehensive list, see ⊕*www.chipublib.org* or pick up a *Free Public Art* guide at a visitor center.

■ The **City Gallery** (⊠*806 N. Michigan Ave.* ☎*312/742–0808*) in the Historic Water Tower hosts rotating exhibits of Chicago-theme photography.

■ Five different galleries showcase contemporary visual art by local artists at the **Chicago Cultural Center** (⊠*78 E. Washington St.* ☎*312/744–6630* ⊕*www.cityofchicago*.org).

Free Concerts

■ Grant Park and Millennium Park host regular classical and pop concerts in summer. For a schedule, pick up the *Chicago Reader* or buy a copy of *Time-Out Chicago*.

■ Chicago is a festival town, celebrating blues, jazz, country, gospel, Celtic, and world music during the warm months. For a schedule, see ⊕*www.cityofchicago.org*.

■ Free jazz and classical concerts are performed Monday through Wednesday and Friday at 12:15 in the **Chicago Cultural Center** (⊠*78 E. Washington St.* ☎*312/744–6630* ⊕*www.cityofchicago.org*).

Free Movies

Every Tuesday night in summer, Grant Park shows classic films at sundown on a giant screen. The films tend to be popular, so go early, spread out a blanket, and have a picnic a couple hours beforehand. There's even a free bike valet. Local library branches and parks also have free movies—check the city's Web site for details.

Free Dance Lessons

Learn to swing, polka, step, waltz, and salsa to the beat of a live band in Grant Park during the summer-long Chicago SummerDance Festival. Chicagoans of all ages and abilities sashay around the dance floor during the lessons and the free dancing afterward. For more information, see ⊕*www.chicagoparkdistrict.com*.

Free Fireworks

Every Wednesday and Saturday night in summer, Navy Pier puts on a showy display of colorful explosives. Watch from the pier or along the waterfront opposite Buckingham Fountain.

Free Trolley Rides

A free trolley circles downtown attractions like the museums and Navy Pier every 20 minutes until 9 PM on weekdays and 11 PM on weekends. For more information, call ☎877/244–2444.

Free Improv

The world-famous Second City comedy troupe has a free improv set following the last performance every night but Friday. For more information, go to ⊕*www.secondcity.com* or call ☎312/337–3992.

Free Museum Days

ALWAYS FREE

Jane Addams Hull-House Museum
Museum of Contemporary Photography
National Museum of Mexican Art
Oriental Institute
Ukrainian Institute of Modern Art
Smart Museum

SUNDAY:

DuSable Museum of African American History

MONDAY:

Adler Planetarium & Astronomy Museum (selected months only)
Chicago Children's Museum (for those 15 and younger the first Monday of each month)

TUESDAY:

Adler Planetarium & Astronomy Museum (selected months only)
Museum of Contemporary Art
Swedish American Museum Center (second Tuesday each month)

THURSDAY:

Art Institute of Chicago (after 5 PM)
Chicago Children's Museum (5–8 PM only)
Peggy Notebaert Nature Museum

Free TV-Show Tickets

Oprah Winfrey and Jerry Springer tape their shows in front of live audiences in Chicago. Though tickets are free, they are at a premium and must be reserved far in advance. Oprah's shows are filmed at **Harpo Studios** (✉*1058 Washington St.* ☎*312/591–9222 for tickets* ⊕*www. oprah.com*). *The Jerry Springer Show* is filmed at **NBC Tower** (✉*454 N. Columbus Dr.* ☎*312/321–5365* ⊕*www.jerryspringertv.com*).

Sightseeing Walks

THAT GREAT STREET

The Loop—defined by the oval created by the El tracks—is the heart of downtown, and the heart of downtown is State Street. Begin at the south end of the Michigan Avenue Bridge, with your back to the Chicago Tribune's Gothic tower. Walk west along the river past Marina City's iconic corn-cob towers, perhaps taking the stairs down to the Riverwalk for a drink at one of the cafés. Once you're back to street level, make a left on State Street, cruising by the famous Chicago Theatre sign that marks the beginning of the theater district. Window-shop at local landmarks Carson Pirie Scott (now closed) and Marshall Field's, which is now Macy's.

ZOOTOPIA

In two hours on a beautiful day you can breeze through the Lincoln Park Zoo, stroll beside the park's lagoons, and explore the quaint, upscale neighborhood of Old Town. Beginning on North Avenue and Lake Shore Drive, walk north through the park next to the lagoons. Watch the crew shells try to navigate past the fishing lines, or throw a line into the stocked lagoon yourself. Take your time through the zoo or the Lincoln Park Conservatory and then circle west to Wells Street, where the Second City improv troupe's theater and a host of tony shops and restaurants line bricked streets.

CHICAGO WITH KIDS

Chicago sometimes seems to have been designed with kids in mind. There are many places to play and things to do, from building sand castles at one of the lakefront's many beaches to playing indoor minigolf at the Navy Pier in winter. Here are some suggestions for ways to show kids the sights.

Museums

Several area museums are specifically designed for kids. At the **Chicago Children's Museum** (⊠ *700 E. Grand Ave., Navy Pier*), three floors of exhibits cast off with a play structure in the shape of a schooner, where kids can walk the gangplank and slide down to the lower level. Also at **Navy Pier** you'll find a Ferris wheel and Viennese swings (the kind that go around in a circle like a merry-go-round). In winter a Chicago-theme minigolf course is set up in the Crystal Ballroom, an atriumlike space with fountains that spring from one potted plant to another in synchronized motion.

Many other Chicago museums are also kid-friendly, especially the butterfly haven at the **Peggy Notebaert Nature Museum,** the replica coal mine at the **Museum of Science and Industry,** the dinosaur exhibits at the **Field Museum,** and the sharks at the **John G. Shedd Aquarium.**

Parks, Zoos & Outside Activities

Chicago's neighborhoods are dotted with area play lots that have playground equipment as well as several ice-skating rinks for winter months. On scorching days, visit the **63rd Street Beach House,** at 63rd Street and Lake Shore Drive in Woodlawn. The interactive spiral fountain in the courtyard jumps and splashes, leaving kids giggling and jumping. **Millennium Park** (⊠ *55 N. Michigan Ave.*) has a 16,000-

MORE IDEAS FROM
FODORS.COM FORUMS

- Holiday Lights Festival on Michigan Ave.

- Bulls, Cubs, or White Sox Game

- Day trip to Oak Park

- Gospel Brunch at House of Blues (call 312/923–2000)

- Chicago Architecture Foundation Cruise (visit www.architecture.org)

square-foot ice-skating rink. Skaters have an unparalleled view of downtown as they whiz around the ice.

For more structured fun, there are two zoos: the free **Lincoln Park Zoo** (⊠ *2200 N. Cannon Dr. at Lake Shore Dr. and Fullerton Pkwy.*) and the large, suburban **Brookfield Zoo** (⊠ *1st Ave. and 31st St., Brookfield*), which has such surprising exhibits as a wall of pulsing jellyfish. The **Buccaneer Pirate Adventure Cruise** (Wagner Charter Cruise Co. Dock, Lower Wacker Dr. between Wells St. and Franklin/Orleans St. bridges) sets sail with wannabe pirates, teaching them about the river's locks and entertaining kids with magic tricks.

FABULOUS FESTIVALS

Chicago festivals range from local neighborhood get-togethers to citywide extravaganzas. People fly in for the Chicago Blues Festival, but try to catch a neighborhood street fair for some great people-watching and fried dough if you're in town between June and September. On some weekends, there are several festivals at once. For details, see ⊕ *www.chicagoreader.com*.

The **St. Patrick's Day parade** (☎ *312/942-9188*) turns the city on its head: the Chicago River is dyed green, shamrocks decorate the street, and the center stripe of Dearborn Street is painted the color of the Irish from Wacker Drive to Van Buren Street. This is your chance to get your fill of bagpipes, green beer, and green kneesocks. You probably won't see the whole thing—the parade can clock in at over four hours.

The **Chicago Blues Festival** (☎ *312/744-3315* ⊕*www.chicagobluesfestival.org*), in Grant Park, is a popular four-day, three-stage event in June starring blues greats from Chicago and around the country. If you see only one festival in Chicago, this is the one.

The medium-size **Chicago Gospel Fest** (☎*312/744-3315*) brings its joyful sounds to Grant Park in early June.

Taste of Chicago (✉ *Grant Park, Columbus Dr. between Jackson and Randolph Sts.* ☎*312/744-3315*) dishes out pizza, cheesecake, and other Chicago specialties to 3.5 million people over a 10-day period before the July Fourth holiday that includes top pop acts as well as novelties—like high divers who torpedo into small swimming pools.

The **Chicago Jazz Festival** (☎*312/744-3315*) holds sway for four days during Labor Day weekend in Grant Park.

At the **Celtic Fest,** Celtic food, art, storytelling, dance, and a bagpiper's circle celebrate everything Irish. It's held in Grant Park during the month of September.

At the weeklong **World Music Festival,** international artists play traditional and contemporary music at venues across the city in September.

Street fairs are held every week in summer, but two stand out as the best. **Halsted Market Days**, in August, is the city's largest street festival. It's held in the heart of the gay community of Lakeview and has blocks and blocks of vendors as well as some wild entertainment such as zany drag queens and radical cheerleaders. The **Taste of Randolph** is more sedate, featuring dishes from the fine restaurants lining the western end of Randolph Street in June.

Chicago's holiday season officially starts with the **Magnificent Mile Lights Festival** (⊕*www.themagnificentmile.com*), a weekend-long event at the end of every November with tons of family-friendly activities including musical performances, ice-carving contests, and stage shows. The fanfare culminates in a parade and the illumination of more than one million lights along Michigan Avenue.

GET OUT OF TOWN

You could spend a month or two just exploring the city of Chicago, but the surrounding towns are likewise rich in history, culture, and activity. The closest suburbs offer theaters and museums; the farther out you go, the more likely you are to find wooded parks and quiet places.

Brush Up Your Ernest Hemingway

Ernest Hemingway Birthplace. Part of the literary legacy of Oak Park, this three-story turreted Queen Anne Victorian, which stands in frilly contrast to the many streamlined Prairie-style homes elsewhere in the neighborhood, contains period-furnished rooms and many photos and artifacts pertaining to the writer's early life. Museum curators have redecorated rooms to faithfully depict the house as it looked at the turn of the 20th century; you can poke your head inside the room in which the author was born on July 21, 1899. ⊠ *339 N. Oak Park Ave.* ☎ *708/848–2222* ⊕ *www.hemingway.org* ✉ *Joint ticket with Hemingway Museum $7* ◔ *Sun.–Fri. 1–5, Sat. 10–5.*

Ernest Hemingway Museum. How did the author's first 20 years in Oak Park impact his later work? Check out the exhibits and videos here to find out. Don't miss his first "book," a set of drawings with captions written by his mother, Grace. Holdings include reproduced manuscripts and letters. ⊠ *200 N. Oak Park Ave.* ☎ *708/848–2222* ⊕ *www.hemingway.org* ✉ *Joint ticket with Hemingway Birthplace $7* ◔ *Sun.–Fri. 1–5, Sat. 10–5.*

Follow the Chicago Symphony Orchestra

If you enjoy music under the stars, the outdoor concerts at **Ravinia Park** are a stellar treat. The **Ravinia Festival** is the summer home of the Chicago Symphony Orchestra. Come for jazz, chamber music, pop, and dance performances. Pack a picnic and blanket and sit on the lawn for a little more than the cost of a movie ($10 to $20). Seats are also available in the pavilion for a significantly higher price ($20 to $80). Restaurants and snack bars are on park grounds. Concerts usually start at 8 PM; be at the park at 6:30 to park and get settled. ⊠ *Green Bay and Lake Cook Rds., in Highland Park, 26 mi north of downtown Chicago* ☎ *847/266–5100* ⊕ *www.ravinia.org.*

ERNEST HEMINGWAY: OAK PARK PROTÉGÉ

It seems unlikely that the rough-and-tumble adventurer and writer Ernest Hemingway was born in 1899 amid the manicured suburb of Oak Park, Illinois, a town he described as having "wide lawns and narrow minds." He excelled at writing for the high school paper—a skill that turned into his life's work. A volunteer stint as an ambulance driver introduced him to World War I and its visceral horrors—he used that experience and the lessons he learned as a reporter for the *Kansas City Star* to craft emotionally complex novels built from deceptively simple sentences, like his master work, *A Farewell to Arms*. Hemingway later lived in Toronto and Chicago. Though his return visits to Oak Park were infrequent, the residents celebrate him there to this day.

Unwind Outdoors

Fodor's Choice See the spectacular spring blooming season or the beautiful display of mid-June roses at the **Chicago Botanic Garden.** Among the 23 different gardens are a three-island Japanese garden, a waterfall garden, a sensory garden, and a 4-acre fruit-and-vegetable garden. Three big greenhouses showcase a desert, a rain forest, and a formal garden with flowers that bloom all winter long. Standout special events are the Antiques and Garden Fair in April and the Railroad Garden in summer. ✉ *Lake Cook Rd. and U.S. 41* ☎ *847/835–5440* ⊕ *www. chicagobotanic.org* 🎫 *Free; parking $12, tram tour $5* ☉ *Daily 8 AM–sunset; 45-min summer tours through Oct., daily 10–3, weather permitting.*

Take a quiet hike around the **Morton Arboretum,** full of woodlands, wetlands, and display gardens. Trees, shrubs, and vines flower year-round, but in spring the flowering trees are particularly spectacular. You can drive your car through some of the grounds, but we think it's much nicer to walk. There are lots of trails to take, and most take about 15 to 30 minutes. Don't miss the Daffodil Glade in early spring. Tours are scheduled most Sunday afternoons. ✉ *4100 Illinois Rte. 53, 25 mi southwest of downtown Chicago* ☎ *630/719–2400 or 630/719–2466* ⊕ *www.mortonarb.org* 🎫 *$7, Wed. $4; tram tours $4* ☉ *Daily 7–7 (or at sunset, whichever is earlier).*

Samuel Insull, partner of Thomas Edison and founder of Commonwealth Edison, built the mansion at the **Cuneo Museum and Gardens** in 1916 as a country home. After Insull lost his fortune, John Cuneo Sr., the printing press magnate, bought the estate and fashioned it into something far more spectacular. The sky-lighted great hall in the main house resembles the open central courtyard of an Italian palazzo; the private family chapel has stained-glass windows; and a gilded grand piano graces the ballroom. The house is filled with antiques, porcelains, 17th-century Flemish tapestries, and Italian paintings. The gardens appeared in the film *My Best Friend's Wedding.*

To get to Cuneo by car (about a 45-minute drive from downtown Chicago), take Interstate 94 West to IL Route 60 West. Turn right (north) onto IL Route 21 (Milwaukee Avenue). It's half a mile to the entrance. To get here by train, take Metra's Milwaukee District North Line from Union Station to Libertyville. Hail a cab to the mansion; it's about 5 mi from the station to Cuneo. ✉ *1350 N. Milwaukee Ave., 15 mi west of Lake Forest, 40 mi northwest of downtown Chicago* ☎ *847/362–3042* ⊕ *www.cuneomuseum.org* 🎫 *$5 per car; $12 per person for mansion tours* ☉ *Tues.–Sun. 10–5; beginning in mid-May, guided mansion tours are Tues.–Sat. at 11, 1, and 3, self-guided on Sun.*

■TIP➔ **For details about Frank Lloyd Wright's Oak Park, see page 141.**

CHICAGO THEN & NOW

The Early Days

Before Chicago was officially "discovered" by the team of Father Jacques Marquette, a French missionary, and Louis Jolliet, a French–Canadian mapmaker and trader, in 1673, the area served as a center of trade and seasonal hunting grounds for several Native American tribes, including the Miamis, Illinois, and Pottawattomie. Villages kept close trading ties with the French, though scuffles with the Fox tribe kept the French influence at bay until 1779. That year, black French trader Jean Baptiste Point du Sable built a five-room "mansion" by the mouth of the Chicago River on the shores of Lake Michigan.

The Great Fire

The city grew until 1871, when a fire in the barn of Catherine and Patrick O'Leary spread across the crowded wooden buildings of the city, destroying 18,000 structures within 36 hours. A year later, the city was on its way to recovery, and the fire led to an explosion of architectural innovation.

Gangsters to the Great Migration

World War I (aka the Great War) changed the face of Chicago. Postwar—and especially during Prohibition (1920–1933)—the Torrio–Capone organization expanded its gambling and liquor distribution operations, consolidating its power during the violent "beer wars" from 1924 to 1930. Hundreds of casualties include the seven victims of the infamous 1929 St. Valentine's Day massacre.

The Great War also led to the Great Migration, when African-Americans from the South moved to the northern cities between 1916 and 1970. World War I slowed immigration from Europe, but increased jobs in Chicago's manufacturing industry. More than 500,000 African-Americans came to the city to find work; the black population, which was 2% before the Great War, was 33% by 1970. By the mid-20th century, African-Americans were a strong force in Chicago's political, economic, and cultural life.

IMPORTANT DATES IN CHICAGO HISTORY

1673	Chicago discovered by Marquette and Jolliet
1779	Jean Baptiste Point du Sable, a "free Negro," and his wife Catherine, a Pottawattamie Indian, are the first Chicago settlers.
1837	Chicago incorporated as a city
1860	First national political convention. Abraham Lincoln nominated as the Republican candidate for president
1871	Great Chicago Fire

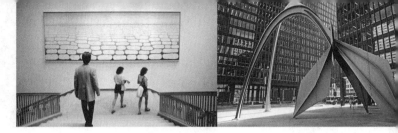

Mayor Daley & the Notorious 1968 Democratic Convention

The Daley dynasty began when Richard J. Daley became mayor in 1955. He was reelected five times and his son, Richard M. Daley, currently runs the city.

The first Mayor Daley redrew Chicago's landscape, overseeing the construction of O'Hare International Airport, the expressway system, the University of Illinois at Chicago, and a towering skyline. He also helped John F. Kennedy get elected, thanks to his control of Chicago's Democratic party.

Despite these advances, Mayor Richard J. Daley is perhaps best known for his crackdown on student protesters during the 1968 Democratic National Convention. Americans watched on their televisions as the Chicago police beat the city's youth with sticks and blinded them with tear gas. That incident, plus his "shoot to kill" order during the riots that followed the assassination of Dr. Martin Luther King Jr., and his use of public funds to build giant, disastrous public housing projects like Cabrini–Green, eventually led to the temporary dissolution of the Democratic machine in Chicago. After Daley's death, Chicago's first black—and beloved—mayor, Harold Washington, took office in 1983.

Chicago Today

The thriving commercial and financial "City of Broad Shoulders" is spiked with gorgeous architecture and set with cultural and recreational gems, including the Art Institute, Millennium Park, 250 theater companies, and 30 mi of shoreline. Three million residents live within city limits. The current Mayor Daley gave downtown a makeover, adding wrought-iron street furniture, regular fireworks, planters of flowers, and Millennium Park. Spectacular lights brighten buildings along Michigan Avenue after dark. There are always controversies, but most Chicagoans are proud to call the city home.

1885	First skyscraper in the country, Home Insurance Building (no longer standing), is built
1886	Haymarket Riot
1893	World's Columbian Exposition
1929	St. Valentine's Day Massacre
1968	Democratic National convention
1973	Sears Tower, tallest building in North America, completed
2005	Chicago White Sox win the World Series

FOR THE FANATICS

Michael Jordan, Scottie Pippin, Walter Payton, William "the Refrigerator" Perry, Ernie Banks, Sammy Sosa, Shoeless Joe Jackson. You can't mention Chicago without talking about sports. Chicagoans are fiercely devoted to their teams, whether it's baseball, basketball, or football—and whether their team's winning or losing. Come opening day for baseball season, die-hard Cubs and Sox fans take the day off work to cheer on their teams; during football season, tailgaters chow down in the parking lot before kickoff, even if it's snowy and in the single digits. One of the most fun ways to get into the Chicago spirit is to go to a game, so throw on your team's colors and join the screaming fans.

Chicago Bears

Chicago football is messy and dirty and sometimes even exciting. Don't expect to be wowed by star quarterbacks and amazing passing, but do get ready for the team's smash-mouth style that reflects the city's blue-collar persona. Legends like Walter Payton have come and gone, but after several mediocre seasons, things have started to look up: they made it to the Super Bowl in 2006 but did not come away the champs.

- **Where They Play: Soldier Field,** *425 E. McFetridge Dr., South Loop*

- **Season:** August–December

- **How to Buy Tickets:** Through Ticketmaster, at ☎ *312/559–1212* or ⊕ *www.chicagobears.com*

- **Most Notable Players:** Dick Butkas, Mike Ditka, Walter Payton, William "the Refrigerator" Perry, Jim McMahon

- **Past Highlights:** Although the Bears didn't win the 2007 Super Bowl, they won it in 1986. During that game, defensive tackle William "the Refrigerator" Perry scored a touchdown, highly rare for a defensive player.

Chicago Bulls

It's been years since Michael Jordan and Phil Jackson's "dynasty" teams played in the United Center, but the Bulls' six championships are still revered here. After Jordan's departure in 1998, the franchise became a shadow of its former self—but a new squad of fresh faces is starting to turn things around. Coach Scott Skiles and the "Baby Bulls" are back in the playoffs (2005 and 2006), and the United Center is starting to rock again.

- **Where They Play: United Center,** *1901 W. Madison St., Near West Side*

- **Season:** November–April

- **How to Buy Tickets:** From the ticket office, ☎ *312/455–4000* or ⊕ *www.bulls.com*

- **Most Notable Players:** Michael Jordan, Dennis Rodman, Scottie Pippen, Toni Kukoc

- **Past Highlights:** The Bulls won six NBA Championship Trophies: 1991, 1992, 1993, 1996, 1997, 1998

- **Note:** Avoid leaving the game early or wandering around this neighborhood at night

TAKE ME OUT
TO THE BALLGAME

In a city where you can get a debate going about all sorts of things—best deep-dish pizza, best blues bar, best big city (Chicago or New York?)—nothing can inspire a passionate discussion quite like Chicago baseball, an argument that's been going strong since 1901.

Your favorite team says more about you than just whether you prefer the National or American League. The rivalry plays out along geographical and class lines. South Siders, who include everyone living south of the Loop, are die-hard Sox fans. North Siders sell out afternoon Cubbies games even when the team is losing—as they do most years.

There's a legendary rivalry between Sox fans and Cubs fans. When the Sox won the World Series in 2005 for the first time in 88 years, most Cubs fans didn't even watch the games. The traitors who did were called "BiSoxual." When the Cubs made the playoffs in 2003, Sox fans actively rooted for the other team

(as the song "Ballad of the South Side Irish" goes, "When it comes to baseball there are two teams that I love, it's the go-go White Sox and whoever plays the Cubs.") One reason that the division has lasted so long is class tension. South Siders, besides the intellectual Hyde Park pocket, tend to be blue collar. North Siders tend to be professionals.

The teams have only played against each other once post-season: the 1906 World Series. The Cubs were favored, but the White Sox won. Fans on both the North and South sides agree on one thing: it would be "an El of a series" if the teams ever faced each other postseason again. As Cubs fans say, "You Gotta Believe."

NATIONAL LEAGUE 1907

SCHULTE · ZIMMERMAN · REULBACH · McCORMICK · SHECKARD · KLING · BROWN · LUNDGREN · CHANCE mgr. · PFEISTER · HOWARD · STEINFELDT · SLAGLE

CHICAGO CUBS

Just the Facts

Nickname: Cubbies

Mascot: None

Founded: 1870

Last World Series appearance: 1945

World Series wins: 1907 and 1908

Most famous players: Sammy Sosa, Ron Santo, Ryne Sandberg, Ernie Banks, Billy Williams

Original name: White Stockings

Did you know?

Most hated fan: Steve Bartman, who, in the eighth inning of Game 6 in the 2003 playoffs, reached for—and caught—a foul ball at the same time as left fielder Moises Alou. Before Bartman, the Cubs were five outs away from advancing to the World Series. After Bartman's catch, the Cubs fell apart, giving up eight runs.

Lifelong Chicagoans: The Cubs are the only team to play continually in the same city since the founding of the National League in 1876.

Curse: William Sianis, the old owner of the Billy Goat Tavern, bought two tickets for one of the 1945 Cubs–Tigers World Series games: one for himself, and one for his goat. The goat was turned away, and Sianis vowed that the Cubs would never again win a World Series.

HARRY CARAY: "HOLY COW!"

Beloved for his hoarse, off-key rendition of "Take Me Out to the Ballgame," the way he mashed up players names, and his infamous "Holy Cow!", the Cubs' exuberant play-by-play broadcaster, Harry Caray (1914–1998), was as much a fixture of Wrigley Field as the bleacher bums.

Caray broadcast 8,300 games in his 53-year career. (Don't tell Cubs fans—before he came to Wrigley field, he was the voice of the St. Louis Cardinals for 25 years, the White Sox for 10.) After his death in 1998, every single player wore a caricature of Caray—with his infectious smile and goggle glasses—on their sleeves.

The curse persists, it seems, even though the current Billy Goat owner, son Sam Sianis, occasionally drags a goat back onto the field.

Best seat in the house: The bleachers. Tradition has it that the most serious fans (known as bleacher bums) sit here, on either side of the ivy covered, hand-operated scoreboard. When rival teams hit a ball into the bleachers, the fans throw it back. The Cubs' owners, The Chicago Tribune Company, have expanded the bleachers for the first time since 1938.

1

CHICAGO WHITE SOX

Just the Facts

Mascot: Southpaw, a fuzzy, green character of indeterminate origin. He appeared in 2004.

Founded: 1893 in Sioux City, Iowa. Moved to Chicago in 1900.

Last World Series appearance: 2005

World Series wins: 1906, 1917, 2005

Notable players: "Shoeless" Joe Jackson, Roberto Hernandez, Roberto Alomar, Johnny Mostil, Frank Thomas, Germaine Dye.

Original name: White Stockings, which was also the first name of the Chicago Cubs. Charles Comiskey hoped to buy some goodwill for the new team by taking on the Cubs' former name.

Did you know?

Theme song: "Na Na Hey Hey (Kiss Him Goodbye)," is played every home game by organist Nancy Faust.

From White Sox to Black: Eight players—outfielder "Shoeless Joe" Jackson, outfielder Oscar "Happy" Felsch, pitchers Eddie Cicotte and Claude "Lefty" Williams, third baseman Buck Weaver, shortstop "Swede" Risberg, and infielders Fred McMullen and Arnold "Chick" Gandi—were accused of throwing the 1919 World Series on behalf of a group of gamblers. They were never convicted, though they were banned from baseball for life. That season's team has been known as the Black Sox ever since.

Most Famous Quote: As Shoeless Joe Jackson was leaving a Black Sox scandal hearing, a newsboy supposedly shouted out, "Say it ain't so, Joe!" This inspired headline writers after the 2005 World Series win to write: "Say it IS so!"

Strangest promotional event: Disco Demolition Night, July 12, 1979, at the old Comiskey Park. Fans were asked to bring unwanted disco records to the park for a Sox–Tigers double header; in return, the admission was lowered to a mere 98 cents. After the first game, chaos erupted—fans threw their records like Frisbees and ran onto the field where they started bonfires and mini-riots.

Fireworks: After every home run and every win, the Sox shoot fireworks into the sky from U.S. Cellular Field. They can be heard across the South Side.

WRIGLEY FIELD

Getting There

Address: 1060 West Addison St., at the corner of Addison St. and Clark St.

Phone: 773/404–CUBS

Public transportation: The Red Line's Addison stop is right outside the park. The #22 Clark bus stops at the entrance.

Driving directions: Try not to drive, but if you do, take Lake Shore Drive north to Belmont Avenue. Travel west on Belmont to North Clark Street, and north on Clark to Wrigley Field.

Parking: Parking is difficult to find around Wrigley, though business owners tend to open up their lots for exorbitant prices, as do lucky home owners with garages.

The Park: The Friendly Confines, as it's known, was built in 1914, which makes it the second-oldest ballpark in the country.

Tours: The Cubs offer 90-minute tours that provide an insider's look at 90 years of Wrigley history. Tickets are $25 per person and you must buy tickets in advance.

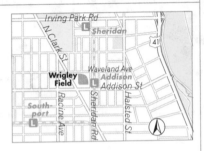

Box Office Hours: Mon.–Fri. 10–6. Sat.–Sun. 10–4. On game days, box office opens at 9 AM.

What to bring: Don't forget your sunscreen and umbrella/rain gear if you're in the bleachers. Bring water—the container must be one liter or less. Don't bring hard-sided coolers, large bags, thermoses, bottles, cans, or alcoholic beverages.

PLAY BALL

Tickets: Prices can range between $10 to $70. Don't expect to score tickets on short notice—games sell out early in the season.

Wrigley Field Alternatives:
- Join the crowd at Harry Caray's Restaurant in River North (⇨ see Where to Eat chapter, pg. 222).
- Check out the ticketless fans in their lawnchairs on Sheffield Avenue.
- Opt for a White Sox game (tickets are easier to come by).

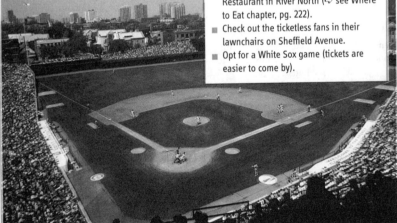

THE CELL

Getting There

Address: 333 W. 35th St.

Phone: 312/674–1000

Public transportation: Take the CTA Red Line to the 35th Street/Sox Park station of the CTA Red Line.

Driving directions: I-94 West to 35th Street; follow signs to "Sox Parking".

Parking: Parking is $18 in the lots surrounding the park. The lots open two hours prior to game time and close one hour after the game. There is no street parking.

About the name: Now it's "The Cell." But until 2003, when the White Sox made a deal to call it U.S. Cellular Field, it was Comiskey Park, named for former White Sox owner Charles A. Comiskey.

What to bring: Sunscreen and hats on hot days; jackets and small umbrellas if it looks like rain. Food in small, clear, see-through plastic bags and one sealed plastic bottle of water per person is OK–all other beverages, coolers, and large bags are not. Leave beach balls and large radios at home. The area around The Cell is sketchy—don't leave valuables in your car.

Tickets: Prices for tickets can range between $8 for a nosebleed seat to $64 for a box seat. Kids who are shorter than the turnstiles—about 36"—get in free but must sit in someone's lap. Monday home games are half price; get a second ticket free when you redeem an empty Pepsi product at ticket windows on the day of the game.

Box Office Hours:

Non-game days: Mon.–Fri., 10–6, Sat. and Sun., 10–4.

Game days: Mon.–Fri. 9–bottom of 5th inning (day games); 9–bottom of 5th inning (night games)

Sat. 9–6 (day games); 9–8 (night games) Sun. 9–4 (day games); 9–9 (night games).

Kids: Pontiac FUNdamentals, huge play area for kids, includes baseball and softball clinics, batting cages, and places to practice base running and pitching. It's above the left field concourse, opens 90 minutes before the game, and stays open throughout the game.

Speed pitch machine: Test your pitching speed and accuracy near section 164.

Fan Deck: Get a panoramic view of the field from a two-tiered deck. It's atop the center field concession stands. Free for all fans holding a main level ticket.

Baggage Check: Outside Gate 5 between parking lots A and B. $2 fee per bag.

ATMs: Sections 139, 531, centerfield, outside the Bullpen Sports Bar, and outside Gate 4.

Concessions: Burgers and veggie burgers, hot dogs and veggie hotdogs, and ice cream are available throughout the park. The Bullpen Sports Bar, offering more substantial food, is near ramp 2. For a small charge, you can sit in the two-tiered, open-air section. Ages 21 and over only.

FIRST GAME CERTIFICATE
The White Sox offer a certificate for guests to commemorate their first time at U.S. Cellular Field. Visit any Guest Relations Booth behind home plate to pick one up.

TAKE ME OUT TO THE BALLGAME

BEHIND THE SCENES

For a look at what (or who) makes the city tick, check out the following activities.

Black & White & Read All Over

Chicago Tribune Freedom Center. Tour the Chicago Tribune's printing plant and the *New York Times'* Midwest distribution center. ⊠*777 W. Chicago Ave., West Loop* ☎*312/222–3040* ✉*Free, but there are no regular tours and you must call ahead.*

Movers & Shakers

Graceland Cemetery. A comprehensive guide available at the entrance walks you by the graves and tombs of the people who made Chicago great, including merchandiser Marshall Field and railroad-car builder George Pullman. ⊠*4001 N. Clark St., Far North Side* ☎*773/525–1105* ⊕*www. gracelandcemetery.org* ✉*Free.*

See Green

Federal Reserve Bank. Though they don't hand out money here, they sure do handle a lot of the green stuff. The facility processes currency and checks, scanning bills for counterfeits, destroying unfit currency, and repackaging fit currency. A visitor center in the lobby has permanent exhibits of old bills, counterfeit money, and a million dollars in $1 bills. One-hour tours explain how money travels and show a high-speed currency-processing machine. Call in advance for tour reservations, since it's often booked in spring and fall with school groups. ⊠*230 S. LaSalle St., Loop* ☎*312/322–2400* ⊕*www.chicago-fed.org* ✉*Free.*

Tour a Factory

Though Chicago isn't the industrial center it once was, you can still watch all sorts of things being made in the Chicago area, from cheesecakes to harps. Log on to ⊕*www.factorytoursusa.com* for a complete list.

Neighborhoods

WORD OF MOUTH

"Lincoln Square is a charming old German community and Anderson-ville is the same for the Swedish. Also, explore Hyde Park—there's Jackson Park with the Japanese Gardens, a few small museums on the University of Chicago Campus, and the Robie House. The National Museum of Mexican Art in Pilsen is really cool, and there is, of course, some great Mexican food and shopping there."

—flamingomonkey

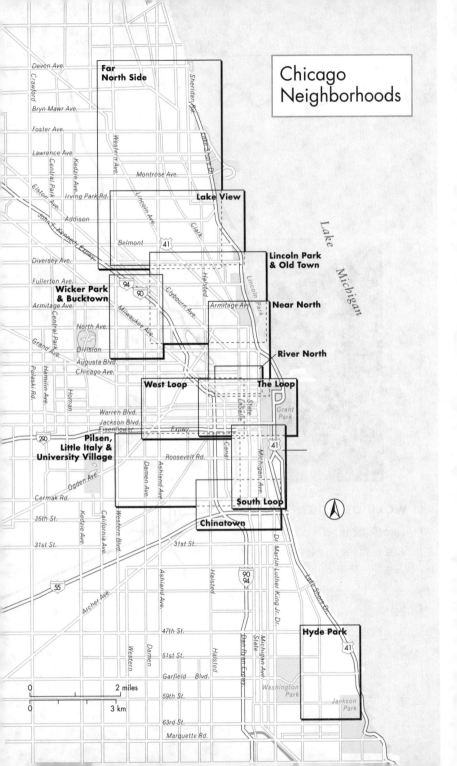

2

LOOP

Sightseeing
★★★★☆

Dining
★★★☆☆

Lodging
★★★☆☆

Shopping
★★☆☆☆

Nightlife
★★★☆☆

The Loop is a living architectural museum, where shimmering modern towers stand side by side with 19th-century buildings. Striking sculptures by Picasso, Miró, and Chagall watch over plazas alive with music and farmers' markets in summer. There are noisy, mesmerizing trading centers, gigantic department stores, internationally known landmarks like the Sears Tower and the Art Institute, and the city's newest playground, Millennium Park. Rattling overhead, encircling it all, is the train system Chicagoans call the El.

Known as the Loop since the cable cars of the 1880s looped around the central business district, downtown Chicago comprises the area south of the Chicago River, west of Lake Michigan, and north of Congress Parkway/Eisenhower Expressway. The western boundary used to be the Chicago River, but the frontier continues to push westward. Handsome skyscrapers line every foot of South Wacker Drive east of the river, and new construction across the bridges is now a near constant.

WHAT'S HERE

Getting around the Loop is easy. It's laid out like a grid: State Street intersects north–south blocks, and Madison Street intersects east–west blocks. Where State and Madison converge is the zero point from where the rest of the city fans out. It's also where you find the building that once housed the department store **Carson Pirie Scott & Co.**, with its breathtaking decorative cast-iron facade—an outstanding example of Louis Sullivan's work. (The company closed the downtown location of the department store in early 2007; for the time being the building stands vacant.) Farther north on State Street—the Loop's most famous thoroughfare—is a **Macy's** department store that until 2006 had been the flagship location for the much mourned Marshall Field's. Despite

GETTING ORIENTED

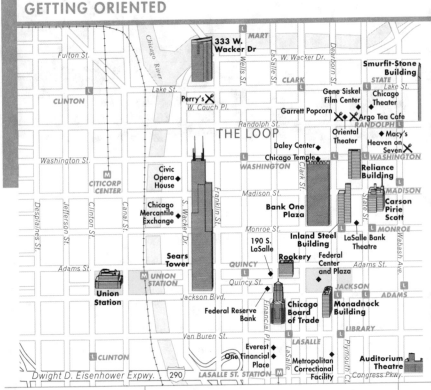

MAKING THE MOST OF YOUR TIME

If you have the time, give yourself a whole day to explore the Loop. You can easily spend half a day at the Art Institute. The rest of your day you can spend sunning yourself in Millennium Park, shopping up and down State Street, taking a trip to the top of the Sears Tower, or meandering among the architectural masterpieces and sculptures. And, of course, you'll want to allow yourself time to stand in line for Garrett Popcorn.

GETTING HERE

Take a bus to Michigan Avenue and Wacker Drive. From the north, you can take Bus 3, 145, 147, or 151. Coming from the south, you can take Bus 3, 6, 145, 146, 147, or 151.

The Lake stop on the El's Red Line will put you at State and Lake streets. The Washington, Monroe, and Jackson stops are also in the Loop, just blocks from one another. The Brown, Green, Orange, Pink, and Purple lines stop at State, aboveground, at Lake Street. These lines also stop at Randolph, Madison, and Adams in the Loop. If you arrive by car, you can park it in the subterranean Grant Park North Garage, with an entrance on Michigan Avenue. Most streets in the Loop prohibit parking weekdays from 7 AM to 6 PM.

KEY

L CTA lines

M Metra lines

✕ Restaurant/ Cafe

NEIGHBORHOOD TOP 5

1. Spend an afternoon with Georges Seurat and *A Sunday on la Grande Jatte* at the **Art Institute**.

2. Stand between the 50-foot faces screened onto the two towers of the **Crown Fountain in Millennium Park** and wait for them to spit.

3. Jump in a car and get lost in the underground world of **Lower Wacker Drive**.

4. Spend an afternoon strolling amongst architectural gems throughout the Loop.

5. Follow your nose and line up at one of the Loop locations of **Garret Popcorn** for a tub or two of the good stuff.

QUICK BITES

Choose from dozens of exotic varieties of tea at **Argo Tea Cafe** (⊠ *16 W. Randolph St., Loop* 📞 *312/553–1551*). Light lunch fare and sweet treats round out the menu.

The lines form early and stay long throughout the day at **Garrett Popcorn** (⊠ *26 W. Randolph St., Loop,* 📞 *312/201–0455*).

Heaven on Seven (⊠ *111 N. Wabash Ave., 7th fl., Loop* 📞 *312/263–6443*) is a Loop legend, famous for casual Cajun breakfasts and lunches that have area office workers gladly lining up to chow down.

Perry's (⊠ *180 N. Franklin St., Loop* 📞 *312/372–7557*) is a hit as much for the trivia questions Perry announces over his deli's PA system as it is for the overstuffed sandwiches.

the name change, the landmark turn-of-the-20th-century building is still beguiling.

Continuing on State, just north of Randolph Street, is the old theater district. First is the ornate 1921 Beaux-Arts **Chicago Theatre,** a former movie palace that now hosts live performances. Across the street is the **Gene Siskel Film Center,** which screens art, industrial, foreign, and classic movies. West on Randolph Street is the **Ford Center for the Performing Arts–Oriental Theatre,** with its long, glitzy neon sign. On Dearborn is the **Goodman Theatre,** wrapped in the 1923 art-deco facades of the landmark Harris & Selwyn Twin Theaters. One more block west is the **Cadillac Palace Theatre,** a renovated 1926 vaudeville house that still has its original marble lobby.

Much of the impressive architecture in the Loop can be credited to the Great Chicago Fire of 1871, which leveled the city and cleared the way for the building of skyscrapers using steel-frame construction. One of the best things to do in the Loop is just to stroll around and take in the different types of buildings. For *more information on architecture, see chapter 4.* .

On Washington Street is the **Daley Center,** an outdoor plaza that has concerts and holiday and farmers' markets. Check out the unnamed Picasso sculpture, referred to simply as the *Picasso.* Opposite the Daley Center is the **Chicago Temple,** a Methodist church whose beautiful spire is so tall that it's best seen at some distance. Also on the south side of the street is Joan Miró's giant figure, *Chicago.*

Controversy swirled when the Picasso was unveiled in 1967—everyone wanted to know if it was a woman's head or was inspired by one of the artist's Afghan hounds.

To the west, following the bend of Wacker Drive, is the art-deco **Civic Opera House,** where Chicago's Lyric Opera gives its performances, and the pale-grape-color twin towers of the **Chicago Mercantile Exchange,** where action on the trading floors is frenetic. East on Monroe Street, the sunken, bi-level **Bank One Plaza** has room to rest in the shadow of the sweeping Bank One building that curves skyward in the shape of the letter "A." The Chagall mosaic, *The Four Seasons,* is at the northeast end of the plaza. Just before you get to State Street is the **LaSalle Bank Theatre** (until recently known as the Shubert Theatre). It was the tallest building in Chicago when it opened in 1906; today, it's one of the top destinations in town to see touring Broadway shows.

Back on Michigan Avenue, between Monroe and Randolph streets, is **Millennium Park,** anchored by the immensely popular *Bean* (also known as the *Cloud Gate*) sculpture. On the west side of the intersection of Randolph Street and Michigan Avenue is the **Chicago Cultural Center,** home to the **Chicago Office of Tourism Visitor Information Center.** At 200 East Randolph is the soaring **Aon Center,** the second-tallest building in Chicago after the Sears Tower. Directly west of the Aon Center is the **Prudential Building,** Chicago's tallest building until the late 1960s.

Dining in the Loop

EXPENSIVE DINING

Everest, *French*, 440 S. LaSalle St., Loop

Morton's, The Steakhouse , *Steakhouse* , 65 E. Wacker Pl., Loop

The Palm, *Steakhouse* , Swissotel, 323 E. Wacker Dr. Loop

MODERATE DINING

312 Chicago, *Italian*, Hotel Allegro, 136 N. LaSalle St., Loop

Aria, *International*, Fairmont Chicago, 200 N. Columbus Dr., Loop

Atwood Cafe, *American*, Hotel Burnham, 1 W. Washington St., Loop

Catch 35, *Seafood*, 35 W. Wacker Dr., Loop

The Grillroom, *Steakhouse*, 33 W. Monroe St., Loop

Nick's Fishmarket, *Seafood*, 51 S. Clark St., Loop

Park Grill, *New American*, Millennium Park, 11 N. Michigan Ave., Loop

Petterino's, *Italian*, 150 N. Dearborn St., Loop

Rhapsody, *New American*, 65 E. Adams St., Loop

Russian Tea Time, *Russian*, 77 E. Adams St., Loop

Trattoria No. 10, *Italian*, 10 N. Dearborn St., Loop

Vivere, *Italian*, 71 W. Monroe St., Loop

Behind it rises the rocket ship–like **Two Prudential Plaza,** affectionately nicknamed Pru Two.

The southern part of the Loop balances the hub of the financial district with the fine arts. On one block is the **Art Institute of Chicago,** the grand-looking **Symphony Center** (home to the internationally acclaimed Chicago Symphony Orchestra), and the **Santa Fe Building** (where Daniel Burnham, the architect, had his offices). Farther south on Michigan Avenue is the **Fine Arts Building.**

On Dearborn Street is the **Federal Center and Plaza,** designed by Mies van der Rohe and anchored by Alexander Calder's red mobile *Flamingo* sculpture. The beautiful **Rookery,** an imposing red-stone building that is one of the city's 19th-century showpieces, is on LaSalle Street; make sure to see the Frank Lloyd Wright lobby. Nearby is Phillip Johnson's **190 South LaSalle,** with striking gold-leaf ceilings. Across Quincy Street is the massive **Federal Reserve Bank.** Farther south at Jackson Boulevard the street seems to disappear in front of the commanding **Chicago Board of Trade,** which sits like a throne reigning over the financial district. From Jackson Boulevard and LaSalle Street, look up to the west to see the hulking **Sears Tower,** the tallest building in North America.

SOUTH LOOP INCLUDING PRINTER'S ROW, MUSEUM CAMPUS & BRONZEVILLE

Sightseeing
★★★★☆

Dining
★★★☆☆

Lodging
★★☆☆☆

Shopping
★☆☆☆☆

Nightlife
★★☆☆☆

The South Loop, bounded by Congress Parkway/Eisenhower Expressway on the north, Michigan Avenue on the east, Cermak Avenue on the south, and the Chicago River on the west, presents a striking contrast to the Loop, with its less trafficked streets and a more subdued—and, in some spots, grittier—vibe. Though it was one of Chicago's first residential districts, the area eventually became a symbol of urban blight. A redevelopment boom has transformed it into a residential neighborhood again, this time attracting more and more residents who like its ethnic and racial mix and growing sense of community, as well as its proximity to the Loop, great museums, and hip restaurants.

Trips to the Museum Campus and Printer's Row district here are musts. Perched on the lakefront, Museum Campus is a glorious spot to take in the skyline and watch the boats go by. It's home to the **Field Museum,** the **John G. Shedd Aquarium,** and the **Adler Planetarium & Astronomy Museum,** all of which hold some of the most important and exciting exhibits and artifacts in the country. Printer's Row, a small enclave to the west, was once a thriving commercial area and the center of the printing trades in Chicago. Today it stands as a good example of the South Loop renaissance with coffeehouses, shops, and restaurants inhabiting the area's beautiful buildings. Farther afield, but worth a visit if there's time, is the Bronzeville area, a historic community originally settled by waves of African-Americans fleeing the South after World War I.

WHAT'S HERE

The 57-acre Museum Campus is home to the Big Three—the **Field Museum**, the **John G. Shedd Aquarium**, and the **Adler Planetarium & Astronomy Museum**, all united in one pedestrian-friendly, parklike setting. Park your car in one of the lots just past the Field Museum on McFetridge Drive, or ride the free Museum Campus trolley (☎877/244–2246), which connects the three museums with other downtown tourist attractions and train stations. It operates daily from Memorial Day to Labor Day and on holidays, and runs only on weekends the rest of the year. On the west side of the campus is the Field Museum, which houses a staggering array of culture- and nature-focused exhibits that date from prehistoric times to the present. It's most famous is Sue, the largest and most complete T. rex skeleton in the world. No one's sure if Sue was actually a male or female. She's named for Sue Hendrickson, the fossil hunter who discovered her skeleton.

DID YOU KNOW? The large marble panel in the lobby of the Adler has bronze emblems representing eight planets. The discovery of Pluto, considered the ninth planet until astronomers took away that status in 2006, was announced after the panel had been installed in 1930.

The Shedd Aquarium, on the lakefront just past the Field Museum, has bizarre and fantastically beautiful fish, plus dolphins and beluga whales. On the east side of the campus, at the far end of a peninsula that juts out into Lake Michigan (and provides wonderful views and photo opportunities of Chicago's skyline), is the Adler Planetarium & Astronomy Museum—the first modern planetarium in the Western Hemisphere.

FRUGAL FUN If you're visiting all three museums, plus some of the city's other big attractions, buy a Chicago CityPass (adults $49.50, kids 3–11 $39). You'll avoid long lines and get access to the Field, the Shedd, and the Adler, plus the Hancock Observatory and the Museum of Science and Industry.

Just south of Museum Campus is **Soldier Field,** the building with the massive columns reminiscent of ancient Greece and the home of the Chicago Bears. A modern glass expansion, completed in 2003, appears to grow out of the 1920s sports-palace design.

The Printer's Row district is bounded by Congress Parkway on the north, Polk Street on the south, Plymouth Court to the east, and the Chicago River to the west. It fell into disrepair in the 1960s as the printing industry moved to other areas in the city because of changing needs for space. Sleazy bars, pawnbrokers, and pornography shops filled the area, but a neighborhood resurgence began in the late 1970s with renovations to some of the run-down loft and office buildings. You can still see examples here of buildings by the group that represented the First Chicago School of Architecture (including Louis Sullivan), as well as **Dearborn Station,** a Romanesque revival–style structure that was once the city's main passenger train hub. These days this section of town is best known for the annual **Printer's Row Book Fair,** a weekend-long literary celebration held each June.

GETTING ORIENTED

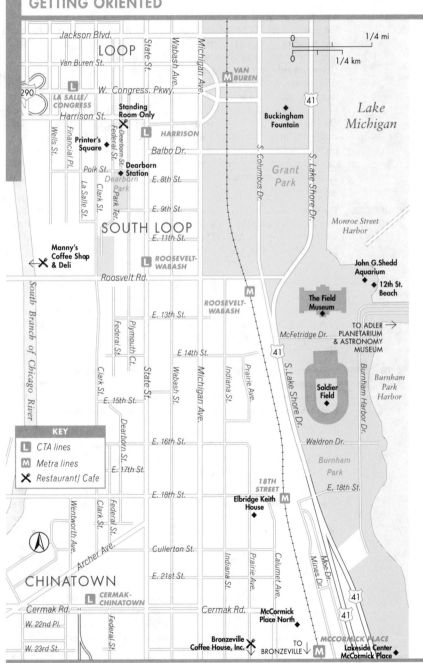

LOOP

Jackson Blvd.

Van Buren St.

W. Congress. Pkwy.

VAN BUREN

290

LA SALLE/ CONGRESS

Harrison St.

Standing Room Only

HARRISON

Printer's Square

Balbo Dr.

Dearborn Station

Polk St.

E. 8th St.

Dearborn Park

E. 9th St.

SOUTH LOOP

E. 11th St.

Manny's Coffee Shop & Deli

ROOSEVELT-WABASH

Roosevelt Rd.

ROOSEVELT-WABASH

E. 13th St.

E 14th St.

E. 15th St.

E. 16th St.

E. 17th St.

E. 18th St.

CHINATOWN

CERMAK-CHINATOWN

Cermak Rd.

W. 22nd Pl.

W. 23rd St.

Buckingham Fountain

Lake Michigan

Grant Park

Monroe Street Harbor

John G.Shedd Aquarium

12th St. Beach

The Field Museum

TO ADLER PLANETARIUM & ASTRONOMY MUSEUM

McFetridge Dr.

Soldier Field

Burnham Park Harbor

Waldron Dr.

Burnham Park

E, 18th St.

18TH STREET

Elbridge Keith House

Cullerton St.

E. 21st St.

Cermak Rd.

McCormick Place North

Bronzeville Coffee House, Inc.

TO BRONZEVILLE

MCCORMICK PLACE

Lakeside Center McCormick Place

0   1/4 mi

0   1/4 km

KEY

- L   CTA lines
- M   Metra lines
- ✕   Restaurant/ Cafe

GETTING HERE

Buses 6, 12, and 146 take you to Museum Campus. If you drive, take Lake Shore Drive to the Museum Campus exit. There's some coveted meter parking as well as pricier lots adjacent to the museums. For Printer's Row, take the El's Brown, Orange, Pink, or Purple Line to the library stop, or the Red Line to Harrison. Buses 6, 22, 36, and 145 will also get you there. Drivers can take Congress Parkway to Dearborn Street. Bronzeville can be easily accessed by buses 49 and 95. To get there by car, take Lake Shore Drive to 31st Street, then travel west to Martin Luther King Drive.

MAKING THE MOST OF YOUR TIME

Plan on at least a day for a visit to the three museums (you could spend a day at the mammoth Field Museum alone). Allow extra time to enjoy the spectacular skyline and lake views from Museum Campus and to stroll along the harbor. Note that traffic can get snarled and special parking rules go into effect around Museum Campus when the Chicago Bears are playing in neighboring Soldier Field. Prairie Avenue is a quick-hit, taking a couple of hours at most. A trip to Bronzeville can take from an hour or two to a half day, depending on whether you opt for one of the longer organized tours.

QUICK BITES

Bronzeville Coffee House, Inc. (⊠ *538 E. 43rd St., South Loop* ☎ *773/536–0494*) is a comfy choice for coffee and pastries.

Have a corned-beef sandwich all the other delis in town aim to beat at **Manny's Coffee Shop & Deli** (⊠ *1141 S. Jefferson St., South Loop* ☎ *312/939–2855*).

"Da Mare" himself, Richard M. Daley, has stood up for the turkey burgers at **Standing Room Only (SRO Chicago)** (⊠ *610 S. Dearborn St., South Loop* ☎ *312/360–1776*).

SAFETY

The South Loop is a changing neighborhood. Some parts can still feel sketchy, so exercise caution, particularly at night, by sticking to populated and well-lighted streets. Group tours of Bronzeville are recommended for those unfamiliar with the area.

TOURS

The **Chicago Office of Tourism** (☎ *312/742–1190*) offers a half-day bus tour of Bronzeville. Other tours are offered by the **Black Metropolis Convention and Tourism Council** (☎ *773/373–2842*), and **Tour Black Chicago** (☎ *773/684–9034*). **Black Cou-Tours** (☎ *773/233–8907*) offers a 2½-hour excursion of black culture including Bronzeville and other highlights.

NEIGHBORHOOD TOP 5

1. Spot your favorite fish at the **John G. Shedd Aquarium**, then stand next to Sue the T. rex at the **Field Museum**.

2. See the stars at the **Adler Planetarium & Astronomy Museum**.

3. Tailgate in the parking lot before a Chicago Bears game at **Soldier Field**.

4. Grab a corned-beef sandwich and potato pancake with a cross-section of Chicago at **Manny's Coffee Shop & Deli**.

5. Take a step back in Chicago's rich African-American history with a guided tour of **Bronzeville**.

Dining in the South Loop

AT A GLANCE

EXPENSIVE DINING
Custom House, *Steakhouse,* 500 S. Dearborn St., South Loop

BUDGET DINING
Chez Joel, *Bistro,* 1119 W. Taylor St., South Loop

Francesca's on Taylor, *Italian,* 1400 W. Taylor St., South Loop

Gioco, *Italian,* 1312 S. Wabash Ave., South Loop

Manny's Coffee Shop and Deli, *American,* 1141 S. Jefferson St., South Loop

Opera, *Chinese,* 1301 S. Wabash St., South Loop

Pompeii, *Italian,* 1531 W. Taylor St., South Loop

The Rosebud on Taylor, *Italian,* 1500 W. Taylor St., South Loop

Tuscany, *Italian,* 1014 W. Taylor St., South Loop

DID YOU KNOW?

That futuristic structure that seems to rise from the river west of Printer's Row on Polk Street is Marina City, a condominium complex and self-contained city within a city. It has its own private 1-acre park, market, clubhouse, dry cleaner, and boat slips.

The historic **Bronzeville** neighborhood, once known as Black Metropolis, roughly covers the area south of McCormick Place and north of Hyde Park between State Street and Cottage Grove Avenue. Following World War I, this neighborhood became a place where African-Americans who had migrated from the South could escape race restrictions prevalent in other parts of the city. Landmarks include the neighborhood's symbolic entrance, a tall statue at 26th Place and Martin Luther King Jr. Drive that depicts a new arrival from the South bearing a suitcase held together with string. The Victory monument at 35th Street and King Drive honors the all-black 8th Illinois Regiment in World War I. Walk along Martin Luther King Jr. Drive between 25th and 35th streets to follow a commemorative trail of more than 90 sidewalk plaques honoring the best and brightest of the community, including Pulitzer Prize–winner Gwendolyn Brooks, whose first book of poetry was called *A Street in Bronzeville.*

WEST LOOP INCLUDING GREEKTOWN

Sightseeing
★☆☆☆☆

Dining
★★★★☆

Lodging
★☆☆☆☆

Shopping
★★☆☆☆

Nightlife
★★★★☆

Most of the West Loop languished for years as a wasteland peppered with warehouses and meatpacking plants. But nowadays, many of the warehouses have been converted to urban lofts, and a thriving contemporary art scene has emerged around Fulton Market. Harpo Studios, the production house of Chicago's grande dame, Oprah Winfrey, is here, and there's also an ultrahip dining and nightclub scene. By day, the neighborhood is a relatively quiet, concrete-laden area where plant workers, white-collar business types, and stroller-pushing power moms alike share the sidewalks. When night falls, the scenesters come out of the woodwork, and the too-cool-for-school vibe reigns.

Greektown, a five-block stretch of Halsted Street within the West Loop, is a world all its own. Here, tourists mingle with people from all over Chicago—they all come to the strip's restaurants, groceries, and shops for a taste of Greece that goes beyond plate breaking.

WHAT'S HERE

The West Loop is bound by Ashland Avenue on the west, the Chicago River on the east, Grand Avenue on the north, and the Eisenhower Expressway on the south.

Randolph Street is the neighborhood's restaurant row and home to some of the city's most notable dining spots, including French-inspired **Marché**, which many credit with jump-starting the neighborhood's turn-

GETTING ORIENTED

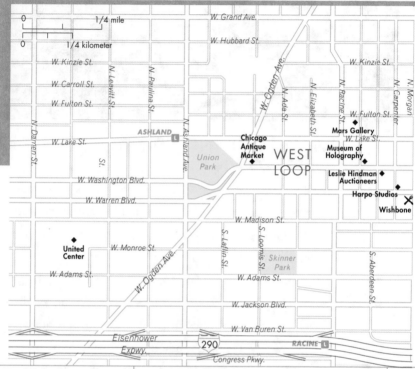

GETTING HERE

By car, take the Kennedy Expressway to the Randolph Street exit. You can also get here by taking the 8 Halsted and 20 Madison buses, or the El's Green Line to Clinton.

For Greektown, take the Blue Line to UIC—Halsted. The 8 Halsted and 20 Madison buses get you here, too. If you're driving to Greektown, exit the Kennedy Expressway at Randolph or Madison streets.

MAKING THE MOST OF YOUR TIME

Start a visit to the West Loop in the late afternoon or early evening, so you have a few hours to browse the galleries before heading to one of the trendy neighborhood restaurants for dinner (plan to eat early if you don't have reservations), and a late-night club to cap off the evening.

If your visit to Chicago happens to coincide with the last Saturday of the month (May–October), check out the Chicago Antique Market around Randolph Street and Ogden Avenue for one-of-a-kind souvenirs, including vintage dishware, clothing, handbags, and jewelry. Afterward, stroll east toward Greektown for a delicious lunch or snack—feta and olives, anyone?

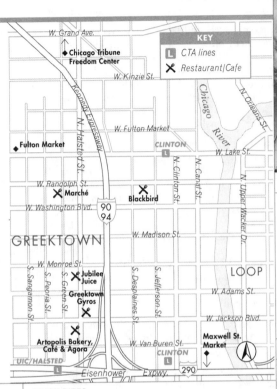

KEY

L CTA lines

X Restaurant/Cafe

◆ Chicago Tribune Freedom Center

W. Grand Ave.

W. Kinzie St.

Kennedy Expressway

N. Halsted St.

W. Fulton Market

CLINTON
L

◆ Fulton Market

W. Lake St.

Chicago River

N. Orleans St.

N. Clinton St.

N. Canal St.

N. Upper Wacker Dr.

W. Randolph St.

X Marché

W. Washington Blvd.

90 94

X Blackbird

GREEKTOWN

W. Madison St.

W. Monroe St.

LOOP

S. Sangamon St.

S. Peoria St.

S. Green St.

X Jubilee Juice

Greektown Gyros

X

S. Desplaines St.

S. Jefferson St.

W. Adams St.

W. Jackson Blvd.

X

Artopolis Bakery, Café & Agora

UIC/HALSTED
L

W. Van Buren St.

CLINTON
L

Maxwell St. Market
◆

Eisenhower Expwy. 290

NEIGHBORHOOD TOP 3

1. Take a picture outside of **Harpo Studios,** where Oprah films her talk show.

2. Check out the funky contemporary art along **Fulton Market.**

3. Order the *saganaki* (flaming cheese) and shout *Opaaa!* along with waiters who set it ablaze for you tableside in **Greektown.**

SAFETY

As you reach the western part of the neighborhood around Ashland Avenue, just a stone's throw from the United Center, the gentrification comes to a halt; the streets around the Fulton Market area are deserted during off times. Exercise caution in both areas.

QUICK BITES

Artopolis Bakery, Café & Agora (⊠ *306 S. Halsted St., West Loop* ☎ *312/559–9000*) has a light menu of salads, soups, sandwiches, and some of the best bread in the city.

For a quick and authentic taste of Greektown, or just a plain old burger and fries anytime day or night, stop in to **Greektown Gyros** (⊠ *239 S. Halsted St., West Loop* ☎ *312/236–9310*), open 24 hours a day, 7 days a week.

Smoothies and salads will fuel you up without weighing you down at the tiny **Jubilee Juice** (⊠ *140 N. Halsted St., West Loop* ☎ *312/491–8500*).

They come from all over town for the cheese grits, blue claw–crab cakes, and other examples of "Southern Reconstructionist" cooking at **Wishbone** (⊠ *1001 W. Washington Blvd., West Loop* ☎ *312/850-2663*). At breakfast and lunch, you can opt for a cafeteria line.

around in the early 1990s, and **Blackbird,** a nouveau American hot spot lauded by critics worldwide as one of the best restaurants anywhere.

The corner of Randolph Street and Des Plaines Avenue is the site of the infamous Haymarket riot, when 11 people were killed in a melee sparked by protests for an eight-hour workday in Chicago. The event led to the creation of May Day, a worker's holiday still observed the first day in May throughout much of Europe. The neighborhood saw more strife in 1969 during the "Days of Rage" riots, which followed the famous "Chicago Seven" trial of seven protestors charged with inciting riots at the Democratic National Convention here a year earlier.

On Carpenter Street between Randolph Street and Washington Boulevard is **Harpo Studios** (✉ *1058 W. Washington Blvd., West Loop* ☎ *312/591–9222* ⊕ *www.oprah.com*), the taping site for Oprah Winfrey's talk show. The studio isn't open to tours, and tickets to the show can be near-impossible to score, so a stop here isn't much more than a fun photo op. However, if you're a die-hard Oprah fan and want to attempt to get tickets, here's what you need to know: The show books audiences only for the current and following month. When you call—and if you're lucky enough to get through—a staffer will give you the taping schedule and a list of available dates. You can reserve up to four seats for any one taping (all attendees must be at least 18). If you can't get tickets in advance, check the Web site for occasional last-minute tickets via e-mail.

LOVE OPRAH? **If you keep your eyes peeled you might spot one of Winfrey's celebrity guests grabbing a bite in the neighborhood after a taping or an assistant walking one of her beloved dogs.**

Just to the west of Harpo on Washington is the **Museum of Holography,** where 10,000 square feet of exhibit space is dedicated to the advancement of—you guessed it—holography as an art form. East along Fulton Market, a number of art galleries are sprinkled in among meatpacking warehouses. The art scene here includes all kinds of work—printmaking, sculpture, photography, paintings, and glass and metalwork. One of the pioneering forces in the art community, **Mars Gallery,** has showcased contemporary pop and outsider art since 1988.

The **Chicago Antique Market,** a seasonal indoor–outdoor flea market held May through October on the last Saturday of the month, has established itself as this city's answer to London's famed Portobello Road market. Centered around Randolph Street and Ogden Avenue, the market offers everything from mid-century furniture to vintage handbags.

Antiques hunters with fat wallets may want to also check the schedule at **Leslie Hindman Auctioneers** (✉ *122 N. Aberdeen St., West Loop* ☎ *312/280–1212*), a fine art auctioneer on Aberdeen Street that's the fifth-largest auction house in the country.

Back on Halsted Street between Madison and Van Buren streets is **Greektown,** a small strip of the West Loop that may as well be half a world away. Greek restaurants are the main draw here.

Dining in the West Loop

EXPENSIVE DINING
Moto, *Cutting-Edge,*
945 W. Fulton Market, at
N. Sangamon St.

MODERATE DINING
Avec, *New American,*
615 W. Randolph St.

Blackbird, *New American,* 619 W. Randolph St.

Carmichael's, *Steakhouse,* 1052 W. Monroe St.

De Cero Taqueria, *Mexican,* 814 W. Randolph St.

Green Zebra, *Vegetarian,* 1460 W. Chicago Ave.

La Sardine, *Bistro,*
111 N. Carpenter St.

Marché, *Brasserie,* 833
W. Randolph St.

N9NE Steakhouse,
Steakhouse,
440 W. Randolph St.

one sixtyblue,
New American,
1400 W. Randolph St.

Red Light, *Pan Asian,*
820 W. Randolph St.

Vivo, *Italian,*
838 W. Randolph St.

West Town Tavern,
American,
1329 W. Chicago Ave.

BUDGET DINING
Costa's, *Greek,*
340 S. Halsted St.

Ina's, *American,*
1235 W. Randolph St.

Lou Mitchell's,
American,
565 W. Jackson Blvd.

The Parthenon, *Greek,*
314 S. Halsted St.

Sushi Wabi, *Japanese,*
842 W. Randolph St.

2

NEAR NORTH INCLUDING THE GOLD COAST, MAGNIFICENT MILE & STREETERVILLE

Sightseeing
★★★★★

Dining
★★★★☆

Lodging
★★★★☆

Shopping
★★★★☆

Nightlife
★★★★☆

The city's greatest tourist magnet reads like a to-do checklist: Navy Pier, the John Hancock Building, art museums and galleries, lakefront activities, and countless shops where you could spend a few dollars or thousands. The Magnificent Mile, a stretch of Michigan Avenue between the Chicago River and Oak Street, owes its name to the swanky shops that line both sides of the street. Shoppers cram the sidewalks in summer and keep the street bustling even in winter, when the trees are twined with thousands of white lights and the buildings are aglow with colored floodlights.

East of the Magnificent Mile is upscale Streeterville, which began as a disreputable landfill that the notorious George Wellington "Cap" Streeter and his wife, Maria, claimed as their own. Along the Lake Michigan shoreline, from North Avenue on the north, Oak Street on the south, and LaSalle Street on the west, is the posh Gold Coast area. Made fashionable after the Great Chicago Fire of 1871 by the social-climbing industrialists of the day, today's Gold Coast neighborhood is still a ritzy place to live, work, shop, and mingle. Architectural styles along East Lake Shore Drive Historic District include baroque, Renaissance, Georgian, and Beaux-Arts—though varied, they blend together beautifully.

WHAT'S HERE

The **Michigan Avenue Bridge** spans the Chicago River as a gateway to North Michigan Avenue from the south. On the east side of the river is the headquarters of the *Chicago Tribune,* in the crenellated **Tribune Tower,** behind which resides the **NBC Tower.**

DID YOU KNOW?

The base of Tribune Tower is studded with pieces from more than 120 famous sites and structures around the world, including the Parthenon, the Taj Mahal, and Bunker Hill.

Across the water and due for completion in late 2008 is the much-hyped Trump International Hotel & Tower, a 92-story mixed-use behemoth on the site of the old *Chicago Sun-Times* headquarters. The construction project has been managed by the Donald's first *Apprentice,* hometown son Bill Rancic. North of the bridge on the west side of Michigan Avenue is the **Wrigley Building,** with its striking wedding-cake embellishments and clock tower. They mark the beginning of the **Magnificent Mile,** the famous stretch of shops. The tapering **John Hancock Center,** the third-tallest building in Chicago, and the elegant Fourth Presbyterian Church, with its peaceful courtyard, are near the north end of the Mile.

SHOP MECCA

This stretch of Michigan Avenue was originally called the Magnificent Mile because of the architecture. Most of those elegant, small buildings are long gone, however, and the moniker now refers to the excellent shopping that attracts visitors and residents alike.

West of the Mag Mile, at Pearson and Rush streets, is Water Tower Park, a Chicago icon. The Water Tower and the matching Water Works Pumping Station across the street are among the few buildings to survive the Great Chicago Fire of 1871. One block east is the imposing **Museum of Contemporary Art,** which concentrates on 20th-century art, principally works created after 1945.

East of the Mag Mile, on Illinois Street and Lake Michigan, is **Navy Pier,** a wonderful place to enjoy lake breezes, hop on an afternoon or evening boat cruise, catch a concert or play, or ride on the giant Ferris wheel. The **Chicago Children's Museum** is part of the Navy Pier complex. North of Navy Pier, hugging Lake Shore Drive, is the Gold Coast neighborhood. Astor Street is the grande dame of Gold Coast promenades. On the northwest corner of Astor and Burton streets, you'll find the Georgian **Patterson-McCormick Mansion** (✉ *20 E. Burton Pl.*), commissioned in 1891 by *Chicago Tribune* chief Joseph Medill. Where Astor Street jogs to meet Schiller Street stands the 1892 **Charnley–Persky House,** designed in part by Frank Lloyd Wright. On Goethe Street is the Ambassador East Hotel, home of the famous **Pump Room** restaurant. In its glory days, celebrities like Frank Sinatra, Humphrey Bogart, and Lauren Bacall held court in the famed Booth One. Where Dearborn Street meets Oak Street is the Gold Coast's famous shopping district. Past the former **Playboy Mansion** (✉ *1340 N. State St.*), all the way to North Avenue, is a beautiful view of Lincoln Park.

GOETHE STREET

If you're ever pressed for conversation in Chicago, just solicit opinions on how Goethe Street should be pronounced. Then sit back and enjoy the fireworks.

GETTING ORIENTED

Armitage Ave.

N. Lincoln Ave.

N. Clark St.

N. Lincoln Ave.

N. Mohawk St.

N. Larrabee St.

N. Sedgwick St.

N. Clark St.

LINCOLN PARK

41

North Ave.

North Ave.

Clybourn Ave.

Wells St.

La Salle Blvd.

E. Burton Pl.

Astor Pl.

E. Schiller St.

Charnley-Persky House ◆

E. Burton Pl.

Astor St.

Lake Michigan

Stanton Park

GOLD COAST

Division St.

Division St.

Division St.

Larrabee St.

Elm St.

RIVER NORTH

Maple St.

Oak St.

Clarke St.

Dearborn St.

Parkway St.

Hudson St.

Oak St. Beach

41

Signature Room at the 95th ✕

John Hancock Center

Walton St.

Franklin St.

Michigan Ave.

L'Appetito ✕

Delaware St.

Delaware St.

KEY

✕ Restaurant/Cafe

Chestnut St.

Water Works

Bistro 110 ✕

Pearson St.

Chicago Ave.

N. Br. Chicago

Kingsbury St.

Sedgwick St.

Orleans St.

La Salle Blvd.

Clark St.

Dearborn St.

State St.

Wabash St.

Rush St.

Museum of Contemporary Art ◆

Superior St.

NEAR NORTH

Huron St.

Erie St.

Garrett Popcorn Shop ✕

Ontario St.

J. F. Kennedy Expwy.

Ohio St.

Fairbanks Ct.

Grand Ave.

River

Illinois St.

Tribune Tower

NBC Tower

Hubbard St.

Kinzie St.

Wrigley Building

✕ Billy Goat Tavern

0 — 1/4 mi

Michigan Ave. Bridge

0 — 1/4 km

TO NAVY PIER & CHICAGO CHILDREN'S MUSEUM

Wacker Dr.

LOOP

GETTING HERE

If you're arriving from the north by car, take Lake Shore Drive south to the Michigan Avenue exit. From the south, you can start your exploring by exiting at Grand Avenue, the exit for Navy Pier. Numerous buses run along Michigan Avenue, including the 3, 4, 144, 145, 146, 167, and 151. Buses 29, 65, and 66 all service Navy Pier. If you're using the El, take the Red Line to Chicago Avenue to get closest to the action.

MAKING THE MOST OF YOUR TIME

You can spend a day at a number of the attractions (or just shopping), depending on your interests. Navy Pier takes at least a couple of hours (especially if you have children); you could spend a few hours in the Chicago Children's Museum alone. Art lovers will want to set aside at least one or two hours for the Museum of Contemporary Art. A stroll through the Gold Coast can be done in an hour, but what's the hurry? Make an afternoon of it. Our favorite times are weekend afternoons in spring or fall or just before dusk any day in summer, when the neighborhood's leafy tranquility and big-city energy converge.

NEIGHBORHOOD TOP 3

1. Have a drink or a meal at the **Signature Room** at the 95th.

2. Sunbathe with the beautiful people at **Oak Street Beach.**

3. Take one of the Chicago Architecture Foundation's amazing **boat tours** along the river.

QUICK BITES

For an inexpensive, hearty lunch, try **L'Appetito** (⊠ *875 N. Michigan Ave.* ☎ *312/337–0691*), a deli and grocery off the Hancock Center's lower-level plaza that has some of the best Italian sandwiches in Chicago.

Behind and one-level down from the Wrigley Building is the (in)famous **Billy Goat Tavern** (⊠ *430 N. Michigan Ave.* ☎ *312/222–1525*), the inspiration for *Saturday Night Live*'s classic "cheezborger, cheezborger" skit and a longtime haunt of local journalists, most notably the late columnist Mike Royko. Grab a greasy burger (and chips, of course) at this no-frills grill, or just have a beer and absorb the comic undertones.

Make a meal out of appetizers at **Bistro 110** (⊠ *110 E. Pearson St.* ☎ *312/266–3110*). The artichoke hearts are heavenly, and the gooey French onion soup is not to be missed. There are ample choices of wine by the glass. The front bar-café area is perfect for casual dining.

Garrett Popcorn Shop (⊠ *670 N. Michigan Ave.* ☎ *312/944–4730*) is a Chicago institution that has been selling popcorn on the Mag Mile for more than 50 years. Tourists and locals alike line up outside—even in the frigid months—to buy tasty warm popcorn mixed with things like macadamia nuts and caramel. (Warning: The cheese and caramel combo is a well-known diet killer.)

AT A GLANCE

Dining in Near North

EXPENSIVE DINING

Avenues, *Cutting-Edge*, Peninsula Hotel, 108 E. Superior St., Near North

Gibsons Steakhouse, *Steakhouse*, 1028 N. Rush St., Near North

Les Nomades, *French*, 222 E. Ontario St., Near North

NoMI, *New American*, Park Hyatt Hotel, 800 N. Michigan Ave., Near North

Primehouse, *Steakhouse*, 616 N. Rush St., Near North

Seasons Restaurant, *New American*, Four Seasons Hotel, 120 E. Delaware Pl., Near North

TRU, *New American*, 676 N. Saint Clair St., Near North

MODERATE DINING

Bistro 110, *Bistro*, 110 E. Pearson St., Near North

Bistrot Margot, *Bistro*, 1437 N. Wells St., Near North

The Caliterra Bar & Grille, *Italian*, Wyndham Chicago Hotel, 633 N. St. Clair St., Near North

The Capital Grille, *Steakhouse*, 633 N. St. Clair St., Near North

Cru Café & Wine Bar, *American*, 25 E. Delaware Ave., Near North

McCormick and Schmick's, *Seafood*, 41 E. Chestnut St., Near North

Mike Ditka's Restaurant, *Steakhouse*, Tremont Hotel, 100 E. Chestnut St., Near North

Pump Room, *American*, 1301 N. State Pkwy, Near North

Riva, *Seafood*, 700 E. Grand Ave., Near North

RL, *American*, 115 E. Chicago Ave., Near North

Roy's, *Pan Asian*, 720 N. State St., Near North

Salpicon, *Mexican*, 1252 N. Wells St., Near North

Shanghai Terrace, *Chinese*, Peninsula Hotel, 108 E. Superior St., Near North

Signature Room at the 95th, *American*, John Hancock Center, 875 N. Michigan Ave., Near North

Spiaggia, *Italian*, 980 N. Michigan Ave., Near North

Viand, *American*, 155 E. Ontario St., Near North

BUDGET DINING

Billy Goat Tavern, *Burger*, 430 N. Michigan Ave., lower level, Near North

Fox & Obel Food Market Cafe, *Cafe*, 401 E. Illinois St., Near North

Heaven on Seven, *Southern*, 600 N. Michigan Ave., Near North

Joe's Be-Bop Cafe and Jazz Emporium, *Southern*, E. Grand Ave., Near North

Kamehachi, *Japanese*, 1400 N. Wells St., Near North

Pierrot Gourmet, *Cafe*, 108 E. Superior St., Near North

2

RIVER NORTH

Sightseeing
★★☆☆☆

Dining
★★★★☆

Lodging
★★★★☆

Shopping
★★★★☆

Nightlife
★★★★☆

Technically a part of Near North, River North is a neighborhood that commands a strong presence all its own. Bounded on the south and west by branches of the Chicago River, River North has eastern and northern boundaries that can be hard to define. As in many other Chicago neighborhoods, the limits have expanded as the area has grown more attractive; today they extend roughly to Oak Street on the north and Rush Street on the east. Richly served by waterways and railroad tracks that ran along its western edge, the neighborhood was settled by Irish immigrants in the mid-19th century. As the 20th century approached, the area developed into a busy commercial, industrial, and warehouse district.

But as economic conditions changed and factories moved away, the neighborhood deteriorated, and River North became just another down-on-its-luck urban area. In the 1970s, artists attracted by low rents and spacious abandoned storage areas and shop floors began to move into the neighborhood, and it eventually became the go-to spot for art lovers to gallery hop. Then developers caught the scent and began buying up properties with an eye to renovation. Today, struggling artists might find it hard to afford a cup of coffee in this high-rent district dotted with tourist-pleasing restaurants and upscale retail shops.

GETTING ORIENTED

GETTING HERE

The Merchandise Mart has its own stop on the El's Brown and Purple lines. By car, take Wells Street to Chicago Avenue to put you at the northern tip of the neighborhood.

You can also walk west from the Mag Mile a few blocks to get to the area.

MAKING THE MOST OF YOUR TIME

You can see all there is to see in about two hours, but add another hour or more if you want to wander leisurely in and out of the shops at Tree Studios or the galleries on Superior Street and the surrounding area. A meal at one of the touristy restaurants can entail a wait on weekends and nice days. Most galleries are closed Sunday and Monday.

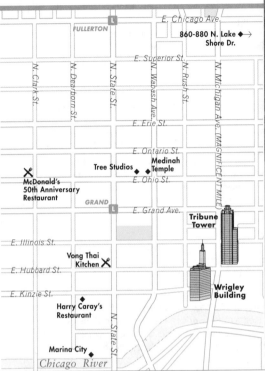

NEIGHBORHOOD TOP 4

1. Treat yourself to music during a Friday lunch at the infamous Andy's Jazz Club's **Jazz at Noon** series.

2. Spend an afternoon browsing the **art galleries**.

3. Pick up some ideas for your next home improvement project at **LuxeHome** in the Merchandise Mart.

4. Cheer on the Chicago Cubs from the comfort of a cozy bar stool at **Harry Caray's Restaurant** at 33 W. Kinzie Street.

QUICK BITES

For quality over kitsch, try the **Big Bowl Café** (✉ *159 W. Erie St.*), or fill up on both while chowing down on yummy Chicago deep-dish pizza at the graffiti-covered, tourist-happy **Gino's East** (✉ *633 N. Wells St.*).

Nestled under the El tracks at Superior and Franklin streets is **Brett's Kitchen** (✉ *233 W. Superior St., River North* ☎ *312/664–6354*), an excellent spot for a sandwich or an omelet Monday through Saturday.

Want some fries to go with that shake, honey? The purposefully snarky waitstaff at **Ed Debevic's** (✉ *640 N. Wells St.*), a '50s-style diner, keeps the crowds entertained.

The great John-Georges Vongerichten gets casual at **Vong Thai Kitchen** (✉ *6 W. Hubbard St., River North* ☎ *312/664–8664*), where sharing satays, noodle dishes, and curries is encouraged.

WHAT'S HERE

The huge **Merchandise Mart,** on the river between Orleans and Wells streets, is so commanding that it has its own zip code as well as its own stop on the El's Brown and Purple lines. Miles of corridors on its top floors are lined with trade-only furniture and home-design showrooms. LuxeHome, a collection of 30 or so upscale stores with an emphasis on home design and renovation, takes up the bottom two floors.

At Dearborn and Kinzie streets is the splendid ornamental brickwork of **33 West Kinzie Street,** the home of Harry Caray's restaurant. (The loud—and delicious—restaurant, filled with flags and giant drawings of the late Cubs broadcaster and his big glasses, is on "Harry Caray Drive," an honorary designation.) Southeast of here, just shy of the bridge that crosses the Chicago River, you can see the distinctive twin corncobs of **Marina City,** a residential complex that also includes the Hotel Sax Chicago (formerly a House of Blues hotel), the House of Blues nightclub, and a bowling alley. Fans of the old *Bob Newhart Show* may recognize Marina City from the backdrop in the show's opening credits.

A few blocks north, at the intersection of State and Ohio streets, are the **Tree Studios** shops and galleries, and the adjacent Medinah Temple, on Wabash Avenue, which houses a **Bloomingdale's Home & Furniture Store.**

THE
ROOTS

The original Tree Studios were intended as living spaces for artists who were in town for the World's Columbian Exposition at the turn of the 20th century. They were used as live-work spaces by generations of creative types and were considered an artistic oasis until 2001, when a development group bought the studio buildings and the Medinah Temple.

Head west on either Ohio or Ontario streets, and as you approach LaSalle, then Wells streets, see the neighborhood transform into something of a dining Disneyland, with enormous outposts of national chains like Rainforest Café, Hooters, and the Hard Rock Cafe. Tourists clog the streets, eager to mob them all.

Things get a little more civilized again north on Wells Street to Superior Street, where you run into the area known as the **River North Gallery District.** Dozens of art galleries show every kind of work imaginable in the area bounded by Wells, Orleans, Chicago, and Erie streets—in fact, virtually every building on Superior Street between Wells and Orleans streets houses at least one gallery. Galleries welcome visitors, so feel free to stop into any that catch your eye. On periodic Fridays throughout the year, the galleries coordinate their exhibitions and open their doors to the public for a special night to showcase new works. Art lovers take note: though River North is still a good bet for great art, a growing number of artists have ditched the high-rent district for the cheaper, more industrial West Loop and Pilsen neighborhoods.

Dining in River North

2

EXPENSIVE DINING

Fogo de Chao, *Brazilian*, 661 N. LaSalle St., River North

Keefer's, *Steakhouse*, 20 W. Kinzie St., River North

Smith and Wollensky, *Steakhouse*, 318 N. State St., River North

MODERATE DINING

Aigre Doux, *New American*, 230 W. Kinzie St., River North

Allen's, *New American*, 217 W. Huron St., River North

Bin 36, *American*, 339 N. Dearborn St., River North

Blue Water Grill, *Seafood*, 520 N. Dearborn St., River North

Brasserie Jo, *Brasserie*, 59 W. Hubbard St., River North

Coco Pazzo, *Italian*, 300 W. Hubbard St., River North

Crofton on Wells, *New American*, 535 N. Wells St., River North

DeLaCosta, *Latin*, 465 E. Illinois St., River North

Frontera Grill, *Mexican*, 445 N. Clark St., River North

Gene and Georgetti, *Steakhouse*, 500 N. Franklin St., River North

Harry Caray's, *Italian*, 33 W. Kinzie St., River North

Japonais, *Japanese*, 606 W. Chicago Ave., River North

Joe's Seafood, *Prime Steaks & Stone Crab*, Seafood, 60 E. Grand Ave., River North

Kevin, *Asian Fusion*, 9 W. Hubbard St., River North

Le Lan, *Asian Fusion*, 749 N. Clark St., River North

Maggiano's Little Italy, *Italian*, 516 N. Clark St., River North

mk, *New American*, 868 N. Franklin St., River North

Nacional 27, *Latin*, 325 W. Huron St., River North

Naha, *New American*, 500 N. Clark St., River North

Osteria via Stato, *Italian*, 620 N. State St., River North

Rockit Bar & Grill, *American*, 22 W. Hubbard St., River North

Ruth's Chris Steak House, *Steakhouse*, 431 N. Dearborn St., River North

Scoozi!, *Italian*, 410 W. Huron St., River North

Shaw's Crab House and Blue Crab Lounge, *Seafood*, 21 E. Hubbard St., River North

SushiSamba Rio, *Japanese*, 504 N. Wells St., River North

Topolobampo, *Mexican*, 445 N. Clark St., River North

BUDGET DINING

Ben Pao, *Chinese*, 52 W. Illinois St., River North

Cafe Iberico, *Spanish*, 739 N. LaSalle St., River North

Cyrano's Bistrot Wine Bar & Cabaret, *Bistro*, 546 N. Wells St., River North

Ed Debevic's, *American*, 640 N. Wells St., River North

Mr. Beef, *American*, 666 N. Orleans St., River North

Pizzeria Due, *Italian*, 619 N. Wabash Ave., River North

Pizzeria Uno, *Italian*, 29 E. Ohio St., River North

LINCOLN PARK & OLD TOWN

Sightseeing
★★★★☆

Dining
★★★★☆

Lodging
★★☆☆☆

Shopping
★★☆☆☆

Nightlife
★★★★☆

What began in the 1850s as a modest neighborhood of working-class German families, Old Town now accommodates a diverse population and has some of the oldest—and most expensive—real estate in Chicago. It's bordered by Division Street to the south, Armitage Avenue to the north, Clark Street on the east, and Larrabee Street on the west, but its heart lies at the intersection of North Avenue and Wells Street. Besides its notable architecture, Old Town is home to the famous comedy clubs Zanies and The Second City.

When you get to Lincoln Park, just north of Old Town, don't be confused: the neighborhood near the southern part of the city's oldest and most popular lakefront park also bears its name. Lincoln Park—the *park*—today extends from North Avenue to Hollywood Avenue. It became the city's first public playground in 1864, named after the then recently assassinated president. The neighborhood adjacent to the original park, bordered by Armitage Avenue on the south, Diversey Parkway on the north, the lake on the east, and the Chicago River on the west, also became known as Lincoln Park. It was a sparsely settled community of truck farms and orchards that grew produce for the city of Chicago, 3 mi to the south.

In some ways, Lincoln Park today epitomizes all the things that people love to hate about yuppified urban areas: stratospheric housing prices, teeny boutiques with big-attitude salespeople, and plenty of fancy-schmancy coffee shops, wine bars, and cafés. That said, it's also got some of the prettiest residential streets in the city, that gorgeous park, a great nature museum, and a thriving arts scene. So grab a nonfat half-caf extra-shot grande latte and go with the flow—you'll be happy you did.

WHAT'S HERE

There's a lot going on in Old Town and Lincoln Park. The yuck-it-up comedy clubs on Wells Street and raucous nightlife along North Lincoln Avenue and Halsted Street are a sharp contrast to the tranquility at the lagoon in Lincoln Park at Fullerton Parkway, where sometimes, all the noise you hear is the flapping wings of the resident waterfowl. Between the two are plenty of historic landmarks as well as some cultural gems.

You can hear the laughs emanating from Wells Street in Old Town most any night of the week. **Zanies** has been hosting stand-up shows by some of the country's most famous comics, from Jay Leno to Dave Chappelle, for 30 years. Just up the street is **The Second City,** the legendary improv company that's served as a training ground for generations of would-be superstars.

FRUGAL FUN

Whether or not you go to a show, visit the lobby at The Second City to check out the who's who collection of photographs and caricatures of past troupe members: Alan Alda, John Belushi, Bonnie Hunt, Mike Meyers, Steve Carell, and Amy Sedaris represent just a few of the famous funny alums.

The **Chicago History Museum** (✉*1601 N. Clark St., Lincoln Park* ☎*312/642–4600*) (formerly the Chicago Historical Society), at North Avenue and Clark Street, is housed in a Georgian structure built in 1932. The beautiful people strut their stuff just to the east along the lake at **North Avenue Beach,** while the beasts roar nearby on Stockton Drive at **Lincoln Park Zoo,** which is free to the public. A few blocks ahead, there's a rather inconspicuous patch of grass where a garage once stood bearing the address **2122 N. Clark Street.** There's no marker, but it's the site of the infamous St. Valentine's Day massacre, when seven men were killed on the orders of Al Capone on February 14, 1929.

DID YOU KNOW?

Another infamous Lincoln Park locale is the Biograph Theater (✉N. Lincoln Ave., Lincoln Park ☎773/871–3000), now home to the Victory Gardens Theater company, where notorious bank robber John Dillinger was shot and killed by the FBI in 1934.

One of the largest Catholic universities in the country, **DePaul University** has a 28-acre campus in Lincoln Park, bounded roughly by Webster Avenue on the south, Fullerton Avenue on the north, Halsted Street on the east, and Racine Avenue on the west. It serves more than 17,000 students, and has four other campuses in the Loop and suburbs. You might have a celebrity sighting or two on Halsted Street if you time a visit right to **Steppenwolf Theatre Company,** where ensemble members including Joan Allen, John Mahoney, Gary Sinese, and John Malkovich often perform or direct. The **Peggy Notebaert Nature Museum,** back in the park at Fullerton Parkway, is geared to kids, but outdoorsy adults will dig it, too.

GETTING ORIENTED

GETTING HERE

Take the Howard (Red Line) train or the Ravenswood (Brown Line) train to either Armitage or Fullerton avenues. Sheffield Avenue will be the nearest north–south street in both cases. Buses 11, 22, 36, and 151 take you through the area, too. If you're driving, take Lake Shore Drive to Fullerton Avenue and drive west on Fullerton Avenue to Sheffield Avenue. Parking is scarce, especially evenings and weekends, so public transit or a cab is recommended.

MAKING THE MOST OF YOUR TIME

You could take an hour or a whole day for Lincoln Park, depending on how you prefer to spend your time. Set aside at least a couple of hours if you plan on a leisurely shopping experience along Armitage, Halsted, and Webster avenues. Tack on a couple more hours for the Peggy Notebaert Nature Museum, especially with kids. And if it's a beautiful summer day, ditch whatever else you had planned and surrender yourself to hours of frolicking in the park and on the beach. If you have kids in tow, or simply love visiting urban beasts, set aside some time for the Lincoln Park Zoo.

Come nightfall, make a beeline for The Second City or the Steppenwolf Theatre Company; do a little research ahead of time to decide what kind of performance you want to see—and how much you want to spend. Then you can plan to make a day out of enjoying Lincoln Park and Old Town. It's quintessential Chicago!

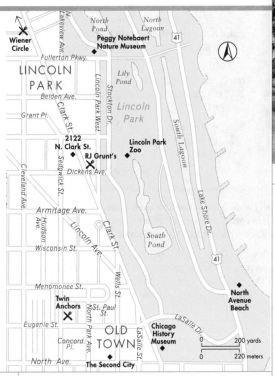

Map labels:
Wiener Circle
Lakeview Ave.
N. Lakeview Ave.
North Pond
North Lagoon
Peggy Notebaert Nature Museum
41
Fullerton Pkwy.
LINCOLN PARK
Lincoln Park West
Stockton Dr.
Lily Pond
Belden Ave.
Grant Pl.
Lincoln Park
Clark St.
2122 N. Clark St.
RJ Grunt's
Lincoln Park Zoo
Dickens Ave.
Sedgwick St.
South Lagoon
Cleveland Ave.
Armitage Ave.
Hudson Ave.
Clark St.
Lincoln Ave.
Wisconsin St.
South Pond
Lake Shore Dr.
41
Menomonee St.
Wells St.
Twin Anchors
North Park Ave.
St. Paul St.
North Avenue Beach
Eugenie St.
LaSalle Dr.
LaSalle St.
OLD TOWN
Chicago History Museum
Concord Pl.
North Ave.
The Second City
0   200 yards
0   220 meters

1. Take a walk—or a run, or a bike ride—along the **lakefront path** heading south from North Avenue beach, and take in the breathtaking views of the city along Lake Michigan.

2. Catch the free improv after the show every night except Friday at **The Second City**.

3. See some of Hollywood's greats come home to their roots to perform in a play at the **Steppenwolf Theatre Company**.

4. Satisfy your late-night cravings after a stint at the bars with a stop at the **Wiener Circle** (at N. Clark St. and Wrightwood Ave.; walk north on Clark from Fullerton Pkwy.), where the surly service is part of the fun.

5. For a very different dining experience, splurge on a degustation at **Charlie Trotter's**.

QUICK BITES

Cafe Luigi (✉ *2548 N. Clark St., Lincoln Park* ☎ *773/404-0200*) is a blink-and-you'll-miss-it storefront that sells New York–style pizza slices, calzones, and sausage rolls to grateful East Coast expats.

Nookies, too (✉ *2114 N. Halsted St., Lincoln Park* ☎ *773/327-1400*) is open 24 hours on Friday and Saturday and serves heaping breakfasts anytime, making it a favorite of the neighborhood's late-night partying crowd. Cash only.

Just outside the park, **R. J. Grunt's** (✉ *2056 N. Lincoln Park W, Lincoln Park* ☎ *773/929-5363*) has been serving killer milk shakes and burgers and stocking a salad bar for healthy types since 1971.

Twin Anchors (✉ *1655 N. Sedgwick St., Lincoln Park* ☎ *312/266-1616* ⊘ *No lunch weekdays*), a popular Old Town restaurant and tavern for more than 60 years, is famous for its barbecued ribs.

Dining in Lincoln Park

EXPENSIVE DINING
Alinea, *Cutting-Edge*, 1723 N. Halsted St., Lincoln Park

Charlie Trotter's, *New American*, 816 W. Armitage Ave., Lincoln Park

Geja's, *French*, 340 W. Armitage Ave., Lincoln Park

MODERATE DINING
Boka, *New American*, 1729 N. Halsted St., Lincoln Park

North Pond, *American*, 2610 N. Cannon Dr., Lincoln Park

Sola, *New American*, 3868 N. Lincoln Ave., Lincoln Park

Twin Anchors Restaurant & Tavern, *Barbecue*, 1655 N. Sedgwick St., Old Town

BUDGET DINING
Café Ba-Ba-Reeba!, *Spanish*, 2024 N. Halsted St., Lincoln Park

Mon Ami Gabi, *Bistro*, 2300 N. Lincoln Park W, Lincoln Park

OUR TIP **All ages get especially wide-eyed in the Notebaert's Judy Istock Butterfly Haven, where you get to commingle with 75 different species of free-flying, brightly colored beauties—roughly 1,000 at any time.**

Film buffs shouldn't leave Lincoln Park without a visit to **Facets Cinematheque,** which presents an eclectic selection of artistically significant films from around the world on its two screens. It also has a well-stocked video store (Facets Videotheque) that's got more than 60,000 foreign, classic, and cult films.

WICKER PARK & BUCKTOWN

Sightseeing
★★☆☆☆

Dining
★★★★☆

Lodging
★☆☆☆☆

Shopping
★★★★☆

Nightlife
★★★★☆

Creative types still cluster in Bucktown and Wicker Park, a hip, somewhat grungy enclave of side-by-side neighborhoods centered on Milwaukee, Damen, and North avenues. But they no longer lay exclusive claim to this funky part of town. These days, you'll find young families, thirtysomething working types, and university students thrown into the mix along with the immigrant communities who have lived here for generations. Within this Petri dish of gentrification, there are also cutting-edge galleries, coffeehouses, nightclubs, and a bizarre bazaar of shops. A sign of the changing times: chains like American Apparel and Urban Outfitters have opened outposts in this neighborhood, once considered a haven from corporate retail. Still, this definitely ain't where you'll find anything akin to your momma's suburban strip malls.

Bucktown—which is said to have taken its name from the goats kept by the area's original Polish and German immigrants—encompasses the neighborhood surrounding Milwaukee Avenue north of North Avenue. The area south of North Avenue to Division Street is Wicker Park. Farther south still is Ukrainian Village, where the artsy types are now encroaching, but which still has a number of sights that are a testimony to the ethnic roots that remain strong in this neighborhood. If you're ambitious, in one afternoon's walk you can visit Bucktown and Wicker Park and even make a detour into Ukrainian Village.

GETTING ORIENTED

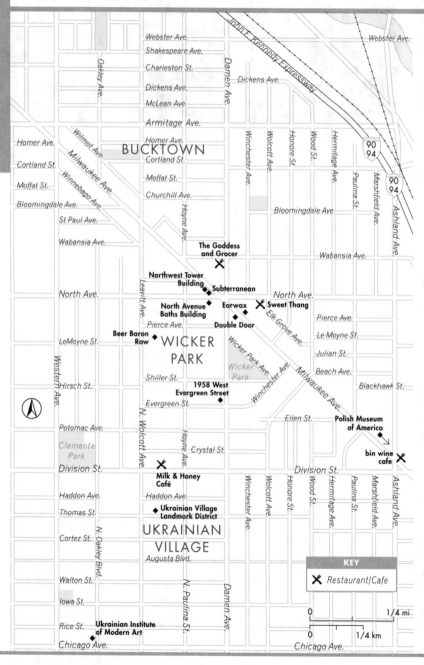

Webster Ave.
Shakespeare Ave.
Charleston St.
Dickens Ave.
McLean Ave.
Armitage Ave.

Oakley Ave.

Damen Ave.

John F. Kennedy Expressway

Dickens Ave.

Webster Ave.

90 94

90 94

Ashland Ave.

Homer Ave.

BUCKTOWN

Homer Ave.
Cortland St.

Wilmot Ave.

Milwaukee Ave.

Winchester Ave.

Wolcott St.

Honore St.

Wood St.

Hermitage Ave.

Paulina Ave.

Marshfield Ave.

Cortland St.
Moffat St.

Winnebago Ave.

Moffat St.
Churchill Ave.

Bloomingdale Ave.
St Paul Ave.

Hoyne Ave.

Bloomingdale Ave.

Wabansia Ave.

Wabansia Ave.

The Goddess and Grocer ✕

Northwest Tower Building ◆
Subterranean

Leavitt Ave.

North Ave.
North Avenue Baths Building
Earwax ✕ **Sweet Thang**

Elk Grove Ave.

North Ave.

Pierce Ave.
Le Moyne St.

Beer Baron Row ◆
Pierce Ave.
Double Door

WICKER PARK

Wicker Park Ave.

Winchester Ave.

Milwaukee Ave.

Julian St.
Beach Ave.

LeMoyne St.

Western Ave.

Hirsch St.

N. Wolcott Ave.

Shiller St.

1958 West Evergreen Street ◆

Wicker Park

Blackhawk St.

Evergreen St.

Polish Museum of America ◆

Potomac Ave.

Hoyne Ave.

Ellen St.

Clemente Park

Crystal St.

bin wine cafe ✕

Division St.

✕
Milk & Honey Café

Division St.

Wood St.

Hermitage Ave.

Paulina St.

Marshfield Ave.

Ashland Ave.

Haddon Ave.
Thomas St.

N. Oakley Blvd.

Haddon Ave.

◆ **Ukrainian Village Landmark District**

Winchester Ave.

Wolcott Ave.

Honore St.

Cortez St.

UKRAINIAN VILLAGE

Augusta Blvd.

Walton St.
Iowa St.

Ukrainian Institute of Modern Art ◆
Chicago Ave.

N. Paulina St.

Damen Ave.

Chicago Ave.

KEY
✕ Restaurant/Cafe

0 ——— 1/4 mi
0 ——— 1/4 km

GETTING HERE

If you're driving, take the Kennedy to North Avenue, then go west on North Avenue until you reach the triangular intersection where North meets Milwaukee and Damen avenues. Metered street parking is available. By El train, take the Blue Line to the Damen–North Avenue stop.

QUICK BITES

bin wine cafe (✉ *1559 N. Milwaukee Ave., Wicker Park* ☎ *773/486-2233*) is a cozy little storefront where you can pair top-notch wines by the glass with global menu options.

To us, former caterer to the stars Debby Sharpe is both **The Goddess and Grocer** (✉ *1646 N. Damen Ave., Bucktown* ☎ *773/342-3200*), serving up to-die-for sandwiches and salads that please vegans and carnivores alike at her gourmet takeout shop. You can eat at the small dining room next door.

A sunny spot with a fireplace for cold winter days, **Milk & Honey Café** (✉ *1920 W. Division St., Wicker Park* ☎ *773/395-9434*) packs in neighborhood types who crave the French toast at breakfast and inventive lunchtime sandwiches served with housemade potato chips.

Fuel up with fluffy French croissants, palmiers, and cappuccinos at **Sweet Thang** (✉ *1921 W. North Ave., Bucktown* ☎ *773/772-4166*), a cute little bistro with a rich red sofa in the window and red-leather chairs with heart-shape backs. If you want to practice your French, place your order for a slice of quiche or a croque monsieur in *la belle langue*. Then settle back and imagine you're in gay Paris.

NEIGHBORHOOD TOP 3

1. Order a cup of coffee or a glass of wine and perch yourself at the window seat in a café—or at an outdoor table in warm weather—and get ready for some of the best **people-watching** in the city.

2. Catch some cutting-edge music at the **Double Door**.

3. **Shop for funky finds** at the shops along Division Street, Milwaukee Avenue, and Damen Avenue.

MAKING THE MOST OF YOUR TIME

The best times for people-watching are in the evenings when the clubs and bars draw crowds, or during Sunday brunch when the restaurants do steady business. May through October you can take your place at an outdoor patio to savor the view of hipsters and young families strolling by, soaking up the sun.

The most lively times to visit are late August, when Bucktown hosts its annual Arts Fest, and September, during the Around the Coyote Arts Festival and the indie favorite Renegade Craft Fair.

WHAT'S HERE

The anchor of the North-Milwaukee-Damen intersection is the striking triangular Northwest Tower Building, used as a reference point from miles around. The beautiful facade of the **North Avenue Baths Building** (⊠ *2039 W. North Ave., Bucktown*), near the intersection of Milwaukee and Damen avenues, is a clue to its past life when it was a storied meeting spot for politicians who cut deals in the hot steam rooms, where it was difficult to plant wire taps.

Across the street is **Subterranean** (⊠ *2011 W. North Ave., Bucktown* ☎ *773/278–6600*), a bar and dance club resting atop tunnels once used to flee authorities in the Prohibition era. Also near this intersection is the **Double Door,** a late-night music venue where homegrown acts like Veruca Salt and Liz Phair and legends like the Rolling Stones have played, and the colorful **Earwax Cafe,** a vegan- and vegetarian-friendly hangout with a video-rentals department.

FRUGAL FUN

Art spills onto the streets of Bucktown and Wicker Park every September, when the weekend-long Around the Coyote Fall Arts Festival attracts thousands of collectors and browsers who scour every nook and cranny of the neighborhood.

For a reality-television fix, check out the building at the corner of Winchester and North avenues, a former *Real World* house. Back on Damen, head north for some shopping—window or otherwise—at a collection of shops selling wares you won't likely find elsewhere. Hip fashionistas from around the city head to p. 45 to check out the latest finds from up-and-coming designers, while homebodies *oooh* and *ahhh* over the luxurious tabletop finds at **Stitch.** The neighborhood's well known to antiques hunters, too, who hunt for treasures at shops like **Pavilion** and **Pagoda Red.**

Along Hoyne and Pierce streets you'll find some of the biggest and best examples of Chicago's Victorian-era architecture. So many brewery owners built homes in this area that it was once dubbed **"Beer Baron Row".** ■ TIP→ **As you're walking the neighborhood, note the Anglophile street names (Webster, Shakespeare, Dickens, Churchill). These were changed around the time of World War I to distance the neighborhood from its Russian, German, and Polish roots.**

DID YOU KNOW?

Novelist Nelson Algren, whose book Chicago: City on the Make still wins praise for capturing the essence of the city, lived in the three-story home at 1958 West Evergreen Street.

For a glimpse of how the working class lived at the turn of the 20th century, head a little farther south to the **Ukrainian Village Landmark District** (on Haddon Avenue and Thomas and Cortez streets between Damen and Leavitt avenues), a well-preserved group of worker cottages and flats. Another place to glimpse the old immigrant populations' squat leaded-glass brick homes is on Homer Street between Leavitt and Oakley streets.

AT A GLANCE

Dining in Wicker Park

MODERATE DINING

Café Absinthe, *New American*, 1954 W. North Ave., Bucktown

Hot Chocolate, *Cafe*, 1747 N. Damen Ave., Wicker Park

Le Bouchon, *Bistro*, 1958 N. Damen Ave., Bucktown

Mas, *Latin*, 1670 W. Division St., Wicker Park

Meritage Café and Wine Bar, *New American*, 2118 N. Damen Ave., Bucktown

Mirai Sushi, *Japanese*, 2020 W. Division St., Wicker Park

Spring, *New American*, 2039 W. North Ave., Wicker Park

BUDGET DINING

Feast, *International*, 1616 N. Damen Ave., Bucktown

Piece, *Pizza*, 1927 W. North Ave., Wicker Park

Smoke Daddy, *Southern*, 1804 W. Division St., Wicker Park

Milk & Honey Café, *Cafe*, 1920 W. Division St., Wicker Park

Nearby on Chicago Avenue is the **Ukrainian Institute of Modern Art** (⊠*2320 W. Chicago Ave.* ☎*773/227–5522*), which has three galleries that focus on sculpture, mixed media, and paintings.

LAKE VIEW INCLUDING WRIGLEYVILLE

Sightseeing
★★☆☆☆

Dining
★★★★☆

Lodging
★☆☆☆☆

Shopping
★★★★☆

Nightlife
★★★★☆

Lake View is a massive North Side neighborhood made up of smaller enclaves that each have their own distinct personalities. There's the beer-swilling, Cubby-blue-'til-we-die sports-bar fanaticism of Wrigleyville, home of the esteemed Wrigley Field; the out-and-proud colors of the gay bars, shops, and clubs along Halsted Street in Boys Town; and an air of urban chicness along Southport Avenue (a street that's really a bit too far west to enjoy any lake views, but part of the neighborhood still the same), where young families stroll amid the trendy boutiques and ice-cream shops. It's a mix that means that a few blocks' walk in one direction or another will surely lead to some interesting finds.

Lake View's first white settler was Conrad Sulzer, a grim-looking Swiss native and the son of a Protestant minister. Sulzer arrived in 1837, but the community was really established in the 1850s by James E. Rees and E. E. Hundley. Rees and Hundley built the Hotel Lake View—from which the neighborhood got its name—and then its first main road, which is now Broadway. By 1889 Chicago took the town for its own. Lake View had, and continues to have, a large Irish population, with pubs dotting many of its streets. It's also an area that's densely populated with young urban professionals and one of the main centers of Chicago's gay and lesbian community.

WHAT'S HERE

The venerable **Wrigley Field,** the ivy-covered home of the Chicago Cubs and the nation's second-oldest major league ballpark, is on the corner of Addison and Clark streets. Check out the **Harry Caray statue** commemorating the late Cubs announcer and sing "Take Me Out to the Ballgame" in his honor. Diagonally across the street is the **Cubby Bear Lounge** (⊠*1059 W. Addison St.* ☎*773/327–1662*), a Chicago institution since 1953. If you look up along Sheffield Avenue on the eastern side of the ballpark, you can see the rooftop patios where baseball fans pay high prices to root for the home team. Ticketless fans sit in lawn chairs on Sheffield during the games, waiting for foul balls to fly their way.

A long fly ball north of Wrigley is **Metro** (⊠*3730 N. Clark St.*), a former theater that's been converted to one of the city's best live-music venues. The Smashing Pumpkins got their start here. East on Grace Street is the 3800 north block of **Alta Vista Terrace,** a lovely residential street where 40 town houses completed as part of a single development in 1904 mirror one another diagonally across the block for a striking, harmonious effect. North again on Clark Street is **Graceland Cemetery,** which has crypts that are almost as strikingly designed as the city skyline.

DID YOU KNOW?

The names on the grave sites at Graceland read like a who's who from a Chicago history book: Marshall Field, George Pullman, Louis Sullivan, and Daniel Burnham are a few of the notables buried here. You can buy a walking-tour map at the entrance Monday through Saturday to explore on your own.

Right on Halsted Street is "Boys Town," as locals often call it. Distinctive rainbow pylons line the street between Belmont and Addison avenues, marking the gay district. In June, Halsted is a sea of people when Chicago's gay pride parade floats down the block.

Belmont Avenue is a strip with a different character entirely. There are tattoo parlors and vintage-clothing stores, and just past the El tracks at Sheffield is the **Vic Theatre,** originally a luxurious vaudeville theater. Today it's a live-music venue that's most popular for Brew & View nights, when second- or third-run movies are screened, three bars are open, and the mood is festive.

LOCAL LIFE

Where Belmont meets up with Clark Street is a place the locals like to call "Punkin' Donuts." It's just a plain old Dunkin' Donuts, really, on a strip where lots of heavily pierced, spiky-haired types hang out.

A few blocks farther west you hit Southport Avenue, where the shopping seems to get more interesting all the time. There's not a Gap or Pottery Barn in sight—rather, the streets that travel north to Irving Park Road are lined with independent shops, many of which cater to well-dressed young women with money to burn. **Red Head Boutique** and neighboring **Krista K** are big favorites. Hipsters of both sexes, meanwhile, drool over the goods at **Jake.** Southport's main claim to fame, though, is the **Music Box Theatre,** a 1929 movie house where you can still see twinkling stars and clouds on the ceiling and hear live organ music before the independent and classic films are shown on its two screens.

GETTING ORIENTED

GETTING HERE

If you're driving, take Lake Shore Drive north from the Loop to Belmont, but keep in mind that parking can be scarce.

Buses 22 and 36 will bring you here from points downtown, as will the Brown and Purple lines to Belmont or the Red Line to Addison. To get to the Southport Avenue shops, take the Brown Line to Southport.

MAKING THE MOST OF YOUR TIME

A quick walk through Wrigleyville and Lake View will take about an hour and a half. Add another half hour if you're wading through the post-Cubs-game crowds.

If you want to get a feel for the rest of the neighborhood, head to Graceland Cemetery—allow about an hour or two for a visit—or go shopping along Southport Avenue. You'll need a few hours more for watching an afternoon game at Wrigley Field, a pastime we consider one of the best ways to experience the *real* Chicago.

NEIGHBORHOOD TOP 5

1. If you can score a ticket, sit in the bleachers with the locals at **Wrigley Field**—and be ready to throw the ball back onto the field if the opposing team nearly hits a homer into the stands.

2. If you can't score a ticket, hang out with the fans on **Sheffield Avenue,** who wait there to catch one of the long fly balls out of the park.

3. Catch a vintage flick at the vintage **Music Box Theatre.**

4. Indulge in a scoop of Daley (as in Mayor Richard J. Daley's) Fudge Addiction at the homegrown **Bobtail Soda Fountain.**

5. Thumb through the extensive selection of vintage vinyl and new tracks at **Reckless Records.**

QUICK BITES

The original Swedish **Ann Sather** (✉929 W. Belmont Ave., Lake View ☎773/348–2378) has legendary breakfasts: lingonberry pancakes or giant cinnamon buns.

Bobtail Soda Fountain (✉2951 N. Broadway, Lake View ☎773/880–7372) serves ice cream based on an old family recipe, with specialty flavors like Lakeview Bourbon Barhopper and Daley Fudge Addiction.

The **Chicago Diner** (✉3411 N. Halsted St., Lake View ☎773/935–6696) is known for its yummy vegetarian food.

Goose Island Wrigleyville (✉3535 N. Clark St., Wrigleyville ☎773/832–9040) has a variety of its own beers and root beers on tap, plus good burgers.

Uncommon Ground (✉3800 N. Clark St., Wrigleyville ☎773/929–3680) might look like a typical neighborhood coffeehouse, until you try the Jamaican jerk pork chops and Guinness French onion soup.

AT A GLANCE

Dining in Lake View

MODERATE DINING

Bistro Campagne, *Bistro*, 4518 N. Lincoln Ave., Lake View

Erwin, *New American*, 2925 N. Halsted St., Lake View

Green Dolphin Street, *American*, 2200 N. Ashland Ave., Lake View

Yoshi's Cafe, *Asian Fusion*, 3257 N. Halsted St., Lake View

BUDGET DINING

Ann Sather, *Scandinavian*, 929 W. Belmont Ave., Lake View

Brett's, *New American*, 2011 W. Roscoe St., Lake View

Coobah, *Latin*, 3423 N. Southport Ave., Lake View

Heaven on Seven, *Southern*, 3478 N. Clark St., Lake View

Hot Doug's, *Hot Dogs*, 3325 N. California Ave., Lake View

Julius Meinl Cafe, *Cafe*, 3601 N. Southport Ave., Lake View

Kitsch'n on Roscoe, *American*, 2005 W. Roscoe St., Lake View

Mia Francesca, *Italian*, 3311 N. Clark St., Lake View

Orange, *American*, 3231 N. Clark St., Lake View

Platiyo, *Mexican*, 3313 N. Clark St., Lake View

Thai Classic, *Thai*, 3332 N. Clark St., Lake View

Turquoise Cafe, *Turkish*, 2147 W. Roscoe St., Lake View

2

FAR NORTH SIDE

Sightseeing
★★☆☆☆

Dining
★★★★☆

Lodging
★☆☆☆☆

Shopping
★★★★☆

Nightlife
★★★☆☆

The far north side of Chicago is home to several of the city's most colorful, eclectic neighborhoods. History-rich Uptown was a once-thriving entertainment district; there, you can take in the beautiful architecture and striking old marquees. Though it's been a bit gritty for decades, new condo developments and chains like Borders and Starbucks are arriving in the area. The area centered around Broadway and Argyle Street is known alternately as Little Saigon, Little Chinatown, and North Chinatown.

Andersonville was named for the Swedish community that settled near Foster Avenue and Clark Street in the 1960s, and the area still has one of the largest concentrations of Swedes in the United States. A water tower above Clark Street is painted with the colors of the Swedish flag and a bunch of businesses sell goodies like strudel and lingonberry pancakes.

Devon Avenue is a true mix of immigrant communities. In places its double street signs attest to its diversity: for a while it's Gandhi Marg, then Golda Meir Avenue. By any name, it's a sensory safari best undertaken on foot.

One of the best ways to explore the ethnic diversity of these areas is by sampling the offerings at restaurants and food stores, so set out hungry. Uptown is just north of Lake View, and Andersonville is north and west of Uptown. Devon Avenue is the farthest north and west of the three.

WHAT'S HERE

Uptown is filled with an interesting mix of entertainment venues that attract, well, a pretty interesting mix of people to the area on any given night. Just outside the Lawrence train station is the **Aragon Ballroom** (⌂ *1106 W. Lawrence Ave.* ☎ *773/561–9500*), its large sign heralding

GETTING ORIENTED

Three Sisters Delicatessen
Rosemblum's Wold of Judaica
Tiffin
Udupi Palace
Rosemont Ave.
Granville Ave.
Glenlake Ave.
Peterson St.
Thorndale Ave.
Ardmore Ave.
Hollywood Ave.
Bryn Mawr St.
Catalpa Ave.
Balmoral Ave.
Foster Ave.
Carmen Ave.
Ainslie St.
Gunnison Ave.
Lawrence Ave.
Wilson Ave.
Montrose Ave.
Cullom Ave.
Berteau Ave.
Irving Park Rd.
Addison St.

California Ave.
Western Ave.
Ridge Ave.
Rosehill Cemetery
Winnemac Park
Winnemac Ave.
Damen Ave.
Ravenswood Ave.
RAVENSWOOD

Devon Ave.
Clark St.
Glenwood Ave.
Broadway
Sheridan Rd.
EDGEWATER   Lake Michigan

Ridge Ave.
14

Bryn Mawr St.
ANDERSONVILLE   Catalpa Ave.
BRYN MAWR
Women & Children First
Swedish Bakery
Reza's
Swedish American Museum Center
Ann Sather
Balmoral Ave.
Berwyn Ave.

BERWYN
ARGYLE
Argyle Strip
St Boniface Cemetery
Green Mill
Lawrence Ave.
Riviera Theater
LAWRENCE

UPTOWN
Aragon Ballroom

Lincoln Park

Lake Shore Drive

41

LINCOLN SQUARE
Leland Ave.
Sunnyside Ave.
MONTROSE
Welles Park
Lincoln Ave.

Ashland Ave.
WILSON
Montrose Ave.
Graceland Cemetery

Sheridan Rd.
Montrose Beach

41

Belle Plaine Ave.
IRVING PARK
Byron St.
Grace St.
Waveland Ave.
ADDISON

Irving Park Rd.
SHERIDAN

Clark St.
Broadway

WRIGLEYVILLE
Wrigley Field
ADDISON
Halsted St.

Cornelia St.
Roscoe St.
School St.
Belmont St.
Barry Ave.

SOUTHPORT
PAULINA
BELMONT
WELLINGTON

Racine Ave.
Lincoln Ave.
Ashland Ave.

LAKE VIEW

Clark St.

KEY
L *CTA lines*
M *Metra lines*
X *Restaurant/Cafe*

0   1/2 mile
0   1/2 kilometer

GETTING HERE

Take the El's Red Line north from the Loop (toward Howard) and get off at the Lawrence stop for Uptown. In a car, take Lake Shore Drive north to Lawrence Avenue for Uptown or Foster Avenue for Andersonville. Devon Avenue is reachable via the El's Red Line (exit at the Morse Avenue station), then the 155 (Devon Avenue) bus. By car, head north up Western Avenue.

MAKING THE MOST OF YOUR TIME

If you're planning on hitting all three neighborhoods, allow most of a day. Uptown will take about an hour; allow a couple of hours for Andersonville if you pop into the shops, and another hour to see the Swedish Museum. Devon Avenue takes about two hours—the street is crowded, especially on evenings and weekends, so walking is slow going there.

LOCAL LIFE

Andersonville is one of the best places in Chicago to stock up on Swedish and other European foods and treats. If you have a sweet tooth, try the **Swedish Bakery** (⊠ *5348 N. Clark St., Far North Side* ☎ *773/561–8919*). Among its delicious baked goods are Swedish *limpa* and Jutland bread, *pepparkakor* (gingerbread) cookies, and flaky strudels and turnovers.

SAFETY

Be cautious in all of Uptown, especially at night. The neighborhood is slowly undergoing a resurgence, but there's still quite a bit of gang activity. Nevertheless, daytime walking, in pairs or groups, is just fine if you stick to the main drags of Broadway and Argyle.

QUICK BITES

Ann Sather (⊠ *5207 N. Clark St., Far North Side* ☎ *773/271–6677*) carries what may be the world's most addictive and enormous cinnamon rolls (you can buy some to carry out) and light lingonberry pancakes.

At **Reza's** (⊠ *5255 N. Clark St., Far North Side* ☎ *773/561–1898*), you can dine on such outstanding Persian cuisine as kebabs, *dolmeh* (stuffed grape leaves), pomegranate juice, and charbroiled ground beef with Persian rice.

Another consistent favorite down the street is **Tiffin** (⊠ *2536 W. Devon, Far North Side* ☎ *773/338–2143*), where the consistent crowds are a good testament to the quality of the curry.

The decor is reminiscent of a hotel lobby, and the music sounds like Indian Muzak, but the South Indian vegetarian cuisine is scrumptious at **Udupi Palace** (⊠ *2543 W. Devon, Far North Side* ☎ *773/338–2152*).

NEIGHBORHOOD TOP 3

1. Gorge yourself on cinnamon rolls at **Ann Sather.**

2. Haggle over the prices of electronics, fabric, and jewelry on **Devon Avenue.**

3. Catch a Sunday-night poetry slam at the **Green Mill,** where it all began.

upcoming bands—who play everything from metal to mariachi—in its dreamy, piazzalike setting. South is the marquee of the **Riviera Theatre** (⊠*4746 N. Racine Ave.* ☎*773/275–6800*), which draws a mosh-pit-diving crowd to see grungy bands.

DID YOU KNOW?

The Green Mill, a cramped jazz club that has drawn top names for over a century, also sparked the national Poetry Slam movement.

Nearby, Little Saigon (also known as Little Chinatown and North Chinatown) is a part of the **Argyle Strip,** which is anchored by the El's Argyle Street stop with its red pagoda. The Strip is teeming with store-front noodle shops and grocery stores. Roasted ducks hang in shop windows and fish peer out from large tanks.

Andersonville, just north of Uptown, still shows many signs of the Swedish settlers who founded the neighborhood. The **Swedish American Museum Center** has an interesting mix of exhibits, a separate museum complete with a Viking ship for kids, and a gift shop packed with Scandinavian items. The section of Clark Street north and just to the south of Foster Avenue is a lively mix of restaurants, bakeries, delicatessens, and boutiques. Victorian-looking street lamps and bricked crosswalks complement the well-kept storefronts. An anchor of the area is the **Women & Children First** bookstore, which stocks an extensive selection of feminist and children's books.

Farther north, **Devon Avenue** is where Chicagoans go when they crave Indian food, or, as the avenue moves west, a good Jewish challah. The Indian restaurants and shops start popping up just east of Western Avenue. Besides authentic, inexpensive Indian and Pakistani food, you find the latest Bollywood flicks, electronics, jewelry, and beautifully embellished saris and fabrics. Restaurants and stores change over rapidly, however, so if the place you're looking for has closed, simply step into the next alluring spot you find. At Talman Avenue, the multicultural wares transform to Jewish specialties. There are butchers and bakers and windows decorated with Russian newspapers and handmade *matrioshkas* (nesting dolls), evidence of this section's concentration of Russian Jews. At **Interbook** (⊠*2754 W. Devon Ave.* ☎*773/973–5536*) you can listen to rowdy rebel Russian rock or read recent romances. At **Three Sisters Delicatessen** (⊠*2854 W. Devon Ave.* ☎*773/973–1919*) you can pick up an imported teapot or a doll with your Russian rye. Pick up menorahs, mezuzahs, and even stuffed matzo-ball dog toys at **Rosenblum's World of Judaica** (⊠*2906 W. Devon Ave.* ☎*773/262–1700*).

PILSEN, LITTLE ITALY & UNIVERSITY VILLAGE

Sightseeing
★★☆☆☆

Dining
★★★★☆

Lodging
★☆☆☆☆

Shopping
★★☆☆☆

Nightlife
★☆☆☆☆

Stretching from the South Branch of the Chicago River to the Eisenhower Expressway (Interstate 290) this area west of the Loop on the south side of the city is a jumble of ethnic neighborhoods that has been home to immigrants of all cultures over the 20th century, most notably the Mexican community of Pilsen and the enclaves of Italian-Americans living in the shadow of the University of Illinois's Medical District and its Circle Campus.

Formerly a neighborhood of immigrants from Bohemia, Czechoslovakia, the enclave of Pilsen is now home to the largest Mexican community in the Midwest—making up roughly 85% of the neighborhood's population. Pilsen is known for its dramatic, colorful murals that show scenes from Mexican history, culture, and religion. It's also home to a thriving arts community—if you're a gallery-hopping art collector, you must visit this neighborhood. Pilsen is bordered by Halsted Street on the east and Western Avenue on the west and extends from 16th Street to the south branch of the Chicago River.

Chicago's Little Italy is to the north of Pilsen. This traditional ethnic neighborhood has been encroached upon by the expansion of the nearby university in recent years, but there are still plenty of yummy Italian restaurants, bakeries, groceries, and sandwich shops to explore. Stretching to Ashland Avenue on the west and Roosevelt on the south, Little Italy blends into University Village in its northeast corner.

The University of Illinois at Chicago anchors University Village. This booming residential area lies west of Roosevelt Road, primarily made up of a massive new mixed-use development that centers around Halsted Street and spans south to 14th Street.

GETTING ORIENTED

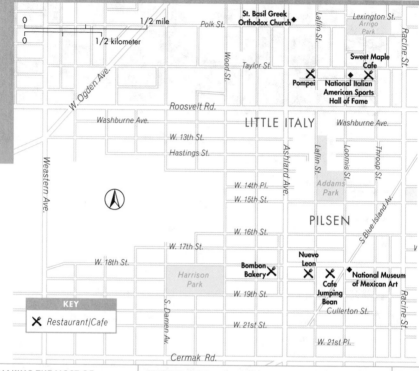

St. Basil Greek Orthodox Church

Lexington St.
Arrigo Park

Polk St.

Laflin St.

Racine St.

Wood St.

Taylor St.

Sweet Maple Cafe

W. Ogden Ave.

✕ Pompei

National Italian American Sports Hall of Fame

✕

Roosevelt Rd.

Weastern Ave.

Washburne Ave.

LITTLE ITALY   Washburne Ave.

W. 13th St.

Hastings St.

Ashland Ave.

Laflin St.

Loomis St.

Throop St.

W. 14th Pl.

W. 15th St.

Addams Park

W. 16th St.

PILSEN

S. Blue Island Av.

W. 17th St.

W. 18th St.

Nuevo Leon

Harrison Park

Bombon Bakery ✕

✕

✕ Cafe Jumping Bean

National Museum of Mexican Art ✕

W. 19th St.

Cullerton St.

Racine St.

S. Damen Av.

KEY
✕ Restaurant/Cafe

W. 21st St.

W. 21st Pl.

Cermak Rd.

0 — 1/2 mile
0 — 1/2 kilometer

MAKING THE MOST OF YOUR TIME

Pilsen is busiest on weekends and on the first weekend of August during the Fiesta del Sol festival, as well as on Second Fridays (the second Friday of every month), when the neighborhood's art galleries stay open late for an art crawl. Little Italy is busier at night when the restaurants and bars draw crowds. A visit to the University Village area is most rewarding on weekdays when there's plenty of student activity on campus, or on Sunday when you can check out the nearby Maxwell Street Market.

GETTING HERE

Take Interstate 290 west to the Damen Street exit. Go south on Damen to 19th Street. There's parking at the National Museum of Mexican Art. You can also take the El's Blue Line from downtown to the 18th Street station. It's a station covered with colorful murals and when you reach street level, take a look at the mosaic mural depicting Mexican women from pre-Columbian time to now.

To get to University Village, take the Blue Line to UIC/Halsted. The 9 Ashland bus will take you to UIC and Little Italy. If you're driving to Little Italy and University Village, take the Kennedy Expressway from either direction to the Taylor Street exit, then head west.

2

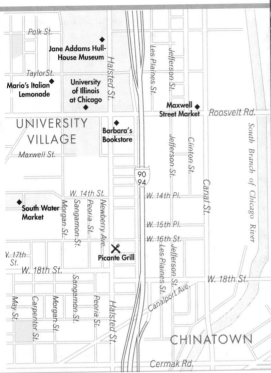

NEIGHBORHOOD TOP 4

1. Try the Italian lemonade—really a slushy Italian ice that comes in a rainbow of flavors—at **Mario's Lemonade Stand** on Taylor Street.

2. Gallery hop on **Second Fridays** in Pilsen, the monthly event when the art galleries stay open late.

3. Haggle over everything from TVs to tube socks at the legendary **Maxwell Street Market** on Sunday.

4. Three words: tres leches cake. Sample it at **BomBon Bakery in Pilsen.** Yum.

SAFETY

The area between Pilsen and Little Italy is railway tracks and vacant lots, and it isn't safe to walk between the two neighborhoods. If at all possible, try to drive to this area, park your car as you explore each individual neighborhood, and drive between the two. Or, take the Blue Line to either UIC–Halsted or Racine to explore University Village and Little Italy, then hop back on and take it two more stops to 18th Street for Pilsen. Cabs aren't too common in this area.

QUICK BITES

Cafe Jumping Bean (✉ 1439 W. 18th St., Pilsen ☎ 312/455–0019), a cozy neighborhood coffee shop, displays original art by local artists on its walls. This eclectic gathering place has hot chocolate with Mexican spices, panini pizzas, and fresh sandwiches.

Picante Grill (✉ 1626 S. Halsted St., Pilsen ☎ 312/455–8500) is an upscale taqueria.

Pompei (✉ 1531 W. Taylor St., Little Italy ☎ 312/421–5179) started as a bakery selling thick, bready squares of pizza back in 1909. Today it's a part of a growing local empire of restaurants that serve salads, housemade pasta, and that same delicious pizza.

Sweet Maple Cafe (✉ 1339 W. Taylor St., Little Italy ☎ 312/243–8908) has a loyal following for their Southern-inspired breakfast. If you can stand the crowds on the weekends, it's worth the wait for grits, salmon cakes, and sweet-milk biscuits.

WHAT'S HERE

The **National Museum of Mexican Art** (formerly the Mexican Fine Arts Center Museum), the nation's largest Latino museum, has traditional and contemporary creations by international and local artists. Its annual Day of the Dead celebration around Halloween is the largest in the city.

The murals of Pilsen are one of the things that give this neighborhood its distinctive flair. You'll run into their bright colors and bold images at many turns during a walk through the neighborhood. At Ashland Avenue and 19th Street are two large murals ruminating on Latino family life and Latinos at work. More murals created by community youth groups and local artists brighten up the blocks along 18th to the east; Aztec sun-god inserts decorate the sidewalk stones.

Pilsen's main commercial strip, 18th Street, is loaded with tempting restaurants, bakeries, and Mexican grocery stores. East on 18th past the BIENVENIDOS A PILSEN sign is **Nuevo Leon,** a brightly painted family restaurant that has been an anchor in the neighborhood since the Guiterrez family set up shop in 1962. Inhale deeply if the doors to the tortilla factory next door are open. A number of art galleries are in the area around Halsted and 18th streets; many keep their doors open late on the second Friday of each month for informal walks (they're open to the public and free).

SWEET TOOTH

If you like sweets or have kids in tow, keep an eye out for BomBon Bakery (⊠1508 W. 18th St. ☎312/733–7788), which stocks a mind-boggling array of treats with a Latino verve to them.

Halsted near 18th Street is home to an ever-growing cluster of art galleries that have put Pilsen on the map with the West Loop and River North as a go-to gallery destination. But while the other neighborhoods have defined themselves as homes to contemporary and fine art, respectively, the Pilsen community doesn't represent a definitive style.

In Little Italy, the main thoroughfare is **Taylor Street,** which is best known for its Italian restaurants, though Thai food, tacos, and other ethnic-food options are starting to fill in the street as well.

The **National Italian American Sports Hall of Fame** (⊠1431 W. Taylor St., Little Italy ☎312/226–5566) pays tribute to athletes like Rocky Marciano, Yogi Berra, and Phil Rizzuto.

NEED A BREAK?

If you visit Taylor Street from May to early September, be sure to stop at Mario's Italian Lemonade (⊠1068 W. Taylor St. ☎No phone) where everyone from politicians like Jesse Jackson to neighborhood families lines up for old-fashioned slush-like Italian ices.

On Polk Street is **St. Basil Greek Orthodox Church** (⊠733 S. Ashland Ave., Little Italy ☎312/243–3738), a gorgeous Greek-revival building originally used as a Jewish synagogue. The bronze statue of Italian explorer Christopher Columbus that anchors **Arrigo Park** on Loomis Street was cast in Rome and brought to Chicago for the 1893 World's Columbian Exposition.

In **University Village,** new luxury town homes and loft conversions intermix with row houses and two-flats on a stretch of the city that not long ago was considered a wasteland. Retailers, including **Barbara's Bookstore** (⊠*1218 S. Halsted St., University Village* ☎*312/413–2665*), a small local chain, have been lured to the area along with the new residents. The **Jane Addams Hull-House Museum** on the UIC campus (⊠*800 S. Halsted St., University Village* ☎*312/413–5353*) is a city landmark as well as a memorial to Jane Addams, who launched innovative settlement house programs. Nearby, you find the new home of the legendary **Maxwell Street Market,** which was not-so-gently nudged to the east at Canal Street and Roosevelt Road to make way for the new development. The year-round Sunday flea market is where odds and ends are sold at hundreds of stalls operated mostly by Latino immigrants. There's also live blues and food.

DID YOU KNOW?

The Jane Addams Hull-House Museum is filled with exhibits about the first Hull House settlement, an innovative model for urban reform at the turn of the 20th century.

PRAIRIE AVENUE & CHINATOWN

Sightseeing
★★★☆☆

Dining
★★★★☆

Lodging
★☆☆☆☆

Shopping
★★☆☆☆

Nightlife
★☆☆☆☆

Geography is the main link between the Prairie Avenue Historic District and Chinatown. Prairie Avenue (two blocks east of Michigan Avenue, between 18th and 22nd streets) was Chicago's first Gold Coast. Many prominent merchants and manufacturers, including George Pullman and Marshall Field, built their homes here in the 1870s through the 1890s. Today only a handful of buildings recall this vanished era, and this stretch of Prairie Avenue is a neighborhood in flux. New condominium construction has helped give this neighborhood more of its old vim, but it's nothing compared to the compact commotion to the west in Chinatown, a neighborhood packed with restaurants and shops. Tour the historic commercial district along Wentworth and Archer avenues and you might just forget you're in a Midwestern city.

WHAT'S HERE

The **National Vietnam Veterans Art Museum,** on the corner of 18th Street and Indiana Avenue, shows art inspired by combat and created by veterans, providing a unique view of war. Explore a different period in history at the **Clarke House,** half a block south on Indiana Avenue. Built in 1836, it holds the distinction of being the oldest still-standing building in Chicago. Today it functions as a museum, revealing what life was like for a middle-class family in the early part of the 19th century.

WIDE LOAD
Clarke House has been moved three times from its original location on Michigan Avenue between 16th and 17th streets. The last time, in 1977, it had to be hoisted above the nearby elevated train tracks.

Just around the corner to the east on Prairie Avenue is the main entrance to the **Glessner House Museum.** Designed by Henry Hobson Richardson, who also designed Trinity Church in Boston, it evokes the revolutionary Richardson Romanesque style (stone construction and short towers).

At the intersection of Calumet and Cullerton avenues is the **Wheeler Mansion,** another of the area's great mansions that was nearly replaced by a parking lot before it was saved and painstakingly restored in the late 1990s. Today it's a contemporary boutique hotel, and a fun alternative to more traditional chain lodging options nearby. ⊠*2020 S. Calumet Ave., Prairie Avenue* ☎*312/945–2020.*

Three blocks farther west, on Michigan Avenue, is the handsome Gothic-revival **Second Presbyterian Church** (⊠*1936 S. Michigan Ave., Prairie Avenue* ☎*312/225–4951*). Be sure to go inside this National Historic Landmark and take a look at the Tiffany stained-glass windows—one of the largest collections anywhere.

Next, walk south another block on Michigan Avenue for a tour of the **Willie Dixon's Blues Heaven Foundation,** housed in the former Chess Records office and studios (⊠*2120 S. Michigan Ave.*), where a cadre of music legends, from Etta James and Bo Diddley to Aretha Franklin and John Lee Hooker, have recorded.

DID YOU KNOW?
The Rolling Stones immortalized the Willie Dixon address in a blues track they recorded here in 1964 entitled—you guessed it—"2120 S. Michigan Avenue."

South of the Prairie Avenue district, where Wentworth Avenue and Cermak Road/22nd Street meet, is the entrance to Chinatown. Our favorite part about Chinatown is the plethora of gift shops spilling over with eye candy in **Chinatown Square** (on bustling Archer Avenue), and the mouthwatering smells from the area's many restaurants and bakeries. The 11-block neighborhood is anchored by the Chinatown Gate and the enormous green-and-red pagoda towers of the Pui Tak Center, a church-based community center, in the former On Leong Tong Building.

Be sure to see the **Nine Dragon Wall** on Cermak Road, next to the El's Red Line Cermak-Chinatown stop, one of only four replicas worldwide of the Beijing original, and **Ping Tom Memorial Park** (⊠*300 W. 19th St., Chinatown*), a multi-acre site dedicated to a neighborhood civic leader, that has views of the Chicago River and incorporates Chinese landscaping elements.

GETTING ORIENTED

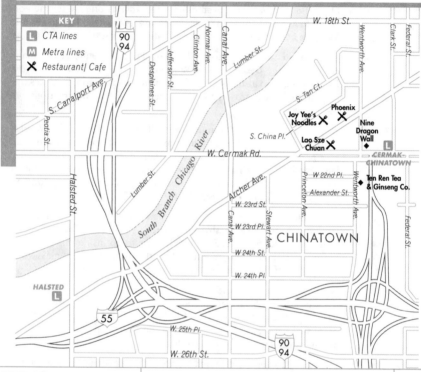

KEY
- L CTA lines
- M Metra lines
- ✕ Restaurant/ Cafe

GETTING HERE

To get to Chinatown by car, drive south on Michigan Avenue and take a left at 18th Street, and travel four blocks to Cermak Road/East 22nd Street. For the Prairie Avenue Historic District, take Michigan Avenue to East 21st Street, then travel west to Prairie Avenue. Buses 1, 3, and 4 cover both of these areas, or you can take the El's Red Line to the Cermak–Chinatown stop.

MAKING THE MOST OF YOUR TIME

You can easily spend a few hours browsing the shops and sampling the goodies along Wentworth Avenue or at Chinatown Square. Add an hour or two more if you're going to tour one or more of the Prairie Avenue homes. Chinatown is particularly busy on weekends throughout the year but the big draws are Chinese New Year in January or February and the summer fair in July.

SAFETY

Both of these areas are a little removed from the heart of the city and bordered by slowly gentrifying neighborhoods, so be cautious and aware if you are walking around the neighborhood after dark.

2

NEIGHBORHOOD TOP 3

1. Forgo traditional weekend brunch for dim sum with the locals at **Phoenix**.

2. Check out the digs where Chicago greats like Marshall Field and George Pullman lived in the **Prairie Avenue Historic District**.

3. Shop for tea and learn about ancient traditions at Chinatown shops like **Ten Ren Tea & Ginseng Co.** (⌧ 2247 S. Wentworth Ave.; ☎ 312/842–1171)

QUICK BITES

Joy Yee's Noodles (⌧ 2159 S. China Pl., in Chinatown Square Mall, Chinatown ☎ 312/328–0001) has a mile-long menu of Pan-Asian dishes that arrive in a flash; they claim to have introduced bubble teas to Chicagoland. Who are we to argue while we sip away?

Lao Sze Chuan (⌧ 2172 S. Archer Ave., Chinatown ☎ 312/326–5040) is the go-to spot for the best Szechuan in town. Try the twice-cooked pork and dry chili string beans. They're served super fast.

Phoenix (⌧ 2131 S. Archer Ave., Chinatown ☎ 312/328–0848) a widely popular choice, is busiest during weekend dim sum, when cart after cart of tempting dumplings and other dishes are rolled before eager diners. The food's all about comfort, but we'll warn you that the service isn't.

TOURS

Package guided tours of both the Clarke House and the Glessner House Museum are available Wednesday through Sunday, and are free on Wednesday (☎ 312/326–1480).

The Chinatown Chamber of Commerce (☎ 312/326–5320) conducts one-hour walking tours in English and can help you arrange lunch at a neighborhood restaurant.

HYDE PARK

Sightseeing
★★★★☆

Dining
★★☆☆☆

Lodging
★☆☆☆☆

Shopping
★☆☆☆☆

Nightlife
★★☆☆☆

Hyde Park is something of a trek from downtown Chicago, but it's worth the extra effort. Best known as the home of the University of Chicago, the neighborhood only began to see significant growth in the late 19th century, when the university opened in 1892 and the Columbian World's Exposition attracted an international influx a year later. The exposition spawned the Midway Plaisance and numerous classical-revival buildings, including the behemoth Museum of Science and Industry. The Midway Plaisance, which surrounded the heart of the fair, still runs along the southern edge of the University of Chicago's original campus. Sprawling homes were soon erected for school faculty in neighboring Kenwood, and the area began to attract well-to-do types who commissioned famous architects to build them spectacular homes.

Today the neighborhood is considered a vibrant, eclectic part of the city. A number of architecturally riveting buildings are here, including two by Frank Lloyd Wright, the **Robie House** and **Heller House.** There's also a thriving theater scene and several art and history museums. Most impressive, though, is the diverse population with a strong sense of community pride and fondness for the neighborhood's pretty tree-lined streets, proximity to the lake, and slightly-off-the-beaten path vibe.

WHAT'S HERE

To get a good overview of the neighborhood, stop by the **Hyde Park Historical Society** (⊠*5529 S. Lake Park Ave., Hyde Park* ☎*773/493–1893* ☼ *Weekends 2–4*), which sponsors lectures and tours.

One of Hyde Park's gems is **Jackson Park** (⊠*Bounded by E. 56th and 67th Sts., S. Stony Island Ave., and the lakefront*), which was designed by Frederick Law Olmsted (who also designed Central Park in New York City) for the World's Columbian Exposition of 1893. It has lagoons, a Japanese garden with authentic Japanese statuary, and the Wooded Island, a nature retreat with wildlife and 300 species of birds.

THE BIRDS

Jackson Park has a notable parrot population. It all started back during the World's Columbian Exposition of 1893, when parrots were imported for an exhibit. The Exposition left, but the parrots settled right down and seem to brave the cold winters just fine.

The **University of Chicago** (⊠*S. Ellis Ave.* ☎*773/702–1234*) dominates the physical and cultural landscape of Hyde Park and South Kenwood, and it's visually arresting. Much of the original campus was designed by Henry Ives Cobb. Especially of note is the International House and the Rockefeller Memorial Chapel, which has a carillon with 72 bells; a university carillonneur gives regular performances. The university's stately Gothic-style quadrangles look like something straight out of Cambridge and Oxford.

DID YOU KNOW?

"The toasters" are two U of C apartment buildings that sit on an island in the middle of the street, so named because, fittingly enough, the buildings look like two pieces of toast. They were designed by I. M. Pei, architect for the Louvre's controversial glass pyramids.

Frank Lloyd Wright's **Robie House** is a Prairie-style masterpiece and one of the most remarkable designs in modern American architecture. (It's also a place of interest for many young readers of the children's book *The Wright 3,* a fictional mystery that takes place at Robie House, which now conducts weekly tours geared to the book's fans.) **Heller House,** nearby on Harper Avenue between 52nd and 53rd streets, was designed in 1897 by Wright, 12 years prior to Robie House. Though not open to the public, the house's exterior is a good indication of his progression toward the Prairie style he achieved with Robie. The area is loaded with other architecturally significant buildings, including the **Windermere House** and **Promontory Apartments.**

Hyde Park has a bunch of smaller museums that stand in the shadow of the Museum of Science and Industry. **The DuSable Museum of African American History** has a notable permanent exhibit on slavery, and offers a cinema series and jazz and blues concerts, as well as children's programs. The **David and Alfred Smart Museum of Art** houses the fine art collection of the University of Chicago. **The Oriental Institute,** also a part of the university, is filled with art and artifacts from the ancient Near East, many that are more than 3,000 years old.

GETTING ORIENTED

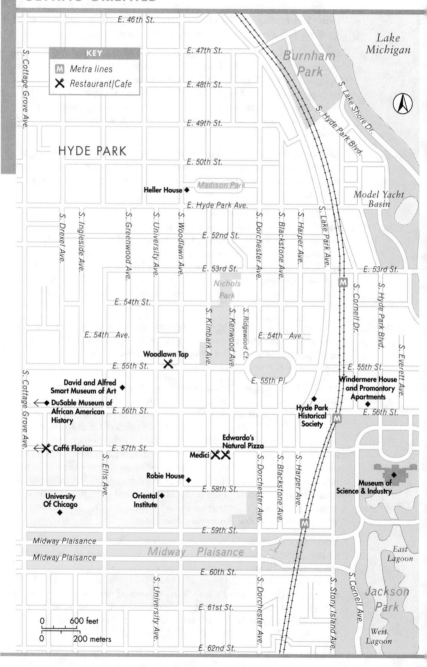

E. 46th St.

Lake
Michigan

Burnham
Park

E. 47th St.

S. Cottage Grove Ave.

KEY
Ⓜ Metra lines
✗ Restaurant/Cafe

E. 48th St.

E. 49th St.

S. Lake Shore Dr.

S. Hyde Park Blvd.

HYDE PARK

E. 50th St.

Model Yacht
Basin

Heller House ◆

Madison Park

E. Hyde Park Ave.

S. Drexel Ave.

S. Ingleside Ave.

S. Greenwood Ave.

S. University Ave.

S. Woodlawn Ave.

E. 52nd St.

S. Dorchester Ave.

S. Blackstone Ave.

S. Harper Ave.

S. Lake Park Ave.

E. 53rd St.

E. 53rd St.

Ⓜ

S. Cornell Dr.

S. Hyde Park Blvd.

Nichols
Park

E. 54th St.

E. 54th Ave.

S. Kimbark Ave.

S. Kenwood Ave.

S. Ridgewood Ct.

E. 54th Ave.

S. Everett Ave.

Woodlawn Tap
✗

E. 55th St.

E. 55th Pl.

Windermere House
and Promontory
Apartments

David and Alfred
Smart Museum of Art ◆

← ◆ DuSable Museum of
African American
History

E. 56th St.

Hyde Park ◆
Historical
Society

E. 55th St.

E. 56th St.

Ⓜ

S. Cottage Grove Ave.

← ✗ Caffé Florian

E. 57th St.

Edwardo's
Natural Pizza

Medici ✗✗

S. Ellis Ave.

Robie House ◆

E. 58th St.

S. Dorchester Ave.

S. Blackstone Ave.

S. Harper Ave.

Museum of ◆
Science & Industry

University
Of Chicago ◆

Oriental ◆
Institute

Ⓜ

E. 59th St.

Midway Plaisance

Midway Plaisance

Midway Plaisance

East
Lagoon

S. University Ave.

E. 60th St.

Jackson
Park

0   600 feet

0   200 meters

E. 61st St.

S. Dorchester Ave.

S. Stony Island Ave.

S. Cornell Ave.

West
Lagoon

E. 62nd St.

2

GETTING HERE

By car, take Lake Shore Drive south to the 57th Street exit and turn left into the parking lot of the Museum of Science and Industry. You can also take the Metra Railroad train from Randolph Street and Michigan Avenue; get off at the 55th Street stop and walk east through the underpass two blocks, then south two blocks. Or, for a longer trip, take the El's Red Line to the State Street and Lake Street stop, then pick up either the No. 6 or No. 10 bus heading southward.

MAKING THE MOST OF YOUR TIME

If you're visiting the Museum of Science and Industry, you'll probably be spending most of your day there. Try to go during the week to avoid crowds. You could wind down the day meandering through Jackson Park or the University of Chicago.

QUICK BITES

Caffé Florian (⊠ *1450 E. 57th St., Hyde Park* ☎ *773/752–4100*) serves pizza and Italian entrées as well as hearty sandwiches, homemade soups and salads, decadent desserts, and lots of java.

The deep-dish pies at **Edwardo's Natural Pizza** (⊠ *1321 E. 57th St., Hyde Park* ☎ *773/241–7960*) are considered by some to be the best in the city.

You'll find several spots on 57th Street where you can get a quick bite and relax. **Medici** (⊠ *1327 E. 57th St., Hyde Park* ☎ *773/667–7394*) has served up its specialty pizzas, burgers, and sandwiches to generations of University of Chicago students who've carved their names into the tables.

Woodlawn Tap (⊠ *1172 E. 55th St., Hyde Park* ☎ *773/643–5516* ⊘ *Daily 11 AM–2 AM*) is a favored spot where locals and university students gather for a spoken-word reading or jazz concert along with pub grub.

SAFETY

Hyde Park is bordered to the west, south, and north by some less prosperous, and at times dangerous, areas. Use caution, especially in the evening, if you're uncertain about where you're heading.

TOURS

Tours of Frank Lloyd Wright's Robie House are conducted daily (☎ 773/834–1847). Themed tours based on the children's book *The Wright 3* by Blue Balliett take place Saturday at 1:30 PM (☎ 773/834–1847; adults $12, children 11–18 $10; 10 and under $5).

A self-guided tour of University of Chicago architecture, *A Walking Guide to the Campus,* is available for purchase in the University of Chicago Bookstore (⊠ *Visitor Center: Reynolds Club 5706 S. University* ☎ *773/702–9739* ⊕ *www.uchicago.edu* ⊘ *Weekdays 9–5*).

NEIGHBORHOOD TOP 4

1. Get lost in the massive wonder of the **Museum of Science and Industry.**

2. Do some exotic-bird-watching in **Jackson Park,** where a tropical-parrot population roosts.

3. Tour Frank Lloyd Wright's fantastic **Robie House.**

4. Pack a picnic and enjoy the views from the beautiful **Promontory Point.**

Museums

WORD OF MOUTH

"The Art Institute of Chicago is so impressive—I could spend hours there."

—Manisha

"The Shedd Aquarium has a great exhibit of beluga whales—so fun to watch them swimming and playing. We're big fans of the Adler Planetarium, in addition to the Museum of Science and Industry."

—SusanEva

MUSEUMS PLANNER

Free Days

Always free:
Jane Addams Hull-House
   Museum
Museum of Contemporary
   Photography
National Museum of
   Mexican Art
Oriental Institute
Smart Museum
Ukrainian Institute of
   Modern Art

Sunday:
DuSable Museum of African
   American History

Monday:
Adler Planetarium &
   Astronomy Museum (selected
   months only)
Chicago Children's Museum
   (for kids 15 and younger first
   Mon. each month)

Tuesday:
Adler Planetarium &
   Astronomy Museum (selected
   months only)
Museum of Contemporary Art
Swedish American Museum
   Center (second Tues. each
   month)

Thursday:
Art Institute of Chicago (after
   5 only)
Chicago Children's Museum
   (5–8 PM only)
Peggy Notebaert Nature
   Museum

Save Money

All the major museums are expensive; consider purchasing
a Chicago CityPass instead of buying a single ticket. For
about the price of admission to two museums, the pass lets
you bypass the long lines and visit all of the big five—the
Art Institute, Field Museum, Museum of Science and Industry, Adler Planetarium, and the Shedd Aquarium—plus the
Hancock Observatory, anytime within nine days. For more
information, see ⊕www.citypass.com.

Late Hours

Adler Planetarium & Astronomy Museum, first Friday of the
month to 10 PM
Art Institute of Chicago, Thursday to 8 PM
Chicago Children's Museum, Thursday & Saturday to 8 PM
Museum of Contemporary Art, Tuesday to 8 PM
Museum of Contemporary Photography, Thursday to 8 PM
Oriental Institute, Wednesday to 8:30 PM
John G. Shedd Aquarium, Thursday to 10 PM (summer only)
Smart Museum, Thursday to 8 PM

Special Events

Tuesdays on the Terrace is a weekly summer event for min-
gling and live local jazz at the Museum of Contemporary
Art. Cash bar. June–Sept., Tues. 5:30–8 PM.

DJs and local bands get things going at the Museum of
Contemporary Art's First Fridays, a monthly preview of
new work by Chicago artists. First Friday of every month,
6–10 PM. $15.

Feel like dinner, drinks, live jazz, and a view of the lake
and the skyline? Get thee to Shedd Aquarium's Jazzin at
the Shedd on the museum's terrace. June–Sept., Thurs.
5–10 PM. $10.

How Much Time?

Less than an hour:
Balzekas Museum of Lithuanian Culture
Museum of Contemporary Photography
Museum of Holography
National Vietnam Veterans Art Museum
Peace Museum
Polish Museum of America
Smart Museum of Art

1–2 hours
DuSable Museum of African American History
Jane Addams Hull-House Museum
Oriental Institute

2–3 hours
Adler Planetarium & Astronomy Museum
Chicago Children's Museum
Chicago History Museum
National Museum of Mexican Art
Peggy Notebaert Nature Museum

Half-Day
Museum of Contemporary Art
John G. Shedd Aquarium

Full Day
Art Institute of Chicago
Field Museum
Museum of Science and Industry

Best Gift Shops

Art Institute of Chicago. Find silk scarves, fine jewelry, glass paperweights, and other items that are reproduced from art works in the museum.

Field Museum. Everything dinosaur is sold in Field gift shops, but our guilty pleasure is the Mold-A-Rama vending machines on the lower level. These 1960s relics take heated colorful plastic and inject it into dinosaur molds.

Museum of Science and Industry. The Big Idea gift shop, on the entrance level, is packed with objects to tickle your mind, including chemistry sets, radio-controlled blimps, robot kits, and a kinetic solar-system model.

Museum of Contemporary Art. Pick up a Calder mobile or electronic chirping bird—you know, the stuff you never knew you always wanted.

Best Quirky Exhibits

Judy Istock Butterfly Haven, Peggy Notebaert Nature Museum. More than 20 local and international species of butterfly flutter through the small butterfly room. Even more interesting are the cocoons in various stages of development. You might even catch a butterfly struggling out of its chrysalis.

Colleen Moore's Fairy Castle, Museum of Science and Industry. The MSI is full of quirky exhibits that make us wonder if we're still in a technology museum—there are live baby chicks and a moving exhibit of circus wagon miniatures—but one of the most beloved is the Fairy Castle. Built between 1928 and 1935, the final cost for this 8-foot-high palace with its 2,000 miniatures was $500,000.

Mesopotamian Gallery, Oriental Institute. The OI's largest gallery covers the entire sweep of Mesopotamian history, and includes a caveman's axe with the first trace of human blood and tablets that trace the history of writing.

Thorne Miniature Rooms, Art Institute. The 68 dollhouse-like rooms were designed by a Chicago socialite to display the miniatures she collected through her travels in Europe and America.

Updated by
Kelly Aiglon

Chicago's museums are the cultural heart of the city—so vital that the mayor rerouted Lake Shore Drive to create a verdant Museum Campus for the Adler Planetarium, Shedd Aquarium, and Field Museum. Treasures in Chicago's museums include Grant Wood's iconic painting *American Gothic,* at the Art Institute; "Sue," the largest T. rex ever discovered, at the Field Museum; and the only German U-boat captured during World War II, at the Museum of Science and Industry.

JUST THE HIGHLIGHTS, PLEASE

Head to the Art Institute for a quick art fix. For a tour of superlatives, see *Sky Above Clouds IV,* Georgia O'Keefe's largest painting; the largest holding of Monet's *Grainstacks* anywhere; and *A Sunday on La Grande Jatte—1884,* Georges Seurat's greatest piece.

CULTURE VULTURE

Tour the world without leaving the city. First stop? Europe. Hit the **Balzekas Museum of Lithuanian Culture,** the **Swedish American Museum Center,** the **Polish Museum of America,** and the **Ukrainian Institute of Modern Art.** Swing by the **Oriental Institute** for relics of the Near East, or brush up on Latino history at the **National Museum of Mexican Art.**

IF YOU HAVE KIDS

Besides the Chicago Children's Museum, these are our favorite kids' exhibits, sure to capture the imagination of your young ones. Don't miss the **Fairy Castle** at the Museum of Science and Industry, **"Sue,"** the T. rex, at the Field Museum, and the **dolphin show** at the Shedd Aquarium's Oceanarium. For an extra-colorful experience, **chase butterflies** at the Peggy Notebaert Nature Museum.

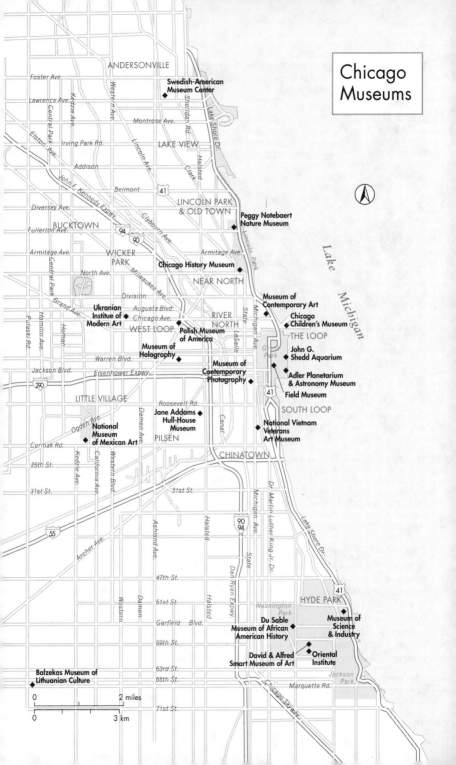

Chicago Museums

ANDERSONVILLE

Foster Ave.

Swedish-American
Museum Center ◆

Lawrence Ave.

Montrose Ave.

LAKE VIEW

Irving Park Rd.

Addison

Belmont

41

LINCOLN PARK
& OLD TOWN

Diversey Ave.

Peggy Notebaert
Nature Museum ◆

BUCKTOWN

Fullerton Ave.

94

90

Armitage Ave.

WICKER
PARK

Armitage Ave.

Chicago History Museum ◆

North Ave.

NEAR NORTH

Division

Museum of
Contemporary Art ◆

Augusta Blvd.

Ukranian
Institute of
Modern Art ◆

Chicago Ave.

RIVER
NORTH

Chicago
Children's Museum ◆

WEST LOOP

Polish Museum
of America ◆

THE LOOP

Museum of
Holography ◆

John G.
Shedd Aquarium ◆

Warren Blvd.

Eisenhower Expwy.

Museum of
Contemporary
Photography ◆

Adler Planetarium
& Astronomy Museum ◆

Jackson Blvd.

290

41

Field Museum ◆

LITTLE VILLAGE

Roosevelt Rd.

SOUTH LOOP

Jane Addams
Hull-House
Museum ◆

National
Museum
of Mexican Art ◆

National Vietnam
Veterans
Art Museum ◆

Cermak Rd.

PILSEN

25th St.

31st St.

CHINATOWN

31st St.

90
94

47th St.

51st St.

HYDE PARK

41

Garfield   Blvd.

Washington
Park

Museum of
Science
& Industry ◆

59th St.

Du Sable
Museum of African
American History ◆

63rd St.

David & Alfred
Smart Museum of Art ◆

Oriental
Institute ◆

Balzekas Museum of ◆
Lithuanian Culture

65th St.

Jackson
Park

Marquette Rd.

0   2 miles

0   3 km

71st St.

Lake
Michigan

Lake Shore Dr.

Sheridan Rd.

Lincoln Ave.

Clark

Halsted

Clybourn Ave.

Lincoln Park

State

Michigan Ave.

LaSalle

Grant
Park

Canal

Foster Ave.

Western Ave.

Kedzie Ave.

Central Park

Elston Ave.

John F. Kennedy Expwy.

Milwaukee Ave.

Grand Ave.

Ogden Ave.

Damen Ave.

Pulaski Rd.

Hamlin Ave.

Homan

Central Park Ave.

California Ave.

Kedzie Ave.

Western Blvd.

Ashland Ave.

Halsted

State

Dan Ryan Expwy.

Michigan Ave.

Dr. Martin Luther King Jr. Dr.

Lake Shore Dr.

Chicago Skyway

Archer Ave.

55

Western

Damen

A GUIDE TO THE ART INSTITUTE

The Art Institute of Chicago, nestled between the contemporary public art showplace of Millennium Park and the Paris-inspired walkways of Grant Park, is both intimate and grand, a place where the rooms are human-scale and the art is transcendent.

Come for the sterling collection of Impressionists and Old Masters (an entire room is dedicated to Monet), linger over the extraordinary and comprehensive photography collection, take in a number of fine American works, and discover paintings, drawings, sculpture, design, and photography spanning the ancient to the contemporary world.

The Institute is more than just a museum; in fact, it was originally founded by a small group of artists in 1866 as a school with an adjoining exhibition space. Famous alumni include political cartoonist Herblock and artists Grant Wood and Ed Paschke. Walt Disney and Georgia O'Keeffe both took classes, but didn't graduate. The School of the Art Institute of Chicago, one of the finest art schools in the country, is across the street from the museum; occasionally there are lectures and discussions that are open to the public.

ORIENTATION TO THE MUSEUM

Take in the museum's grandeur.

✉ 111 S. Michigan Ave., South Loop

☎ 312/443-3600

🌐 www.artic.edu/aic/

🎟 Suggested $12, Students and Seniors $7, Free Thursday 5–8

🕐 Mon.–Wed. and Fri. 10:30–5, Thu. 10:30–8, Sat.–Sun. 10–5

The Art Institute is a complicated jumble of three difficult-to-navigate buildings—you can only change buildings on the first level of the museum, and the map the museum gives out isn't very helpful. Here are some tips to help you find your way around:

Photo op: Pose with one of the two bronze lions.

- On the lower level are textiles, decorative arts, the Thorne Miniature Room, and the Kraft Education Center. The first level includes the non-European galleries, contemporary art, and American art to 1890. The second level holds American art from 1900 to 1950, European art from all periods, and Impressionism.

- Pinpoint the five or six works you'd really like to see or pick two or three galleries and wander around after getting yourself there.

- Guards expect visitors to ask for directions, so don't be shy.

- Buy the audio tour ($6) by the coatroom as you enter—it provides descriptions for every gallery and work in the museum. All you do is key in the gallery number and the voices of curators will guide you around the room.

- Note that a massive construction project, due to be completed in 2009, may cause the temporary closure of some exhibits (including the celebrated Chagall stained glass windows) or the relocation of some galleries.

FOR THE KIDS

Kids love the Kraft Education Center, which has rotating exhibits of child-friendly art (like paintings from picture books) and a permanent, interactive exhibit called *Faces, Places & Inner Spaces* that helps teach children how to look at different kinds of art. There's also a small stage with Kabuki costumes, actual paintings hung at kid-friendly levels, and computer-enhanced games. Nearby is the Touch Gallery, which was originally designed for the blind. You can run your fingers over several bronze works. For more suggestions, check out *Behind the Lions: A Family Guide to the Art Institute of Chicago*, available at the museum bookstore.

BEST PAINTINGS

AMERICAN GOTHIC (1930). GALLERY 263
Grant Wood won $300 for his iconic painting of a solemn farmer and his wife (really his sister and his dentist). Wood saw the work as a celebration of solid, work-based Midwestern values, a statement that rural America would survive the Depression and the massive migration to cities.

American Gothic (1930).

NIGHTHAWKS (1942). GALLERY 262
Edward Hopper's painting of four figures in a diner on the corner of a deserted New York street is a noir portrait of isolated lives and is one of the most recognized images of 20th-century art. The red-haired woman is the artist's wife, Jo.

THE CHILD'S BATH (1893). GALLERY 273
Mary Cassatt was the only American to become an established Impressionist and her work focused on the daily lives of women and children. In this, her most famous work, a woman gently bathes a child who is tucked up on her lap. The Bath was unconventional when it was painted because the bold patterns and cropped forms it used were more often seen in Japanese prints at the time.

Nighthawks (1942).

SKY ABOVE CLOUDS IV (1965). GALLERY 249
(not pictured) Georgia O'Keeffe's massive painting, the largest canvas of her career, is of clouds seen from an airplane. The rows of white rectangles stretching toward the horizon look both solid and ethereal, as if they are stepping stones for angels.

THE OLD GUITARIST (1903/04). GALLERY 263
(not pictured) One of the most important works of Pablo Picasso's Blue Period, this monochromatic painting is a study of the crooked figure of a blind and destitute street guitarist, singing sorrowfully. When he painted it, Picasso was feeling particularly empathetic toward the downtrodden—perhaps because of a friend's suicide—and the image of the guitarist is one of dignity amid poverty.

The Child's Bath (1893).

GRAINSTACK (1890/91). GALLERY 206
The Art Institute has the largest collection of Monet's Grainstacks in the world. The stacks rose 15 to 20 feet tall outside Monet's farmhouse in Giverny and were a symbol to the artist of sustenance and survival.

Grainstack (1890/91)

A SUNDAY ON LA GRANDE JATTE 1884 (1884-86).
GALLERY 205

Georges Seurat's greatest work has inspired generations of painters and even spawned a musical—Stephen Sondheim's *Sunday in the Park with George*. A precise pattern of tiny dots creates a scene of mixed-class serenity in Paris, with rounded figures of soldiers, genteel women, children, and a monkey.

SELF-PORTRAIT (1887). GALLERY 205

Twenty-four self portraits were painted by Vincent Van Gogh, and this early example is an expressive picture made up of colorful dots and dashes. The artist's intense eyes gaze directly into yours, inviting you into his soul.

A Sunday on La Grande Jatte 1884 (1884-86).

OTHER DON'T-MISS EXHIBITS

PAPERWEIGHT COLLECTION. GALLERY 69

In the mid-nineteenth century, a newly dependable mail service made writing implements and desk accessories chic—including glass paperweights. The Art Institute's famous Arthur Rubloff Collection houses over 1,400 of these surprisingly intricate paperweights, with examples from all periods, techniques, designs, and manufacturers.

Self-Portrait (1887).

STOCK EXCHANGE TRADING ROOM.

Architects Louis Sullivan and Dankmar Adler used art glass and stenciled decorations to build a glorious trading room for the Chicago Stock Exchange. Though the Exchange was demolished in 1972, it's recreated here with pieces from the original.

TADAO ANDO. GALLERY 109

Many visitors miss this serene room of pottery and painted screens, half hidden behind a closed glass door in the Asian galleries on the first floor. The room, designed by Japanese architect and artist Tadao Ando, is notable for its rows of large wooden columns; Ando said he wanted viewers to "feel as if the wind is passing through."

Paperweight collection.

THORNE MINIATURE ROOMS. GALLERY 11

Sixty-eight tiny rooms showcase interior design and decorative arts from the 13th century to 1940. Master craftsmen built them (1932–1940) for Mrs. James Ward Thorne to a scale of one inch to one foot. The rooms look like dollhouses.

Thorne Miniature Rooms.

ADLER PLANETARIUM & ASTRONOMY MUSEUM

✉ 1300 S. Lake Shore Dr., South Loop

☎ 312/922–7827

🌐 www.adlerplanetarium.org

🎫 $16 museum admission and 1 show, $20 museum admission and 2 shows. Free Mon. and Tues. Jan., Feb., Oct., and Nov. Discount weeks throughout the year

🕐 9:30 AM–4:30 PM (except 1st Fri. of month when open until 10 PM); summer hours 9:30 AM–6:30 PM (except 1st Fri. of month when open until 10 PM).

Navigate your way through the solar system with interactive and state-of-the-art exhibits that appeal to planetarium traditionalists as well as technology-savvy kids and adults. The museum uses computer games, videos, short films, and hands-on devices to teach physics and astronomy basics like the Doppler effect. Two different planetariums unlock the mysteries of the stars.

HIGHLIGHTS

The Adler's traditional in-the-round Zeiss planetarium (called the Sky Theater) shows constellations and planets in the night sky. It's been around since the Adler opened in 1930 as the first public planetarium in the Western Hemisphere.

See the restored Gemini 12, the spacecraft flown by Captain Jim Lovell and Buzz Aldrin in 1966, in the new permanent exhibit "Shoot for the Moon." A collection of space artifacts once owned by Lovell is also on exhibit.

Take a digital journey into space on the interactive Star-Rider Theater, inside the high-tech Sky Pavilion. For some shows, you use control buttons on your armrest to vote for what you see on screen. (Part of the technology is based on aircraft flight simulators.) Other shows wrap you in a 3-D universe of stars. Also in the Sky Pavilion are a telescope terrace and interactive exhibition galleries that include computer animations of the Milky Way and of the birth of the solar system.

TIPS

■ Additional charges apply for the Sky Theater planetarium shows and the Star-Rider interactive shows *(see admission prices, above)*, but don't skip them—they're the reason to go.

■ Take a quick (free) ride in the Atwood Sphere, a large metal globe with punched-out stars. It provided the nation's very first planetarium experience.

■ No need to purchase the museum's audio tour. The signs in the museum are comprehensive and the narrative doesn't add much to the experience.

CHICAGO CHILDREN'S MUSEUM

✉ Navy Pier, 700 E. Grand
Ave., Near North

☎ 312/527-1000

⊕ www.chichildrensmuseum.
org

💳 $8, free Thurs. 5–8 PM and
1st Mon. of the month for
children 15 and younger

🕙 Sun.–Wed. and Fri. 10
AM–5 PM, Thurs. and Sat.
10 AM–8 PM.

3

TIPS

■ The museum issues read-
mission bracelets that let you
leave the museum and come
back on the same day—great
idea for weary families that
want to take a break to get a
bite to eat, or simply explore
other parts of Navy Pier
before coming back to
the museum.

■ Grab a bite at the nearby
space-themed McDonald's
(☎312/832–1640) or bring a
picnic and grab a sunny seat
outside (in warm weather) or
gather in the Crystal Ballroom
(amid tropical plants and
fountains).

■ Most families spend an
average of three hours visiting
the museum.

■ Hour-long art workshops
at Artabounds are free.

■ The museum is designed
for children 2 to 12 years.

■ Adults may not enter the
museum without a child.

■ Try each of the artist-created benches to figure out
which one makes music when
you sit on it.

"Hands-on" is the operative concept for this brightly colored Navy Pier anchor. Kids play educational video games,
climb through multilevel tunnels, run their own TV stations, and, if their parents allow it, get soaking wet.

HIGHLIGHTS

Kids can don raincoats before they start splashing around
in the WaterWays exhibit, which has oversize water tubs
with waterwheels, pumps, brightly colored pipes, and
splashing fountains. If everyone pumps hard enough,
water squirts 50 feet into the air.

In the Big Backyard exhibit, children "shrink" to the size
of bugs amid giant giggling flowers. Butterflies seem to
flutter around their bodies and water appears to splash
down on their heads, all through the magic of a tall
video screen.

Parents, get ready for a workout. You and your children
can scurry up a three-story-high rigging complete with
crow's nest and gangplank on the Kovler Family Climb-
ing Schooner. It's reminiscent of the boats that once
sailed Lake Michigan. If you make it to the rope tunnels at the top, you can take in bird's-eye views of the
museum, then slide back down to the lower level, where
there are tanks of fish.

Crouch beside your child to search for fossils in Dinosaur Expedition. Brush away dirt to discover the bones
of a Suchomimus, a kind of fish-eating dinosaur that's
on display nearby. The exhibit re-creates a trip to the
Sahara led by University of Chicago paleontologist Paul
Sereno.

Collaboration is the watchword at Artabounds Gallery,
where kids participate in rotating group art projects
that include activities like creating a castle out of clay.

FIELD MUSEUM

✉ 1400 S. Lake Shore Dr., South Loop

☎ 312/922–9410

🌐 www.fieldmuseum.org

💲 $12

🕐 Daily 9 AM–5 PM; last admission at 4 PM.

TIPS

■ It's impossible to see the entire Field in one visit. Try to get tickets to the special exhibit of the season (go to the Web site if you'd like to order in advance) and then choose a couple subjects you'd like to explore, like North American birds or Chinese jade.

■ The Sue Store sells a mind-boggling assortment of dinosaur-related merchandise.

■ Bring young ones to 20-minute story times, when staff and volunteers read a dinosaur-themed book and direct an art project (weekends year-round and daily July and August).

■ The lobby of the museum includes the Corner Bakery. The dining room tucked in the back has sparkling views of the lake and the Museum Campus.

■ Check the Web site for up-to-date details on special performances and lectures.

★ More than 6 *acres* of exhibits fill this gigantic museum, which explores cultures and environments around the world. Interactive exhibits examine such topics as Egyptian mummies, the people of Africa and the Pacific Northwest, and living creatures in the soil. Funded by Chicago retailer Marshall Field, the museum was founded in 1893 to hold material gathered for the World's Columbian Exposition; its current classical-style home opened in 1921.

HIGHLIGHTS

Shrink to the size of a bug to burrow beneath the surface of the soil in the Underground Adventure exhibit ($7 extra). You'll come face-to-face with a giant, animatronic wolf spider twice your size, listen to the sounds of gnawing insects, and have other encounters with the life that teems under our feet.

Spend a couple hours taking in contemporary and ancient Africa. Dioramas let you feel like you're stepping inside the homes and lives of Africans from Senegal, Cameroon, and the Sahara, while the remarkable Inside Ancient Egypt complex includes a working canal, a living marsh where papyrus is grown, a shrine to the cat goddess Bastet, burial-ceremony artifacts, and 23 mummies.

The Field's dinosaur collection is one of the world's best. You can't miss 65-million-year-old "Sue," the largest and most complete Tyrannosaurus rex fossil ever found—it's on permanent exhibit in the lobby.

Figure out which exhibit is your favorite. The most popular are the Pawnee Earth Lodge, a reconstruction of a Native American dwelling; the man-eating Lions of Tsavo; McDonald's Fossil Preparation Laboratory, where you can watch paleontologists cleaning up bones; and Evolving Planet, which uses video technology to explain the dawn of single-cell organisms and the advent of dinosaurs.

MUSEUM OF CONTEMPORARY ART

✉ 220 E. Chicago Ave., Near North

☎ 312/280–2660

⊕ www.mcachicago.org

💳 $10, free Tues.

⊙ Tues. 10 AM–8 PM, Wed.–Sun. 10 AM–5 PM.

3

TIPS

■ The back of the MCA is one of the best spots to have lunch or Sunday brunch in the city. Run by Wolfgang Puck and called Puck's Café

■ Try to catch one of the cutting-edge music and theater performances; one year, for example, the entire front of the museum was turned into a puppet theater. Performances happen quite frequently; check the Web site for information on what will be happening when you're in town.

■ In summer come for Tuesdays on the Terrace and be serenaded by local jazz bands. There's a cash bar from 5:30 to 8 PM and a full menu at the café

■ On the first Friday of every month the museum hosts a party ($15) with live music and hors d'oeuvres from 6 PM to 10 PM.

★ Fodor's Choice A group of art patrons who felt the great Art Institute was unresponsive to modern work founded the MCA in 1967, and it's remained a renegade art museum ever since. It doesn't have any permanent exhibits; even the works from its collection are constantly rotating. This gives it a feeling of freshness, but it also makes it impossible to predict what will be on display at any time. Special exhibits are devoted mostly to original shows you can't see anywhere else— past exhibits have included solo shows by light artist Dan Flavin and photographer Catherine Opie, and group shows with new work from China and Brazil. See the MCA Web site for details.

HIGHLIGHTS

The MCA's dramatic quarters were designed by Berlin architect Josef Paul Kleihues. From the outside, the building looks like a home for modern art—it's made of square metal plates, with round bolts in each corner.

The MCA's growing 7,000-piece collection, which includes work by René

The museum showcases work in all media, including paintings, sculpture, works on paper, photography, video, film, and installations.

The MCA Store is the place to go for well-designed jewelry and items for the home, from a porcelain egg shell from which a flower sprouts to a clock with a face that's a psychedelic swirl of color.

MUSEUM OF SCIENCE AND INDUSTRY

✉ 5700 S. Lake Shore Dr., Hyde Park

☎ 773/684–1414

🌐 www.msichicago.org

💲 $11; museum and Omnimax admission $17; parking $12

🕙 Memorial Day–Labor Day, Mon.–Sat. 9–5:30, Sun. 11–5:30; Labor Day–Memorial Day, Mon.–Sat. 9:30–4, Sun. 11–4.

TIPS

■ Use the museum map to plan out your visit. Your best bet is to hit a couple of highlights (the U-boat tour alone will take at least an hour) and then see a couple of quirky exhibits.

■ If the kids get grouchy, bring them to the Idea Factory, a giant playroom where they can play with water cannons, blocks, and cranks. Limited to ages 10 and younger.

■ Relax with some ice cream in the old-fashioned ice-cream parlor, tucked away in a genteel re-creation of an Illinois main street.

■ On nice days, hordes of sunbathers and kite-flyers camp out on the giant lawn out front—it's almost as entertaining as the museum itself. Lake Michigan is across the street.

■ The museum has free-admission days, but the schedule changes often. Check the Web site for details.

★ **Fodor's Choice** The MSI is one of the most visited sites in Chicago. The sprawling open space has 2,000 exhibits on three floors, with new exhibits being added constantly. The museum's high-tech interior is hidden by the classical-revival exterior; it was designed in 1892 by D.H. Burnham & Company as a temporary structure to house the Palace of Fine Arts for the World's Columbian Exposition. It's the fair's only surviving building. On a nice day, walk behind the museum to Jackson Park and its Osaka Garden.

HIGHLIGHTS

Descend into the depths of a simulated coal mine on a "miner"-led tour that explores the technology behind digging energy out of the ground.

Get a close-up view of a plane's flaps and wheels as a cantilevered Boeing 727 "takes off" above visitors every hour. Former United pilots explain what's going on to those sitting inside the jet as the airplane flaps raise and lower.

The opulent and detailed-as-a-film-set Fairy Castle (really a giant dollhouse) has tiny chandeliers that flash with real diamonds and floors that are laid with intricate stone patterns. It's enough to make us daydream about what the world's fairy-tale characters might have lived in.

Tour the cramped quarters of the only U-505 German submarine captured during World War II (there's an additional fee). Don't feel like waiting in line? Explore just the free interactive exhibits surrounding the sub, which give stunning insight into the strategy behind the war at sea.

Learn how scientists can make frogs' eyes glow or watch baby chicks tap themselves out of their shells at the "Genetics–Decoding Life" exhibit.

The Omnimax Theater shows science- and space-related films on a giant screen.

JOHN G. SHEDD AQUARIUM

✉ 1200 S. Lake Shore Dr., South Loop

☎ 312/939–2438

🌐 www.sheddaquarium.org

🎫 $23 all-access pass

🕐 Memorial Day–Labor Day, daily 9–6, Thurs. until 10; Labor Day–Memorial Day, weekdays 9–5, weekends 9–6.

TIPS

■ Catch live jazz on the Shedd's north terrace on Thursday evenings from 5 to 10 PM June through August. A gorgeous view of the lake and skyline can make for a magical night. Food and a bar are available.

■ Lines for the Shedd often extend all the way down the neoclassical steps. Buy a ticket in advance to avoid the interminable wait, or spring for a CityPass.

■ Soundings restaurant is an elegant stop for lunch. The menu is pricey, but the quiet tables look over Lake Michigan—and there are very few Chicago eateries that can say that.

■ Discount admission days are offered throughout the year. Check the Web site for updates.

★ Fodor's Choice Take a plunge into an underwater world at the world's largest indoor aquarium. Built in 1930, the Shedd is one of the most popular aquariums in the country, housing more than 8,000 aquatic animals in realistic waterscapes.

HIGHLIGHTS

"Amazon Rising" gives you an up-close look at the animals of the Amazon River, including piranhas, snakes, and stingrays.

Sharks swim by in their 400,000 gallon tank as part of the permanent exhibit "Wild Reef," which explores the marine biodiversity and coral reefs in the Indo-Pacific. Wild Reef also has colorful corals, stingrays that slide by under your feet, and other surprising creatures, all from the waters around the Philippines.

Stare down one of the knobby-headed beluga whales (they love to people-watch), observe Pacific white-sided dolphins at play, and explore the simulated Pacific Northwest nature trail in the spectacular Oceanarium, which has pools that seem to blend into Lake Michigan. We like the daily educational dolphin presentation, during which the playful animals show off their natural behaviors, including vocalizing, breaching, and tail-walking, for delighted audiences. Be sure to get an underwater glimpse of the dolphins and whales through the viewing windows on the lower level, where you can also find a bunch of information-packed, hands-on activities.

In the 90,000-gallon Caribbean Reef exhibit in the main building, divers feed sharks, stingrays, a sea turtle, and other denizens of the deep.

3

OTHER MUSEUMS

Sometimes the best museums are ones that you can see in an hour or less. We like Chicago's smaller museums for the unexpected, interesting, and simply fun things you can find. Some of them highlight the diverse origins that built the city; others dedicate their space to history, archaeology, or specific types of art.

FOR HIDDEN
GEMS

Balzekas Museum of Lithuanian Culture. Though many of the people who come here do so for research (the museum is a large repository for genealogical information), the Balzekas has a stunning collection of Lithuanian amber. Other exhibits—armor, rare maps, stamps, and coins—chronicle Lithuanian history. ✉6500 S. Pulaski Rd., Englewood☎773/582–6500 💲$5, free Mon. ⊘Daily 10–4.

WINDY CITY
HISTORY
★

Chicago History Museum. The museum went through a major rehaul in late 2006 when it changed its name from the Chicago Historical Society in honor of its 150th birthday. The new permanent sights include a Costume and Textile Gallery and the exhibit entitled "Chicago: Crossroads of America," which demystifies historic tragedies like the Great Chicago Fire and Haymarket Affair. ✉1601 N. Clark St., Lincoln Park ☎312/642–4600 ⊕www.chicagohistory.org 💲$12, Mon. free ⊘Mon.–Wed., Fri., and Sat. 9:30–4:30, Thurs. 9:30–8, Sun. noon–5.

David and Alfred Smart Museum of Art. If you want to see art masterpieces but don't want to spend a long day wandering one of the major art museums, the Smart may be just your speed. The diverse, 10,000-piece permanent collection includes works by old masters; photographs by Walker Evans; furniture by Frank Lloyd Wright; sculptures by Degas, Matisse, Rodin, and Henry Moore; ancient Chinese bronzes; and modern Japanese ceramics. Temporary exhibits are a great way to see startlingly good art in a smaller, intimate space. ✉5550 S. Greenwood Ave., Hyde Park ☎773/702–0200 ⊕www.smartmuseum.uchicago.edu 💲Free ⊘Tues., Wed., and Fri. 10–4, Thurs. 10–8, weekends 11–5.

DuSable Museum of African American History. The DuSable is a colorful—and haunting—exploration of the African-American experience, set alongside the lagoons of Washington Park. There are handwritten lyric sheets from Motown greats, letters and memorabilia of scholar W. E. B. DuBois and poet Langston Hughes, and a significant African-American art collection. The most moving exhibit is one on slavery; the poignant, disturbing artifacts include rusted shackles used on slave ships. ✉740 E. 56th Pl., Hyde Park ☎773/947–0600 ⊕www.dusablemuseum.org 💲$3, free Sun. ⊘Tues.–Sat. 10–5, Sun. noon–5.

Jane Addams Hull-House Museum. The redbrick Victorian Hull House was the birthplace of social work, which makes it an American landmark. Social welfare pioneers and peace advocates Jane Addams and Ellen Gates Starr started the American settlement house movement in this house in 1889 and wrought near miracles in their surrounding community, which was then a slum for new immigrants. Pictures and letters add context to the two museum buildings, which re-create the homey setting the residents experienced. ✉800 S. Halsted St., Uni-

QUIET SPACES

North Terrace, Shedd Aquarium. The entire aquarium is mesmerizing; you might find yourself staring at placidly swimming fish for hours without getting bored. But for a truly peaceful experience during mild weather, push through the doors of the North Terrace and sit at a table overlooking Lake Michigan and the city skyline. The terrace is usually deserted even on the busiest summer days.

Mammal dioramas, Field Museum. Few visitors linger amid the long, darkened hallways of the North American mammal dioramas. Take a seat on a curved wooden bench and you won't be disturbed—unless the sight of stuffed and mounted bears and buffalo makes you queasy.

Main Street theater and Jackson Park, Museum of Science and Industry. Olde Chicago is re-created in a corner of the MSI, complete with cobblestones and iron lamps. At the end of the street is a small theater showing silent shorts of Buster Keaton. If you'd rather be in the sunshine, take a walk around Jackson Park's lagoons and bridges behind the museum, one of the most peaceful—and overlooked—spots in all of Chicago.

versity Village ☎ *312/413–5353* ⊕ *www.uic.edu/jaddams/hull* ✉ *Free* ⊗ *Tues.–Fri. 10–4, Sun. noon–4.*

IF YOU ONLY
HAVE TIME
FOR ONE
★

National Museum of Mexican Art. Formerly the Mexican Fine Arts Museum Center, this sparkling site, the largest Latino museum in the country, is half art museum, half cultural exploration. After the big downtown museums, this is the one you shouldn't miss. Galleries house impressive collections of contemporary, traditional, and meso-American art from both sides of the border, as well as vivid exhibits that trace immigration woes and political fights. Every fall, the giant Day of the Dead exhibit stuns Chicagoans with its altars from artists across the country. ✉ *1852 W. 19th St., Pilsen* ☎ *312/738–1503* ⊕ *www.nationalmuseumofmexicanart.org* ✉ *Free* ⊗ *Tues.–Sun. 10–5.*

Museum of Contemporary Photography. "Contemporary" is defined here as anything after 1936. Over 7,000 works from American-born and American-resident photographers make this an impressive collection. Don't-miss works include exhibits by Dorothea Lange, Ansel Adams, and Nicholas Nixon. Curators constantly seek out new talent and under-appreciated established photographers, which means that there are artists here you probably won't see elsewhere. Rotating exhibits have included photojournalism and scientific photography. ✉ *600 S. Michigan Ave., South Loop* ☎ *312/663–5554* ⊕ *www.mocp.org* ✉ *Free* ⊗ *Mon.–Wed., Fri., and Sat. 10–5, Thurs. 10–8, Sun. noon–5.*

The Local Art Scene

You don't need to be an art expert to explore the city's growing web of local neighborhood galleries. Just do like a local and ready yourself with a free copy of *The Chicago Reader,* which has gallery and exhibition listings (available in many street dispensers, coffee shops, and record stores), or grab the *Chicago Gallery News* (or check it out on the Web at ⊕ *www. chicagogallerynews.com*)—it's the best source for maps, gallery information, and exhibition listings. Most galleries provide complimentary copies.

Here's the skinny: Chicago is divided into gallery "districts," or communities. They each have their own feel and flavor. Stop by anytime during gallery hours—no need to make an appointment—even if you're just browsing. Gallery directors and staff are always available to answer questions or provide further information on their artists.

RIVER NORTH DISTRICT

The city's first organized art neighborhood remains a vibrant community and the hub of the gallery scene.

Zolla/Lieberman (*contemporary multimedia* ⊠ *325 W. Huron St.* ☎ *312/944–1990*).

Roy Boyd (*contemporary painting and sculpture* ⊠ *739 N. Wells St.* ☎ *312/642–1606*).

Carl Hammer (*American folk and outsider* ⊠ *740 N. Wells St.* ☎ *312/266–8512*).

Ann Nathan Gallery (*contemporary painting and sculpture* ⊠ *212 W. Superior St.* ☎ *312/664–6622*).

Stephen Daiter Gallery (*vintage black-and-white photography* ⊠ *311 W. Superior St.* ☎ *312/787–3350*).

WEST LOOP DISTRICT

Lots of galleries have opened in multilevel warehouses on Randolph Street and throughout the rest of the neighborhood.

Packer Schopf Gallery (*emerging and mid-career artists* ⊠ *942 W. Lake St.* ☎ *312/226–8984*).

Rhona Hoffman (*established and emerging contemporary artists* ⊠ *118 N. Peoria St.* ☎ *312/455–1990*).

Donald Young Gallery (*local and international contemporary art* ⊠ *933 W. Washington Blvd.* ☎ *312/455–0100*).

EAST PILSEN DISTRICT

Most artists live in their galleries in this district south and west of the Loop, and the line between reality and fantasy is often outrageously blurred.

4ArtInc. (*contemporary, artist-run* ⊠ *1932 S. Halsted St.* ☎ *312/850–1816*) and **Dubhe Carreñ** (*contemporary ceramic art* ⊠ *1841 S. Halsted St.* ☎ *312/666–3150*).

WICKER PARK/BUCKTOWN

The area is home to a respectable chunk of the city's artists, but most show their work privately or in independent group shows. You can still see artists' studios if you wander around the **Flat Iron Building** (⊠ *1714 N. Damen Ave.*). Check out **Pagoda Red** (*Chinese and Tibetan art objects* ⊠ *1714 N. Damen Ave.* ☎ *773/235–1188*).

Museum of Holography. Holography seems almost quaint in our age of 3-D digital renderings. Still, it's fun to spend an hour walking from side to side in front of these glowing, three-dimensional, laser-etched portraits and pictures. ⊠*1134 W. Washington Blvd., West Loop* ☎*312/226–1007* ⊕*www.holographiccenter.com* 🖾*$4* ⊘ *Wed.–Sun. 12:30–5.*

National Vietnam Veterans Art Museum. The chimelike sounds of more than 58,000 imprinted dog tags hanging from the ceiling entranceway are a melancholy memorial to the soldiers who lost their lives in the unpopular war. Take in the visual journal of the experiences of more than 122 artists who served in Vietnam through the 1,000-plus pieces of art on display here. ⊠*1801 S. Indiana Ave., South Loop* ☎*312/326–0270* ⊕*www.nvvam.org* 🖾*$10, free to service members* ⊘ *Tues.–Fri. 11–6, Sat. 10–5.*

MAKE LIKE
INDIANA
JONES **Oriental Institute.** This gem began with artifacts collected by University of Chicago archaeologists in the 1930s (one is rumored to have been the model for Indiana Jones) and has expanded into an interesting, informative museum with a jaw-dropping collection from the ancient Near East, including the largest U.S. collection of Iraqi antiquities. There are amulets, mummies, limestone reliefs, gold jewelry, ivories, pottery, and bronzes from the 4th millennium BC through the 13th century AD. You won't be able to miss the 17-foot-tall statue of King Tut, excavated from the ruins of a temple in western Thebes in 1930. ⊠*1155 E. 58th St., Hyde Park* ☎*773/702–9520* ⊕*www.oi.uchicago.edu* 🖾*Free* ⊘ *Tues. and Thurs.–Sat. 10–6, Wed. 10–8:30, Sun. noon–6.*

★ **Peggy Notebaert Nature Museum.** Walk among hundreds of Midwest species of butterflies and learn about the impact of rivers and lakes on daily life at this modern museum washed in natural light. Like Chicago's other science museums, it's geared to kids, with educational computer games to play and water turbines to control. But even jaded adults will be excited when bright yellow butterflies land on their shoulders. The idea is to study nature inside without forgetting graceful Lincoln Park outside. ⊠*2430 N. Cannon Dr., Lincoln Park* ☎*773/755–5100* ⊕*www.naturemuseum.org* 🖾*$7, free Thurs.* ⊘ *Weekdays 9–4:30, weekends 10–5.*

POLISH YOUR
POLISH **Polish Museum of America.** Chicago has the largest Polish population of any city outside Warsaw, and this museum in Ukrainian Village, just

---

ARTSY FESTIVALS

VISION (☎*312/649–0065* ⊕*www.chicagoartdealers.org*) is a cool summertime art fest in its 13th year. Opening night is always a madhouse, with crowds spilling out of gallery doors onto the sidewalk, but things settle down in the following weeks for gallery tours and talks. Wicker Park/Bucktown throws a biannual festival called **Around the Coyote** (☎*773/342–6777* ⊕*www. aroundthecoyote.org*), with exhibitions and performance art taking place in and around the Flat Iron Building.

3

south of Wicker Park, celebrates that fact. Take a trip to the old country by strolling through exhibits of folk costumes, memorabilia from Pope John Paul II, Hussar armor, American Revolutionary War heroes Tadeusz Kosciuszko and Casimir Pulaski, pianist and composer Ignacy Paderewski, and an 8-foot-long sleigh in the shape of a dolphin that's carved from a single log. It's also a good place to catch up on your reading; the library has 60,000 volumes. ⊠*984 N. Milwaukee Ave., Wicker Park* ☎*773/384–3352* ⊕*pma.prcua.org* ⊠*$5* ☉*Fri.–Wed. 11–4.*

★ **Swedish American Museum Center.** Though this tiny and welcoming museum does have changing exhibits that focus on the art and culture of Sweden, you don't have to be Swedish to find it interesting—much of the museum focuses on the immigrant experience. On permanent display, for example, are trunks immigrants brought with them to Chicago, and a map showing where in the city different immigrant groups settled. On the third floor, in the only children's museum in the country dedicated to immigration, kids can climb aboard a colorful Viking ship or "milk" a wooden cow, pulling rubber udders to collect streams of water in a bucket. ⊠*5211 N. Clark St., Far North Side* ☎*773/728–8111* ⊕*www.samac.org* ⊠*$4, free 2nd Tues. of month* ☉*Tues.–Fri. 10–4, weekends 11–4.*

Ukrainian Institute of Modern Art. Modern and contemporary art fans head out to this small museum at the far western edge of the Ukrainian Village, near Wicker Park. Three permanent galleries feature mixed media, sculpture, painting, and even some digital art. Some of the most interesting works are abstract or playful versions of old-world themes, like Evan Prokopov's 1998 abstract bronze of a mother cradling her child. ⊠*2320 W. Chicago Ave., Wicker Park* ☎*773/227–5522* ⊕*www.uima-art.org* ⊠*Free* ☉*Wed.–Sun. noon–4.*

Architecture

WORD OF MOUTH

"I love walking on Michigan Avenue and the lakefront early in the morning. Hardly anyone is out except photographers. You can really appreciate some of the details of the buildings."

—buttercup

"Chicago is such a wonderful city and has so much to offer. Go to the top of the John Hancock building, which has an incredible view of the city and the lake from its observation deck."

—lisa

ARCHITECTURE PLANNER

In a Chicago Mood

Chicago has long been known as America's Second City, but, as a visit here makes clear, this is no burg. A metropolis if there ever was one, Chicago hums with activity while its lakeside location lends a relaxed, breezy ambience. A great way to take advantage of this intermingling is to sit a spell in Millennium Park or Grant Park and enjoy the march of buildings up Michigan Avenue. Known to some as the "Michigan Avenue Cliff," this stretch just west of the parks comprises a slew of noteworthy structures, including the Auditorium Building, the Santa Fe Center, and the Chicago Cultural Center.

Good Reads

Architecture geeks won't need much introduction to the city's architectural history, but if you don't count yourself among that special breed, you might pick up *Chicago Architecture and Design*, a beautifully illustrated book with a good perspective by George A. Larson and Jay Pridmore. For a more in-depth yet highly readable study of some of the big names who worked here, check out Peter Blake's *The Master Builders*. And if you don't mind a bit of murder with your history lesson, there's Erik Larson's magnificent *The Devil in the White City*.

Walking Tours

The Chicago Architecture Foundation has a gigantic selection of expertly guided tours. Chicago Greeter and InstaGreeter are two free city services that match savvy Chicagoans with visitors for neighborhood tours. Friends of the Chicago River leads Saturday-morning tours during the warmer months.

Contacts **Chicago Architecture Foundation** (⊠ *Santa Fe Bldg., 224 S. Michigan Ave.* ☎ *312/922–3432* ⊕ *www. architecture.org*). **Chicago Greeter/InstaGreeter** (⊠ *Visitor Information Center at Chicago Cultural Center, 77 E. Randolph St.* ☎ *312/744–8000* ⊕ *www.chicagogreeter.com*). **Friends of the Chicago River** (⊠ *407 S. Dearborn St., Suite 1580* ☎ *312/939–0490* ⊕ *www.chicagoriver.org*).

Bus & Trolley Tours

A narrated bus or trolley tour is a fun way to enjoy Chicago's architecture. Tours cost roughly $20 and last about two hours.

Contacts **Gray Line Tours** (☎ *800/621–4153* ⊕ *www. grayline.com*). **Chicago Architecture Foundation** *(See Walking Tours.)* **Chicago Trolley and Double Decker Co.** (☎ *773/648–5000* ⊕ *www.chicagotrolley.com*).

Boat Tours

The Chicago Architecture Foundation river tour on *Chicago's First Lady* is the most authoritative, if a tad pricier than some others ($26 weekdays; $28 on weekends and holidays). You can purchase tickets at the Chicago ArchiCenter, 224 South Michigan Avenue, or through Ticketmaster at 312/902–1500 or www.ticketmaster.com. The boat-tour season usually runs from the end of April to mid-November—always call ahead.

Other options include: **Mercury Chicago Skyline Cruiseline** (☎ *312/332–1353* ⊕ *www.mercuryskylinecruiseline.com*). **MetroDucks** (☎ *800/298–1506* ⊕ *www.metroducks.com*). **Shoreline Sightseeing** (☎ *312/222–9328* ⊕ *www.shorelinesightseeing.com*). **Wendella Sightseeing Boats** (⊠ *400 N. Michigan Ave.* ☎ *312/337–1446* ⊕ *www.wendellaboats. com*). **Windy of Chicago Ltd** (☎ *312/595–5555* ⊕ *www. tallshipwindy.com*).

Revised by
Kelly Aiglon

Every great city has great buildings, but Chicago *is* its great
buildings. Art, culture, food, and diversion are all part of
the picture here, but everything Chicagoans do is framed
by some of the most remarkable architecture to be found
anywhere. From the sky-scraping of its tall towers to the
horizontal sweep of the Prairie School, Chicago's built environment is second to none.

DECISIONS, DECISIONS, DECISIONS

Even if you're pressed for time, you can't leave town without seeing
a few of the city's important buildings. The lovely **Reliance Building** on
State Street (home to trendy Hotel Burnham) is steps away from **The
Harold Washington Library** and just blocks from the Art Institute and
Millennium Park. Mies van der Rohe's **860–880 North Lake Shore Drive**
buildings are right on the lake and not too far from high-end shopping
on the Magnificent Mile.

With so many significant skyscrapers packed into the Loop, it's tough
to elevate any one above the rest. When it comes to early buildings,
the **Rookery** is hard to beat. Looking like an impenetrable terra-cotta
mass from the street, its heart is a graceful, covered court done up
by Frank Lloyd Wright. And no matter how much you may dislike
modern architecture, the **Inland Steel Building** is a beauty. Also worth
a visit is the dizzying atrium of the squat **James R. Thompson Center,** a
bold interpretation of a public building. Finally, for a swanky art-deco
number, stop by the **Carbide and Carbon Building,** home to the Hard
Rock Hotel Chicago.

A TALL ORDER

If you came looking for tall buildings, Chicago certainly won't let you
down. Among the tallest are the famous **Sears Tower,** with its 103rd-
floor observatory (on clear days you can see four states); the instantly
recognizable **John Hancock Center,** with its crisscross braces and two
huge antennae (not to mention a showy bar and restaurant on the
95th floor); and the formidable **Aon Center,** which towers over Millen-

nium Park. And no building proclaims its sky-scraping ambition quite like **311 South Wacker Drive**, whose Gothic crown is ablaze with light at night.

IT'S WORTH THE TRIP

Nearby **Oak Park** is Frank Lloyd Wright's old stomping ground. The leafy community is chock-full of his work, from early examples of Prairie style to a fascinating Unitarian church. A visit to **Glessner House**—H.H. Richardson's 1887 masterpiece in the Prairie Avenue Historic District—offers the voyeuristic appeal of poking through a great home. It's enough to motivate even those who don't know an I beam from a flying buttress.

THE LOOP

Defined by the El (the elevated train that makes a circuit around the area), the Loop is Chicago at its big-city best. A hub of retail, cultural, financial, and governmental activity, it's also home to the city's most notable skyscrapers. Ambitious walkers can cover a good part of the Loop and the surrounding areas in a day, but even a relatively short stroll will reveal some top sites.

HISTORIC BUILDINGS

★ **Auditorium Building.** Hunkered down across from Grant Park, this 110,000-ton granite-and-limestone behemoth was an instant star when it debuted in 1889, boasting a 400-room hotel, offices, and a 4,300-seat theater. It didn't hurt the careers of its designers, Dankmar Adler and Louis H. Sullivan, either. The state-of-the-art theater included electric lighting and an air-conditioning system that used 15 tons of ice per day. Adler managed the engineering—the theater's acoustics are renowned—while Sullivan ornamented the space using mosaics, cast iron, art glass, wood, and plaster. During World War II, the building was conscripted for use as a Servicemen's Center. Then Roosevelt University moved in. Thanks to Herculean restoration efforts, the theater—rechristened as the Auditorium Theatre of Roosevelt University—is once again one of the city's premiere performance venues. If you can't book a performance, call for tour details. ⊠ *50 E. Congress Pkwy., Loop* ☎ *312/431–2389* ⊕ *www.auditoriumtheatre.org* ⊠ *Tour $6.*

> #### FINDING FACTS
>
> For more information about the city's architectural treasures, contact the Chicago Architecture Foundation at 312/922–8687 or 312/922–3432 (online at ⊕ *www. architecture.org*) or the Chicago Convention and Tourism Bureau at 312/567–8500 (online at ⊕ *www. choosechicago.com/architecture. html*).

Carson Pirie Scott & Co. Built in 1899, the old-fashioned department store's flagship location closed its doors in 2007. While shopping—window or otherwise—is no longer an option, it's worth checking out the building's facade. The work of one of Chicago's most renowned architects, it combines Louis H. Sullivan's visionary expression of modern design with intricate cast-iron ornamentation. The eye-catching rotunda and the 11 stories above it are actually an addition Sullivan made to his original building. In later years, D. H. Burnham & Co. and Holabird & Root extended Sullivan's smooth, horizontal scheme farther down State Street. ⊠*1 S. State St., Loop* ☎*312/641–7000.*

WORLD'S
LARGEST
TIFFANY DOME
★

Chicago Cultural Center. Built in1897 as the city's original public library, this huge building houses the **Chicago Office of Tourism Visitor Information Center,** as well as a gift shop, café, galleries, and a concert hall. Designed by the Boston firm Shepley, Rutan & Coolidge—the team behind the Art Institute of Chicago—it's a palatial affair of Carrara marble, mosaics, gold leaf, and the world's largest Tiffany glass dome. Building tours are offered Wednesday, Friday, and Saturday at 1:15 PM. There's live music on Monday, Tuesday, Wednesday, and Friday at 12:15 PM in the café. ⊠*78 E. Washington St., Loop* ☎*312/346–3278 or 312/744–6630* ⊕*www.ci.chi.il.us/Tourism/CulturalCenter/* ⊗*Mon.–Thurs. 10–7, Fri. 10–6, Sat. 10–5, Sun. 11–5.*

> **FOR SULLIVAN FANS**
>
> Bear north to Lincoln Park to see the **Louis Sullivan row houses.** The love of geometric ornamentation that Sullivan eventually brought to such projects as the Carson Pirie Scott building is already visible in these row houses built in 1885. The terracotta cornices and decorative window tops are especially noteworthy. ⊠*E 1826–1834 N. Lincoln Park W, Lincoln Park.*

Fine Arts Building. This creaky building was constructed in 1895 to house the showrooms of the Studebaker Company, then makers of carriages. Publishers and artists have used its spaces; today the principal tenants are professional musicians. Take a look at the handsome exterior then step inside the marble-and-woodwork lobby. The motto engraved in the marble as you enter says, ALL PASSES—ART ALONE ENDURES. The building has an interior courtyard, across which strains of piano music and soprano voices compete with tenors as they run through exercises. There's also a gallery on the fourth floor (open Wed.–Sun. from noon to 6). ⊠*410 S. Michigan Ave., Loop* ☎*312/913–0537.*

CHECK OUT
THE CHICAGO
WINDOWS
★

Marquette Building. Like a slipcover over a sofa, the clean, geometric facade of the Marquette Building expresses what lies beneath: in this case, a structural steel frame. Sure, the base is marked with roughly cut stone and a fancy cornice crowns the top, but the bulk of the building mirrors the cage around which it is built. Inside is another story. The intimate lobby of this 1895 Holabird & Roche building is a jewel box of a space, where a single Doric column stands surrounded by a Tiffany glass mosaic depicting the exploits of French Jesuit missionary Jacques Marquette, an early explorer of Illinois. The building is a clear example of the Chicago style, from the steel skeleton to the Chicago Windows to the terra-cotta ornamentation. ⊠*140 S. Dearborn St., Loop.*

Monadnock Building. Built in two segments a few years apart, the Monadnock captures the turning point in high-rise construction. Its northern

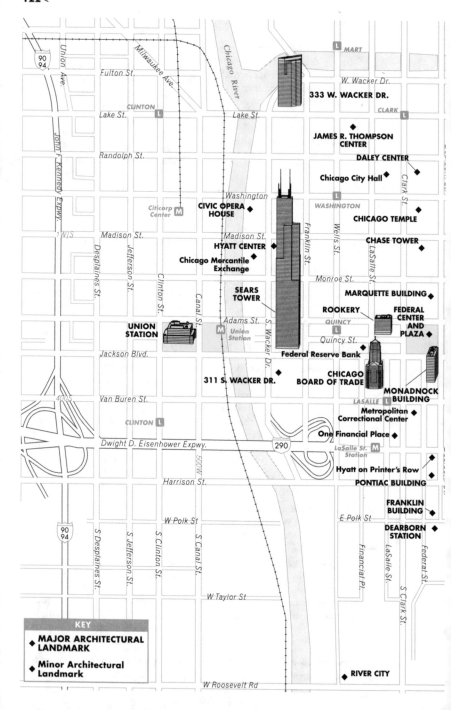

MART

W. Wacker Dr.

333 W. WACKER DR.

CLARK

Union Ave.

Fulton St.

Milwaukee Ave.

Chicago River

CLINTON

Lake St.

Lake St.

**JAMES R. THOMPSON
CENTER**

DALEY CENTER

Clark St.

Randolph St.

Chicago City Hall

John F. Kennedy Expwy.

Washington

Citicorp
Center

**CIVIC OPERA
HOUSE**

WASHINGTON

CHICAGO TEMPLE

Wells St.

Franklin St.

I-90/I-94

I-95

Madison St.

Madison St.

HYATT CENTER

CHASE TOWER

LaSalle St.

Desplaines St.

Jefferson St.

**Chicago Mercantile
Exchange**

Monroe St.

MARQUETTE BUILDING

Clinton St.

**SEARS
TOWER**

ROOKERY

**FEDERAL
CENTER
AND
PLAZA**

Canal St.

**UNION
STATION**

Union
Station

Adams St.

S. Wacker Dr.

QUINCY

Quincy St.

Federal Reserve Bank

Jackson Blvd.

311 S. WACKER DR.

**CHICAGO
BOARD OF TRADE**

**MONADNOCK
BUILDING**

4005

Van Buren St.

LASALLE

**Metropolitan
Correctional Center**

CLINTON

One Financial Place

Dwight D. Eisenhower Expwy.

290

LaSalle St.
Station

500W

Hyatt on Printer's Row

Harrison St.

E Polk St

PONTIAC BUILDING

**FRANKLIN
BUILDING**

90/94

S Desplaines St.

S Jefferson St.

S Clinton St.

S Canal St.

**DEARBORN
STATION**

W Polk St

Financial Pl.

LaSalle St.

Federal St.

S Clark St.

W Taylor St

KEY

◆ **MAJOR ARCHITECTURAL
LANDMARK**

◆ **Minor Architectural
Landmark**

W Roosevelt Rd

RIVER CITY

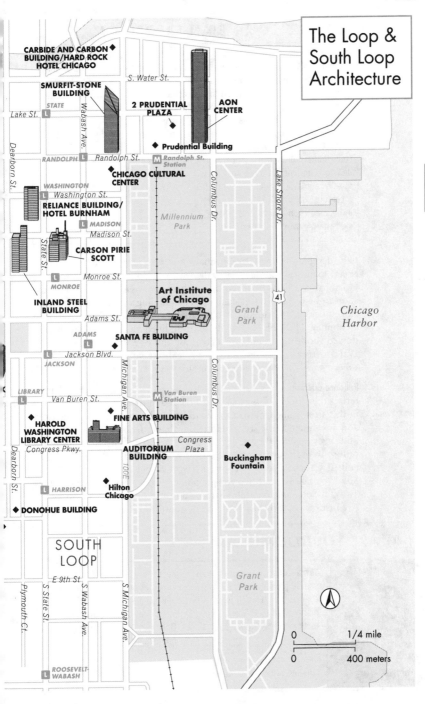

WORLD'S COLUMBIAN EXPOSITION

In 1893 the city of Chicago hosted the **World's Columbian Exposition.** The fair's mix of green spaces and Beaux-Arts buildings offered the vision of a more pleasantly habitable metropolis than the crammed industrial center that rose from the ashes of the Great Fire. However, a ruffled Louis Sullivan prophesied that "the damage wrought to this country by the Chicago World's Fair will last half a century." He wasn't entirely wrong in his prediction—the classicist style vied sharply over the next decades with the native creations of the Chicago and Prairie schools, all the while incorporating their technical advances. One of Hyde Park's most popular destinations—the Museum of Science and Industry—was erected as the fair's Palace of Fine Arts. It's the exposition's only building that is still standing.

half, designed in 1891 by Burnham & Root, was erected with traditional load-bearing masonry walls (6 feet deep at the base). In 1893, Holabird & Roche designed its southern half, which rose around the soon-to-be-common steel skeleton. The building's stone and brick exterior, shockingly unornamented for its time, led one critic to liken it to a chimney. The lobby is equally spartan: lined on either side with windowed shops, it's essentially a corridor, but one well worth traveling. Walk it from end to end and you'll feel like you're stepping back in time. ⊠ *53 W. Jackson Blvd. at S. Dearborn St., Loop.*

A CHICAGO
LANDMARK
Fodor'sChoice
★

Reliance Building. The clearly expressed, gleaming verticality that characterizes the modern skyscraper was first and most eloquently articulated in this steel-frame tower in the heart of the Loop. Completed in 1895 and now home to the stylish **Hotel Burnham,** the building was a crumbling eyesore until the late 1990s, when the city initiated a major restoration. In the early and mid-1900s, it was a mixed-use office building, and Al Capone's dentist reportedly worked out of what's now Room 809. Don't be misled when you go looking for this masterpiece—a block away, at State and Randolph streets, a dormitory for the School of the Art Institute of Chicago shamelessly mimics this trailblazing original

WHAT ARE YOU LOOKIN' AT?

Terra-cotta, a baked clay that can be produced as tiles or shaped ornamentally, was commonly used by Chicago architects after the Great Fire of 1871.

Heat resistant and malleable, the material proved an effective and attractive fireproofing agent for the metal-frame buildings that otherwise would melt and collapse. The facade of the Marquette Building at 140 S. Dearborn Street is a particularly fine example.

by Burnham, Root, and Charles Atwood. Once you've found the real thing, don't miss the mosaic floor and ironwork in the reconstructed elevator lobby. The building boasts early examples of the Chicago Window, which define the entire building's facade by adding a shimmer and glimmer to the surrounding white terra-cotta. ⊠*1 W. Washington St., Loop* ☎*312/782–1111* ⊕*www.burnhamhotel.com.*

> **GREAT CORNERS TO LOOK UP!**
>
> ■ North Michigan Avenue and East Wacker Drive
>
> ■ West Adams and South LaSalle streets
>
> ■ North Michigan Avenue and East Chestnut Street

4

Fodor'sChoice
★
Rookery. This 11-story structure, with its eclectically ornamented facade, got its name from the pigeons and politicians who roosted at the city hall that once stood on this site. Designed in 1885 by Burnham & Root, who used both masonry and the more modern steel-frame construction, the Rookery was one of the first buildings in the country to feature a central court that brought sunlight into interior office spaces. Frank Lloyd Wright, who kept an office here for a short time, renovated the two-story lobby and light court, eliminating some of the ironwork and terra-cotta and adding marble scored with geometric patterns detailed in gold leaf. The interior endured some less tasteful alterations after that, but it has since been restored to the way it looked when Wright completed his work in 1907. ⊠*209 S. LaSalle St., Loop.*

Santa Fe Building. Also known as the Railway Exchange Building, this structure was designed in 1904 by Daniel Burnham, who later moved his office here. The SANTA FE sign on its roof was put up early in the 20th century by the Santa Fe Railroad, one of several railroads that had offices here when Chicago was the rail center of the country. The fantastic **ArchiCenter of the Chicago Architecture Foundation** (☎*312/922–3432* ⊕*www.architecture.org* ☉*Tues.–Sun. 9:30–4*) occupies this historic space. ⊠*224 S. Michigan Ave., Loop.*

Symphony Center. Orchestra Hall, home to the acclaimed Chicago Symphony Orchestra (CSO), lies at the heart of this music center. The hall was built in 1904 under the supervision of Daniel Burnham. The Georgian building has a symmetrical facade of pink brick with limestone quoins, lintels, and other decorative elements. Backstage tours are available by appointment for groups of 10 or more. ⊠*220 S. Michigan Ave., Loop* ☎*312/294–3000.*

FINDING THE ART DECO

FROM BUBBLY
INSPIRATION
★
Carbide and Carbon Building. Designed in 1929 by Daniel and Hubert Burnham, sons of the renowned architect Daniel Burnham, this is arguably the jazziest skyscraper in town. A deep-green terra-cotta tower rising from a black granite base, its upper reaches are embellished with gold leaf. The original public spaces are a luxurious composition in

marble and bronze. The story goes that the brothers Burnham got their design inspiration from a gold-foiled bottle of champagne. So perhaps it's fitting that the building now houses the **Hard Rock Hotel Chicago,** party central for those who wouldn't be caught dead at the Four Seasons. ✉*230 N. Michigan Ave., Loop.*

★ **Chicago Board of Trade.** Rising dramatically at the end of LaSalle Street—heart of the city's financial district—Holabird & Root's building is a streamlined giant from the days when art deco was all the rage. The artfully lit marble lobby soars three stories; atop the roof stands Ceres, the Roman goddess of agriculture. Erected in 1930, this 45-story structure reigned as the city's tallest skyscraper until 1955, when the Prudential Center grabbed that title. ✉*141 W. Jackson Blvd., Loop* ☎*312/435–3590.*

Civic Opera House. The handsome home of the Lyric Opera of Chicago is grand indeed, with pink-and-gray Tennessee marble floors, pillars with carved capitals, crystal chandeliers, and a sweeping staircase to the second floor. Designed by Graham, Anderson, Probst & White, it combines lavish art-deco details with classical touches. And the show goes on, with the Lyric Opera performing regularly on the great stage within. ✉*20 N. Wacker Dr., Loop* ☎*312/419–0033 Civic Opera House, 312/332–2244 Lyric Opera* ⊕*www.civicoperahouse.com.*

1950S & BEYOND: MEET MODERNISM

Daley Center. Named for the late mayor Richard J. Daley, this boldly plain high-rise is the headquarters of the Cook County court system, but it's best known as the site of a sculpture by Picasso. Known simply as the *Picasso,* this monumental piece provoked an outcry when it was installed in 1967; baffled Chicagoans tried to determine whether it represented a woman or an Afghan hound. In the end, they gave up guessing and simply embraced it as a unique symbol of the city. The building was constructed in 1965 of Cor-Ten steel, which weathers naturally to an attractive bronze. In summer the building's plaza is the site of concerts, political rallies, and a weekly farmers' market (Thursday); during the holidays, the city's official Christmas tree is erected here. ✉*Bounded by Washington Blvd., Randolph, Dearborn, and Clark Sts., Loop.*

MIES MEETS CALDER   **Federal Center and Plaza.** Designed in 1959, but not completed until 1974, this severe constellation of buildings around a sweeping plaza

★ was Mies van der Rohe's first mixed-use urban project. Fans of the International Style will groove on this pocket of pure modernism, while others can take comfort in the presence of the Marquette Building, which marks the north side of the site. In contrast to this dark ensemble are the great red arches of Alexander Calder's *Flamingo.* The piece was dedicated on the same day in 1974 that the artist's *The Universe* was unveiled at Sears Tower. Calder went from one event to the other, riding through the streets in a brightly colored circus wagon accompanied by calliopes. The area is bound by Dearborn, Clark, and Adams streets and Jackson Boulevard. ☒*Dirksen: 219 S. Dearborn St., Loop* ☒*Kluczynski: 230 S. Dearborn St., Loop.*

★ **Inland Steel Building.** A runt compared to today's tall buildings, this crisp, sparkling structure from Skidmore, Owings & Merrill was a trailblazer back in the late 1950s. It was the first skyscraper built with external supports (allowing for wide-open, unobstructed floors within); the first to employ steel pilings (driven 85 feet down to bedrock); the city's first fully air-conditioned building; and the first to feature underground parking. As for looks, well, you might say it combines the friendly scale of the Reliance Building with the cool rigor of a high-rise by Mies. ☒*30 W. Monroe St., Loop.*

4

LATE MODERNISM GIVES WAY TO POSTMODERNISM

ENJOY THE **James R. Thompson Center.** People either hate or love the center: former
17-STORY governor James Thompson, who selected the Helmut Jahn design for
ATRIUM this state government building, hailed it in his dedication speech in
★ 1985 as "the first building of the 21st century." For others, it's a case of postmodernism run amok. A bowl-like form topped by a truncated cylinder, the building's sky-blue and salmon color scheme scream 1980s. But the 17-story atrium, where exposed elevators zip up and down and sunlight casts dizzying patterns through the metal-and-glass skin, is one of the most animated interiors to be found anywhere in the city. The sculpture in the plaza is Jean Dubuffet's *Monument with Standing Beast.* It's nearly as controversial as the building itself. The curved shapes, in white with black traceries, have been compared to a pile of melting Chicago snow. The **Illinois Artisans Shop** (☎312/814–5321), on the second level of the Center, sells crafts, jewelry, and folk art by Illinois artists. ☒*100 W. Randolph St., Loop.*

Smurfit-Stone Building. Some wags have said this building, with its diamond-shape top, looks like a giant pencil sharpener. The slanted top carves through 10 floors of this 1984 building. The painted, folded-aluminum sculpture in the plaza is Yaacov Agam's *Communication X9.* You'll see different patterns in the sculpture depending on your vantage point. ☒*150 N. Michigan Ave., Loop.*

333 West Wacker Drive. This green-glazed beauty doesn't follow the rules. Its riverside facade echoes the curve of the Chicago River just in front of it, while the other side of the building is all business, conforming neatly to the straight lines of the street grid. This 1983 Kohn Pedersen Fox design is roughly contemporary to the James R. Thompson Center—but it has enjoyed a much more positive public reception. ☒*333 W. Wacker Dr., between W. Lake Street and N. Orleans St., Loop.*

CHECK OUT **Harold Washington Library Center.** Gargantuan and almost goofy (the huge,
THE ROOF gargoyle-like sculptures atop the building look like something out of
OWLS Harry Potter), this granite-and-brick edifice is a uniquely postmodern
★ homage to Chicago's great architectural past. The heavy, rusticated
☾ ground level recalls the Rookery; the stepped-back, arched windows are a reference to the great arches in the Auditorium Theatre of Roos-

Continued on page 132

THE SKY'S THE LIMIT

Talk about baptism by fire. Although Chicago was incorporated in 1837, it wasn't until after the Great Fire of 1871 that the city really started to take shape. With four square miles gone up in flames, the town was a clean slate. The opportunity to make a mark on this metropolis drew a slew of architects, from Adler & Sullivan to H. H. Richardson and Daniel H. Burnham—names renowned in the annals of American architecture. A Windy City tradition was born: the city's continuously morphing skyline is graced with tall wonders designed by architecture's heavy hitters, including Mies van der Rohe; Skidmore, Owings & Merrill; and, if he has his way, Santiago Calatrava. In the next four pages, you'll find an eye-popping sampling of Chicago's great buildings and how they've pushed—and continue to push—the definition of even such a lofty term as "skyscraper."

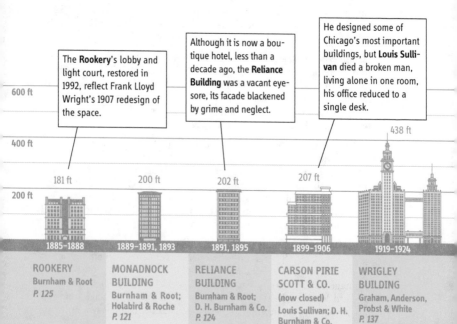

The **Rookery**'s lobby and light court, restored in 1992, reflect Frank Lloyd Wright's 1907 redesign of the space.

Although it is now a boutique hotel, less than a decade ago, the **Reliance Building** was a vacant eyesore, its facade blackened by grime and neglect.

He designed some of Chicago's most important buildings, but **Louis Sullivan** died a broken man, living alone in one room, his office reduced to a single desk.

600 ft
400 ft
200 ft

181 ft — 200 ft — 202 ft — 207 ft — 438 ft

| 1885–1888 | 1889–1891, 1893 | 1891, 1895 | 1899–1906 | 1919–1924 |

ROOKERY
Burnham & Root
P. 125

MONADNOCK BUILDING
Burnham & Root;
Holabird & Roche
P. 121

RELIANCE BUILDING
Burnham & Root;
D. H. Burnham & Co.
P. 124

CARSON PIRIE SCOTT & CO.
(now closed)
Louis Sullivan; D. H. Burnham & Co.
P. 120

WRIGLEY BUILDING
Graham, Anderson, Probst & White
P. 137

THE BIRTH OF THE SKYSCRAPER

Houses, churches, and commercial buildings of all sorts rose from the ashes after the blaze of 1871, but what truly put Chicago on the architectural map was the tall building. The earliest of these barely scrape the sky—especially when compared to what towers over us today—but in the late 19th century, structures such as William Le Baron Jenney's ten-story Home Insurance Building (1884) represented a bold push upward. Until then, the sheer weight of stone and cast-iron construction had limited how high a building could soar. But by using a lighter yet stronger steel frame and simply sheathing his building in a thin skin of masonry, Jenney blazed the way for ever taller buildings. And with only so much land available in the central business district, up was the way to go.

Although the Home Insurance Building was razed in 1931, Chicago's Loop remains a rich trove of early skyscraper design. Some of these survivors stand severe and solid as fortresses, while others manifest an almost ethereal quality. They—and their descendants along Wacker Drive, North Michigan Avenue, and Lake Shore Drive—reflect the technological, economic, and aesthetic forces that have made this city on the prairie one of the most dramatically vertical communities in the country.

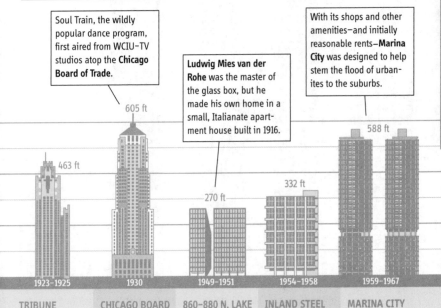

Soul Train, the wildly popular dance program, first aired from WCIU-TV studios atop the **Chicago Board of Trade**.

Ludwig Mies van der Rohe was the master of the glass box, but he made his own home in a small, Italianate apartment house built in 1916.

With its shops and other amenities—and initially reasonable rents—**Marina City** was designed to help stem the flood of urbanites to the suburbs.

605 ft

588 ft

463 ft

332 ft

270 ft

1923–1925	1930	1949–1951	1954–1958	1959–1967
TRIBUNE TOWER	CHICAGO BOARD OF TRADE	860–880 N. LAKE SHORE DRIVE	INLAND STEEL BUILDING	MARINA CITY
Howells & Hood	Holabird & Root	Ludwig Mies van der Rohe	Skidmore, Owings & Merrill	Bertrand Goldberg Associates
P. 136	P. 126	P. 139	P. 127	P. 139

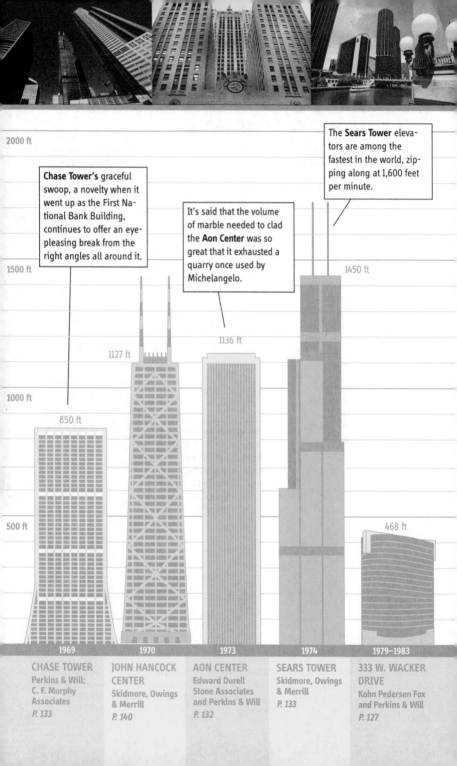

2000 ft

Chase Tower's graceful swoop, a novelty when it went up as the First National Bank Building, continues to offer an eye-pleasing break from the right angles all around it.

It's said that the volume of marble needed to clad the **Aon Center** was so great that it exhausted a quarry once used by Michelangelo.

The **Sears Tower** elevators are among the fastest in the world, zipping along at 1,600 feet per minute.

1500 ft

1127 ft

1450 ft

1136 ft

1000 ft

850 ft

500 ft

468 ft

1969	1970	1973	1974	1979–1983
CHASE TOWER	**JOHN HANCOCK CENTER**	**AON CENTER**	**SEARS TOWER**	**333 W. WACKER DRIVE**
Perkins & Will; C. F. Murphy Associates	Skidmore, Owings & Merrill	Edward Durell Stone Associates and Perkins & Will	Skidmore, Owings & Merrill	Kohn Pedersen Fox and Perkins & Will
P. 133	*P. 140*	*P. 132*	*P. 133*	*P. 127*

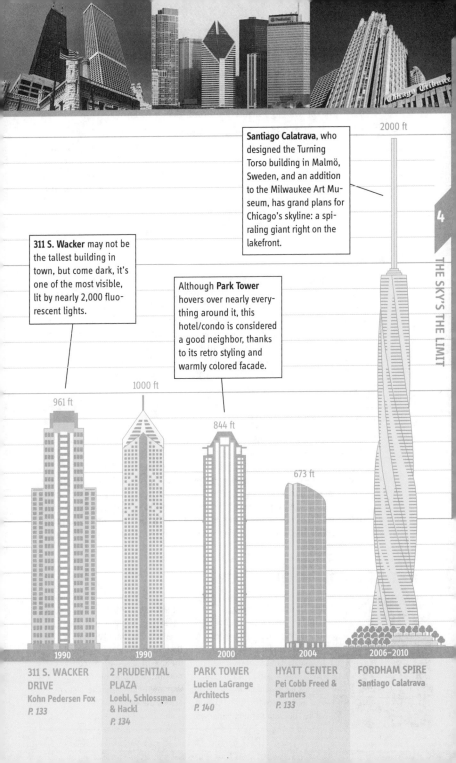

2000 ft

Santiago Calatrava, who designed the Turning Torso building in Malmö, Sweden, and an addition to the Milwaukee Art Museum, has grand plans for Chicago's skyline: a spiraling giant right on the lakefront.

311 S. Wacker may not be the tallest building in town, but come dark, it's one of the most visible, lit by nearly 2,000 fluorescent lights.

Although **Park Tower** hovers over nearly everything around it, this hotel/condo is considered a good neighbor, thanks to its retro styling and warmly colored facade.

1000 ft

961 ft

844 ft

673 ft

1990

1990

2000

2004

2006–2010

311 S. WACKER DRIVE
Kohn Pedersen Fox
P. 133

2 PRUDENTIAL PLAZA
Loebl, Schlossman & Hackl
P. 134

PARK TOWER
Lucien LaGrange Architects
P. 140

HYATT CENTER
Pei Cobb Freed & Partners
P. 133

FORDHAM SPIRE
Santiago Calatrava

evelt University; the swirling terra-cotta design is pinched from the Marquette Building; and the glass curtain wall on the west side is a nod to 1950s modernism. The library was named for the first African-American mayor of Chicago, and the primary architect was Thomas Beeby, of the Chicago firm Hammond, Beeby & Babka.

The excellent **Children's Library** on the second floor, an 18,000-square-foot haven, has vibrant wall-mounted figures by Chicago imagist Karl Wirsum. Works by noted Chicago artists are displayed along a second-floor walkway above the main lobby. There's also an impressive Winter Garden with skylights on the ninth floor. Free programs and performances are offered regularly at the center. ⊠ *400 S. State St., Loop* ☎ *312/747–4300* ⊕ *www.chipublib.org* ⊙ *Mon.–Thurs. 9–9, Fri. and Sat. 9–5, Sun. 1–5.*

SKY-HIGH SANCTUARY

Chicago Temple. The Gothic-inspired headquarters of the First United Methodist Church of Chicago were built in 1923 by Holabird & Roche, complete with a first-floor sanctuary, 21 floors of office space, a sky-high chapel, and an eight-story spire (best viewed from the bridge across the Chicago River at Dearborn Street). Outside, along the building's east wall at ground level, stained-glass windows relate the history of the church in Chicago. Joan Miró's sculpture *Chicago* (1981) is in the small plaza just east of the church. ⊠ *77 W. Washington St., Loop.*

UP, UP, UP: THE SKYSCRAPERS

Aon Center. With the open space of Millennium Park at its doorstep, the Aon Center really stands out—even if its appearance isn't much to write home about. Originally built as the Standard Oil Building, the structure has changed names and appearances twice. Not long after it went up, its marble cladding came crashing down and the whole building was resheathed in granite. The massive building sits on a handsome (if rather sterile) plaza, where Harry Bertoia's wind-chime sculpture in the reflecting pool makes interesting sounds when a breeze blows. ⊠ *200 E. Randolph Dr., Loop.*

WHAT ARE YOU LOOKIN' AT?

The **Chicago Window,** a popular window design used in buildings all over America (until air-conditioning made it obsolete), consists of a large fixed central pane with smaller moveable windows on each side. The picture window offered light, while the double-hung windows let in the Lake Michigan breeze. Developed in Chicago by engineer and architect William Le Baron Jenney, who pioneered the use of metal-frame construction in the 1880s, the Chicago Window helps to define buildings across the city.

PLAZA
BLISS: VISIT
THE MARC
CHAGALL
MOSAIC

Chase Tower. This building's graceful swoop—a novelty when it went up—continues to offer an eye-pleasing respite from all the right angles surrounding it. And its spacious plaza, with a mosaic by Marc Chagall called **The Four Seasons,** is one of the most enjoyable public spaces in the neighborhood. Designed by Perkins & Will and C. F. Murphy Associates in 1969, the building has been home to a succession of financial institutions (its most recent name was Bank One Plaza); names aside, it remains one of the more distinctive buildings around, not to mention one of the highest buildings in the Loop's true heart. ✉ *Bounded by Dearborn, Madison, Clark, and Monroe Sts., Loop.*

Hyatt Center. At 48 stories, the headquarters of this hospitality group is no giant, but it more than makes its mark on South Wacker Drive with a bold elliptical shape, a glass-faced street-level lobby rising 36 feet, and a pedestrian-friendly plaza. One of the city's newer towers, it displays a noticeable tweaking of the unrelieved curtain wall that makes many city streets forbidding canyons. Designed by Pei Cobb Freed & Partners, the building was completed in 2004. ✉ *71 S. Wacker Dr., Loop.*

CHECK OUT
THE 103RD
FLOOR
Fodor's Choice
★
☺

Sears Tower. In Chicago, size matters. This soaring 110-story skyscraper, designed by Skidmore, Owings & Merrill in 1974, was the world's tallest building until 1996 when the Petronas Towers in Kuala Lumpur, Malaysia, claimed the title. However, the folks at the Sears Tower are quick to point out that Petronas counts its spire as part of the building. If you were to measure the 1,450-foot-high Sears Tower in terms of highest occupied floor, highest roof, or highest antenna, the Sears Tower would win hands down.

Those bragging rights aside, the **Skydeck** is really something to boast about. Enter on Jackson Boulevard to take the ear-popping ride to the 103rd-floor observatory. Video monitors turn the 70-second elevator ride into a fun-filled, thrilling trip. On a clear day a whopping four states are visible: Illinois, Michigan, Wisconsin, and Indiana. (Check the visibility ratings at the security desk before you decide to ride up and take in the view.) At the top, interactive exhibits tell about Chicago's dreamers, schemers, architects, musicians, and sports stars. Computer kiosks in six languages help international travelers key into Chicago hot spots. Knee-High Chicago, a 4-foot-high exhibit with cutouts of Chicago sports and history at a child's eye-level, will entertain the kids. The Sears Tower also has spruced up the lower level with a food court, new exhibits, and a short movie about the city. Security is very tight, so figure in a little extra time for your visit to the Skydeck. Before you leave, don't miss the spiraling Calder mobile sculpture *The Universe* in the ground-floor lobby on the Wacker Drive side. ✉ *233 S. Wacker Dr.; for the Skydeck, enter on Jackson Blvd. between Wacker Dr. and Franklin St., Loop* ☎ *312/875–9696* ⊕ *www.the-skydeck.com* 🎫 *$12* ☺ *Apr.–Sept., daily 10–10; Oct.–Mar., daily 10--8.*

NIGHT LIGHTS
SUPREME
★

311 South Wacker Drive. The first of three towers intended for the site, this pale pink building is the work of Kohn Pedersen Fox, who also designed 333 West Wacker Drive, a few blocks away. The 1990 building's most distinctive feature is its Gothic crown, blindingly lighted at night. During migration season so many birds crashed into the illuminated tower that the building management was forced to tone down the lighting. The building has an inviting atrium, with palm trees and a splashy, romantic fountain. ⊠*333 S. Wacker Dr., at W. Jackson Blvd., Loop* ⊕*www.311southwacker.com.*

Two Prudential Plaza. Nicknamed "Two Pru," this glass-and-granite giant is the older sibling of the 1955 tower at its feet (looking very 1950s indeed). Together with their neighbors they form a block-long business-oriented minicity. Two Prudential is the tallest reinforced concrete building in the city, and its blue detailing and beveled roof are instantly recognizable from afar. ⊠*180 N. Stetson Ave., Loop* ⊕*www. pruplazachicago.com.*

SOUTH LOOP

Heading south from the heart of the Loop, you'll find Printer's Row, where lofts that once clattered with linotype machines are now luxury real-estate morsels, as well as Dearborn Park, a residential enclave reclaimed from old rail yards.

HISTORIC BUILDINGS

Dearborn Station. Chicago's oldest standing passenger train station, a South Loop landmark, now serves as a galleria. Designed in Romanesque-revival style in 1885 by the New York architect Cyrus L.W. Eidlitz, it has a wonderful clock tower and a red-sandstone and red-brick facade ornamented with terra-cotta. Striking features inside are the marble floor, wraparound brass walkway, and arching wood-frame doorways. ⊠*47 W. Polk St., South Loop* ☎*312/554–8100* ⊙*Daily 7 AM–9 PM.*

Donohue Building. The first major printing facility in Printers Row, this 1883 building's main entrance is flanked by marble columns topped by ornately carved capitals, with tile work over the entrance set into a splendid granite arch. Note the beautiful ironwork and woodwork ornamenting the first-floor retail establishments. ⊠*711 S. Dearborn St., South Loop.*

Franklin Building. Built in 1888 and initially the home of the Franklin Company, a printing concern, this building has intricate decoration. The tile work on the facade leads up to *The First Impression*—a medieval scene illustrating the first application of the printer's craft. Above the entryway is a motto: THE EXCELLENCE OF EVERY ART MUST CONSIST IN THE COMPLETE ACCOMPLISHMENT OF ITS PURPOSE. ⊠*720 S. Dearborn St., South Loop.*

CURVES ON THE MARINA

River City. These concrete curves may look familiar; the complex was built in 1986 by Bertrand Goldberg, who also built the "corncobs" of Marina City. This apartment complex features a 10-story atrium, commercial space, and 62-slip marina. It has great views of the water from the lobby. ⊠*800 S. Wells St., South Loop.*

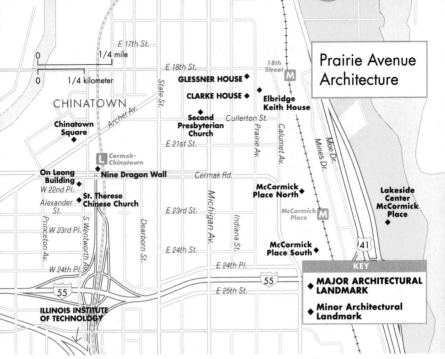

KEY

◆ **MAJOR ARCHITECTURAL LANDMARK**

♦ **Minor Architectural Landmark**

OLD SCHOOL **Pontiac Building.** An early Chicago School skyscraper—note its classic
HOLABIRD & rectangular shape and flat roof—the simple, redbrick, 14-story Pontiac
ROCHE was designed by Holabird & Roche in 1891 and is their oldest existing
building in Chicago. ⊠ *542 S. Dearborn St., South Loop.*

PRAIRIE AVENUE & BEYOND

Heading even farther south parallel to the lakeshore, you'll find the Prairie Avenue Historic District; this was the neighborhood of choice for the city's movers and shakers in the mid-19th century. If you're a die-hard Mies van der Rohe fan, continue your journey south to check out his buildings on the campus of the Illinois Institute of Technology.

HISTORIC BUILDINGS

Clarke House. This Greek revival dates from 1836, making it Chicago's oldest surviving building. It's a clapboard house in a masonry city, built for Henry and Caroline Palmer Clarke to remind them of the East Coast they left behind. The Doric columns and pilasters were an attempt to civilize Chicago's frontier image. The everyday objects and furnishings inside reveal a typical 1830s–60s middle-class home. ⊠ *1827 S. Indiana Ave., Prairie Avenue District* ☎ *312/745-0040* 🖺 *$10; see Glessner House listing for combo-ticket information* ⊙ *Tours: Wed.–Sun. at noon, 1, and 2* PM.

Fodor'sChoice **Glessner House.** This fortresslike, Romanesque revival 1886 residence is
★ the only surviving building in Chicago by architect H. H. Richardson,

MIES VAN DER ROHE, KOOLHAAS & JAHN

Illinois Institute of Technology. "Less is more" claimed Mies van der Rohe, but for fans of the master's work, more is more at IIT. The campus holds an array of the kind of glass-and-steel structures for which he is most famous. Crown Hall is the jewel of the collection and has been designated a National Historic Landmark, but don't overlook the Robert F. Carr Memorial Chapel of St. Savior.

Additions to the campus include the McCormick Tribune Campus Center,

designed by Dutch architect Rem Koolhaas and new student housing by Helmut Jahn. The campus is about 1 mi west of Lake Shore Drive on 31st Street. Or take the El train's Green or Red Line to the 35th Street stop, and walk east two blocks to campus. ⊠ *S. State St. between 31st and 35th Sts., Douglas, south of Chinatown* ☎ *312/567–3000* ⊕ *www. iit.edu.*

who also designed Boston's Trinity Church. It's also one of the few great mansions left on Prairie Avenue, once home to such heavy hitters as retailer Marshall Field and meat-packing magnate Philip Armour. The area has lately seen the arrival of new, high-end construction, but nothing beats a tour of Glessner House, a remarkable relic of the days when merchant princes really lived like royalty. Enjoy the lavish interiors and the many artifacts, from silver pieces and art glass to antique ceramics and Isaac Scott carvings and furnishings. ⊠ *1800 S. Prairie Ave., Prairie Avenue* ☎ *312/326–1480* ⊕ *www.glessnerhouse.org* ☞ *$10. Combined admission to Glessner and the nearby Clarke House $15. Free Wed.* ⊙ *Tours Wed.–Sun. at 1, 2, and 3* PM.

NEAR NORTH & RIVER NORTH

Just a hop, skip, and a jump from the Loop's northern reaches and across the Chicago River are the Near North and River North neighborhoods. The magnet for most folks is North Michigan Avenue—aka the Magnificent Mile—a glittering stretch studded with shops and hotels. Saunter up this thoroughfare from the Michigan Avenue Bridge (or head south from Oak Street) and you'll see such sights as the Wrigley Building, the Tribune Tower, the Historic Water Tower, and the John Hancock Center.

HISTORIC BUILDINGS

Tribune Tower. In 1922 *Chicago Tribune* publisher Colonel Robert McCormick chose a Gothic design for the building that would house his paper, after rejecting a slew of functional modern designs by such notables as Walter Gropius, Eliel Saarinen, and Adolf Loos. Embedded in the exterior walls of the tower are chunks of material taken from famous sites around the world. Look for bits from the Parthenon, Westminster Abbey, the Alamo, St. Peter's Basilica, the Taj Mahal,

A REVERED SCHOOL

The **Chicago School** had no classrooms and no curriculum. It didn't confer degrees. The Chicago School wasn't an institution at all, but a name given to the collection of architects whose work, beginning in the 1880s, helped free American architecture from the often rigid styles of the past. Nonetheless, a number of their buildings echoed a classical column, with the lower floors functioning as the base, the middle floors as the shaft, and the cornice on top being the equivalent of a capital. In pioneering the "tall building," these architects utilized steel-frame construction; they also reduced ornamentation. Alumni include Daniel Burnham, William Le Baron Jenney, Louis Sullivan, Dankmar Adler, John Root, William Holabird, and Martin Roche.

and the Great Wall of China. On the ground floor are the studios of WGN radio, part of the *Chicago Tribune* empire, which also includes WGN-TV, cable-television stations, and the Chicago Cubs. (Modesty was not one of Colonel McCormick's prime traits: WGN stands for the *Tribune*'s self-bestowed nickname, World's Greatest Newspaper). ✉*435 N. Michigan Ave., Near North* ☎*312/222–3232* ⊕*www. chicagotribune.com.*

Historic Water Tower. This famous Michigan Avenue structure, completed in 1867, was originally built to house a 137-foot standpipe that equalized the pressure of the water pumped by the similar pumping station across the street. Oscar Wilde uncharitably called it "a castellated monstrosity" studded with pepper shakers. Nonetheless, it remains a Chicago landmark and a symbol of the city's spirit of survival following the Great Chicago Fire of 1871. The small gallery inside has rotating art exhibitions of local interest. ✉*806 N. Michigan Ave., at Pearson St., Near North* 🎫*Free* ◷*Mon.–Sat. 10–6:30, Sun. 10–5.*

Water Works Pumping Station. Water is still pumped to some of the city residents at a rate of about 250 million gallons per day from this Gothic-style structure, which, along with the Water Tower across the street, survived the Great Chicago Fire of 1871. The acclaimed **Lookingglass Theatre** calls this place home. The station also houses a **Chicago Water Works Visitor Information Center** (☎*877/244–2246* ⊕*www.877chicago. com* ◷*Mon.–Thurs. 8 AM–7 PM; Fri. 8 AM–6 PM; Sat. 9 AM–6 PM; Sun. 10 AM–6 PM*), which has a sandwich shop. ✉*163 E. Pearson St., at Michigan Ave., Near North.*

A NOD TO SEVILLE

★ **Wrigley Building.** Two structures built several years apart and later connected, the gleaming white Wrigley Building sports a clock tower inspired by the bell tower of the grand cathedral in Seville, Spain. The landmark headquarters of the chewing gum company—designed by Graham, Anderson, Probst & White—was instrumental in transforming Michigan Avenue from an area of warehouses to one of the most desirable spots in the city. Be sure to check it out at night, when lamps bounce light off the building's gleaming terra-cotta facade. ✉*400 and 410 N. Michigan Ave., Near North* ⊕*www.wrigley.com/wrigley/about/ about_story_building.asp.*

Near North & River North Architecture

KEY

◆ **MAJOR ARCHITECTURAL LANDMARK**

◆ Minor Architectural Landmark

Armitage Ave.

N. Lincoln Ave.

N. Clark St.

N. Mohawk St.

N. Larrabee St.

N. Sedgwick St.

N. Clark St.

Baha'i House of Worship (18 mi north of downtown)

LINCOLN PARK

GOLD COAST

North Ave.

Wells St.

La Salle Blvd

Clarke St.

Dearborn St.

North Ave.

Parkway St.

Astor Pl.

41

Schiller St.

CHARNLEY–PERSKY HOUSE

Astor St.

Lake Michigan

Clybourn Ave.

Division St.

Elm St.

Bellevue St.

Larrabee St.

RIVER NORTH

Maple St

Oak St

Lake Shore Dr.

FOURTH PRESBYTERIAN CHURCH

JOHN HANCOCK BUILDING

860–880 N. LAKE SHORE DRIVE

Kingsbury St.

Hudson St.

Sedgwick St.

Franklin St.

Walton St.

Delaware St.

Quigley Seminary

Chestnut St.

HISTORIC WATER TOWER

Pearson St.

41

Orleans St.

Chicago Ave.

PARK TOWER

Holy Name Cathedral

Wabash St.

Rush St.

Michigan Ave.

WATER WORKS PUMPING STATION

Fairbanks Ct.

Superior St

Huron St

Erie St

La Salle Blvd

Clark St.

Dearborn St.

State St.

St. James Cathedral

NEAR NORTH

J. F. Kennedy Expwy

Ontario St

Ohio St

N. Branch Chicago River

Grand Ave

Illinois St

Hubbard St

Kinzie St

Carroll St

TRIBUNE TOWER

Navy Pier →

WRIGLEY BUILDING

NBC Tower

MARINA CITY

MICHIGAN AVENUE BRIDGE

Centennial Fountain and Arc

Wacker Dr.

LOOP

0   1/4 mi

0   1/4 km

TWO INTERPRETATIONS OF "TWINS"

Fodor'sChoice ★ **860–880 N. Lake Shore Drive.** These twin apartment towers overlooking Lake Michigan were an early and eloquent realization of Mies van der Rohe's "less is more" credo, expressed in the high-rise. I beams running up the facade underscore the building's verticality while, inside, mechanical systems are housed in the center so as to leave the rest of each floor free and open to the spectacular views. Completed in 1951, the buildings were built in the famed International Style, which played a key role in transforming the look of American cities. ✉*860–880 N. Lake Shore Dr., at E. Chestnut St., River North.*

SOME CALL THEM CORNCOBS **Marina City.** Likened to everything from corncobs to the towers of Antonio Gaudi's Sagrada Familia in Barcelona, Goldberg's twin towers were a bold departure from the severity of the International Style, which began to dominate high-rise architecture beginning in the 1950s. Completed in 1967, the towers house condominium apartments (all pie-shape, with curving balconies). In addition to the apartments and marina, the complex now has four restaurants, the House of Blues nightclub, the new Hotel Sax Chicago, and a huge bowling alley. ✉*329 N. Dearborn St., River North* ☎*312/923–2000.*

> OFF THE BEATEN PATH:
> HARMONY UP NORTH
>
> About 18 mi north of downtown Chicago (in Wilmette), rising near the lake, the ★ **Baha'i House of Worship** is an intriguing, nine-sided building that incorporates architectural styles and symbols from many of the world's religions. With its delicate lacelike details and massive dome, the Louis Bourgeois design emphasizes the 19th-century Persian origins of the Baha'i religion. As symmetrical and harmonious as the building are the formal gardens that surround it. The temple is the U.S. center of the Baha'i faith, which advocates spiritual unity, world peace, race unity, and equality of the sexes. The visitor center has exhibits explaining the Baha'i faith; here you can also ask for a guide to show you around. ✉*100 Linden Ave.* ☎*847/853–2300* ⊕*www.us.bahai.org* ✉*Free* ⊙*May–Sept., daily 10–8; Oct.–Apr., daily 10–5*

BRIDGE OF BRIDGES

★ **Michigan Avenue Bridge.** Chicago is a city of bridges, and this is one of its most graceful. Completed in 1920, it features impressive sculptures on its four pylons representing major Chicago events: its exploration by Marquette and Joliet, its settlement by trader Jean Baptiste Point du Sable, the Fort Dearborn Massacre of 1812, and the rebuilding of the city after the Great Chicago Fire of 1871. The site of the fort, at the southeast end of the bridge, is marked by a commemorative plaque. As you stroll Michigan Avenue, be prepared for a possible delay; the bridge rises regularly to allow boat traffic to pass underneath. ✉*Michigan Ave. at Wacker Dr., Near North.*

SKYSCRAPERS DELUXE

SKY-HIGH
"BIG JOHN"
Fodor'sChoice
★

John Hancock Center. Designed by the same team that designed the Sears Tower (Skidmore, Owings & Merrill), this multi-use skyscraper is distinguished by its tapering shape and the enormous X braces, which help stabilize its 100 stories. Soon after it went up in 1970, it earned the nickname "Big John." No wonder: at 1,127 feet (1,502 feet counting the antennae at the top), 2.8 million square feet, and 46,000 tons o' steel, there's nothing little about it. Packed with retail, parking, offices, a restaurant, and residences, it has been likened to a city within a city. Impressive from any angle, it offers mind-boggling views from a 94th floor observatory (as with the Sears Tower, you can see to four states on clear days). For anyone afflicted with vertigo, a sensible option is a seat in the bar of the 95th floor Signature Room. The tab will be steep, but you'll be steady on your feet—*maybe.* ✉*875 N. Michigan Ave., Near North* ☎*312/751–3681* ⊕*www.hancock-observatory.com and www.johnhancockcenterchicago.com* ✉*Observatory $10* ☉*Daily 9* AM–*11* PM; *last ticket sold at 10:45* PM.

Park Tower. A relative newcomer to the neighborhood (2000), this high-end hotel–condo combines retro touches (note the pitched roof) and quirky contemporary flourishes (check out the protruding bank of windows on the seventh floor). Designed by Lucien LaGrange Architects, the 67-story tower seems even taller than it really is (almost 900 feet), thanks to its unobstructed location across from the small park where the Historic Water Tower stands. ✉*800 N. Michigan Ave., at Chicago Ave., Near North* ⊕*www.parkhyatt.com.*

CHICAGO'S ANSWER TO A GOTHIC-REVIVAL CHURCH

REST YOUR
FEET IN THE
GRASSY
COURTYARD

Fourth Presbyterian Church. A welcome visual and physical oasis amid the high-rise hubbub of North Michigan Avenue, this Gothic revival house of worship was designed by Ralph Adams Cram. Local architect Charles van Doren Shaw devised the cloister and companion buildings. The first big building erected on the avenue after the Chicago Fire, it counted among its congregants the city's elite. Noontime concerts are given every Friday in the sanctuary. ✉*126 E. Chestnut St., Near North* ☎*312/787–4570* ⊕*www.fourthchurch.org.*

WHAT ARE YOU LOOKIN' AT?

"Curtain Wall" is the term for the largely glass exterior surface of many modern buildings.

Unlike masonry construction, in which stone or brick support the weight of the building, a curtain wall is not a load-bearing system; rather, it is hung on

the steel or concrete frame that holds the building up.

The Reliance Building (an early example), the Sears Tower, and 333 W. Wacker Drive are all curtain-wall buildings.

FRANK LLOYD WRIGHT

1867–1959

The most famous American architect of the 20th century led a life that was as zany and scandalous as his architectural legacy was great. Behind the photo-op appearance and lordly pronouncements was a rebel visionary who left an unforgettable imprint on the world's notion of architecture. Nowhere else in the country can you experience Frank Lloyd Wright's genius as you can in Chicago and its surroundings.

Born two years after the Civil War ended, Wright did not live to see the completion of his late masterpiece, the Guggenheim Museum. His father preached and played (the Gospel and music) and dragged the family from the Midwest to New England and back before he up and left for good. Wright's Welsh-born mother, Anna Lloyd Jones, grew up in Wisconsin, and her son's roots would run deep there, too. Although his career began in Chicago and his work took him as far away as Japan, the home Wright built in Spring Green, Wisconsin—Taliesin—was his true center.

Despite all his dramas and financial instability (Wright was notoriously bad with money), the architect certainly produced. He was always ready to try something new—as long as it fit his notion of architecture as an expression of the human spirit and of human relationship with nature. By the time he died in 1959, Wright had designed over 1,000 projects, more than half of which were constructed.

Robie House, Chicago

WELCOME TO OAK PARK!

★ Fodor's Choice

Oak Park is a leafy, quiet community just 10 miles west of downtown Chicago. When you arrive, head to the **Oak Park Visitors Center** (⊠ 158 N. Forest Ave. ☎ 708/848–1500 ⊕ www.visitoakpark. com ☉ Daily 10–5, until 4 in winter) and get oriented with a free map.

Next wander to the **Frank Lloyd Wright Home and Studio** (⊠ 951 Chicago Ave. ☎ 708/848–1976 🖶 708/848–1248 ⊕ www.wrightplus.org ✉ $12; walking tour $12; combined $20 ☉ Weekday tours at 11, 1, and 3; weekend tours 11–3:30, every 20 mins. Tickets can be purchased in advance via the Web site). From the outside, the shingle-clad structure may not appear all that innovative,

but it's here that Wright developed the architectural language that still has the world talking.

Financed with a $5,000 loan from his mentor, Louis Sullivan, Wright designed the home when he was only 22. The residence manifests some of the spatial and stylistic characteristics that became hallmarks of Wright's work: there's a central fireplace from which other spaces seem to radiate and an enticing flow to the rooms. In 1974, the local Frank Lloyd Wright Home and Studio Foundation, together with the National Trust for Historic Preservation, embarked on a 13-year restoration that returned the building to its 1909 appearance.

GETTING HERE

To get to the heart of Oak Park by car, take the Eisenhower Expressway (I-290) west to Harlem Avenue. Head north on Harlem and take a right on Lake Street to get to the Oak Park Visitors Center at Forest Avenue and Lake Street (158 N. Forest Avenue), where there's ample free parking. You can also take the Green Line of the El to the last stop, the Harlem Avenue exit, or Metra's Union Pacific West Line from the Ogilvie Transportation Center in Citicorp Center downtown (500 W. Madison) to the Oak Park stop at Marion Street.

WOMEN, FIRE, SCANDAL ... AND OVER 1,000 DESIGNS

The southeast entrance to the Frank Lloyd Wright Home & Studio in Oak Park.

1885 Wright briefly studies engineering at the University of Wisconsin.

1887 Wright strikes out for Chicago. He starts his career learning the basics with J. L. Silsbee, a residential architect. Later he joins the office of Adler & Sullivan as a drafter, just as the firm begins work on the massive Auditorium building.

1889 Wright marries Catherine Tobin; he builds her a home in suburban Oak Park, and they have six children together.

> "WHILE NEW YORK HAS REPRODUCED MUCH AND PRODUCED NOTHING, CHICAGO'S ACHIEVEMENTS IN ARCHITECTURE HAVE GAINED WORLD-WIDE RECOGNITION AS A DISTINCTIVELY AMERICAN ARCHITECTURE."

Strolling Oak Park

A leisurely stroll around the neighborhood will introduce you to plenty of **Frank Lloyd Wright houses**. All are privately owned, so you'll have to be content with what you can see from the outside. Check out 1019, 1027, and 1031 Chicago Avenue. These are typical Victorians that Wright designed on the sly while working for Sullivan.

For a look at the "real" Wright, don't miss the **Moore–Dugal Home** (1895) at 333 N. Forest Avenue, which reflects Wright's evolving architectural philosophy with its huge chimney and overhanging second story. Peek also at numbers 318, 313, 238, and 210, where you can follow his emerging modernism. Around the corner at 6 Elizabeth Court is the **Laura Gale House,** a 1909 project whose cantilevered profile foreshadows the thrusting planes Wright would create at Fallingwater decades later.

Between 1889 and 1913, Wright erected over two dozen buildings in Oak Park, so unless you're making an extended

A landmark profile: the eastern facade of the architect's home and studio, Oak Park.

visit, don't expect to see everything. But don't leave town without a visit to his 1908 **Unity Temple** (✉ 875 W. Lake St. ☎ 708/383–8873), a National Historic Landmark. Take a moment to appreciate Wright's fresh take on a place of worship; his bold strokes in creating a flowing interior; his unfailing attention to what was outside (note the skylights); and his dramatic use of concrete, which helps to protect the space from traffic noise.

Interior, Unity Temple, Oak Park

1893	Wright launches his own practice in downtown Chicago.
1898	As his practice grows, Wright adds a studio to his Oak Park residence.
1905	Wright begins designing the reinforced concrete Unity Temple.
1908	Construction begins on the Robie House in Chicago's Hyde Park neighborhood.

Guided Tours

A great way to get to know Oak Park is to take advantage of the guided tours. Well-informed local guides take small groups on tours throughout the day, discussing various architectural details, pointing out artifacts from the family's life, and often telling amusing stories of the rambunctious Wright clan. Reservations are required for groups of 10 or more for the home and studio tours. Note that you need to arrive as early as possible to be assured a spot. Tours begin at the **Ginkgo Tree Bookshop**, which is part of the home and studio. The shop carries architecture-related books and gifts. You can pick up a map ($3.95) to find other examples of Wright's work that are within easy walking or driving distance, or you can join a guided tour of the neighborhood led by volunteers.

The Hemingway Connection

Frank Lloyd Wright wasn't the only creative giant to call Oak Park home. Ten years after Wright arrived, Ernest Hemingway was born here in 1899 in a proper Queen Anne, complete with turret. Wright was gone by the time Hemingway began to sow his literary oats. Good thing, too. It's doubtful the quiet village could have handled two such egos. *See* Get Out of Town: Brushing up your Ernest Hemingway pg. 26.

Frank Lloyd Wright's distinctive take on a modern dining room.

TIPS

Tickets go on sale every March 1 for the eagerly awaited annual **Wright Plus Benefit Housewalk**, your chance to see the interiors of some of Oak Park's most architecturally notable homes. Check out ⊕ www.wrightplus.org for more details.

Note that you can save time (or rest your feet) on the free **Oak Park Shuttle** (☎ 708/615–1830). Operated by PACE and the Village of Oak Park, the shuttle bus runs every 30 minutes and makes 21 stops at Oak Park sights. Regular hours are 10–5:30 daily. You can catch the shuttle outside the Frank Lloyd Wright Home and Studio.

Interior, Rookery, Chicago

1909   Wright leaves for Europe with Mamah Cheney, the wife of a former client; this puts an abrupt end to his family life, but Mrs. Wright does not consent to a divorce.

1911   Wright and Cheney settle at Taliesin, in Spring Green, Wisconsin.

1914   Mrs. Cheney, her two children, and several other people are killed by a deranged employee, who also sets fire to Taliesin. Wright rebuilds, as he does when the house burns again in 1922.

1915   With new mistress Miriam Noel in tow, the architect heads for Japan to oversee the building of the Imperial Hotel.

PRAIRIE STYLE PRIMER

Primarily a residential mode, Wright's Prairie style is characterized by ground-hugging masses; low-pitched roofs with deep eaves; and ribbon windows. Generally, Prairie houses are two-story affairs, with single story wings and terraces that project into the landscape. Brick and stone, earth tones, and unpainted wood underscore the perception of a house as an extension of the natural world. Wright designed free-flowing living spaces defined by alternating ceiling heights, natural light, and architectural screens. Although a number of other Chicago architects pursued this emerging aesthetic, Wright became its

> "ALL FINE ARCHITECTURAL VALUES ARE HUMAN VALUES, ELSE NOT VALUABLE."

acknowledged master. Though Wright designed dozens of Prairie style homes, the most well-known is Robie House, in Chicago's Hyde Park neighborhood. A dynamic composition of overlapping planes, it seems both beautifully anchored to the ground and ready to sail off with the arrival of a sharp breeze.

4

FRANK LLOYD WRIGHT

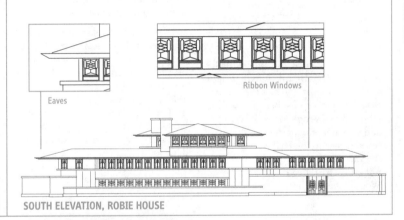

Eaves

Ribbon Windows

SOUTH ELEVATION, ROBIE HOUSE

The architect discusses a project with his assistants in Oak Park, 1958.

1922   Wright and his wife Catherine divorce.

1924   Wright marries Miriam Noel, but Noel is emotionally unsteady and the marriage implodes three years later.

1928   Wright marries Olga (Olgivanna) Lazovich Milanoff, who remains a compelling helpmate for the remainder of his life. They have one daughter together.

1930   The Taliesin Fellowship is launched; eager apprentices arrive at Spring Green to learn from the master.

WRIGHT BACK IN THE CITY

If you can't make it to Oak Park, there are a handful of notable—and memorable—Frank Lloyd Wright experiences to be had in the city.

★ **Fodor's Choice** Long and low, **Robie House** (1908–1910) grabs the ground and sends the eye zipping westward. Massive overhangs shoot out from the low-pitched roof and windows run along the facade in a glittering stretch. Inside, Wright's "open plan" echoes the great outdoors, as one space flows into another, while sunlight streaming through decorative leaded windows bathes the rooms in patterns. Robie House is midway through a 10-year renovation but remains open to visitors. ✉ 5757 S. Woodlawn Ave., Hyde Park ☎ 773/834–1847 ⛉ $12 ⊙ Tour weekdays at 11, 1, and 3; weekends every ½ hr 11–3:30.

When he designed the **Isidore Heller House** in 1897, Frank Lloyd Wright was still moving toward the mature Prairie style achieved in the Robie House. As was common with Wright—and very uncommon then and now—the entrance to the Heller House is on the side of the structure. The house is not open to the public. ✉ 5132 S. Woodlawn Ave., Hyde Park.

Frank Lloyd Wright designed the **Charnley–Persky House** with his mentor Louis Sullivan. This almost-austere residence represents one of Wright's first significant forays into residential design. Historians still squabble about who designed what here, but it's easy to imagine that the young go-getter had a hand in the cleanly rendered interior. Note how the geometric exterior looks unmistakably modern next to its fussy neighbors. ✉ 1365 N. Astor St., Near North ☎ 312/915–0105 ⛉ Free Wed., $9 for Sat. tour that includes Madlener House. ⊙ Apr.–Nov., tours Wed. at noon, Sat. at 10 AM and 1 PM; Dec.–Mar., 10 AM only. For larger groups, make reservations well in advance.

Stand outside the **Rookery** with its dizzyingly detailed facade and you'll think you've taken a wrong turn in your search for Wright. This early high-rise was designed by Burnham & Root. In 1905, Wright was hired to spruce up the building's interior court, which he lightened up by replacing terra-cotta with gilded white marble; adding pendant light fixtures; and gracing the stairway with urns, one of his favorite motifs. ✉ 209 S. LaSalle St., Loop.

A New York icon: Wright's Guggenheim Museum.

1935 Fallingwater, the country home of Pittsburgh retailer Edgar J. Kaufmann, is completed at Bear Run, Pennsylvania.

1937 Wright begins construction of his winter getaway, Taliesin West, in Scottsdale, Arizona.

1956 Wright designs the Guggenheim Museum in New York. It is completed in 1959.

1957 Wright joins preservationists in saving Robie House from demolition.

1959 Wright dies at the age of 91.

Shopping

WORD OF MOUTH

"Check out the boutique shopping in neighborhoods like Lincoln Park, where you'll find smaller, non-chain, funkier stores. Not cheap, but much more affordable than Oak Street."

—jlm–mi

"Definitely have a drink at the top of the Hancock Building, then do a little retail therapy along Michigan Avenue."

—parisandelle

SHOPPING PLANNER

Itineraries for the Obsessed

If art is your thing, then head to River North and the West Loop, which are quick cab rides from one another and loaded with fabulous galleries.

If you're looking to head home with funky fashions, go to Bucktown and Wicker Park. Must-hits include **p. 45** (*1643 N. Damen Ave., 773/862–4523*) for women's styles; **G Boutique** for va-va-va-voom lingerie (*2131 N. Damen Ave., 773/235–1234*); and **shebang** (*1616 N. Damen Ave., 773/486–3800*) for pretty accessories.

Need to buy some things for the little ones in your life? Hit Lincoln Park's **Stinky Pants** (*808 W. Armitage Ave., 773/281–2001*) and **LMNOP** (*2570 N. Lincoln Ave., 773/975–4055*). Find treats for tiny feet at **Piggy Toes** (*2205 N. Halsted St., 773/281–5583*). For stuff for the home, best bets are **Bellini** (*2100 N. Southport Ave., 773/880–5840*) and **The Land of Nod** (*900 W. North Ave., 312/475–9903*), for stylish bedding, bath items, books, and toys.

Cold Weather Considerations

Visiting during winter or one of Chicago's chilly days? Don't let the cold keep you from scoring some serious stash. Take a cue from weather-savvy local shoppers, who hit indoor urban malls like Water Tower Place and 900 North Michigan on the Mag Mile when the winds whip up.

If you're willing to brave the elements, dress wisely. The weather can change on a dime here, so wear layers that are easy to peel off and carry—something that'll make dressing-room acrobatics go quicker, too. We're talking warm undershirt, long-sleeved shirt, sweater or warm jacket, and windbreaker—substitute heavy winter coat for that last one if you're visiting in the dead of winter, along with the necessary accoutrements (scarf, hat, gloves). Happily, you'll find plenty of places along the way for a hot cocoa, coffee, or tea if the cold is getting the best of you.

Getting Around

Second only in size to that of New York City, the public transportation system in Chicago serves roughly 1.5 million riders a day and can get you to the city's main shopping drags with relative ease. With so many riders, it can get pretty crowded during weekday rush hours; also improvement and repair projects can cause delays on many train lines, so plan accordingly.

■ Fares are $2 (cash) for both the bus and train (called the El, for the elevated tracks that run around the Loop).

■ If you plan on riding frequently, buy a transit card at any El station vending machine or at many grocery and drug stores. Bus rides cost $1.75 with a transit card, and transfers on both the bus and El cost an additional 25 cents.

■ Some of the neighborhoods we mention here are easy to walk between, like the Mag Mile and River North, and parts of Lincoln Park and Lake View, but it's best to consult a map to determine whether the distances you're planning to travel warrant wheels.

Chicago Hours

Keep these timing tips in mind as you plan out your day:

■ Most stores keep traditional retail hours, opening around 10 AM and closing at 6 or 7 PM, though different neighborhood styles and street traffic can dictate otherwise. In Bucktown and Wicker Park, for example, many shops don't open until 11 AM or noon, and may stay open later in the evening.

■ Count on mall stores to keep later hours, usually until 7 or 8 PM. Most are open (with shorter hours than other days) on Sunday.

■ If there's a particular boutique you want to visit, call ahead. Simply flip through this chapter and you'll find all the contact information you'll need.

Pamper Your Pet

Chicago is a pet-lover's city, and it's filled with fun places to shop for them. Check out **The Down Town Dog** (Macy's, 111 N. State St., 312/782–4575), a delightful boutique within Macy's that's stocked with everything for the urban pooch (and kitty). In Bucktown, **Red Dog House** (2031 N. Damen Ave., 773/227–7341) keeps pace with the fashionable 'hood by selling spa products (such as paw balm), high-end treats (biscotti for pups) and sculptural bowls and beds. If your dog comes along for the trip, there are some retail stores that let well-behaved pups on leashes do a little browsing. Our favorite: **Neiman Marcus** (737 N. Michigan Ave., 312/642–5900), where pedigree types can peruse Burberry carriers and other fancy items.

Word of Mouth

"Even if you are coming to Chicago on a budget, you have to do a shopping day–even if you don't buy anything. I window-shop in Chicago all the time. If you are coming around Christmastime, you might want to check out all the ornaments and stores on State Street. Then head to North Michigan Avenue and hit Saks, and Disney Store and American Girl Place (if you're holiday shopping for little ones), Water Tower Place, and Bloomingdales. You'll have a great time! Walking down Michigan Avenue during the holidays is a great feeling."

–Vanessa

5

Updated by
Judy Sutton
Taylor

A POTENT CONCENTRATION OF FAMOUS retailers around Michigan Avenue and neighborhoods bursting with one-of-a-kind shops combine to make Chicago a shopper's city. Michigan Avenue's world-class Magnificent Mile lures thousands of avid shoppers every week. How often can you find Neiman Marcus, Macy's, Nordstrom, Saks Fifth Avenue, Lord & Taylor, and Barneys New York within walking distance of one another? Neighborhood shopping areas, like fun-but-sophisticated Lincoln Park or the hipster haven of Bucktown/Wicker Park, have singular stores for specialty interests, whether Prairie-style furniture, cowboy boots, or outsider art. Those averse to paying retail won't have to venture far to unearth bargains on everything from fine jewelry to business attire. When it comes to shopping, this is one city that has it all.

Be forewarned that a gulp-inducing 9% city sales tax is added to all purchases except groceries and prescription drugs. Neighborhood shops on the North Side, especially those in Bucktown and Wicker Park, tend to open late—around 11 or noon. Most stores, particularly those on North Michigan Avenue and the North Side, are open on Sunday, although this varies by type of business; where applicable, more information is provided at the beginning of each area or category.

THE LOOP & SOUTH LOOP

This area—named for the elevated train track that encircles it—is the heart of Chicago's business and financial district. Two department stores that long defined shopping here, Marshall Field's and Carson Pirie Scott, departed **State Street** in early 2007, a double hit for the stretch that had been striving to regain the stature it had when it was immortalized as "State Street, that great street." Carson's is empty for the time being, while Macy's has taken over the Marshall Field's building. State Street is more enticing for shoppers than it was in the 1980s and early 1990s, particularly for those interested in discount department stores, but it's still a far cry from the shopping mecca that is the Mag Mile. The blocks surrounding the intersection of Wabash Avenue and Madison Street are designated as Jewelers Row; five high-rises cater to the wholesale trade, but many showrooms sell to the public at prices 25% to 50% below retail. Despite the preponderance of working moms who spend their weekday lunch hours shopping in the area, the Loop lacks a strong presence of retail for kids, with some of the discount chains even pulling their children's lines from Loop outposts. Not all Loop stores maintain street-level visibility: several gems are tucked away on upper floors of office buildings.

Department stores and major chains are generally open on Sunday. Smaller stores are likely to be closed on Sunday and keep limited Saturday hours. Loop workers tend to start their day early, so many stores keep pace by opening by 8:30 and closing at 5 or 6.

DEPARTMENT STORES

Filene's Basement. Patience can pay off at Filene's, where shoppers flip through racks of discounted clothing for a great find or two. Women can do well at either the State Street or Michigan Avenue location, but

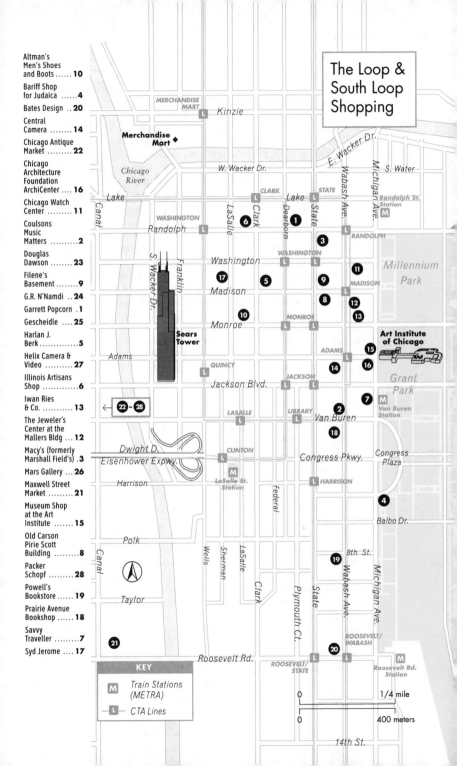

Altman's
Men's Shoes
and Boots **10**

Bariff Shop
for Judaica **4**

Bates Design .. **20**

Central
Camera **14**

Chicago Antique
Market **22**

Chicago
Architecture
Foundation
ArchiCenter **16**

Chicago Watch
Center **11**

Coulsons
Music
Matters **2**

Douglas
Dawson **23**

Filene's
Basement **9**

G.R. N'Namdi .. **24**

Garrett Popcorn . **1**

Gescheidle **25**

Harlan J.
Berk **5**

Helix Camera &
Video **27**

Illinois Artisans
Shop **6**

Iwan Ries
& Co. **13**

The Jeweler's
Center at the
Mallers Bldg ... **12**

Macy's (formerly
Marshall Field's) . **3**

Mars Gallery ... **26**

Maxwell Street
Market **21**

Museum Shop
at the Art
Institute **15**

Old Carson
Pirie Scott
Building **8**

Packer
Schopf **28**

Powell's
Bookstore **19**

Prairie Avenue
Bookshop **18**

Savvy
Traveller **7**

Syd Jerome **17**

The Loop &
South Loop
Shopping

MERCHANDISE
MART

Kinzie

Merchandise
Mart

Chicago
River

W. Wacker Dr.

E. Wacker Dr.

S. Water

S. Wacker Dr.

Lake

CLARK

Lake

STATE

Randolph St.
Station

WASHINGTON

Randolph

RANDOLPH

Millennium
Park

Franklin

LaSalle

Clark

Dearborn

State

Wabash Ave.

Michigan Ave.

Washington

WASHINGTON

6

1

3

11

Madison

17

5

9

MADISON

8

12

Monroe

10

MONROE

13

Sears
Tower

Adams

QUINCY

15

Art Institute
of Chicago

16

Jackson Blvd.

JACKSON

14

Grant
Park

LASALLE

LIBRARY

Van Buren

7

2

Van Buren
Station

22–**28**

18

Dwight D.
Eisenhower Expwy.

CLINTON

Congress Pkwy.

Congress
Plaza

Harrison

LaSalle St.
Station

HARRISON

4

Balbo Dr.

Polk

Federal

Canal

Taylor

Wells

Sherman

LaSalle

Clark

Plymouth Ct.

State

Wabash Ave.

Michigan Ave.

19

8th St.

ROOSEVELT/
WABASH

Powell's
Bookstore **19**

21

20

Roosevelt Rd.

ROOSEVELT/
STATE

Roosevelt Rd.
Station

KEY

Ⓜ Train Stations
(METRA)

Ⓛ CTA Lines

0   1/4 mile

0   400 meters

14th St.

men will find a superior selection of designer names at State Street. Watch newspaper ads midweek for special shipments. ✉*1 N. State St., Loop* ☎*312/553–1055* ✉*830 N. Michigan Ave., Magnificent Mile* ☎*312/482–8918.*

★ **Macy's.** In the fall of 2006, Marshall Field's, Chicago's most famous - and perpetually struggling - department store, became a Macy's. Some of the higher-end designers Field's carried are gone from the racks, but overall, the store remains the same, still standing as a glorious reminder of how grand department stores used to be. Founder Marshall Field's motto was "Give the lady what she wants!" and for many years both ladies and gentlemen had been able to find everything from furs to personalized stationery on one of the store's nine levels. The ground floor and lower level are fashioned in the model of European department stores to include leased boutiques. These stores-within-the-store include national companies like Yahoo!, selling Internet service and computer equipment, and an Yves St. Laurent accessories boutique, as well as local retailers like Merz Apothecary, a pharmacy that opened on the North Side of Chicago in 1875 and specializes in homeopathic remedies. You can still buy Field's famous Frango mints (though they're no longer made locally), and the Walnut Room restaurant on the 7th floor is still a magical place to dine at Christmas. And, the famous Tiffany Dome—designed in 1907 by Louis Comfort Tiffany—is visible from the 5th floor. ✉*111 N. State St., Loop* ☎*312/781–1000* ✉*Water Tower Place, 835 N. Michigan Ave., Magnificent Mile* ☎*312/335–7700.*

SPECIALTY STORES

BOOKS & MUSIC **Coulsons Music Matters.** Musicians come here to find sheet music that suits their style—whether it's jazz, classical, pop, or just about anything else. You'll also find handy accessories like piano lights and metronomes. ✉*77 E. Van Buren St., Loop* ☎*312/461–1989.*

Powell's Bookstore. Marxism, the occult, and philosophy all have their own sections at Powell's, which focuses on used, rare, and discounted books and remainders with an intellectual bent. ✉*828 S. Wabash Ave., South Loop* ☎*312/341–0748* ✉*1501 E. 57th St., Hyde Park* ☎*773/955–7780* ✉*2850 N. Lincoln Ave., Lincoln Park* ☎*773/248–1444.*

Prairie Avenue Bookshop. Massive tables amid architectural artifacts in the Prairie-style interior give browsers room to peruse nearly 20,000 new, rare, and out-of-print titles on architecture, interior design, and urban planning. ✉*418 S. Wabash Ave., Loop* ☎*312/922–8311.*

The Savvy Traveller. Along with every travel guidebook you might want to get your hands on, you'll find an impressive selection of gadgets to improve the quality of life on the road, plus maps, luggage, and videos for everyone from on-the-go business executives to traveling toddlers. ✉*310 S. Michigan Ave., Loop* ☎*312/913–9800.*

SHUTTERBUGS **Central Camera.** This century-old, third-generation-owned store is FodorsChoice a Loop institution, stacked to the rafters with cameras and dark-
★ room equipment at competitive prices. ✉*230 S. Wabash Ave., Loop* ☎*312/427–5580.*

CLOTHING & SHOES

Altman's Men's Shoes and Boots. Price tags are still written by hand at this 75-year-old institution, which has 27 stockrooms holding 50,000 pairs of men's shoes in sizes from 5 to 19 and in widths from AAAA to EEE. You can find anything from Timberland and Tony Lama boots to Allen-Edmonds and Alden oxfords, all at a decent discount. ⊠*120 W. Monroe St., Loop* ☎*312/332–0667.*

Bates Design. Barbara Bates has been designing upscale fashions with a distinct urban edge since 1986 for a who's-who client list that includes Oprah Winfrey, Michael Jordan, Will Smith, and Mary J. Blige. But she's still invested in her community: her eponymous foundation donates custom prom dresses and tuxedos to disadvantaged inner-city teens set to graduate high school. This new studio showcases her couture and traditional labels. ⊠*1130 S. Wabash Ave., Suite 407, South Loop* ☎*312/427–0284.*

Syd Jerome. Board of Trade types who like special attention and snazzy designers come to this legendary clothier for Giorgio Armani, Ermenegildo Zegna, and on-the-spot custom alterations. Home and office consultations are available. ⊠*2 N. LaSalle St., Loop* ☎*312/346–0333.*

DISCOUNT JEWELRY & WATCHES

Chicago Watch Center. This large street-side booth in the Wabash Jewelers Mall has one of the city's most outstanding inventories of used luxury watches. ⊠*Wabash Jewelers Mall, 21 N. Wabash Ave., Loop* ☎*312/609–0003.*

The Jeweler's Center at the Mallers Building. The largest concentration of wholesale and retail jewelers in the Midwest has been housed in this building since 1921 and is open to the general public. Roughly 185 retailers span 13 floors, offering all kinds of jewelry, watches, and related repairs and services. ⊠*5 S. Wabash Ave., Loop* ☎*312/424–2664.*

MUSEUM STORES

Bariff Shop for Judaica. Come here for all your modern Jewish musthaves, like Moses action figures and Jonathan Adler yarmulkes. There's also more traditional holiday ware, books, and music. The shop's inside the Spertus Institute of Jewish Studies. ⊠*618 S. Michigan Ave., Loop* ☎*312/322–1740.*

Museum Shop at the Art Institute of Chicago. Museum reproductions in the form of jewelry, posters, and Frank Lloyd Wright–inspired decorative accessories, as well as books and toys, fill the Art Institute's gift shop. If you're keen on one of the museum's current big exhibits, chances are you'll find some nifty souvenirs to take away. ⊠*111 S. Michigan Ave., Loop* ☎*312/443–3583.*

SOUVENIRS OF CHICAGO

Fodor'sChoice

★

Chicago Architecture Foundation ArchiCenter Shop & Tour Center. Daniel Burnham's 1904 Santa Fe Building is a fitting home for the Chicago Architecture Foundation. Chock-full of architecture-related books, home accessories, and everything and anything related to Frank Lloyd Wright, the store is also the place to sign up for one of the foundation's acclaimed walking tours conducted by foot, bus, bicycle, and river cruise. ⊠*224 S. Michigan Ave., Loop* ☎*312/922–3432.*

★ **Garrett Popcorn.** Bring home a tub of Chicago's famous popcorn instead of a giant pencil or T-shirt, and you'll score major points. The lines can be long, but trust us—this stuff is worth the wait. ⊠*26 E. Randolph St., Loop* ☎*312/630–0127* ⊠*4 E. Madison St., Loop* ☎*312/263–8466* ⊠*2 W. Jackson Blvd., Loop* ☎*312/360–1108* ⊠*670 N. Michigan Ave., Near North* ☎*312/944–2630.*

5

Illinois Artisans Shop. This store run by the Illinois State Museum culls the best jewelry, ceramics, glass, and dolls from craftspeople around the state and sells them at very reasonable prices. There are also exhibits on anything from quilting to Celtic design. ⊠*James R. Thompson Center, 100 W. Randolph St., Suite 2–100, Loop* ☎*312/814–5321* ⊙*Closed weekends.*

SPECIAL STOPS **Harlan J. Berk.** Travel back to antiquity amid this wondrous trove of classical Greek, Roman, and Byzantine coinage and artifacts. Don't miss the gallery rooms in the back. ⊠*31 N. Clark St., Loop* ☎*312/609–0016.*

★ **Iwan Ries and Co.** Iwan Ries did not just jump on the cigar bandwagon; the family-owned store has been around since 1857. Cigar smokers are welcome to light up in the smoking area, which also displays antique pipes. ■TIP→ **Almost 100 brands of cigars are available, as are 10,000 or so pipes, deluxe Elie Bleu humidors, and all manner of smoking accessories.** ⊠*19 S. Wabash Ave., 2nd fl., Loop* ☎*312/372–1306.*

> ### ONE-OF-KIND SOUVENIRS
>
> **Chicago Architecture Foundation ArchiCenter Shop & Tour Center** (*224 S. Michigan Ave., Loop, 312/922–3432*) is chock-full of treasures to remind you of the city's glorious architecture.
>
> **Garrett Popcorn** (*26 E. Randolph St., Loop, 312/630–0127*) lures people off the street with its mouthwatering aromas.
>
> **City of Chicago Store** (*163 E. Pearson St., Near North, 312/742–8811*) makes you forget the snow globes and lets you bring home something really authentic—like an old city parking meter.

WEST LOOP

Art aficionados and gallery owners are taking a new direction in Chicago. After years of doing business in River North and along Michigan Avenue, their new credo is to go west—specifically, to the West Loop, an area just west of downtown marked by Halsted Street to the east, Fulton Market (still a busy meat-packing center) to the north, Ogden Avenue to the west, and Roosevelt Avenue to the south. Large former warehouses and loft spaces coupled with more reasonable rents have led many galleries from more established neighborhoods to join what was once a sparse number of experimental artists and dealers here. Most are clustered around the northern section of the neighborhood.

ART GALLERIES

Douglas Dawson. Douglas Dawson has 8,000 square feet of space plus a sculpture garden in his West Loop space to showcase ancient and historic art from Africa, Oceania, and the Americas. ⊠*400 N. Morgan St., West Loop* ☎*312/226–7975.*

G.R. N'Namdi. This gallery represents contemporary painters and sculptors, with an emphasis on African-American and Latin American artists. ⊠*110 N. Peoria St., West Loop* ☎*312/563–9240.*

Gescheidle. Susan Gescheidle's focus is on representational paintings and drawings. Veteran Chicago artist Michael Paxton is represented here. ⊠*118 N. Peoria St., West Loop* ☎*312/226–3500.*

Mars Gallery. A neighborhood pioneer that showcases contemporary pop and outsider artwork, Mars Gallery shows work by Peter Mars and other well-known locals like Kevin Luthardt. ✉*1139 W. Fulton Market, West Loop* ☎*312/226–7808.*

Packer Schopf Gallery. Browse through an extensive collection of vintage photography and contemporary art with a special emphasis on folk and outsider pieces at this gallery run by well-known local owners Aron Packer and William Schopf. ✉*942 W. Lake St., West Loop* ☎*312/226–8984.*

CAMERAS & ELECTRONICS

Helix Camera & Video. Professional photographers buy and rent camera and darkroom equipment at this eight-story warehouse on Racine Avenue just west of Greektown (1½ mi west of the Loop). A good selection of used equipment is available. Underwater photography equipment is a specialty. ✉*310 S. Racine Ave., West Loop* ☎*312/421–6000.*

NOTABLE MARKETS

Fodor'sChoice ★ **Chicago Antique Market.** This indoor–outdoor flea market is similar to the ones you might find in London and Paris. On the last Sunday of the month in season, more than 200 stalls line Randolph Street selling furniture, jewelry, books, and more. ■TIP➔ **The vibe is more funky fashions and vintage treasures than tube socks and refurbished vacuums.** There's also an Indie Designer Fashion Market, showcasing one-of-a-kind wearables by up-and-coming local designers. Children under 12 get in free. ✉*Randolph St. between Ogden Ave. and Ada St., West Loop* 🎟*$8* ☉*May–Oct., last Sun. of month.*

Maxwell Street Market. A legendary outdoor bazaar that is part of the cultural landscape of the city, the Maxwell Street Market was closed by the city of Chicago amid much controversy in the 1990s. Soon after, it reopened in its current location as the New Maxwell Street Market, where it remains a popular spot, particularly for Latino immigrants, to buy and sell wares. The finds aren't so fabulous, but the atmosphere sure is fun: live blues and stalls selling Mexican street food keep things lively. ✉*Intersection of Canal St. and Roosevelt Rd., West Loop* ☎*312/922–3100* 🎟*Free* ☉*Sun. 7 AM–3 PM.*

NEAR NORTH

The Near North section of Chicago encompasses the Gold Coast, which, yes, is as swanky as its name suggests. Filled with old, exclusive apartment buildings, luxury hotels, and top-notch restaurants, it also has some of the best shopping in the city. This is where you'll find the Magnificent Mile, Chicago's most famous shopping strip, as well as a bevy of significant shopping streets in the surrounding area. Check out the boutiques on Rush Street, which offers something for everyone—from young hipsters to ladies who lunch. Along the big avenues like Chicago and Ohio, you'll find hyper-sized versions of familiar fare.

SPECIALTY STORES

BOOKS, MUSIC & ART **Europa Books.** Europa is the place for foreign-language books, newspapers, and magazines. This well-stocked bookstore carries French, Spanish, German, and Italian titles and is known for its selec-

Near North &
River North
Shopping

Maple St.

Bellevue Pl

E.

W. Oak St.

Washington
Square
Park

N. Orleans St.

N. Franklin St.

Locust St.

N. Clark St.

N. Dearborn St.

Rush St.

① 1

② 2
③ 3 ⑤ 5
④ 4
⑥ 6
⑦ 7

⑧ 8

⑨ 9

⑯ 16 ⑮ 15
⑱ 18 ⑲ 19 ⑳ 20 ⑬ 13 Chicago Ave.
⑰ 17 ㉑ 21 ⑭ 14
㉓ 23 ㉒ 22 W. Superior St.
㉔ 24 ㉗ 27 – 29 ㉙ ㉚ 30 W. Huron St.
㉕ 25 ㉖ 26

㉛ 31 N. Wells St. W. Erie St. N. State St. N. Wabash Ave. ㊽ 48

N. LaSalle St.

W. Ontario St.

㊼ 47 ㊾ 49
㊻ 46

㉜ 32 ㉝ 33 W. Ohio St.

W. Grand Ave.

㉞ 34 W. Illinois St.

㉟ 35 ㊱ 36 ㊺ 45

㊹ 44

㊸ 43

㊲ 37 ㊶ 42 Kinzie St. N. Wate

㊵ 40

㊶ 41

㊳ 38 Merchandise
Mart
㊴ 39 Carroll St.

5

tion of Latin American literature. ⊠*832 N. State St., Near North* ☎*312/335–9677.*

Jazz Record Mart. Billing itself as the world's largest jazz record store, this "mart" sells tens of thousands of new and used titles on CD, vinyl, and cassette. You'll also find a broad selection of world music. Who are we to argue? A vast, in-depth selection of jazz and blues and knowledgeable sales staff make the store a must for music lovers. Sometimes you can catch a live performance here on a Saturday afternoon. ⊠*25 E. Illinois St., Near North* ☎*312/222–1467.*

Museum of Contemporary Art Store and Bookstore. This outstanding museum gift shop has out-of-the-ordinary decorative accessories, tableware, and jewelry, as well as a superb collection of books on modern and contemporary art. The shop has its own street-level entrance. ⊠*220 E. Chicago Ave., Near North* ☎*312/397–4000* ⊘*Closed Mon.*

BUTTONS **Tender Buttons.** You can find lots and lots of anything-but-routine buttons here. These antique and vintage works of art will up the style quotient of any clothing they grace, and are priced accordingly. ⊠*946 Rush St., Near North* ☎*312/337–7033.*

FOR KIDS **American Girl Place.** American Girl attracts little girls from just about everywhere with their signature dolls in tow. There's easily a day's worth of activities here—shop at the boutique, take in a live musical revue, and have lunch or afternoon tea at the café, where dolls can partake in the meal from their own "sassy seats." ⚠**Brace yourself for long lines just to get into the store during high shopping seasons.** ⊠*111 E. Chicago Ave., Near North* ☎*877/247–5223.*

Children in Paradise. Young readers will think they are in paradise at this bookstore dedicated solely to children. There's also a good selection of kid-oriented DVDs and CDs, and free story times on Tuesday and Wednesday mornings. ⊠*909 N. Rush St., Near North* ☎*312/951–5437.*

Madison and Friends. Mini Mag Mile shoppers get their own high-end shopping experience at this boutique, which stocks labels like Hannah Banana and Les Tout Petits in newborn through junior sizes. They also carry top-of-the-line strollers and accessories. Adults can shop in the Denim Lounge downstairs, where the latest styles from Miss Sixty, True Religion, and other of-the-moment brands are available. ⊠*940 N. Rush St., Near North* ☎*312/642–6403.*

CLOTHING & SHOES **Adidas Originals Chicago.** Old-school sneakers and hip urban fashions for a fresh generation of fans are the draw here. ⊠*923 N. Rush St., Near North* ☎*312/932–0651.*

Ikram. A household name in chichi Gold Coast high-rises, this 4,000-square-foot store named for owner Ikram Goldman carries an assortment of new and old fashion icons, from Alexander McQueen and Jean Paul Gaultier to Narciso Rodriguez and Zac Posen. There's also a carefully edited selection of vintage designs. ⊠*873 N. Rush St., Near North* ☎*312/587–1000.*

CLOTHING FOR MEN & WOMEN ★ **Jake.** The motto here is "fashion without victims," and the owners have taken heed to stock clothes for both sexes by up-and-coming designers you don't see elsewhere. This shop is the swanky downtown sibling of the wildly popular Southport Avenue store in Lake View. ⊠*939 N. Rush St., Near North* ☎*312/664–5553.*

Londo Mondo. A great selection of swimwear for buff beach-ready bodies is here. You can also find workout gear and men's and women's in-line skates. ☒*1100 N. Dearborn St., Near North* ☎*312/751–2794* ☒*2148 N. Halsted St., Lincoln Park* ☎*773/327–2218* ☒*444 W. Jackson St., Loop* ☎*312/648–9188.*

FOR THE HOME **Jonathan Adler.** Design guru Adler's store is chock-full of his signature fun, funky pottery and home furnishings, all arranged in a series of small living spaces. ☒*676 Wabash Ave., Near North* ☎*312/274–9920.*

Quatrine. The washable upholstered and slipcovered furniture for dining rooms, living rooms, and bedrooms here looks decidedly chic and not at all what you'd consider child- or pet-friendly. ☒*944 N. Rush St., Near North* ☎*312/649–1700.*

Room & Board. Straightforward yet stylish pieces with a modern sensibility blend quality craftsmanship and materials with affordable pricing. ☒*55 E. Ohio St., Near North* ☎*312/222–0970.*

SOUVENIRS OF CHICAGO **City of Chicago Store.** Nab unusual souvenirs of the city here—anything from a street sign to a real parking meter. It's also a good source for *Fodor's*Choice guidebooks, posters, and T-shirts. ☒*Chicago Waterworks Visitor Information Center, 163 E. Pearson St., Near North* ☎*312/742–8811.*

> **SPOTLIGHT: NAVY PIER**
>
> Extending more than ½ mi onto Lake Michigan from 600 East Grand Avenue, Navy Pier treats you to spectacular views of the skyline, especially from a jumbo Ferris wheel set in slow motion. Stores and carts gear their wares to families and tourists and most don't merit a special trip. But if you're out there, check out **Oh Yes Chicago!** for souvenirs and the **Chicago Children's Museum Store** for educational kids' toys. Many stores are open late into the evening, especially in summer.

RIVER NORTH

Contained by the Chicago River on the south and west, Clark Street on the east, and Oak Street on the north, River North is home to art galleries, high-end antiques shops, home furnishings stores, and a few clothing boutiques. The biggest news in this neighborhood is the resurrection of Tree Studios, part of a controversial restoration project to a building originally designed as an artist's colony. On the verge of demolition a few years ago, the building is again housing retail and tenants involved in the arts, though they are no longer permitted to live here. Most of the businesses in River North have a distinctive style that fits in with this art-minded area. Strangely, it's also a wildly popular entertainment district; touristy theme restaurants such as Ed Debevic's and Rainforest Café peddle logo merchandise as aggressively as burgers.

MERCHANDISE MART

This massive marketplace between Wells and North Orleans streets just north of the Chicago River is more notable for its art-deco design than its shopping. Much of the building is reserved for the design trade, meaning that only interior-design professionals have access to its wares. However, the first two floors have been turned into retail with the unveiling of LuxeHome, a group of 24 high-end kitchen, bath, and building showrooms that are open to the public as well as the design trade. Tenants include de Giulio kitchen design, Waterworks, and Christopher Peacock Cabinetry. The Chopping Block, a local culinary school with a loyal fan base, has a spacious location here. The Mart is usually closed on Sunday, and stores keep relatively short Saturday hours.

SPECIALTY STORES

ANTIQUES &
COLLECTIBLES

Antiquarians Building. Five floors of dealers in Asian and European antiques display their wares; some examples of modernism and art deco are thrown in for good measure. ⊠ *159 W. Kinzie St., River North* 🕾 *312/527–0533.*

Christa's, Ltd. Chests, cabinets, tables, and bureaus are stacked three and four high, creating narrow aisles that are precarious to negotiate but make for adventurous exploring. Look in, over, and under each and every piece to assess the gems stashed in every possible crevice. ⊠ *217 W. Illinois St., River North* 🕾 *312/222–2520.*

Evanstonia Antique Gallery. Dealer Ziggy Osak has a rich collection of fine 19th-century English and Continental antiques that are prized for being as functional as they are striking. ⊠ *120 W. Kinzie St., River North* 🕾 *312/907–0101.*

Fly-by-Nite Gallery. Exceptional decorative and functional art objects (circa 1890–1930) are chosen with a curatorial eye. Fly-by-Nite is especially known for European art glass and pottery and antique jewelry. ⊠ *714 N. Wells St., River North* 🕾 *312/664–8136.*

Jay Robert's Antique Warehouse. Jay Robert's has enough antique merchandise to fill a 50,000-square-foot showroom on his own. He specializes in 18th- and 19th-century European pieces, and has many large-scale armoires, dining sets, sideboards, fireplace mantels, and clocks. ⊠ *149 W. Kinzie St., River North* 🕾 *312/222–0167.*

Michael FitzSimmons Decorative Arts. Works by Frank Lloyd Wright, Louis Sullivan, and Gustav Stickley, along with some quality reproductions, are displayed in a homelike environment. FitzSimmons' collection of furniture and artifacts from the British and American Arts and Crafts movements is renowned. ⊠ *311 W. Superior St., River North* 🕾 *312/787–0496.*

P.O.S.H. It's hard to resist the charming displays of piled-up, never-been-used, vintage hotel and restaurant china here. There's also an impressive selection of silver gravy boats, creamers, and flatware that bear the marks of ocean liners and private clubs. ⊠ *Tree Studios, 613 N. State St., River North* 🕾 *312/280–1602.*

Rita Bucheit, Ltd. Devoted to the streamlined Biedermeier aesthetic, this shop carries choice furniture and accessories from the period along with art deco and modern pieces that are perfect complements to the style. ⊠ *449 N. Wells St., River North* 🕾 *312/527–4080.*

ART GALLERIES

The contemporary art scene continues to thrive in River North, despite losing some of its residents to a slightly lower-rent warehouse district in the nearby West Loop and a burgeoning gallery scene in Pilsen, southwest of the Loop. The neighborhood is chock-full of galleries, most open Tuesday through Saturday. ∎ TIP➜ **Every Saturday morning at 11, the Art Dealers Association of Chicago offers complimentary gallery**

Continued on page 167

THE MAGNIFICENT MILE: A SHOPPER'S SHANGRI-LA

One mile. Nearly 500 shops. Four vertical malls.

Art galleries, haute couture, bargains, and boutiques.

Does it get any better than this?

We've got news for shopaholics who consider the Midwest nothing but flyover country: If you haven't shopped Chicago's Magnificent Mile, dare we say, you simply haven't shopped.

With four lavish malls and more than 460 stores along the stretch of Michigan Avenue that runs from the Chicago River to Oak Street, the Mag Mile is one of the best shopping strips the world over. (Swanky Oak Street is also considered part of the Mag Mile, though neighboring streets technically are not. Shops on those streets are listed in this chapter under "Near North.")

Chanel, Hermès, Gucci, and Armani are just a few of the legendary fashion houses with fabulous boutiques here. Other no-

tables like Anne Fontaine, Kate Spade, and Prada also have Mag Mile outposts, recognizing the everybody-who's-anybody importance of the address.

Shoppers with down-to-earth budgets will find there's plenty on the Mag Mile, as well, with national chains making an extra effort at their multi-level megastores here. But the Mag Mile is much more than a paradise for clothes horses, with stores for techies, furniture fiends, sports fans, art collectors, and almost anyone else with money to spend.

Following is a selective guide to stores in the area. Hours generally run from 10 AM to 7 or 8 PM Monday through Saturday, with shorter hours on Sunday.

Bellevue Pl.

Sugar Magnolia Jil Sander Chasalla Palazzo
Prada Elements Hermès Ultimo
1000 E. Oak St. E. Lake Shore Dr.

Barneys Bravco Colletti Tod's Chanel
New York Beauty Gallery Kate Spade
Centre
Jimmy E. Walton St.
Choo Louis Vuitton
900 North Anne
Michigan Shops Fontaine
(with Bloomingdale's)
900 E. Delaware Pl.

John Hancock
Center
Richard Gray
Gallery

E. Chestnut St.

Water Tower
Place (with
H&M Macy's and
Lord & Taylor)
E. Pearson St.

Water Tower City of Chicago
Store
Giorgio Armani
800 Chicago Ave.

Pola/Ralph Lauren

Pottery Barn
Neiman Marcus

E. Superior St.
Saks Fifth Avenue
Men's Store
Chicago Place The Disney Store
(with Saks Fifth Ave.)
Brooks Brothers
700 E. Huron St.

E. Erie St.

N. Wabash Ave.
N. Rush St.
Michigan Ave.
Mies van der Rohe Way
Clair St.

DEPARTMENT STORES

Barneys New York. A smaller version of the Manhattan store known for austere fashions, this one's heavy on private-label merchandise, though you'll find Donna Karan and several European designers. A Vera Wang salon caters to brides. The cosmetics and Chelsea Passage gift areas have plenty of plum choices. ⊠ 25 E. Oak St. ☏ 312/587-1700.

Bloomingdale's. Chicago's Bloomie's is built in an airy style that is part Prairie School, part postmodern

(quite unlike its New York City sibling), giving you plenty of elbow room to sift through its selection of designer labels. The new Space on 5 has trendier fashions. ⊠ 900 North Michigan Shops ☏ 312/440-4460.

The Disney Store. This Mecca to the Mouse has everything little Disney disciples need for a fix: giant monitors playing Walt's classics, plus a plethora of plush toys, videos, games, and other goodies. ⊠ 717 N. Michigan Ave. ☏ 312/654-9208.

Lord & Taylor. Moderate to upscale clothing for men and women, plus shoes and accessories, form the inventory here, frequently at sale prices. ⊠ Water Tower Place, 835 N. Michigan Ave. ☏ 312/787-7400.

Neiman Marcus. Prices may be high, but they're matched by the level of taste. The selection of designer clothing and accessories is outstanding, and the gourmet top-floor food area tempts with hard-to-find delicacies and impeccable hostess gifts. ⊠ 737 N. Michigan Ave. ☏ 312/642-5900.

Nordstrom. This is a lovely department store with a killer shoe department. Note the Nordstrom Spa on the third floor. ⊠ Westfield North Bridge, 520 N. Michigan Ave. ☏ 312/464-1515.

Saks Fifth Avenue. The smaller, less-crowded cousin of the New York flagship doesn't scrimp on its selection of designer clothes. A men's specialty store is directly across the street. ⊠ Chicago Place, 700 N. Michigan Ave. ☏ 312/944-6500 ⊠ Men's Store, 717 N. Michigan Ave. ☏ 312/944-6500.

CLOTHING FOR WOMEN

Anne Fontaine Paris. The French designer's famous takes on the classic white shirt sport hefty price tags, thanks to her attention to detail. ✉ 909 N. Michigan Ave. ☎ 312/943-0401.

Chanel Boutique. Ensconced in the Drake Hotel, this shop carries the complete line of Chanel products, including ready-to-wear, fragrances, and cosmetics. ✉ 935 N. Michigan Ave. ☎ 312/787-5500.

Palazzo. Chic urban brides trust Jane and Saeed Hamidi for their clean-lined bridal collection. ✉ 49 E. Oak St. ☎ 312/337-6940.

Sugar Magnolia. Named for the Grateful Dead song, Sugar Magnolia has clothes and accessories that tap into trends with a romantic, Bohemian spin. Prices are high, but not

over the top. ✉ 34 E. Oak St. ☎ 312/944-0885.

Ultimo. Check out the well-edited selection of designer goods from such names as John Galliano, Michael Kors, Chloe, and Manolo Blahnik. Oprah is a customer! ✉ 114 E. Oak St. ☎ 312/787-1171.

CLOTHING FOR MEN

Ermenegildo Zegna. The sportswear, softly tailored business attire, and dress clothes of this Italian great are gathered all under one roof. ✉ 645 N. Michigan Ave. ☎ 312/587-9660.

Hugo BOSS. Men will find modern, well-cut suits with attention to tailoring, as well as other signature Boss clothing and accessories here. ✉ Westfield North Bridge, 520 N. Michigan Ave. ☎ 312/660-0056.

Saks Fifth Avenue Men's Store. Spread over 30,000 square feet and three levels, Saks is the city's leading retailer for menswear. ✉ 717 N. Michigan Ave. ☎ 312/944-6500 or 888/643-7257.

CLOTHING FOR MEN & WOMEN

Brooks Brothers. The bastion of ready-to-wear conservative fashion still sells boatloads of their classic 1837 navy blazer. But this one-stop shop for oxfords and khakis also sneaks in the occasional bold color. ⊠ 713 N. Michigan Ave. ☎ 312/915-0060.

Burberry. The label once favored by the conservatively well-dressed is now hot with young fashionistas, who can't get enough of the label's signature plaid on everything from bikinis to baby gear. ⊠ 633 N. Michigan Ave. ☎ 312/787-2500.

Chasalla. Chasalla isn't for the timid—the bold, sexy clothes and accessories of European couture houses such as Dolce & Gabbana, Gianni Versace, and Hugo Boss are the norm here. ⊠ 70 E. Oak St. ☎ 312/640-1940.

Giorgio Armani. An airy, two-floor space displays Armani's discreetly luxurious clothes and accessories, including the top-priced Black Label line. ⊠ 800 N. Michigan Ave. ☎ 312/751-2244.

Gucci. Though the prices aren't for the faint of heart, there are plenty of pieces here that will last a lifetime. ⊠ 900 North Michigan Shops ☎ 312/664-5504.

H&M. Bargain-savvy fashionistas around the world love the cheap-n-chic styles on offer; the constant crowds at the Mag Mile store prove Chicagoans are no different. ⊠ 840 N. Michigan Ave. ☎ 312/640-0060.

Hermès of Paris. The well-heeled and very well-paid shop here for suits, signature scarves, and leather accessories. ⊠ 110 E. Oak St. ☎ 312/787-8175.

Jil Sander. This line has captured the devotion of the fashion flock for its minimalist designs and impeccable tailoring. Prices are at the upper end of the designer range. ⊠ 48 E. Oak St. ☎ 312/335-0006.

Mark Shale. Here you'll find two floors filled with stylish suits and separates from an international array of designers. ⊠ 900 North Michigan Shops ☎ 312/440-0720.

Prada. The store has a spare, cool look that matches its modern inventory of clothing, shoes, and bags. In fact, unless you're a Miuccia devotee, the three-story shop can seem almost bare. ⊠ 30 E. Oak St. ☎ 312/951-1113.

Polo/Ralph Lauren. Manor house meets mass marketing. The upper-crust chic covers men's, women's, and children's clothes and housewares. Fabrics are often enticing (suede, silk, cashmere), but expect to pay a pretty penny. ⊠ 750 N. Michigan Ave. ☎ 312/280-1655.

TECH STUFF

Apple Store. It's a multilevel fantasyland for Mac users, complete with the full range of products—from computers to iPods to digital cameras. There's an Internet café where PC fans can get a glimpse of life on the other side. ⊠ 679 N. Michigan Ave. ☎ 312/981-4104.

SHOES & ACCESSORIES

Avventura. Professional basketball players in need of European-style footwear stop here for sizes up to 16! ⊠ Water Tower Place, 835 N. Michigan Ave. ☎ 312/337-3700.

Coach. Well-designed leather goods, in the form of purses, smart shoes, briefcases, and cell phone and PDA holders, are Coach's specialty. ⊠ 625 N. Michigan Ave. ☎ 312/587-3167 ⊠ 900 North Michigan Shops ☎ 312/440-1777.

Jimmy Choo. These are the heela that have celebs and stylish women the world over drooling. Break out the plastic. ✉ 63 Oak St. ☎ 312/255-1170.

Kate Spade. The goddess of handbags has filled her two-floor boutique in the middle of Oak Street with adorable shoes, pajamas, small leather goods, men's accessories from the Jack Spade line, and, of course, her to-die-for purses. ✉ 101 E. Oak St. ☎ 312/654-8853.

Louis Vuitton. Here you have it all under one roof—the coveted purses, leather goods, and luggage bearing the beloved logo, plus men's and women's shoes and jewelry. ✉ 919 N. Michigan Ave. ☎ 312/944-2010.

Salvatore Ferragamo. The shoes have been the classic choice of the well-heeled for generations, but it's the handbags, with a fresh, contemporary sensibility, that are generating excitement of late. ✉ 645 N. Michigan Ave. ☎ 312/397-0464.

Tod's. Choose from a wide selection of the signature handbags and driving moccasins that made Tod's famous, as well as newer additions to the line, including high heels. ✉ 121 E. Oak St. ☎ 312/943-0070 or 800/457-8637.

GET SPORTY

Niketown. This is one of Chicago's top tourist attractions. Many visitors—including professional

athletes—stop here to take in the sports memorabilia, road test a pair of sneakers, or watch the inspirational videos. ✉ 669 N. Michigan Ave. ☎ 312/642-6363.

ART GALLERIES

Colletti Gallery. Fine antique posters, a serious

collection of European ceramics and glass, and an eclectic selection of furniture transport you to the late 19th century. ✉ 67 E. Oak St. ☎ 312/664-6767.

Joel Oppenheimer, Inc. Established in 1969, this gallery in the Wrigley Building has an amazing collection of Audubon prints and specializes in antique natural-history pieces. ✉ 410 N. Michigan Ave. ☎ 312/642-5300.

R. H. Love Galleries. For three decades, this gallery has specialized in museum-quality American art from the colonial period to the early 20th century. ✉ 645 N. Michigan Ave., 2nd fl. entrance on Erie St. ☎ 312/640-1300.

R. S. Johnson Fine Art.

More than 50 museums can be counted among the clients of R. S. Johnson, a Mag Mile resident for 50 years. The family-run gallery sells old masters along with art by modernists like Pablo Picasso, Edgar Degas, and Goya. ✉ 645 N. Michigan Ave., 2nd fl. entrance on Erie St. ☎ 312/943-1661.

Richard Gray Gallery. This gallery lures serious collectors with pieces by modern masters such as David Hockney and Roy Lichtenstein. ✉ John Hancock Center, 875 N. Michigan Ave., Suite 2503 ☎ 312/642-8877.

MIGHTY VERTICAL MALLS

Forget all your preconceived notions about malls being suburban wastelands. Four decidedly upscale urban malls dot the Mag Mile.

The toniest of the four is 900 North Michigan, with a dazzling list of tenants, plus live weekend piano serenades. A more casual but no less entertaining shopping mecca is just blocks away at Water Tower Place. Fuel up there with a snack from **Wow Bao**, which sells steamed meat and vegetable buns that are *delish*.

Check out the beautiful views from Chicago Place's airy top-floor food court. The newest kid on the block is Westfield North Bridge, which opened in 2000.

Chicago Place. Saks Fifth Avenue is the big tenant here, and there's also a multilevel Ann Taylor. Several boutiques carry distinctive art for the home, including Chiaroscuro, Design Toscano, and Kashmir Handicrafts. ✉ 700 N. Michigan Ave. ☎ 312/642–4811.

900 North Michigan Shops. There's a ritzy feel to the mall that houses the Chicago branch of Bloomingdale's along with dozens of boutiques and specialty stores, such as Gucci, Coach, Lalique, and Fogal. ✉ 900 N. Michigan Ave. ☎ 312/915–3916.

Water Tower Place. The Ritz-Carlton Hotel sits atop this mall, which contains branches of Macy's and Lord & Taylor, as well as seven floors of shops. The more unusual spots here include Teavana (a modern tea shop) and Jacadi (children's wear). **Foodlife**, a step above usual mall food-court fare, is a fantastic spot for a quick bite. ✉ 835 N. Michigan Ave. ☎ 312/440–3165.

Westfield North Bridge. The big draw here is Nordstrom. Chains like Sephora and Ann Taylor Loft share space with specialty stores like Vosges Haut-Chocolat, a local chocolatier with an international following. The third floor is for tots, with a LEGO Store, a play area, and Oilily Kids. ✉ 520 N. Michigan Ave. ☎ 312/327–2300.

THE ANNUAL LIGHTS FESTIVAL

Chicago's holiday season officially kicks off every year at the end of November with the **Magnificent Mile Lights Festival**, a weekend-long event consisting of family-friendly activities that packs the shopping strip to the gills. Music, ice-carving contests, and stage shows kick off the celebration, which culminates in a parade and the illumination of more than one million lights along Michigan Avenue. Neighborhood stores keep late hours to accommodate the crowds. For more information, check out ⊕ www.themagnificentmile.com.

tours. Groups meet at the Starbucks at 750 North Franklin Street and are guided each week by a different gallery owner or director from the area. For more information and to check holiday weekend schedules, call 312/649–0065 or go to www.chicagoartdealers.org.

Alan Koppel Gallery. An eclectic mix of works by modern masters and contemporary artists is balanced by a selection of French and Italian Modernist furniture from the 1920s to 1960s. ⊠*210 W. Chicago Ave., River North* ☎*312/640–0730.*

Ann Nathan Gallery. The specialty here is contemporary paintings, but the gallery also showcases sculpture and singular artist-made furniture. ⊠*212 W. Superior St., River North* ☎*312/664–6622.*

Byron Roche. Contemporary paintings and drawings, many by Chicago artists, are exhibited here. ⊠*750 N. Franklin St., River North* ☎*312/654–0144.*

Carl Hammer Gallery. Lee Godie, Henry Darger, and Jordan Mozer are among the outsider and self-taught artists whose work is shown at this gallery. ⊠*740 N. Wells St., River North* ☎*312/266–8512.*

Catherine Edelman Gallery. This gallery of contemporary photography explores the work of emerging, mixed-media, photo-based artists such as Maria Martinez-Canes and Jack Spencer. ⊠*300 W. Superior St., River North* ☎*312/266–2350.*

Habatat. Collectors of fine studio art glass are drawn here by luminaries such as Dale Chihuly. ⊠*222 W. Superior St., River North* ☎*312/440–0288.*

Primitive Art Works. Find ethnic and tribal art, including textiles, furniture, and jewelry, at this longtime Chicago favorite gallery. ⊠*130 N. Jefferson St., River North* ☎*312/575–9600.*

Stephen Daiter Gallery. This space showcases stunning 20th-century European and American photography, particularly avant-garde photojournalism. ⊠*311 W. Superior St., River North* ☎*312/787–3350.*

ART SUPPLIES & BOOKS **Abraham Lincoln Book Shop.** The shop owner here buys, sells, and appraises books, paintings, documents, and other paraphernalia associated with American military and political history. It's been around since 1938. ⊠*357 W. Chicago Ave., River North* ☎*312/944–3085.*

Pearl Art & Craft Supply. Pearl is the name synonymous with the best selection of art supplies at the best prices. Paints and palettes, crafts, portfolios, tools, easels—it's all here, and it's all discounted. ⊠*225 W. Chicago Ave., River North* ☎*312/915–0200.*

CHEAP CHOCOLATE **Blommer Chocolate Outlet Store.** "Why do parts of River North smell like freshly baked brownies?" is a question you hear fairly often. The oh-so-sweet reason: it's near the Blommer Chocolate Factory, which has been making wholesale chocolates here since 1939. More important, the retail outlet store is also here, so you can snap up your Blommer chocolates and candies at a discount—a handy tip to know when those smells give you a case of the munchies. ⊠*600 W. Kinzie St. at the corner of N. Jefferson St., River North* ☎*312/226–7700.*

CLOTHING FOR WOMEN **Blake.** A no-nonsense boutique without pomp, circumstance, or even signage, Blake displays clean-lined clothes in a pristine setting. You'll find designers like Dries van Noten, Balenciaga, and shoes and accessories of a similar subtle elegance. ⊠*212 W. Chicago Ave, River North* ☎*312/202–0047.*

Clever Alice. This women's boutique carries a well-chosen inventory of fashion from local designers like Alice in Oz and Veronica Martin Riley plus other avant-garde labels like Kitchen Orange and Metalicus. ✉️ *750 N. Franklin St., River North* ☎️ *312/587–8693.*

FOR THE HOME

Fodor's Choice

★

Bloomingdale's Home & Furniture Store. The Medinah Temple once occupied this space, and Bloomie's kept the historically significant exterior intact but gutted the inside to create its first stand-alone furnishings store in Chicago. Naturally, it's stocked to the rafters with everything you need to eat, sleep, and relax in your home in high style. ✉️ *600 N. Wabash Ave., Near North* ☎️ *312/324–7500.*

Cambium. A particularly expansive line of kitchen fittings and accoutrements is one of many temptations at this home-furnishings store. ✉️ *113–119 W. Hubbard St., River North* ☎️ *312/832–9920.*

★ **The Chopping Block.** New and seasoned chefs appreciate an expertly edited selection of pots and pans, bakeware, gadgets, and ingredients here. The intimate cooking classes are hugely popular and taught by a fun, knowledgeable staff. (Students get 10% off store merchandise.) The Lincoln Square location has a wine shop. ✉️ *Merchandise Mart Plaza, Suite 107, River North* ☎️ *312/644–6360* ✉️ *4747 N. Lincoln Ave., Lincoln Square* ☎️ *773/472–6700.*

Golden Triangle. This is a must-stop shop for anyone enamored with the East-meets-West aesthetic. There are 11,000 square feet of choice pieces, including antique Chinese and British colonial Raj furniture from Burma, Asian accessories, and idiosyncratic pieces from Thailand. ✉️ *72 W. Hubbard St., River North* ☎️ *312/755–1266.*

Lightology. This 20,000-square-foot showroom of modern light designs is an essential stop for designers and architects, not to mention passersby drawn to the striking designs visible from the windows. It's the brainchild of Greg Kay, who started out as a roller-disco lighting designer in the 1970s and made a name for himself in Chicago with Tech Lighting, a contemporary design gallery. ✉️ *215 W. Chicago Ave., River North* ☎️ *312/944–1000.*

Luminaire. The city's largest showroom of international contemporary furniture includes pieces by Philippe Starck, Antonio Citterio, Alberta Meda, and Shiro Kuromata. Sleek kitchen designs are from Italian manufacturer Bofi, and a large home accessories section has equally edgy offerings from Alessi, Zani & Zani, Rosenthal, and Mono. ✉️ *301 W. Superior St., River North* ☎️ *312/664–9582.*

Manifesto. In a huge, street-level space, one of the largest design ateliers in the city showcases work by furniture designer (and owner) Richard Gorman, plus contemporary furniture from Armani Casa (Giorgio Armani's furniture line and streamlined Finnish accessories.) ✉️ *755 N. Wells St., River North* ☎️ *312/664–0733.*

Modernica. Find reissues of clean-lined and practical mid-century modernist furniture by the likes of George Nelson and Charles and Ray Eames here, plus a good selection of furniture design books. ✉️ *555 N. Franklin St., River North* ☎️ *312/222–1808.*

Orange Skin. The go-to resource for modern furniture, lighting, and accessories in Chicago carries pieces by Minotti, Alessi, Michael Graves, and Tisettanta. A recent move from Wicker Park to a bi-level space means a bigger inventory of goodies to choose from. ✉ *223 W. Erie St., River North* ☎ *312/335–1033.*

★ **Sawbridge Studios.** Sawbridge Studios displays custom handcrafted furniture by about 40 American artisans. The specialties include Frank Lloyd Wright reproductions, newly designed pieces with an Arts and Crafts or Shaker aesthetic, and contemporary pottery. ✉ *153 W. Ohio St., River North* ☎ *312/828–0055.*

Svenska Mobler. This store carries a hand-picked selection of Swedish antique furniture, lighting, and art, plus some mid-century pieces from Argentina. ✉ *516 N. Wells St., River North* ☎ *312/595–9320.*

GIFTS **Pops for Champagne.** Choose from well-chosen group of bubbly plus assorted accoutrements at the retail shop of this popular champagne bar. ✉ *605 N. State St., River North* ☎ *312/266–7676.*

PAPER **Paper Source.** Reams and reams of different types of paper are sold ★ here; much of it is eclectic and expensive. Chech out the custom invitation department and good selection of rubber stamps and bookbinding supplies. Ask about the classes offered. ✉ *232 W. Chicago Ave., River North* ☎ *312/337–0798* ✉ *919 W. Armitage Ave., Lincoln Park* ☎ *773/525–7300.*

WICKER PARK & BUCKTOWN

Artists and musicians were the first to claim this once run-down area near the intersection of North, Damen, and Milwaukee avenues, and then, some years later, points south on and around Division Street; the trendy coffeehouses, nightclubs, and restaurants followed. Young, hip families were next, and shopping has since snowballed. Now scads of edgy clothing boutiques, art galleries, home-design ateliers, alternative-music stores, and funky kids' shops dot the area. Hipsters have been squawking about gentrification with the opening of chains like Urban Outfitters and American Apparel in the neighborhood, but this is still a one-of-a-kind-shopping destination that deserves a solid chunk of time.

Many stores don't open until at least 11 AM, some shops are closed on Monday and Tuesday, and hours can be erratic. Spend a late afternoon shopping before settling in for dinner at one of the neighborhood's popular restaurants. To get here from downtown on the El, take the Blue Line toward O'Hare and exit at Damen Avenue.

SPECIALTY STORES

ACCESSORIES **Paper Doll.** Doll up your gift with an unusual card and handmade wrap-
& GIFTS ping paper from this Wicker Park shop, where Maude, the owners' pug, holds court on the floor. Finger puppets, candles, and other gift items are also stocked here. The popular store has newer, bigger digs a few doors down from the teeny old shop. ✉ *2048 W. Division St., Wicker Park* ☎ *773/227–6950.*

Red Dog House. Finally, a place in the neighborhood to shop for hipsters' four-legged friends. This boutique has everything Fido and Kitty need to sit, stay, and live pretty, from swank sweaters to made-to-order name collars, beds, and bowls. ✉ *2031 N. Damen St., Bucktown* ☎ *773/227–7341.*

RR#1 Chicago. A wood-paneled 1930s pharmacy is the setting for this charming gift shop, which stocks eclectic ideas for everyone on your list, plus a tempting array of bath and beauty product lines like Barefoot Venus and Pre de Provence. ✉*814 N. Ashland Ave., Wicker Park* ☎*312/421–9079.*

Ruby Room. This Wicker Park spa–boutique sells an eclectic mix of bath and body products from brands like Sage Spirit, Phytologie, and Surly Girl Studios. Check out the spa services, too—everything from intuitive astrology and pet healing to brow waxing and facials. ✉*1743–45 W. Division St., 2nd fl., Wicker Park* ☎*773/635–5000.*

shebang. Accessories junkies meet up-and-coming designers at this shop chock full of handbag, jewelry, and hat finds. Super-contemporary labels include Dutchy, Hayden-Harnett, and Alexis Bittar. ✉*1616 N. Damen Ave., Wicker Park* ☎*773/486–3800.*

Tatine. It's hard to decide which luscious-smelling candle to choose with such eclectic scents as sake, rose tabac, and ginger lily among the offerings. Margo Breznik hand-pours all the candles in this pretty shop herself using soy wax, which is said to burn cleaner than traditional paraffin wax. ✉*1742 W. Division St., Wicker Park* ☎*773/342–1890.*

ANTIQUES & COLLECTIBLES
Pagoda Red. Exceptionally well-priced Asian furnishings from owner Betsy Nathan's frequent overseas trips pack this open loft space. Among the treasures, you'll find Chinese deco chairs, Nepalese rugs, antique lanterns, and a rare collection of 20th-century Chinese advertising posters. ✉*1714 N. Damen Ave., Bucktown* ☎*773/235–1188.*

Pavilion. The specialty here is French, Italian, and Scandinavian antiques, but you'll be lured in by the altogether uncommon mix of industrial and decorative furnishings, accessories, and fixtures. The eclectic selection reflects the collecting acumen of its two idiosyncratic owners, who scour Europe and the Midwest for items in the perfect state of intriguing decay. ✉*2055 N. Damen Ave., Bucktown* ☎*773/645–0924.*

BOOKS & MUSIC
Dusty Groove America. The retail outlet of a massive online business, Dusty Groove stocks an enormous collection of older jazz, funk, soul, and blues in both LP and CD formats. They also buy used records Monday through Saturday, from noon to 5 PM. ✉*1120 N. Ashland Ave., Wicker Park* ☎*773/342–5800.*

★ **Myopic Books.** One of Chicago's largest used-book dealers stocks more than 80,000 titles and buys books from the public on Friday evenings and all day Saturday. ■TIP➜ **A community mainstay, Myopic also hosts regular music and poetry events and is the meeting spot for the Wicker Park Chess Club.** ✉*1564 N. Milwaukee Ave., Wicker Park* ☎*773/862–4882.*

Reckless Records. Look for a varied selection of music at this sister store to the Lake View flagship, including lots of rare stuff and rock paraphernalia. ✉*1532 N. Milwaukee Ave., Bucktown* ☎*773/235–3727.*

FOR KIDS
Goldilocks & Gremlins. Pinball machines and games keep kids busy while parents sort through such items as Robeez and Bobux shoes for the not-quite-walking set and fun tween fashions. ✉*1905 W. Division St., Wicker Park* ☎*773/252–5055.*

Grow. Kids can grow up green with this stock of organic cotton clothes, all-natural bath products and balms, and environmentally friendly

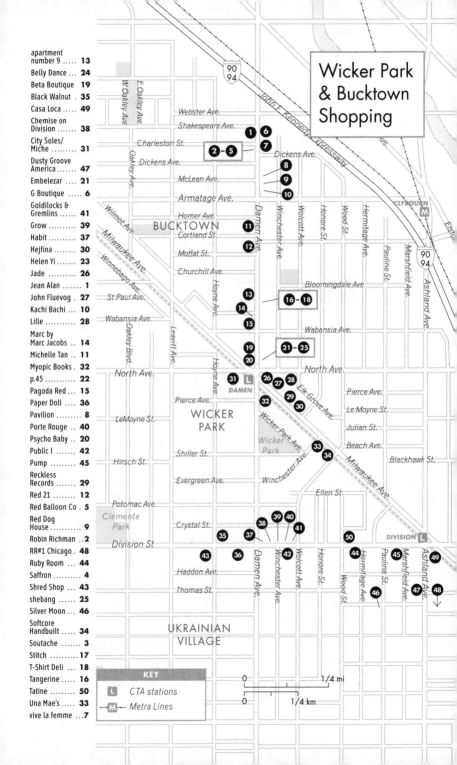

Wicker Park & Bucktown Shopping

W. Oakley Ave.
E. Oakley Ave.
Webster Ave.
Shakespeare Ave.
Charleston St.
Oakley Ave.
Dickens Ave.
Dickens Ave.
McLean Ave.
Armatage Ave.
Homer Ave.
Wilmot Ave.
BUCKTOWN
Cortland St.
Moffat St.
Churchill Ave.
Milwaukee Ave.
Winnebago Ave.
St Paul Ave.
Wabansia Ave.
Oakley Blvd.
Leavitt Ave.
Hoyne Ave.
Damen Ave.
Winchester Ave.
Wolcott Ave.
Honore St.
Wood St.
Hermitage Ave.
Paulina St.
Marshfield Ave.
Ashland Ave.
CLYBOURN
Elston Ave.
Bloomingdale Ave.
Wabansia Ave.
North Ave.
North Ave.
DAMEN
Pierce Ave.
LeMoyne St.
WICKER PARK
Pierce Ave.
Le Moyne St.
Julian St.
Elk Grove Ave.
Wicker Park Ave.
Beach Ave.
Blackhawk St.
Winchester Ave.
Shiller St.
Wicker Park
Hirsch St.
Evergreen Ave.
Ellen St.
Milwaukee Ave.
Potomac Ave.
Clemente Park
Crystal St.
Division St.
DIVISION
Haddon Ave.
Thomas St.
Damen Ave.
Winchester Ave.
Wolcott Ave.
Honore St.
Wood St.
Hermitage Ave.
Paulina St.
Marshfield Ave.
Ashland Ave.
UKRAINIAN VILLAGE

KEY

L *CTA stations*

M *Metra Lines*

0   1/4 mi

0   1/4 km

nursery furniture. ✉*1943 W. Division St., Wicker Park* ☎*773/489–0009.*

Psycho Baby. The best-dressed urban tykes send their parents to this shop to spend a pretty penny on funky duds by designers like Imps & Elves, Rabbi's Daughters, and Paper Denim & Cloth. There's

a great selection of shoes, plus toys and books, and a story hour every Monday and Wednesday for parents brave enough to tote their tykes along. ✉*1630 N. Damen Ave., Bucktown* ☎*773/772–2815.*

The Red Balloon Company. Known for its beautiful handmade children's furniture and stock of colorful Zutano infant wear, this charming store also carries a great selection of classic kids books and toys, as well as blankets and art work that can be personalized. ✉*2060 N. Damen Ave., Bucktown* ☎*773/489–9800* ✉*5407 N. Clark St., Andersonville* ☎*773/989–8500 or 877/969–9800.*

Red 21. Fashion-conscious grown-ups who lament the lack of stylish options for boys have found the answer to their prayers with this store, which caters exclusively to boys sizes 2 to 16 with funky labels like Wes and Willy and City College. There's a plasma TV and basketball hoop to keep junior busy, too. ✉*1858 N. Damen Ave., Bucktown* ☎*773/252–9570.*

CLOTHING FOR MEN **apartment number 9.** Siblings Amy and Sarah Blessing offer sisterly advice to guys born without the metrosexual gene on what styles best suit them. Their store, named for the Tammy Wynette song, carries classic lines like Paul Smith, Marc Jacobs, and Michael Kors. ✉*1804 N. Damen Ave., Bucktown* ☎*773/395–2999.*

Chemise on Division. Button up in dress shirts ranging from classic to cowboy style. All are made with careful attention to detail. ✉*1939 W. Division St., Wicker Park* ☎*773/276–8020.*

CLOTHING FOR MEN & WOMEN **Habit.** Emerging independent designers are stocked by shop owner Lindsey Boland. As most pieces are only made in small quantities, this is where to go if you don't want anyone else wearing what you are. In-house alterations are available, and some lines, including Boland's Superficial, Inc., offer made-to-order designs. ✉*1951 W. Division St., Wicker Park* ☎*773/342–0093.*

Hejfina. This lifestyle boutique carries everything the mod Wicker Parker needs to get through the day stylishly: clothes by of-the-moment designers from across the globe, custom-made furniture from local designers, and books on modern art and architecture. The store also hosts art installations and speakers on design from time to time. ✉*1529 N. Milwaukee Ave., Wicker Park* ☎*773/772–0002.*

Marc by Marc Jacobs. Neighborhood style mavens are rejoicing that Jacobs' first Chicago store is slated to open in Bucktown rather than on the label-conscious Mag Mile (at this writing, the date is set for summer 2007). It seems a fitting locale for the fashion icon, whose whimsical, slightly offbeat designs make hipsters drool. ✉*1714 N. Damen Ave., Bucktown* .

Public I. Public I prides itself on paying attention to its customers, offering plenty of helpful suggestions about which of its smart, hip, won't-find-it-down-the-street designs work best. Their inventory includes designs by How & Wen, Isda for Men, and Emerge London. ✉*1923 W. Division St., Wicker Park* ☎773/772–9088.

Silver Moon. Vintage wedding gowns and tuxedos are a specialty here, but you can also find less formal vintage clothing and accessories. There are also new collections from Vivienne Westwood, housewares, and custom-embellished denim for babies and small kids. ✉*1755 W. North Ave., Bucktown* ☎773/235–5797.

Softcore Handbuilt. Club kids go to Softcore for funky styles from Diesel, Miss Sixty, Octopussy (the store's own label), and local designer Geoffrey Mac. ✉*1420 N. Milwaukee Ave., Wicker Park* ☎773/276–7616.

The T-Shirt Deli. Order up a made-to-order T-shirt with custom iron-on letters or throwback '70s decals. You'll get your T-shirt served up on the spot, wrapped in paper like a sandwich, and packed with a bag of chips for good measure. ✉*1739 N. Damen Ave., Bucktown* ☎773/276–6266.

CLOTHING FOR WOMEN

Belly Dance Maternity. The hippest moms-to-be shop here for up-to-the-minute maternity fashions by Japanese Weekend, Cadeau, and Citizens of Humanity. ✉*1647 N. Damen Ave., Bucktown* ☎773/862–1133.

Beta Boutique. Janice Moskoff built a following bringing occasional sample sales to young fashionistas, and now she's opened up a permanent location to hawk finds from a huge list of designers, from Cynthia Steffe to C. Ronson. The store is open Thursday to Sunday only. ✉*2016 W. Concord Pl., Bucktown* ☎773/276–0905 ⊘*Closed Mon.–Wed.*

G Boutique. Here's an all-in-one stop for women planning for a little romance. There's beautiful lingerie from brands like Aubade and Cosabella, plus massage oils, books, videos, and toys. There's an 18-and-over admission policy. ✉*2131 N. Damen Ave., Bucktown* ☎773/235–1234.

Helen Yi. This loftlike, minimalist boutique stocks sophisticated styles from up-and-coming designers, including Shelly Steffee and local handbag maker Susan Fitch. ✉*1645 N. Damen Ave., Bucktown* ☎773/252–3838.

Jade. Former stylist and fashion writer Laura Haberman's shop stands out from the crowd of women's boutiques in the neighborhood with a carefully chosen stock of must-have cocktail dresses, tops, jeans, and accessories, all displayed against a calming jade-green backdrop. ✉*1557 N. Milwaukee Ave., Wicker Park* ☎773/342–5233.

Michelle Tan. Local indie design star Michelle Tan's shop also serves as a working studio where she creates clothes with an emphasis on interesting textures, most in the $200 to $300 range. You'll also find pieces by other local designers, including some students. ✉ *1872 N. Damen Ave., Bucktown* ☎ *773/252–1888.*

★ **p. 45.** This store is a must-hit for its fashion-forward collection by a cadre of hip designers like Rebecca Taylor and Ulla Johnson. Customers from all over the city and well beyond come here for adventurous to elegant styles and prices that don't get out of hand. ✉ *1643 N. Damen Ave., Bucktown* ☎ *773/862–4523.*

Robin Richman. Robin Richman showcases her famous knitwear alongside designs from lesser-known European labels and local clothes designers. Chicagoland artists contribute to the shops' eclectic displays. ✉ *2108 N. Damen Ave., Bucktown* ☎ *773/278–6150.*

Saffron. Merchandise as indulgent and decadent as the namesake spice lures you into this Bucktown boutique. You'll find fluid, finely finished clothes made of natural fabrics, organically inspired jewelry, and lavish bath products. ✉ *2064 N. Damen Ave., Bucktown* ☎ *773/486–7753.*

Tangerine. Popular designers, such as Three Dots and Ashley, provide the fun, feminine clothes and accessories here. There's also a good denim selection, including styles by Joe's Jeans and Serfontaine. ✉ *1719 N. Damen Ave., Bucktown* ☎ *773/772–0505.*

Una Mae's. This Wicker Park favorite for vintage fashions is bursting at the seams with inventory. The bulk of the bulging stock is from the 1950s through the '80s, but there are also new lines from designers like Hot Sauce and The People Have Spoken. ✉ *1422 N. Milwaukee Ave., Wicker Park* ☎ *773/276–7002.*

vive la femme. The motto is "style beyond size," and the specialty is sexy, exciting clothes for women in sizes 12 to 28 from lines including Anna Scholz, Svoboda, and Z. Cavaricci. ✉ *2048 N. Damen Ave., Bucktown* ☎ *773/772–7429.*

GIFTS & FOR THE HOME

Black Walnut Gallery. The selection of beautiful handcrafted wood furniture, sculpture, and art at this gallery got even more tempting in March 2007, when it merged with neighbor "wag artworks" to add stunning and affordable ($30 to $3,000) contemporary art to the mix. ✉ *2135 W. Division St., Wicker Park* ☎ *773/772–8870.*

Casa Loca. The handsome, rustic pine furniture from Mexico and South America is carved or painted, and the collection is complemented by superb vintage and antique Mexican folk art and tinware from Guanajuato. ✉ *1130 N. Milwaukee Ave., Wicker Park* ☎ *773/278–2972.*

Embelezar. The name is Portuguese for "embellish," and after a visit to this airy shop you'll be able to do just that. Everything's geared for gracious living, from the hand-painted, silk-covered, Venetian fixtures to the sumptuous sofas. ✉ *1639 N. Damen Ave., Bucktown* ☎ *773/645–9705.*

Jean Alan Upholstered. The offerings at this design atelier, owned by a former feature-film set decorator, range from Victorian to mid-20th-century modern. There's always a healthy assortment of sofas and

---

FOR THE MOM-TO-BE

Krista K Maternity + Baby (3530 N. Southport Ave., Lake View, 773/248–4477).

Belly Dance Maternity (1647 N. Damen Ave., Bucktown, 773/862–1133).

Shopgirl (1206 W. Webster Ave., Lincoln Park, 773/935–7467).

chairs recovered in eclectic fabrics, plus pillows made of unusual textiles and refurbished vintage lamps with marvelous shades. ⊠*2134 N. Damen Ave., Bucktown* ☎*773/278–2345.*

Kachi Bachi. What you'll find here are Claudia Ahuile's visions for home design in the way of custom throw pillows, bedding, and window treatments, even though the name (derived from a Spanish slang term for "junk") might suggest otherwise. ⊠*2041 N. Damen Ave., Bucktown* ☎*773/645–8640.*

Lille. Hidden behind a low-profile storefront in the middle of a hectic street, Lille sequesters a carefully selected mix of home furnishings and personal accessories by well-known artists (Bodo Sperlein dinnerware) and lesser-known ones (jewelry by Jeanine Payer). ⊠*1923 W. North Ave., Bucktown* ☎*773/342–0563.*

Porte Rouge. Push through the red door for housewares and pretty painted tableware. Look for copper cookware from Mauviel, Spiegelau stemware, and Mariage Fréres teas. ⊠*1911 W. Division St., Wicker Park* ☎*773/269–2800.*

Soutache. French for "braid," Soutache is all about the extras that make life so much more interesting: high-end trimmings and embellishments like tortoise shell-and-bamboo belt buckles and purse handles; exotic ostrich plumes; suede tassels; and reams and reams of ribbon. It's up to you how to get creative with all this fun stuff. ⊠*2125 N. Damen Ave., Bucktown* ☎*773/292–9110.*

Stitch. Leather goods of every ilk—purses, travel bags, desk accessories—are the main attraction here, but you also find minimalist furniture, tabletop goods, and jewelry. ⊠*1723 N. Damen Ave., Bucktown* ☎*773/782–1570.*

SHOES **City Soles/Niche.** These two shoe stores under one roof represent a version of mecca to many shoe fiends. There's a vast selection of edgy men's and women's shoes from designers like Camper and Tsubo, plus a more upscale selection of sophisticated styles from Blay, Rebecca Sanver, and others. ⊠*2001 W. North Ave., Bucktown* ☎*773/489–2001* ⊠*3432 N. Southport Ave., Lakeview* ☎*773/665–4233.*

John Fluevog. Canadian designer Fluevog's chunky platforms and bold designs have graced the famous feet of Madonna and throngs of other loyal devotees, and they can house your toes, too, if you shop here. ⊠*1539–41 N. Milwaukee Ave., Wicker Park* ☎*773/772–1983.*

Pump. High heels are in high supply here, but so are plenty of other shoe styles from well-heeled designers like Dolce Vita, Via Spiga, and Kenneth Cole. ⊠*1659 W. Division St., Wicker Park* ☎*773/384–6750.*

SPORTING **Shred Shop.** Skaters and snowboarders find their hearts' desires at this
GOODS outpost of the Skokie megastore. The Shred Shop does rentals and servicing, too. ⊠*2048 W. Division St., Wicker Park* ☎*773/384–2100.*

LINCOLN PARK & OLD TOWN

The upscale residential neighborhood of Lincoln Park entices with its mix of distinctive boutiques and well-known national chain stores. **Armitage Avenue** between Orchard Street and Racine Avenue is a great source for of-the-moment clothing, tableware, jewelry, and gifts. There are also some good finds (lingerie, French-inspired goodies) on **Web-**

Ethnic Enclaves

Chicago's ethnic neighborhoods give you the chance to shop the globe without ever leaving the city. Just southwest of the Loop is **Pilsen,** the city's largest Latino neighborhood. A walk along 18th Street between Halsted Street and Western Avenue leads you to a colorful array of bakeries, religious goods shops, and a burgeoning art-gallery district. Stretching south and east from the intersection of Cermak Road and Wentworth Avenue, **Chinatown** has shops selling Far Eastern imports, including jade and ginseng root. On the north side in **Uptown,** a heavy influx of Vietnamese and other Asian trinket shops and imported food stores around the intersection of Broadway and Argyle Street have earned the area the title of "New Chinatown." In the **Lincoln Square** neighborhood on a stretch of Lincoln Avenue between Leland and Lawrence avenues on the city's North Side, you'll still find German delis and stores that sell European-made health and beauty products amid the swell

of newer upscale clothing and gift boutiques attracting the hip singles and young families who now call this area home. Heading east to **Andersonville,** you'll find a slew of Swedish restaurants, bakeries, and gift shops along Clark Street between Foster and Balmoral avenues, plus specialty boutiques that sell everything from fine chocolates to eclectic home furnishings. Many non–U.S. visitors make the trek to a cluster of dingy but well-stocked electronics stores on **Devon Avenue** (between Western and Washtenaw avenues) in an Indian neighborhood on the city's Far North Side. The attraction is a chance to buy electronics that run on 220 volts. Because the United States has no value-added tax, it's often cheaper for international visitors to buy here than at home. ■ TIP→ **The same stretch of Devon Avenue is also home to a cacophony of great Indian groceries, Bollywood video stores, and fabric shops where you can while away your time.**

ster Avenue. On **Halsted Street,** between Armitage Avenue and Fullerton Parkway, are chains geared to the young and thin like bebe and The Blues Jean Bar. The **Clybourn Corridor** section of this neighborhood, which runs along North Avenue and Clybourn Avenue, has become akin to a giant urban strip mall, with standbys like J. Crew (*929 W. North Ave.*) and Restoration Hardware (*938 W. North Ave.*) lining the streets. The star of the show, though, is the flagship three-story Crate&Barrel. You'll also find plenty to buy for the little ones, from children's furniture to plush and pricey clothes and gear. Just east of the Clybourn Corridor, around the intersection of **North Avenue** and **Wells Street,** you'll find the cozy, tree-lined streets of Old Town, with upscale clothiers and accessory shops. The Lincoln Park area is easily reached by taking the Ravenswood (Brown Line) El line to the Armitage stop, or the Howard (Red) El line to Clybourn. To get to Old Town, take the Ravenswood (Brown) El line to Sedgwick.

SPECIALTY STORES

ACCESSORIES **Fabrice.** The only Fabrice boutique outside of Paris stocks an abundance of French accessories: its own line of pins, necklaces, and other jewelry inspired by the gardens of Provence, plus Longchamp handbags, pretty wraps and shawls, and bath products. ✉*1714 N. Wells St., Old Town* ☎*312/280–0011.*

Isabella Fine Lingerie. Lauren Amerine, a self-confessed lingerie addict who herself has inspired many obsessions among her loyal clientele, runs this high-end jewel of a shop. Look for affordable items from Cosabella and Le Mystere mixed in with more exclusive lines like Parah and Julianne, plus bridal pieces and swimwear. The new store on Roscoe Street stocks a smaller selection, with more emphasis on basics. ✉*1101 W. Webster Ave., Lincoln Park* ☎*773/281–2352* ✉*2238 W. Roscoe St., Lakeview* ☎*773/472–3822.*

The Left Bank. An eclectic mix of antique-style French jewelry brings a touch of Paris chic to Chicago. There's also a beautiful selection of French-theme jewelry boxes, perfume bottles, and other accessories. Owner Susan Jablonski has become known for her large assortment of bridal headpieces and tiaras, and she offers wedding-planning services as well. ✉*1155 W. Webster Ave., Lincoln Park* ☎*773/929–7422.*

★ **Mint.** Mint is like a crafts fair inside a pretty storefront, selling only items—from jewelry and purses to cards and candles—from local designers. The prices are reasonable and the selection is fun and funky, not fuddy-duddy. ✉*2150 N. Seminary Ave., Lincoln Park* ☎*773/322–2944.*

Quiltology, the Urban Quilt Space. Quilting is the new knitting for funky DIY-ers, and Colette Cogley's Lincoln Park shop stocks everything they need to keep their habit going, including designs by Amy Butler and Kaffe Fassett. Classes and workshops are available in the back-room sewing lounge, too. ✉*2625 N. Halsted St., Lincoln Park* ☎*773/880–5994.*

★ **1154 Lill Studio.** Creative types design their own handbags (from chic clutches to diaper totes) and ballet flats from tons of fabric and shape options at this super-popular shop housed in a pretty brownstone. Some limited-edition, ready-made bags are available, too. ✉*904 W. Armitage Ave., Lincoln Park* ☎*773/477–5455.*

BEAUTY **Aroma Workshop.** Customize lotions, massage oils, and bath salts with more than 150 essential and fragrance oils in this beauty boutique. The workshop makes its own line of facial-care products, too. ✉*2050 N. Halsted St., Lincoln Park* ☎*773/871–1985.*

Endo Exo. A favorite with gotta-have-it types, this store has vintage pharmacy cabinets filled with a well-chosen stock of trendy and hard-to-find beauty lines such as Jo Wood, Bliss, and Delux Beauty. ✉*2034 N. Halsted St., Lincoln Park* ☎*773/525–0500.*

BOOKS & **Different Strummer.** A sibling to the Different Strummer store in Lincoln
MUSIC Square, this shop within the Old Town School of Folk Music has a good
★ selection of new and used kids' instruments, plus all manner of instruments for rent. ✉*909 W. Armitage Ave., Lincoln Park* ☎*773/751–3410* ✉*4544 N. Lincoln Ave., Lincoln Square* ☎*773/751–3398.*

Gramaphone Records. Local DJs and club kids go to Gramaphone to find vintage and cutting-edge dance releases, from house to hip-hop, and hear them on the spot at one of the store's listening stations. The store also stocks DJ gear. ✉*2843 N. Clark St., Lincoln Park* ☎*773/472–3683.*

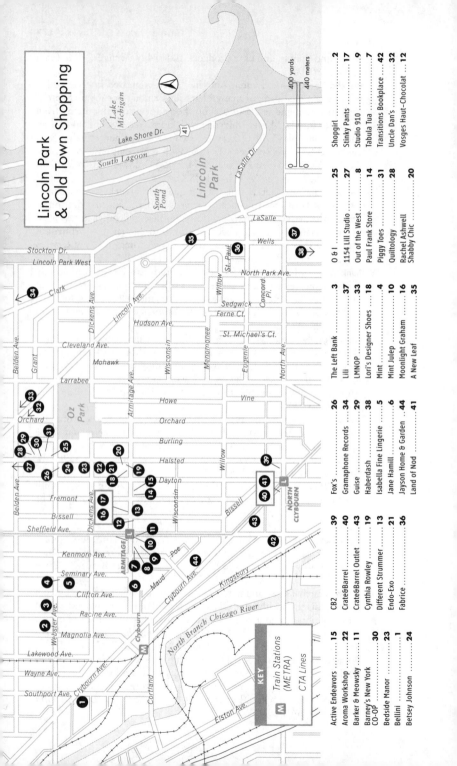

Lincoln Park & Old Town Shopping

Lake Michigan

Lake Shore Dr.

South Lagoon

South Pond

Lincoln Park

LaSalle Dr.

400 yards
440 meters

Stockton Dr.
Lincoln Park West

Clark

Dickens Ave.

Lincoln Ave.

Hudson Ave.

Cleveland Ave.

Mohawk

Larrabee

Oz Park

Orchard

Burling

Halsted

Dayton

Wisconsin

Willow

Bissell

Fremont

Bissell

Sheffield Ave.

Kenmore Ave.

Seminary Ave.

Clifton Ave.

Racine Ave.

Magnolia Ave.

Lakewood Ave.

Wayne Ave.

Southport Ave.

Clybourn Ave.

North Branch Chicago River

Kingsbury

Cortland

Elston Ave.

LaSalle
Wells

St. Paul

North Park Ave.

Sedgwick
Ferne Ct.

St. Michael's Ct.

Concord Pl.

Eugenie

North Ave.

Vine

Orchard

Howe

Armitage Ave.

Menomonee

NORTH/CLYBOURN

ARMITAGE

Belden Ave.

Grant

Orchard

Webster Ave.

Poe

Maud

KEY

M Train Stations (METRA)

CTA Lines

Transitions Bookplace. Alternative healing, religion, mythology, and folklore are among the subjects stocked at one of the country's top New Age bookstores. There's a lively program of author appearances and workshops, plus a café. ✉ *1000 W. North Ave., Lincoln Park* ☎ *312/951–7323.*

FOR KIDS **Bellini.** Virtually everything a stylish baby will need is here, including top-of-the-line wood bedroom furniture, luxury bedding, and accessories. ✉ *2100 N. Southport Ave., Lincoln Park* ☎ *773/880–5840.*

The Land of Nod. Crate&Barrel is next-door neighbor (and business partner) to this quirky-cool children's furniture store. There are plenty of parent-pleasing designs, plus loads of fun accessories, toys, and a great music section, too. ✉ *900 W. North Ave., Lincoln Park* ☎ *312/475–9903.*

> ## FOR BEAUTY-PRODUCT JUNKIES
>
> **Endo Exo** (*2034 N. Halsted St., Lincoln Park, 773/525–0500*) sells the latest makeup lines and offers great advice.
>
> **Bravco Beauty Centre** (*43 E. Oak St., Near North, 312/943–4305*) is a favorite of celebs for its expansive stock (48 types of hair extensions, anyone?), and staff who can explain the differences between them. Cash only.
>
> **Merz Apothecary** (*4716 N. Lincoln Ave., Lincoln Square, 773/989–0900*) has been in business since 1875 and specializes in exclusive European lines and holistic and herbal remedies.

LMNOP. Tykes can get their posh on early with duds from this high-end kids' clothes shop; designers include Flora & Henri and Judith LaCroix and sizes go up to an 8. ✉ *2570 N. Lincoln Ave., Lincoln Park* ☎ *773/975–4055.*

Piggy Toes. This store stocks a good (though pricey) selection of European footwear for well-heeled children. ✉ *2205 N. Halsted St., Lincoln Park* ☎ *773/281–5583.*

Stinky Pants. Parents can shop high-end kids' clothing lines like Eye Spy Baby and Lucy Sykes while their progeny entertain themselves with books and toys in the store's kid-friendly "stinky lounge." ✉ *808 W. Armitage Ave., Lincoln Park* ☎ *773/489–2001.*

CLOTHING FOR MEN **Guise.** For men who want to look good without all the energy it takes to make it happen, Guise is the place to go. This one-stop shop stocks designer clothes from the likes of Theory and Nicole Farhi, offers manicures, shoe shines, haircuts, barbershop-style shaves, and—to make the experience as painless as possible—serves complimentary beer to drink while catching a game on manly sized TVs. ✉ *2217 N. Halsted St., Lincoln Park* ☎ *73/929–6101.*

Haberdash. Owner Adam Beltzman ditched his job as a lawyer to set up shop in Old Town. Tailored clothes and accessories from designers like John Varvatos, Ted Baker, and James Perse plus leather armchairs, plasma TV, and dark wood walls make this store decidedly masculine. ✉ *1350 N. Wells St., Old Town* ☎ *312/440–1300.*

Moonlight Graham. Sports fans love this shop, which pays homage to the nostalgia of baseball. It's named for Archibald "Moonlight"

Graham, famous for appearing in one major league game for the New York Giants in 1905. You'll find sportswear with vintage team logos along with other retro goodies like Tony the Tiger dishware. ✉ *854 W. Armitage Ave., Lincoln Park* ☎ *773/929–3939.*

CLOTHING FOR
MEN & WOMEN

Active Endeavors. Active Endeavors is stocked with trendy clothes for svelte types from designers like Charlotte Ronson and Marc Jacobs. There's an impressive denim selection, too, with brands like Citizens for Humanity and Rag & Bone in the mix. ✉ *853 W. Armitage Ave., Lincoln Park* ☎ *773/281–8100.*

Barneys New York CO-OP. The CO-OP in Chicago has an urban-loft feel, an enormous inventory of designer denim, and lots of hip accessories. ✉ *2209–11 N. Halsted St., Lincoln Park* ☎ *773/248–0426.*

Out of the West. With an inventory that includes saddles, hats, and boots, there's a definite nod to urban cowboys at this Lincoln Park shop. But fashionistas won't feel left out either—especially if they're in the market for fancy-pants blue jeans from premium brands like Seven and Blue Cult. A tailor visits the store weekly to do custom alterations on jeans. ✉ *1021 W. Armitage Ave., Lincoln Park* ☎ *773/404–9378.*

Uncle Dan's. This is the place to go for camping, skiing, and general outdoorsy gear by brands like Marmot and The North Face. There's a good kids' selection, too. ✉ *2440 N. Lincoln Ave., Lincoln Park* ☎ *773/477–1718* ✉ *3551 N. Southport Ave., Lakeview* ☎ *773/348–5800.*

CLOTHING FOR
WOMEN

Betsey Johnson. All of the bold designer's signature fun and over-the-top styles are here. ✉ *2120 N. Halsted St., Lincoln Park* ☎ *773/871–3961.*

Cynthia Rowley. Cynthia Rowley is a Chicago-area native, and she fills her Lincoln Park store with the exuberant, well-priced dresses, separates, and accessories that have made her so popular. ✉ *808 W. Armitage Ave., Lincoln Park* ☎ *773/528–6160.*

Fox's. Snap up canceled and overstocked designer clothes from the likes of Tahari and ABS at 40% to 70% discounts. New shipments come in several times a week, so there's always something new to try on. ✉ *2150 N. Halsted St., Lincoln Park* ☎ *773/281–0700.*

Jane Hamill. Jane Hamill is a local designer who sells must-have looks at reasonable prices to the Lincoln Park set. Dress Fancy by Jane Hamill is the designer's take on bridesmaid dresses—contemporary and feminine without any frightening frills. ✉ *1117 W. Armitage Ave., Lincoln Park* ☎ *773/665–1102.*

Lili. With boho-chic fashions flowing from armoires, pretty chandeliers overhead, and decadent white leather seating, this Old Town store feels like the well-appointed townhouse of a super-stylish friend. She's got good—and expensive—taste, too, filling the drawers and shelves with peasant tops from Bellekat, jeans from Earnest Sewn, and T-shirts from Bonnie Heart Clyde. ✉ *1543 N. Wells St., Old Town* ☎ *312/654–8511.*

Mint Julep. Sarah Eshaghy's keen eye for style developed a loyal following at the long-popular Tribeca on the Avenue. She's outdone herself at her new Lincoln Park boutique, chock-full of fabulous finds from the likes of Nanette Lepore, Tulle, and Glam. The best news: more than half the inventory is priced under $100, so you can stock up without breaking the bank. ✉ *1013 W. Armitage Ave., Lincoln Park* ☎ *773/296–2997.*

Fodor's Choice
★
Shopgirl. A following of devoted customers comes here to find out what to wear next, and fall for pieces by Trina Turk, Ella Moss, and Citizens of Humanity. The owner has moved her fabulous maternity selection into this store, too. ⊠*1206 W. Webster Ave., Lincoln Park* ☎*773/935–7467 or 773/935-7587.*

Studio 910. A friendly sales staff helps shoppers sort through classic pieces from Diane von Furstenburg mixed in with funkier styles by labels like Tessuto. They've moved down the block from the 910 West Armitage location. ⊠*1007 W. Armitage Ave., Lincoln Park* ☎*773/929-2400.*

GIFTS **Barker & Meowsky.** This "paw firm" carries great gifts for dogs, cats, and humans. There are beautiful bowls, plush beds, picture frames, treats, and even pet massage and grooming services—just the things to get tails wagging. ⊠*1003 W. Armitage Ave., Lincoln Park* ☎*773/868–0200.*

Paul Frank Store. Young fans of the designer's famous trademarked monkey, Julius, will find his likeness on stickers, slippers, and sunglasses. Scurvy, a skull and crossbones; Ellie, a pink elephant; and the designer's other kitschy characters are well represented here, too. ⊠*851 W. Armitage Ave., Lincoln Park* ☎*773/388–3122.*

Vosges Haut-Chocolat. Local chocolatier Katrina Markoff's exotic truffles, flavored with spices like curry and ancho chili, have fans across the globe. Her ever-expanding line of goodies now includes caramels, ice cream, chocolate tortilla chips, and even yoga wear and dresses. ⊠*951 W. Armitage Ave., Lincoln Park* ☎*773/296–9866* ⊠*520 N. Michigan Ave., Near North* ☎*312/822–0600.*

FOR THE HOME **Bedside Manor.** Dreamland is even more inviting with these handcrafted beds and lush designer linens, many of which come in interesting jacquard weaves or are nicely trimmed and finished. ⊠*2056 N. Halsted St., Lincoln Park* ☎*773/404–2020.*

Fodor's Choice
★
CB2. A concept store by furniture giant Crate&Barrel, CB2 is unique to Chicago—for now. The idea is stylish, bold basics for trendy urban abodes, all sans big-ticket price tags. ⊠*800 W. North Ave., Lincoln Park* ☎*312/787–8329.*

Crate&Barrel. There's plenty to "Oooh" and "Aaah" about throughout the three floors of stylish home furnishings and kitchenware at Crate&Barrel's flagship location. There's plenty of free parking, and you can even take a break from your heavy-duty shopping at the top-floor café. ⊠*850 W. North Ave., Lincoln Park* ☎*312/573–9800.*

Crate&Barrel Outlet. Around the corner from the massive outpost of the flagship store, the outlet carries odds and ends from the company's housewares and kitchen lines. Look for discounts of up to 75% on out-of-season items. ⊠*1864 N. Clybourn Ave., Lincoln Park* ☎*312/787–4775.*

Jayson Home & Garden. Loaded with new and vintage European and American furnishings, this decor store carries the Mitchell Gold line. Look for oversize cupboards and armoires and decorative accessories, plus stylish garden furniture and a bevy of beautiful floral arrangements. ⊠*1885 N. Clybourn Ave., Lincoln Park* ☎*773/248–8180.*

★ **A New Leaf.** You'll find one of the best selections of fresh flowers in town here. The breathtaking Wells Street space, designed by architect

CLOSE UP

Unpacking Crate&Barrel

Gordon and Carole Segal saw a void in the Chicago retail market in 1962, and they set out to fill it by opening the first Crate&Barrel store in an abandoned elevator factory in the then-questionable Old Town neighborhood.

"I was doing the dishes—classic Arzberg dishes we had picked up on our Caribbean honeymoon—and I said to Carole, 'How come nobody is selling this dinnerware in Chicago?,'" Gordon Segal recalls. "I think we should open a store." And, as they say, the rest is history. With "more taste than money," the Segals displayed their unique housewares en masse on the crates and barrels they were shipped in, and found a niche and a name.

At a time when gas station give-away glasses were common kitchen table fixtures, shoppers were immediately drawn to the grocery store-style displays of contemporary merchandise at reasonable prices. As the business grew, store displays became more sophisticated and the inventory more diverse.

Before the age of home-improvement cable television shows, the Segals brought accessible design into the American home. They added the Finnish fabric line Marimekko to their inventory in the late 1960s, and the bold, colorful prints became a signature style of the era.

Carole retired to raise their family, but Gordon Segal still runs the Chicago-based company they founded together 43 years ago, now a dominant home-furnishings chain with 123 stores across the United States. Always keeping his motto, "Stay humble, stay nervous," in the back of his mind, Segal has continued to fine-tune Crate&Barrel throughout its history, creating shopping environments that engage the senses. He pays close attention to the exteriors, too, focusing on building stores with architectural merit. Stores in Illinois, Pennsylvania, and Chicago have received awards for their outstanding architectural design.

The home furnishings industry has exploded since Crate&Barrel's humble beginnings, and Segal has kept a keen eye on what interests the buying public. In 2000 Crate&Barrel launched CB2, a new concept store aimed at a young urban market with—again—a single store on Chicago's North Side. And, so that no one in the family feels left out, in 2001 Crate&Barrel formed a partnership with Land of Nod, a quirky children's furniture catalog company. They opened one store—guess where?—on Chicago's North Side to start, and have since expanded to five locations. The Segal empire just keeps growing.

–By Judy Sutton Taylor

Cynthia Weese, is also stocked with singular antique and vintage furnishings and accessories as well as a mind-boggling selection of candles, vases, tiles, and pots. ⊠*1818 N. Wells St., Old Town* ☎*312/642–8553* ⊠*1645 N. Wells St., Lincoln Park* ☎*312/642–1576* ⊠*Chicago Place, 700 N. Michigan Ave., Near North* ☎*773/871–3610.*

Rachel Ashwell Shabby Chic. Pop into this outpost (one of six nationally) of the cushy, slip-covered furniture designer. There are also pretty pastel linens and an extensive lighting collection. ⊠*2146 N. Halsted St., Lincoln Park* ☎*773/327–9372.*

Tabula Tua. The colorful, contemporary, mix-and-match dishes and tabletop accessories here are worlds away from standard formal china. Other offerings include breathtaking mosaic tables handmade to order, rustic furniture crafted from old barn wood, and sleek, polished pewter pieces. ✉ *1015 W. Armitage Ave., Lincoln Park* ☎ *773/525–3500.*

SHOES **Lori's Designer Shoes.** Owner Lori Andre's obsession with shoes takes
Fodor'sChoice her on biannual trips to Europe to scour for styles you won't likely see
★ at department stores. The result is an inventory that many fine-footed women consider to be the best in Chicago. Shoes by designers like Gastone Lucioli, janet & janet, and more well-known ones like Franco Sarto are sold at discounts of 10% to 30% in a self-serve atmosphere. Terrific handbags, jewelry, bridal shoes, and other accessories are also available. ✉ *824 W. Armitage Ave., Lincoln Park* ☎ *773/281–5655.*

O & I Shoes. Chic European footwear by the likes of L.A.M.B. and Miss Sixty is sold at this shop, adjacent to swanky kids-shoe outfitter Piggy Toes. ✉ *2205 N. Halsted St., Lincoln Park* ☎ *773/281–5583.*

5

LAKE VIEW

Lake View, a large neighborhood just north of Lincoln Park, has spawned a number of worthwhile shopping strips, including a smattering of antiques shops around Belmont and Ashland avenues. **Clark Street** between Diversey Avenue and Addison Street has myriad clothing boutiques and specialty stores such as pet boutiques and rug dealers, as well as stores filled to the gills with Chicago Cubs paraphernalia as you approach Wrigley Field at Addison. The area farther north on **Halsted Street** between Belmont Avenue and Addison Street is known as Boy's Town; here you'll find more gift shops and boutiques, many with a gay orientation, as well as vintage-clothing and antiques stores. In West Lake View, the new hot spot is **Southport Avenue** between Belmont Avenue and Grace Street, where a recent onslaught of boutiques with a bent toward trendy upscale fashion has put it on the "must" list. **Broadway** between Diversey Avenue and Addison Street also claims its share of intriguing shops. The **Century Mall,** in a former movie palace at Clark Street, Broadway, and Diversey Parkway, houses some chain stores (Aveda, Victoria's Secret, Express), but has a tired feel compared with the rest of the area. To reach this neighborhood from downtown, take the 22 Clark Street bus at Dearborn Street or the 36 Broadway bus at State Street heading north. Or, take the Howard (Red Line) or Ravenswood (Brown Line) El north to the Belmont stop from downtown, which will drop you into the heart of Lake View, near the intersection of Belmont and Sheffield avenues.

ANTIQUES DISTRICTS

BELMONT Fans of art deco, kitchen collectibles, and bar memorabilia can poke
AVENUE into the shops and malls lining Belmont Avenue, starting a bit west of Ashland Avenue and running to Western Avenue. You may have to scrounge around to unearth treasures in these stores, but the prices are some of the lowest in the city. The shops are usually open weekends but may be closed on one or more weekdays. Call before making a special trip.

Blitz Tour: One-of-a-Kind Finds

Get ready for some serious spending—or at least some serious ogling. This itinerary is geared to the antiques lover in you; find exact addresses in the chapter's store listings.

Chicago tempts furniture buyers with antiques, collectibles, and architectural artifacts at prices that generally beat those on either coast. In fact, dealers from all over regularly troll these shops, which are clustered mostly in neighborhoods or malls, for stock to resell in their own shops. For a rundown on dealers, buy a copy of *Taylor's Guide to Antique Shops in Illinois & Southern Wisconsin* ($6), which is available in some bookstores and many antiques shops (to order, call ☎800/829–5677 or go to ⊕*www. taylorsguide.com*). Many antiques districts also publish free pamphlets that list dealers in the neighborhood; look for them in the shops.

To catch the maximum number of open dealers, it's best to tackle this route after brunch on a weekend or on a Thursday or Friday. Assuming your interest runs more toward 20th-century collectibles than Biedermeier, this tour focuses mostly on the West Lake View neighborhood (north of Lin-coln Park and west of Wrigley Field). Take the 11 Lincoln Avenue bus or a taxi to the **Chicago Antique Centre** to browse through the wares of its 35 dealers. Keep your eyes open for other antiques and vintage-clothing shops along this stretch of Lincoln Avenue. Two superb sources for adventurous, mid-20th-century, modern furnishings and collectibles are **Urban Artifacts** and **Zig Zag**. Venture further north on Lincoln Avenue to check out the dustless vintage finds at **At Home** and the art-deco and art-nouveau treasures at **Smythson Yeats Antiques.**

There are three other compelling destinations for collectors that are short cab rides away. **Architectural Artifacts** is an amazing repository for statuary, garden ornaments, and the like. **Lincoln Antique Mall** stockpiles everything from kitchenware to furniture, mostly post-1920. There's also a huge selection of estate jewelry and photographs. Farthest north on the antiques trail is the **Broadway Antique Market,** with its excellent stash of mid-20th-century pieces that range from art deco and Arts and Crafts to modernism and beyond.

Antique Resources. Choice Georgian antiques are sold at fair prices. This is an excellent source for stately desks and dignified dining sets, but the true find is a huge trove—numbering more than 300—of antique crystal and gilt chandeliers from France. ✉*1741 W. Belmont Ave., Lake View* ☎*773/871–4242.*

Father Time Antiques. Father Time bills itself as the Midwest's largest restorer of vintage timepieces; it also stocks vintage Victorian and art-deco European furniture. ✉*2108 W. Belmont Ave., Lake View* ☎*773/880–5599.*

LINCOLN AVENUE & ENVIRONS
A 1½-mi stretch of Lincoln Avenue is worth a visit for its funky antiques, collectibles, and vintage clothing. The shops start around the intersection of Lincoln Avenue and Diversey Parkway and continue until Irving Park Road. A car or the 11 Lincoln Avenue bus is the best way to navigate this area. To get the bus from downtown, take the Howard (Red

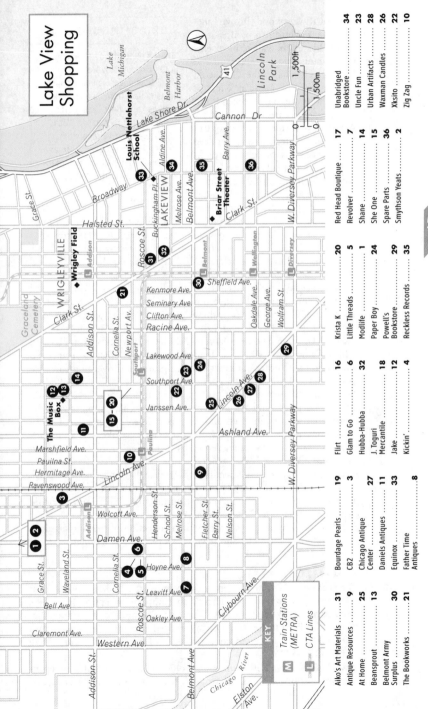

Lake View Shopping

Lincoln Park

Louis Nettlehorst School

Briar Street Theater

The Music Box

Wrigley Field

KEY

Train Stations (METRA)

CTA Lines

Aiko's Art Materials	31
Antique Resources	9
At Home	25
Beansprout	13
Belmont Army Surplus	30
The Bookworks	21

Bourdage Pearls	19
CB2	3
Chicago Antique Center	27
Daniels Antiques	11
Equinox	33
Father Time Antiques	8

Flirt	16
Glam to Go	6
Hubba-Hubba	32
J. Toguri Mercantile	18
Jake	12
Kickin'	4

Krista K	20
Little Threads	5
Modlife	1
Paper Boy	24
Powell's Bookstore	29
Reckless Records	35

Red Head Boutique	17
Revolver	7
Shane	14
She One	15
Spare Parts	36
Smythson Yeats	2

Unabridged Bookstore	34
Uncle Fun	23
Urban Artifacts	28
Waxman Candles	26
Xksito	22
Zig Zag	10

Line) or Ravenswood (Brown Line) El to the Fullerton stop; after exiting the El station, walk ½ block east to the intersection of Fullerton and Lincoln. Then catch the 11 Lincoln Avenue bus to your stop. Most of these shops are open weekends but may be closed early in the week.

At Home. If antiques shopping can be made to feel like a modern experience, this place succeeds at it. It's clean instead of musty and is stocked with a beautiful selection of such items as armoires and vintage glassware, plus some new home accessories. ✉3062 N. Lincoln Ave., Lake View ☎773/472–0800.

Chicago Antique Centre. Open seven days a week, this one-stop spot houses 35 dealers on two levels, some with especially good selections of vintage dishes and jewelry. ✉3036 N. Lincoln Ave., Lake View ☎773/929–0200.

Daniels Antiques. Five blocks north of the six-way Lincoln, Belmont, and Ashland intersection, this cavernous shop shelters a huge stash of Victorian and 20th-century furnishings, especially larger pieces and complete sets. ✉3711 N. Ashland Ave., Lake View ☎773/868–9355.

Modlife. The emphasis here is on mid-20th-century finds from Herman Miller, Eames, Hans Olsen, and other well-known designers. You'll also find original abstract paintings and sculptures and overall affordable price points. ✉3856 N. Lincoln Ave., Lake View ☎773/868–0844.

Smythson Yeats Antiques. An always-changing selection here includes plenty of art-deco and art-nouveau treasures, with an impressive selection of lamps, chandeliers, and ceramics. There are plenty of fabulous larger pieces, too—dark wood sideboards, bookcases, and plush leather chairs. Lamp-repair service is available. ✉3851 N. Lincoln Ave., Lake View ☎773/244–6365.

Urban Artifacts. A superb selection of furniture, lighting, and decorative accessories from the 1940s to the '70s emphasizes the industrial designs that are a popular theme in modern furnishings. ✉2928 N. Lincoln Ave., Lake View ☎773/404–1008.

Zig Zag. Zig Zag displays a well-edited collection of pristine art-deco and modern furnishings and jewelry. ✉3419 N. Lincoln Ave., Lake View ☎773/525–1060.

SPECIALTY STORES

BOOKSTORES **The Bookworks.** The stock here includes more than 40,000 titles, most of them used and/or rare. There's an emphasis on sports (for Cubs fans strolling by from nearby Wrigley Field) and contemporary fiction. Check out the vintage-vinyl-record section. The store buys used books in good condition, too. ✉3444 N. Clark St., Lake View ☎773/871–5318.

Powell's Bookstore. This is one of the oldest and most reliable independent bookshops around; the strength here is the section featuring art, architecture, and photography. Also check out the impressive collection of rare books. ✉*2850 N. Lincoln Ave., Lake View* ☎*773/248–1444* ✉*828 S. Wabash Ave., South Loop* ☎*312/341–1078.*

Unabridged Bookstore. This independent bookshop has maintained a loyal clientele for more than 20 years who love its vast selection and dedicated staff. Known for having one of the most extensive gay and lesbian selections in the city, it also has an impressive children's section and great magazines, too. ✉*3251 N. Broadway, Lake View* ☎*773/883–9119.*

CLOTHING FOR MEN & WOMEN **Belmont Army Surplus.** Puma, Diesel, and other funky brands get mixed in with fatigues, flak jackets, and even faux-fur coats in this neighborhood mainstay, which was forced to move to a new location by a CTA platform expansion project. Despite the name, don't expect too many bargains. ✉*855 W. Belmont Ave., Lake View* ☎*773/975–0626* ✉*1318 N. Milwaukee Ave., Bucktown* ☎*773/384–8448.*

Flirt. You'll find designs for women by Ben Sherman and Left of Center, plus the latest handbag and jewelry finds at this cute boutique. ✉*3449 N. Southport Ave., Lake View* ☎*773/935–4789.*

Hubba-Hubba. Flowy, feminine clothes with a retro-flavor mix with vintage and modern jewelry and accessories at this small, but packed-to-the-gills shop. ✉*3309 N. Clark St., Lake View* ☎*773/477–1414.*

★ **Jake.** The hip and down-to-earth owners of this ever-growing empire (it's expected to soon go national) stock men's and women's clothing by up-and-coming designers. An instant favorite from the moment it opened its doors, Jake's sister store just off the Mag Mile has the same great aesthetic, but is not as jeans-and-T-shirt heavy as the original. ✉*3740 N. Southport Ave., Lake View* ☎*773/929–5253* ✉*939 N. Rush St., Near North* ☎*312/664–5533.*

Kickin'. Hip, urban women snap up their maternity wear at this new shop. There's an emphasis on workout and yoga gear. ✉*2142 W. Roscoe St., Lake View* ☎*773/281–6577.*

Krista K Boutique. An inventory of must-haves for women from designers like Citizens of Humanity, Theory, and Helen Wang reflects the style of the neighborhood. The shop has become the go-to spot for the latest denim trends, too. Down the street is the maternity branch, where stylish expectant moms shop a selection that includes casual non-maternity clothes with a little extra give. ✉*3458 N. Southport Ave., Lake View* ☎*773/248–1967* ✉*3530 N. Southport Ave., Lake View* ☎*773/248–4477.*

Red Head Boutique. This colorful jewel of a shop carries a limited inventory of girly clothes with a fun and funky edge, suitable for young trendoids and cool neighborhood moms alike. Look for local labels like Doris Ruth and hard-to-find ones like Beverly & Monika. ✉*3450 N. Southport Ave., Lake View* ☎*773/325–9898.*

Revolver Chicago. Look effortlessly rock-star cool with threads from this menswear boutique. Video games and complimentary drinks draw in even uninspired shoppers. ✉*2135 W. Belmont Ave., Lake View* ☎*773/832–4866.*

Shane. This is a great stop for the latest in casual urban duds for guys and girls, including Lawd Knows, Three Dots, and a good selection of vintage T-shirts. ✉*3657 N. Southport Ave., Lake View* ☎*773/549–0179.*

She One. A plentiful assortment of bright T-shirts, oh-so-pretty dresses and trendy jewelry dresses the stylish young urban woman. ⊠*3402 N. Southport Ave., Lake View* ☎*773/549–9698.*

FOR KIDS **Beansprout.** Beansprout carries supercute kids' clothes up to size 6x for girls and 6 for boys in fabrics that won't itch, scratch, or (hopefully) become showcases for stains. ⊠*3732 N. Southport Ave., Lake View* ☎*773/472–4780.*

Little Threads. Junk Food, Oink Baby, and Zutano are just some of the funky kids' labels at this cute neighborhood shop. There's also a fun selection of children's reading material and even cool diaper bags for mom. ⊠*2142 W. Roscoe St., Lake View* ☎*773/281–6577.*

GIFTS & **Bourdage Pearls.** Sherry Bourdage sells Chinese freshwater pearls in a
GOODIES staggering array of colors and styles that range from simple and inexpensive to elaborate custom designs. ⊠*3530 N Southport Ave., Lake View* ☎*773/244-1126.*

Glam to Go. The lotions and potions found here will help you stay soft and smelling good, plus there are candles, makeup, and toys for tykes. ⊠*2002 W. Roscoe St., Lake View* ☎*773/525–7004.*

Spare Parts. The selection of fine leather goods here draws on a gamut of sources, including Village Tannery, Jack Spade, and local designer Susan Fitch. Jewelry, bath and body products, and home accessories round out the selection. ⊠*2947 N. Broadway, Lake View* ☎*773/525–4242.*

Uncle Fun. The astonishing and goofy inventory of new and vintage tricks, gags, party favors, and more, delight young and old—as do the reasonable prices. ■TIP➔ **Think trendy bobble-head dolls and the Official John Travolta Picture/Postcard book.** The store is closed Monday. ⊠*1338 W. Belmont Ave., Lake View* ☎*773/477–8223.*

Xksito Latin Boutique. The bright and cheery interior of this Southport Avenue shop is loaded with funky finds from Latin America, including silver jewelry, leather goods from Argentina, and hand-crafted clothing from Brazil. ⊠*3453 N. Southport Ave., Lake View* ☎*773/525–8785.*

Waxman Candles. The candles sold here are made on the premises and come in countless shapes, colors, and scents. There's an incredible selection of holders for votives and pillars, and incense, too. ⊠*3044 N. Lincoln Ave., Lake View* ☎*773/929–3000.*

FOR THE HOME **CB2.** House-proud locals with tight budgets come to this Crate&Barrel
Fodor$Choice offshoot for kitchenware and accessories that look great but don't break
★ the bank. ⊠*3757 N. Lincoln Ave., Lake View* ☎*773/755–3900.*

Equinox. Equinox literally glows from within, thanks to its Tiffany-style lamps, but the true strength here is the selection of Arts and Crafts–style art tiles and reproduction pottery. ⊠*3401 N. Broadway Ave., Lake View* ☎*773/281–9151* ⊠*609 N. State St., River North* ☎*312/335–8006.*

J. Toguri Mercantile Company. This warehouse-style store carries all things Asian, including tea sets, lacquerware, kimonos, hard-to-find pots, and Japanese music. ⊠*851 W. Belmont Ave., Lake View* ☎*773/929–3500.*

MUSIC STORE **Reckless Records.** Reckless Records ranks as one of the city's leading alternative and secondhand record stores. Besides the indie offerings, you can flip through jazz, classical, and soul recordings, or catch a live appearance by an up-and-comer passing through town. ✉*3161 N. Broadway, Lake View* ☎*773/404–5080.*

PAPER **Aiko's Art Materials Import.** Hundreds of stenciled, marbled, textured, and tie-dyed Japanese papers line the walls at this store that's been in business since the 1950s. You'll also find bookbinding and woodcutting materials, pottery, and books about Japanese culture. ✉*3347 N. Clark St., Lake View* ☎*773/404–5600.*

Paper Boy. A hip sensibility informs the cards, gift wrap, and invitations sold here by the people who bring you the quirky goods at Uncle Fun across the street. ✉*1351 W. Belmont Ave., Lake View* ☎*773/388–8811.*

WORTH A SPECIAL TRIP

ANTIQUES & COLLECTIBLES

Architectural Artifacts. The selection matches the warehouse proportions here. The mammoth two-story space houses oversize garden ornaments (arbors, benches), statuary, iron grills, fixtures, and decorative tiles. Architectural fragments—marble, metal, wood, terra-cotta—hail from American and European historic buildings. ✉*4325 N. Ravenswood Ave., Ravenswood* ☎*773/348–0622.*

★ **Broadway Antique Market.** More than 75 hand-picked dealers, plus quality that is more carefully monitored than at most malls, make it worth the trek to the Broadway Antique Market, affectionately called BAM by its loyal fans. Mid-20th century is the primary emphasis, but items range from Arts and Crafts and art deco to Heywood-Wakefield. Display is the market's strong suit—the furniture, jewelry, and bibelots are wonderfully presented. The building itself is a prime example of deco architecture; it's near the Thorndale stop on the Red Line. The Edgewater Antique Mall (6314 N. Broadway), which specializes in 20th-century goods, is a couple of blocks north. ✉*6130 N. Broadway, Edgewater* ☎*773/743–5444.*

Lincoln Antique Mall. Dozens of dealers carrying antiques and collectibles share this large space. There's a good selection of French and mid-20th-century modern furniture, plus estate jewelry, oil paintings, and photographs, but you can find virtually anything and everything here. ✉*3115 W. Irving Park Rd., Northwest Side* ☎*773/604–4700.*

★ **Salvage One.** An enormous warehouse chock-full of stained lead glass, garden ornaments, fireplace mantels, bathtubs, bars, and other architectural artifacts draws creative home remodelers and restaurant designers from around the country. ■TIP➡ **This is the place to hunt for all kinds of treasures, from vintage dental chairs to Paris street lamps.** ✉*1840 W. Hubbard St., Ukrainian Village* ☎*312/733–0098.*

APOTHECARY

★ **Merz Apothecary.** This old-fashioned druggist stocks all manner of homeopathic and herbal remedies, as well as a great selection of hard-to-find European toiletries, cosmetics, candles, and natural laundry products. It's closed Sunday. There's an outlet in the Macy's on State Street as well. ✉*4716 N. Lincoln Ave., Lincoln Square* ☎*773/989–0900.*

5

AUCTIONS

Susanin's Auctioneers and Appraisers. Live, usually themed, sales occur on Saturday mornings in a 35,000-square-foot location in the South Loop. Preview items are also displayed on the floor for immediate sale at a set price. Preview hours are Monday through Saturday from 10 AM to 5 PM. ⊠*900 S. Clinton St., South Loop* ☎*312/832–9800.*

BOOK & MUSIC STORES

Afrocentric Bookstore. Owner Desiree Sanders's store is dedicated entirely to African-American literature, and the store hosts many notable African-American speakers. ⊠*4655 S. King Dr., Bronzeville* ☎*773/924–3966.*

Women & Children First. This feminist bookstore 6½ mi north of the Loop stocks fiction and nonfiction, periodicals, journals, small-press publications, and a strong selection of gay and lesbian titles. The children's section has a great array of books, all politically correct. ⊠*5233 N. Clark St., Andersonville* ☎*773/769–9299.*

FACTORY OUTLETS & OFF-PRICE STORES

Mark Shale Outlet. Unsold men's and women's clothing from Mark Shale stores is available here for 30% to 70% less than the original retail price. In a strip shopping center about 2¼ mi northwest of the Loop, this outlet stocks corporate and weekend clothing from the likes of Polo and Joseph Abboud. ⊠*2593 N. Elston Ave., Logan Square* ☎*773/772–9600.*

FOR HOME & GARDEN

Rotofugi. A toy store for grown-up kids, Rotofugi specializes in artist-created, limited-edition toys considered art (not playthings) by customers and owners alike. You'll find dozens of specialty lines from the United States, China, and Japan, like CiBoys Mini Destroyers and toys by H. Moto. The store also hosts a series of revolving gallery exhibitions. ⊠*1953 W. Chicago Ave., Ukrainian Village* ☎*312/491–9501.*

Sprout Home. If your tastes run toward modern furnishings, you'll drool over every nook and cranny of this store, which sells lines like Vessel, Pure, and Thomas Paul for your indoor life, plus unusual plants and gardening products for your outdoor one. ⊠*745 N. Damen Ave., Ukrainian Village* ☎*312/226–5950.*

HATS

Optimo Hat Co. One of the last stores of its kind, Optimo makes high-end custom straw and felt hats for men in an atmosphere that evokes 1930s and '40s haberdashery. The store also offers a complete line of hat services, from cleaning and blocking to repairs. ⊠*10215 S. Western Ave., Beverly* ☎*773/238–2999.*

WESTERN

Alcala's Western Wear. Alcala stocks more than 10,000 pairs of cowboy boots—many in exotic skins—for men, women, and children. About 2½ mi west of Michigan Avenue, it's a bit out of the way, but the amazing array of Stetson hats and rodeo gear makes this a must-see for cowboys, caballeros, and country-and-western dancers. ⊠*1733 W. Chicago Ave., Ukrainian Village* ☎*312/226–0152.*

Entertainment

WORD OF MOUTH

"Go to Millennium Park at night to hear a concert, then walk to Buckingham Fountain and watch the light show."

—cheribob

"The Green Mill was frequented by Al Capone. Great place, one of the true must sees in the city."

—exiledprincess

ENTERTAINMENT PLANNER

Find out What's Going On

To find out what's happening in the Windy City, check out the following: the *Chicago Tribune*'s Metromix.com, *Time Out Chicago* magazine or Web site (www.timeout.com/chicago), the *Chicago Reader*, an alternative newsweekly and Web site (www.chicagoreader.com), and Centerstage.net, which has a calendar of music and theater events.

Getting There

Parking in North Side neighborhoods, particularly Lincoln Park and Lake View, is increasingly scarce, even on weeknights. If you're going out in these areas, take a cab or public transportation.

If you do decide to drive, use the curbside valet service available at many restaurants and clubs for about $6 to $7. If you're headed to the South Side, be cautious about public transportation late at night. It's best to drive or cab it here.

Get Tickets

You can save money on seats at **Hot Tix** (⊕ *www.hottix.org*, for listings and booth information only), where unsold tickets are available, usually at half price (plus a service charge) on the day of performance; you won't know what's available until that day. On Friday, however, you can buy tickets for Saturday and Sunday. Hot Tix booths are at the Chicago Tourism Center at 72 East Randolph Street; the Chicago Water Works Visitor Center at the southeast corner of Michigan Avenue and Pearson Street; and the North Shore Center for the Performing Arts at 9501 North Skokie Boulevard, in suburban Skokie. Hot Tix also functions as a Ticketmaster outlet, selling advance, full-price, cash-only tickets.

You can charge full-price tickets over the phone or online at **Ticketmaster** (☏ *312/559–1212 for rock concerts and general-interest events, 312/902–1500 arts line* ⊕ *www.ticketmaster.com*).

For hot, sold-out shows, such as performances by the Chicago Symphony Orchestra or the Lyric Opera of Chicago, call a day or two before the show to see if there are any subscriber returns. Another option is to show up at the box office on concert day—a surprising number of people strike it lucky with on-the-spot tickets due to cancellations.

Small fees can have big payoffs! Many of the smaller neighborhood street festivals (there are hundreds in summer) request $5 to $10 donations upon entry, but it's often worth the expense: big-name bands are known to take the stage of even the most under-publicized festivals. For moment-to moment festival coverage, check out ⊕ *www.metromix.com*.

Festivals

For the first two weeks in October, the **Chicago International Film Festival** (☎ *312/332–3456* ⊕ *www.chicagofilmfestival.org*) screens more than 100 films, including premieres of Hollywood films, international releases, documentaries, short subjects, animation, videos, and student films. Movie stars usually make appearances at the opening events.

Grant Park Music Festival (☎ *312/742–7638* ⊕ *www. grantparkmusicfestival.com*), a program of the Chicago Park District, gives free concerts June through August in the spectacular new Frank Gehry–designed Jay Pritzker Pavilion in Millennium Park. Tote along dinner and make a full night of the performance by the superb Grant Park Orchestra and Chorus. Concerts are usually Wednesday, Friday, and Saturday evenings.

In summer you can enjoy the Chicago Symphony at the **Ravinia Festival** (☎ *847/266–5100* ⊕ *www.ravinia.org*) in Highland Park, a 25-mi train trip from Chicago. The park is lovely, and lawn seats are always available even when those in the pavilion are sold out. Ravinia also draws crowds with jazz, pop, and dance concerts.

In early June, the **Chicago Blues Festival** (☎ *312/744–3370* ⊕ *www.chicagobluesfestival.org*), the largest free blues festival in the world, rocks the city. Blues legends such as B. B. King, Koko Taylor, and Buddy Guy have all headlined the festival, and blues lovers from around the world — most notably Chuck Berry and Keith Richards — have been known to attend (and sometimes take the stage).

Labor Day weekend blasts off with the unmistakable sounds of the **Chicago Jazz Festival** (☎ *312/744–3370*). Set in Grant Park, the four-day festival offers not only a prime lakefront locale, but also free performances by local, national, and international musicians and special tributes to jazz legends.

Raves & Faves

Pointe of Pride: Joffrey Ballet of Chicago

Most Wanted Tickets: Lyric Opera of Chicago

Hits Closest to Home: Steppenwolf Theatre Company

Chicest Sidewalk Café: Cru Café and Wine Bar

Sharpest Wits: The Second City

Hours

Live music starts around 9 PM at bars around town.

Bars close at 2 AM Friday and 3 AM Saturday.

Curtain calls for performances are usually at 7:30 or 8 PM.

6

Updated by
Jessica Volpe

Chicago's arts and nightlife scene is as vivacious and diverse as its neighborhoods. Sing along with a biographical musical at Black Ensemble Theater to the north or zip southwest to Wicker Park's renowned Steppenwolf Theatre, where you just might run into longtime ensemble member John Malkovich. Head for the Loop where renowned companies such as the Lyric Opera and the Joffrey Ballet hold court. And remember that this is the city that gave birth to the often raucous "poetry slam" at the Green Mill jazz club.

Nighttime entertainment options before and after hours are infinite—as long as you're willing to explore. Sip an imported Belgian beer at Hopleaf, a cozy North Side tavern, or tap into your wild side at a downtown dance club such as Le Passage. And we can't forget to mention comedy: Second City Club has been unleashing top comedic talents, including John Belushi and Bill Murray, for decades.

GREAT PERFORMANCES

If you're even mildly interested in the performing arts, Chicago has the means to put you in your seat—be it floor, mezzanine, or balcony. Just pick your preference (theater, dance, or symphony/orchestra), and let Chicago's impressive body of artists do the rest. From critically acclaimed big names to fringe groups that specialize in experimental work, there truly is a performance art for everyone.

Ticket prices vary wildly depending on whether you're seeing a high-profile group or venturing into more obscure territory. Chicago Symphony tickets range from $15 to $200, the Lyric Opera from $30 to $180 (if you can get them). Smaller choruses and orchestras charge from $10 to $30; watch the listings for free performances. Commercial theater ranges from $15 to $75; smaller experimental ensembles might charge $5, $10, or pay-what-you-can. Movie prices range from $9 for first-run houses to as low as $1.50 at some suburban second-run houses.

■TIP→ **For free, live music in summer, head downtown to the Grant Park Music Fest (a classical-music series) and the jam-packed Chicago Blues and Chicago Jazz festivals. Held at the visually stunning Millennium Park and Grant Park, there's no cheaper way to experience some of the best sights and sounds Chicago has to offer. See the Festivals section in the Planner for more information.**

TOP 5 PERFORMANCES

Joffrey Ballet. Fine-tuned performances, such as the glittering production of *The Nutcracker,* make this Chicago's premier classical-dance company. Treat yourself to one of several annual performances at the Auditorium Theatre and help celebrate more than 50 seasons of superb ballet. ☎*312/739–0120* ⊕*www.joffrey.com.*

Lookingglass Theatre Company. Gawk at offbeat and fantastically acrobatic performances inside the belly of the Chicago Water Works building. The company's physically and artistically daring works incorporate theater, dance, music, and circus arts. ☎312/337–0665 ⊕*www.lookingglasstheatre.org.*

Fodor'sChoice **Steppenwolf.** The alumni roster
★ speaks for itself: John Malkovich, Gary Sinise, Joan Allen, and Laurie Metcalf all honed their chops with this troupe. The company's trademark cutting-edge acting style and consistently successful productions have won national acclaim. ☎312/335–1650 ⊕*www.steppenwolf.org.*

☾ **Chicago Symphony Orchestra.** Two internationally celebrated conductors, two in-house award-winning composers, and more than 150 magnificent performances a year make the Chicago Symphony Orchestra a musical tour de force. The impressive annual roster offers regular concerts and special theme series including classical, chamber, and children's concerts. Tickets are sometimes scarce, but they do become available; call or check the Web site for status updates. If you buy your tickets online, click on the "Know Your Seats" section, where you can see photos of the views of the stage from different seats. ☎312/294–3000 or 800/223–7114 ⊕*www.cso.org* ☉*Sept.–June.*

Lyric Opera of Chicago. The big voices of the opera world star in these top-flight productions. This is one of the top two opera companies in America today. Don't worry about understanding German or Italian; English translations are projected above the stage. All of the superb performances have sold out for more than a dozen years, and close to 90% of all Lyric tickets go to subscribers—the key to getting in is to call the Lyric in early August when individual tickets first go on sale. ☎312/332–2244 ⊕*www.lyricopera.org* ☉*Sept.–Mar.*

BEAUTIFUL VOICES: HIGHLY RECOMMENDED VOCAL PERFORMANCES

From a cappella to opera, the City of Big Shoulders has some of the nation's top vocal groups. Treat the kids to a sprightly concert by the Chicago Children's Choir or hear the sacred sounds of Bella Voce reverberate from the walls of a gorgeous church. The following are our picks for the most beautiful voices in the city.

CHORAL & CHAMBER GROUPS

Apollo Chorus of Chicago (☎312/427–5620 ⊕*www.apollochorus.org*), formed in 1872, is one of the country's oldest oratorio societies. Don't miss the annual Handel's *Messiah* if you're here in December. Otherwise, they perform various choral classics throughout the year at area churches.

Bella Voce (☎312/479–1096 ⊕*www.bellavoce.org*). "Beautiful voices," indeed. Formerly known as His Majestie's Clerkes, the 20-person a cappella group performs a variety of sacred and secular music, including everything from early music to works by living composers. Concerts are often held in churches throughout the city, providing a powerful acoustical and visual accompaniment to the music. The season runs October through May.

☾ A performance by the **Chicago Children's Choir** (☎312/849–8300 ⊕*www. ccchoir.org*) is the closest thing we can imagine to hearing angels sing. Its members—ages 8 to 18—are culled from a broad spectrum of racial, ethnic, and economic groups. Performances, culled from an international music base, are given each year during the holiday season and in May. Other concerts are scheduled periodically, sometimes in the Chicago Cultural Center's Preston Bradley Hall.

Take a step back in time with **Music of the Baroque** (☎312/551–1414 ⊕*www.baroque.org*), one of the Midwest's leading music ensembles specializing in baroque and early classical music. See one of seven yearly programs at either Millennium Park's Harris Theater or one of several beautiful Chicago-area churches. Performances run from September to May.

The small but mighty **Oriana Singers** (☎773/262–4558 ⊕*www.oriana. org*) are an outstanding a cappella sextet with an eclectic early, classical, and jazz repertoire. The close-knit traveling group performs from September to June, periodically in conjunction with Joffrey Ballet and other Chicago-area groups.

OPERA

Chicago Opera Theater (☎312/704–8414 ⊕*www.chicagooperatheater.org*) shrugs off esoteric notions of opera, preferring to make productions that are accessible to aficionados and novices alike. The production of "Nixon in China," a contemporary American opera detailing conversations between the former U.S. President and Henry Kissinger (among others), is a shining example of the company's open-mindedness toward the operatic canon. From innovative versions of traditional favorites to important lesser-known works, the emphasis is on both theatrical and musical aspects. Fear not—performances are sung in English, or in Italian with English supertitles projected above the stage. They're held at the Harris Theater for Music and Dance.

Light Opera Works (☎847/869–6300 ⊕*www.light-opera-works.org*) favors the satirical tones of the distinctly British Gilbert and Sullivan operettas, but takes on frothy Viennese, French, and other light operettas and American musicals from June to early January.

HIGHLY RECOMMENDED DANCE & THEATER TROUPES

Chicago's reputation as a dance and theatrical powerhouse was born from its small, independent companies that produce a roster of works, from jazz-inflected ballets to biographical musicals. The groups listed do consistently interesting work, and a few have gained national attention. Be open-minded when you're choosing a show; even a group you've never heard of may be harboring one or two underpaid geniuses.

VENUES WORTH CHECKING OUT

The following host various productions. Call or check their schedules online to see who will be on stage.

The **Athenaeum Theatre** (✉ *2936 N. Southport Ave., Lake View* ☎ *773/935–6860* ⊕ *www.athenaeumtheatre.com*) hosts innovative, small dance companies, and the fall series Dance Chicago, which features all forms of dance from Chicago dance companies.

The **Dance Center of Columbia College Chicago** (✉ *1306 S. Michigan Ave., South Loop* ☎ *312/344–8300* ⊕ *www.dancecenter.org*) presents thought-provoking fare with leading international and national contemporary-dance artists.

The Reader carries complete dance and theater listings, plus reviews of the more avant-garde shows.

DANCE

Hubbard Street Dance Chicago (☎ *312/850–9744* ⊕ *www.hubbardstreetdance.com*), Chicago's most notable success story in dance, exudes a jazzy vitality that has made it extremely popular. The style mixes classical-ballet techniques, theatrical jazz, and contemporary dance.

Muntu Dance Theatre of Chicago (☎ *773/602–1135* ⊕ *www.muntu.com*) showcases dynamic interpretations of contemporary and traditional African and African-American dance. Artistic director Amaniyea Payne travels to Africa to learn traditional dances and adapts them for the stage.

Trinity Irish Dance Co. (☎ *773/549–6135* ⊕ *www.trinitydancers.com*), founded long before *Riverdance,* promotes traditional and progressive Irish dancing. In addition to the world-champion professional group, you can also catch performances by younger dancers enrolled in the Trinity Academy of Irish Dance.

THEATER

About Face Theatre (☎ *773/784–8565* ⊕ *www.aboutfacetheatre.com*) is the city's best-known gay and lesbian performing group, which in its short history has garnered awards for original works, world premieres, and adaptations presented in larger theaters like the Steppenwolf and the Goodman.

Bailiwick Repertory Theatre (✉ *1229 W. Belmont Ave., Lake View* ☎ *773/883–1090* ⊕ *www.bailiwick.org*) stages new and classical material at its namesake Arts Center. Its Pride Performance series, held every summer, focuses on plays by gays and lesbians.

★ **Black Ensemble Theater** (✉ *4520 N. Beacon St., Ravenswood* ☎ *773/769–4451* ⊕ *www.blackensembletheater.org*) has a penchant for long-running musicals based on popular African-American icons. Founder and

6

executive producer Jackie Taylor has written and directed such hits as *The Jackie Wilson Story* and *The Other Cinderella*.

Collaboraction (✉ *437 N. Wolcott Ave., Ukrainian Village* ☎ *312/226–9633* ⊕ *www.collaboraction.org*) lets actors, artists, and musicians share the stage together in an experimental free-for-all that puts the "fun" in dysfunctional. Of its several performances a year, we recommend Sketchbook—a series of 16 seven-minute long plays—for its color and energy.

★ **Chicago Shakespeare Theater** (✉ *800 E. Grand Ave., Near North* ☎ *312/595–5600* ⊕ *www.chicagoshakes.com*) devotes its considerable talents to keeping the Bard's flame alive in the Chicago area, with at least three plays a year. The best part? The Courtyard Theater, on Navy Pier, has sparkling views of the city, and seats are never farther than 30 feet from the thrust stage.

ETA Creative Arts Foundation (✉ *7558 S. Chicago Ave., Grand Crossing* ☎ *773/752–3955* ⊕ *www.etacreativearts.org*), a South Side performing-arts center, has established a strong presence for African-American theater, with six plays each year. It also hosts black cultural presentations. Enjoy your trip to the South Side, but be aware that some areas are sketchier than others. To ensure your safety, avoid public transportation and opt for a cab instead.

Neo-Futurists (✉ *5153 N. Ashland Ave., Uptown* ☎ *773/275–5255* ⊕ *www.neofuturists.org*) perform their long-running, late-night hit *Too Much Light Makes the Baby Go Blind* in a space—oddly enough—above a funeral home. The piece is a series of 30 ever-changing plays performed in 60 minutes; the order of the plays is chosen by the audience. In keeping with the spirit of randomness, the admission price is set by the roll of a die, plus $7.

Fodor'sChoice **Redmoon Theater** (☎ *312/850–8440* ⊕ *www.redmoon.org*) tells imaginative, seasonal stories with the magically creative use of puppets, sets, and live actors. The company's annual outdoor spectacle series presents madcap theater in unlikely places, including undiscovered parks and even on water. The series usually takes place in the fall, but experimental theater would be nothing if not unpredictable, so be sure to call for confirmation. Nonseries performances are held everywhere, from grassroots neighborhood events to Redmoon Central.

★ **Victory Gardens Theater** (✉ *2433 N. Lincoln Ave., Lincoln Park* ☎ *773/871–3000* ⊕ *www.victorygardens.org*) is known for its workshops and Chicago premieres. After buying out the landmark Biograph Theater (site of John Dillinger's infamous demise) in 2006, all company productions now take place on the impressive 299-seat proscenium-thrust stage there. Victory Gardens' original theater, now called the Greenhouse, hosts plays by local production companies on four stages.

CINEMATHEQUE

The rowdy crowd at **Brew and View** come for cheap flicks—usually cult faves—and beer specials. ✉ *Vic Theatre* ☎ *773/929–6713* ⊕ *www. brewview.com.*

Facets Cinematheque shows rare and exotic films in its cinema and video theater. ☎ *773/281–4114.*

Gene Siskel Film Center screens unusual current films and revivals of rare classics; the best part is that filmmakers sometimes give lectures to accompany the movie. ☎ *312/846–2600.*

If you love old theaters, old movies, and ghosts (rumor has it the theater is haunted by the spirit of its original manager) don't miss a trip to **Music Box Theatre.** ☎ *773/871–6604.*

For **IMAX and OMNIMAX theaters** go to **Navy Pier** (☎ *312/595–5629)* or the **Museum of Science and Industry** (☎ *773/684–1414).*

For a change of scenery, watch classic films under the stars at the **Chicago Outdoor Film Festival,** which runs July through August in Grant Park on Tuesday nights. ☎ *312/742–7529.*

AFTER DARK

6

Chicago's entertainment varies from loud and loose to sophisticated and sedate. You'll find classic Chicago corner bars in most neighborhoods, along with trendier alternatives like wine bars. The strains of blues and jazz provide much of the backbeat to the city's groove, and an alternative country scene is flourishing. As far as dancing is concerned, the action has switched from cavernous clubs to smaller spots with DJs spinning dance tunes; there's everything from hip-hop to swing. Wicker Park and Bucktown have the hottest nightlife, but prime spots such as Sound-Bar and Le Passage are spread throughout the city.

The Reader (distributed midweek in bookstores, record shops, and other city establishments) is your best guide to the entertainment scene. This free weekly has comprehensive, timely listings and reviews. Another reliable weekly is *Time Out Chicago* magazine. The Friday editions of the *Chicago Tribune* and *Chicago Sun-Times* are also good sources of information. Daily updates on happenings around town are listed in the *Chicago Tribune's* sister paper, *RedEye,* or on the Web at ⊕ *www.metromix.com.*

Shows usually begin at 9 PM; cover charges generally range from $3 to $20, depending on the day of the week (Friday and Saturday nights are the most expensive). Most bars stay open until 2 AM Friday night and 3 AM Saturday, except for a few after-hours spots and some larger dance clubs, which are often open until 4 AM Friday night and 5 AM Saturday (Berlin, Crobar, and Transit are very popular). Outdoor beer gardens such as Sheffield's and John Barleycorn are the exception; these close at 11 PM on weekdays and midnight on weekends. Some bars are not open seven days a week, so call before you go.

CHECK IT OUT

For complete music and theater listings, check two weeklies, *The Reader* and *TimeOut Chicago*, both published midweek; the Friday and Sunday editions of the *Chicago Tribune* and *Chicago Sun-Times*; and the monthly *Chicago* magazine.

If you're interested in Broadway-scale shows, contact the following theaters to see what's playing while you're in town.

Auditorium Theatre of Roosevelt University (☎ *312/922–2110* ⊕ *www.auditoriumtheatre.org*).

Chicago Theatre (☎ *312/462–6300* ⊕ *www.thechicagotheatre.com*).

Goodman Theatre (☎ *312/443–3800* ⊕ *www.goodman-theatre.org*).

Oriental Theatre (☎ *312/782–2004 or 312/902–1400* ⊕ *www.broadway-inchicago.com*).

LaSalle Bank Theatre (formerly the Shubert Theatre) (☎ *312/902–1400 or 312/977–1700* ⊕ *www.broadwayinchicago.com*).

For other performances, check out:

Cadillac Palace Theatre (☎ *312/977–1700* ⊕ *www.broadwayinchicago.com*).

Joan W. and Irving B. Harris Theater for Music and Dance (☎ *312/334–7777* ⊕ *www.harristheaterchicago.org*).

Storefront Theater (☎ *312/742–8497*).

Athenaeum Theatre (☎ *773/935–6860* ⊕ *www.athenaeumtheatre.com*).

Briar Street Theatre (☎ *773/348–4000 or 800/258–3626*).

Drury Lane Theatre Water Tower Place (☎ *312/642–2000* ⊕ *www.drurylanewatertower.com*).

Royal George Theatre Center (☎ *312/988–9000* ⊕ *www.theroyal-georgetheatre.com*).

Theatre Building (☎ *773/327–5252* ⊕ *www.theatrebuildingchicago.org*).

Theatre on the Lake (☎ *312/742–7994*).

For concerts, try the following halls:

Chicago Cultural Center (☎ *312/346–3278 or 312/744–6630* ⊕ *www.cityofchicago.org*).

Mandel Hall (☎ *773/702–8511 or 773/702–7300*).

Newberry Library (☎ *312/943–9090* ⊕ *www.newberry.org*).

Orchestra Hall (☎ *312/294–3000*).

Three Arts Club (☎ *312/944–6250* ⊕ *www.threearts.org*).

The list of blues and jazz clubs includes several South Side locations: be cautious about transportation here late at night because some of these neighborhoods can be unsafe. Drive your own car or ask the bartender to call you a cab.

BARS

Chicago bars—whether they're sports bars, wine bars, neighborhood bars, or even trendy bars—are surprisingly accessible. With few exceptions, snobbishness and exclusivity are not tolerated throughout the scene, so bring your ID (most places card at the door), pocket some cash, and join the party!

■ TIP➜ If you're sticking to downtown and North Side bars, it's relatively safe to take public transportation. But if you're planning on staying out past midnight, we suggest taking a cab home.

LOOP, SOUTH LOOP & WEST LOOP

Sleek and sexy wine bars and lounges light up Chicago's core business district after work and on weekends. Beware: downtown bars are seldom budget-friendly (but often worth the money).

Fulton Lounge (⊠ *955 W. Fulton Market, West Loop* ☎ *312/942–9500*) is largely responsible for Fulton Market District's now blooming nightlife scene. The stylish lounge is all about clean-lined and understated elegance, from the slender bar right down to the low-slung swivel chairs and seasonal martinis. A sophisticated crowd mingles on the patio in summer months.

Encore (⊠ *171 W. Randolph St., Loop* ☎ *312/338–3788*) is a jazzed-up hotel lounge sandwiched between the Cadillac Palace Theatre and the Hotel Allegro. Clubby seating and a classic cocktail menu make it an appealing downtown destination for post-dinner or -theater drinks, a light bite, and conversation.

Ghost Bar (⊠ *440 W. Randolph St., West Loop* ☎ *312/575–9900*) is a sexy downtown space perched above the restaurant Nine. Cool and futuristic with cushy vinyl banquettes and designer seating, the bar is white as a, well, you know what, and the muted lighting casts the fashion-conscious crowd in silhouette.

Kitty O'Shea's (⊠ *Chicago Hilton and Towers, 720 S. Michigan Ave., South Loop* ☎ *312/922–4400*), a handsome room in the Chicago Hilton and Towers, re-creates an Irish pub with all things Irish, including live music seven nights a week, beer, food, and bar staff.

The **Tasting Room** (⊠ *1415 W. Randolph St., Loop* ☎ *312/942–1313*) makes the short list of nightspots where Chicagoans take guests they want to impress. This two-story wine bar has casual, loft-chic looks and sweeping skyline views. More than 100 wines are poured by the glass or flight, and over 300 by the bottle. Cheese, caviar, and other light bites are the perfect complement. If you love the vintage you taste here, buy a bottle to take home at the adjacent wineshop, Randolph Wine Cellars.

NEAR NORTH & RIVER NORTH

The famous Chicago bar scene known as **Rush Street** has faded into the mists of time, although the street has found resurgent energy with the opening of a string of upscale restaurants and outdoor cafés. For the vestiges of the old Rush Street, continue north to trendy **Division Street**

CLASSIC CHICAGO SPOTS

Imbibe your way through a history lesson at these Chicago institutions.

The Omni Ambassador East's glamorous **Pump Room** (⊠ *1301 N. State Pkwy., Old Town* ☎ *312/943–9200*) is the spot for anyone interested in the Golden Age of Hollywood. Booth One alone has played host to more celebrities like Humphrey Bogart, Lauren Bacall, Irv "Kup" Kupcinet, and Judy Garland, than Oprah Winfrey's couch.

The **Green Mill** (⊠ *4802 N. Broadway, Far North Side* ☎ *773/878–5552*), opened in 1914 in Uptown, has undergone quite a few makeovers and owners (including Al Capone). We like its current incarnation: dark-wood carvings, passionate jazz, and smoke-filled booths.

Since the 1960s, **Original Mother's** (⊠ *26 W. Division St., Near North* ☎ *312/642–7251*) has been a local favorite for cutting-edge music and dance-'til-you-drop partying. The subterranean singles' destination was immortalized by Demi Moore, Jim Belushi, and Rob Lowe in the film *About Last Night.*

between Clark and State streets. The crowd here consists mostly of suburbanites and out-of-towners on the make. The bars are crowded and noisy. Among the better-known singles' bars are **Butch McGuire's** (⊠ *20 W. Division St., Near North* ☎ *312/337–9080*), the **Lodge** (⊠ *21 W. Division St., Near North* ☎ *312/642–4406*), and **Original Mother's** (⊠ *26 W. Division St., Near North* ☎ *312/642–7251*), which was featured in the motion picture *About Last Night.*

Reprieve from the bustling Division Street scene is only a few blocks south, in the Near North and River North neighborhoods. Hunker down in a low-key lounge or sip a hearty pint of Guinness at an authentic Irish pub. Whatever your preference, plenty of conversation-friendly bars are a brief cab ride away.

Cru Café and Wine Bar (⊠ *25 E. Delaware Pl., Near North* ☎ *312/337–4001*) is suffused with a living-large ethos—from the oversize chandeliers to the extensive wine list to the international set that roosts here—in an appropriately sprawling space. In warmer months, a roomy Euro-style sidewalk café extends the seating options.

Motel (⊠ *600 W. Chicago Ave., River North* ☎ *312/822–2900*) has all the comforts of a real, honest-to-goodness motel bar (TVs tuned to sports, classic cocktails, and a retro color scheme), but the whole ordeal is amped-up with sexy, low-rise furniture, and a "room service" menu of upscale bites.

Fado (⊠ *100 W. Grand Ave., River North* ☎ *312/836–0066*) uses imported wood, stone, and glasswork to create its Irish look. The second floor—with bar imported from Dublin—feels more like the real thing than the first. There's expertly drawn Guinness, a fine selection of Irish whiskeys, live Irish music on weekends, and a menu of traditional Irish food.

Designer Nate Berkus assembled **Rockit's** (✉22 W. Hubbard St., River North ☎312/645–6000) hunter-lodge look: wood-plank-framed plasma TVs, antler chandeliers, and brown-leather booths. The crowd, much like the beer list, is diverse and tasteful, and despite the masculine vibe, there's a good mix of men and women. Dress to impress.

★ The **Signature Lounge** (✉875 N. Michigan Ave., Near North ☎312/787–9596) has no competition when it comes to views. Perched on the 96th floor of the John Hancock Center—above even the tower's observation deck—the bar offers stunning vistas of the skyline and lake for only the cost of a pricey drink.

Swirl Wine Bar (✉111 W. Hubbard St., River North ☎312/828–9000) has a cozy, shabby-chic lounge and snob-free approach to wine that is enough to disarm even the most jaded oenophiles. A list of 25 wines are available by the bottle, glass, quartino, and flight, and are thoughtfully arranged by flavor instead of region.

WICKER PARK & BUCKTOWN

Hip cats, artists, and yuppies converge on the famed six corners of North, Milwaukee, and Damen avenues, where the cast of Real World Chicago once resided. Previously scruffy and edgy, the area is now dotted with pricey, upscale bars, though the occasional honky-tonk still exists.

★ **California Clipper** (✉1002 N. California Ave., Wicker Park ☎773/384–2547), in Humboldt Park, just to the west of Wicker Park, has a 1940s vintage look, including a curving 60-foot-long Brunswick bar and tiny booths lining the long room back-to-back like seats on a train. Alternative country acts and soul-gospel DJs are part of the eccentric musical lineup.

The **Map Room** (✉1949 N. Hoyne Ave., Bucktown ☎773/252–7636) might help you find your way around Chicago, if not the world. Maps and travel books decorate the walls of this self-described "travelers' tavern," and the beers represent much of the world. Tuesday is international night, with a free buffet of cuisines from different countries.

The highly stylized **Rodan** (✉1530 N. Milwaukee Ave., Wicker Park ☎773/276–7036) is a restaurant-lounge that caters mostly to the young neighborhood hipsters who arrive at dinnertime (served until 11 PM) and stay put until closing. The narrow space often feels cramped but if you can snag a spot at the bar or on a blue-suede banquette, an evening of major league people-watching is in store. Snacks are served all night, so refuel with a pile of wasabi-tempura fries.

Northside Bar & Grill (✉*1635 N. Damen Ave., Wicker Park* ☎*773/384–3555*) was one of the first anchors of the now-teeming Wicker Park nightlife scene. Arty (and sometimes slightly yuppie) types come to drink, eat, shoot pool, and see and be seen. The enclosed indoor–outdoor patio lets you get the best out of the chancy Chicago weather.

> **WORD OF MOUTH**
>
> "I am a big fan of Sonotheque on Chicago Ave. Easy to get to via cab from downtown. Great space, great music, great crowd. Sometimes there's a cover, but it's minimal and the drinks are reasonable." –superk

Silver Cloud Bar & Grill (✉*1700 N. Damen Ave., Bucktown* ☎*773/489–6212*) might be the only place in the city where you can order a champagne cocktail alongside sloppy Joes and Tater Tots and not open yourself up to a citizen's arrest. For us, that's reason enough to go. Spacious red-leather booths, retro-fringed lamps, friendly service, and an upbeat neighborhood crowd round out the good points.

★ **Sonotheque** (✉*1444 W. Chicago Ave., Wicker Park* ☎*312/226–7600*), with its tasteful, modern design and sparse, podlike seating, is one of the more visually interesting lounges in Chicago. A thoughtful Scotch list, high-profile DJs, and down-to-earth service bring heavy crowds to West Town, a few blocks south of Wicker Park, on weekends.

Vintage Wine Bar (✉*1942 W. Division St., Wicker Park* ☎*773/772–3400*) offers reasonably priced vino (many bottles clock in around $30) in an attitude-free atmosphere. Choose a seat at the glowing lipstick-red bar, or relax in the lounge up front, where there's a working fireplace. Hungry? A serious menu lists everything from gourmet pizzas to artisanal cheese flights.

LINCOLN PARK

One of the most beautiful (and bustling) neighborhoods on the north side of Chicago, Lincoln Park is largely defined by the DePaul students who inhabit the area. Irish pubs and sports bars line the streets with college students, but intimate wine bars attract an older, more sophisticated set.

John Barleycorn (✉*658 W. Belden Ave., Lincoln Park* ☎*773/348–8899*), a historic pub with a long wooden bar, can get somewhat rowdy despite the classical music (played until 8 PM) and the art slides shown on video screens. It has a spacious summer beer garden, a good pub menu, and a wide selection of beers. Sibling locations are at 2142 North Clybourn Avenue in Lincoln Park West and 3524 North Clark Street in Wrigleyville.

There are two reasons to go to **Red Lion** (✉*2446 N. Lincoln Ave., Lincoln Park* ☎*773/348–2695*). The first is the British kitsch: check out the London Metro maps that line the walls, duck into the hulking red phone booth, and feast on fish-and-chips and Guinness or bangers-and-mash and hard cider. The second is the legend: a bookie joint in the 1930s, it's said to be one of America's most haunted places.

Webster's Wine Bar (⊠*1480 W. Webster Ave., Lincoln Park* ☎*773/868–0608*), a romantic place for a date, stocks more than 500 bottles of wine, with at least 30 by the glass, as well as ports, sherries, single-malt Scotches, a few microbrews, and a menu of small tasting entrées at reasonable prices.

Clybar (⊠*2417 N. Clybourn Ave., Lincoln Park* ☎*773/388–1877*) is one of the few Lincoln Park bars not filled to the brim with frat boys. Inside, sophisticates of all ages gather round to sip a stiff drink and carry on conversation. Booths and a roomy backroom couch are perfect for groups of four or more. Singles and smaller parties tend to stick to the bar, where chatty bartenders keep the conversation flowing as briskly as the shaken martinis. Twinkling lights, dark-wood furniture, and a cherrywood fireplace add a touch of romance for those in the mood.

LAKE VIEW & FAR NORTH SIDE

Lake View, Uptown, and Andersonville, all on the Far North Side, have one thing in common: affordability. Unbelievable as it sounds, there are places in the city where $20 stretches beyond the price of admission and a martini. Drink deals are frequently offered at many bars.

6

Gingerman Tavern (⊠*3740 N. Clark St., Lake View* ☎*773/549–2050*), up the street from Wrigley Field, deftly manages to avoid being pigeonholed as a sports bar. Folks here take their beer and billiards seriously, with three pool tables and—our favorite part—a list of more than 100 bottles of beer. New and vintage tunes crank out of the jukebox all night long.

Holiday Club (⊠*4000 N. Sheridan Rd., Far North Side* ☎*773/348–9600*) bills itself as the "Swinger's mecca." Rat Pack aficionados will appreciate the 1950s decor and well-stocked CD jukebox, which has selections ranging from Dean Martin and Frank Sinatra to early punk. Down a pint of good beer (or even bad beer in cans) and scan the typical (but tasty) bar menu.

★ **Hopleaf** (⊠*5148 N. Clark St., Far North Side* ☎*773/334–9851*), an anchor in the Andersonville corridor, continues the tradition of the classic Chicago bar hospitable to conversation (not a TV in sight). Pick one of the too-many-to-choose-from beers on the menu, with special offerings of Belgian beers and regional microbrews. A menu of Belgian bar fare usurps typical bar food options.

Sheffield's (⊠*3258 N. Sheffield Ave., Lake View* ☎*773/281–4989*) spans the seasons with a shaded beer garden in summer and a roaring fireplace in winter. This laid-back neighborhood pub has billiards and more than 100 kinds of bottled beer that change seasonally, including regional microbrews, the bartender's "bad beer of the month"—a cheap can of beer (think PBR)—as well as 18 brands on tap.

Space is so limited at **Joie de Vine** (⊠*1744 W. Balmoral Ave., Lake View* ☎*773/989–6846*), the wine barely has room to breathe. Good design (and sidewalk tables in summer months) saves the space from feeling claustrophobic. Sit at the long wooden bar or opposing banquette and

BARS WITH VIEWS

Vertigo is a small price to pay for these stellar views.

Castaways (✉ *1603 N. Lakeshore Dr., River North* ☎ *773/281–1200*) puts you so close to Lake Michigan, you might consider wearing a swimsuit. Perched atop the North Avenue Beach Boathouse, the breezy, casual bar and grill creates the perfect setup for lazy, summertime sipping.

When it comes to heights, **Signature Lounge** (✉ *875 N. Michigan Ave., Near North* ☎ *312/787–9596*)—set on the 96th floor of the John Hancock Center—is in a category all its own. Drinks and appetizers are pricey, but well worth it: the cityscape views are simply unmatched.

Glittering panoramic views of Lake Michigan and the city draw visitors worldwide to **Whiskey Sky** (✉ *644 N. Lakeshore Dr., Near North* ☎ *312/943–9200*). The W Hotel Lakeshore's plush, low-lit lounge also offers tasty cocktails, a cool vibe, and owner Rande Gerber's seal of approval.

enjoy the real focal point of the room, a glass brick wall lit up in multiple colors. All sorts of tasty delights, from wine (available in flights or by the glass) to olives and cheese, are reasonably priced. Try stopping by on a weeknight when the neighborhood regulars are least likely to crowd the slender bar.

CAFÉS

High-maintenance ("half-caff-double-foam-soy-latte-to-go") and low-maintenance ("cup 'o joe, black") coffee drinkers feel at home in the diverse range of cafés dotting the streets of Chicago's busiest North Side neighborhoods. Expect to spend anywhere from $2 to $6 (depending on your order) for a caffeinated beverage.

NEAR NORTH, WICKER PARK & BUCKTOWN

Caffe de Luca (✉ *1721 N. Damen Ave., Bucktown* ☎ *773/342–6000*) is the place to go when you crave air and light with your caffeine and calories. This sophisticated Bucktown spot hints at Tuscany with richly colored walls and a fine selection of Italian sandwiches, salads, and sorbets.

Earwax (✉ *1561 N. Milwaukee Ave., Wicker Park* ☎ *773/772–4019*) is a mecca for local vegans and vegetarians looking to order scrambled tofu alongside their ordinary cup of coffee. Well-worn, comfy furniture and a quirky staff go hand-in-hand with the relaxed atmosphere. A small selection of secondhand videos is for sale. Stop by for coffee, sweets, or a light meal.

Third Coast Café (✉ *1260 N. Dearborn St., Near North* ☎ *312/649–0730*), the oldest coffeehouse in the Gold Coast, lets you indulge your need for caffeine until midnight seven nights a week, with a full liquor, coffee, and food menu.

Café Ballou's (✉*939 N. Western Ave., near Wicker Park* ☎*773/342–2909*) European charm lies in details like a preserved tin ceiling, a squishy couch, and smooth marble tables. The inviting atmosphere at this café nestled in the Ukrainian Village, near Wicker Park, is a far cry from Starbucks, and you won't find many grab-and-go caffeine addicts here. Choose from a menu of international sippers that are served according to tradition, like Turkish coffee brewed on a hot plate inside a mound of sand, or Russian tea drizzled with cherry compote. The friendly owner speaks fluent Polish and Ukrainian, most often to her customers, many of whom are local neighborhood immigrants.

LAKE VIEW & FAR NORTH SIDE

Intelligentsia (✉*3123 N. Broadway, Lake View* ☎*773/348–8058*) was named to invoke the prechain days when cafés were forums for discussion, but the long, broad farmer's tables and handsome couches are usually occupied by students and other serious types who treat the café like their office. The store does all of its own coffee roasting and sells its custom blends to local restaurants.

Kopi, a Traveler's Cafe (✉*5317 N. Clark St., Far North Side* ☎*773/989–5674*) is a study in opposites, with healthy vegetarian options as well as decadent desserts. In the Andersonville district, a 20-minute cab ride from downtown, this café has a selection of travel books (for sale), foreign artifacts, and artfully painted tables.

The **Pick Me Up Café** (✉*3408 N. Clark St., Lake View* ☎*773/248–6613*) combines the charm of a quirky, neighborhood café with the late-night hours of those chain diners. The thrift-store treasures hanging on the walls are as eclectic as the crowd that comes at all hours of the day and night to drink bottomless cups of coffee or dine on sandwiches, appetizers, and desserts.

Uncommon Ground's (✉*3800 N. Clark St., Lake View* ☎*773/929–3680*) expanded Lake View location is roomier and smoke-free. It continues to deliver the goods with bowls of coffee, hot chocolate, a full bar, and a hearty, all-day food menu. Fun perks include two fireplaces, a sidewalk café, and a steady lineup of acoustic musical acts.

COMEDY & IMPROV CLUBS

Improvisation has long had a successful following in Chicago; stand-up comedy hasn't fared as well. Most comedy clubs have a cover charge ($5 to $20); many have a two-drink minimum on top of that. In the stand-up circuit, keep an eye out for performances by Steve Harvey, star of his own WB television series.

Barrel of Laughs (✉*10345 S. Central Ave., Oaklawn* ☎*708/499–2969*), in the city's southwest suburbs (a 30-minute drive from downtown), spotlights local and national comics. The dinner package includes a meal at the adjacent Senese's restaurant and reserved seats at the show.

ComedySportz (⊠*929 W. Belmont Ave., Lake View* ☎*773/549–8080*) specializes in "competitive improv," in which two teams vie for the audience's favor.

I.O. (⊠*3541 N. Clark St., Lake View* ☎*773/880–0199*) (formerly called ImprovOlympic) has shows with student and professional improvisation in two intimate spaces every night of the week. Team members present long-form comedic improvisations drawn on audience suggestions, including an improvised musical and a Monday-night alumni show. No drink or age minimum.

★ **Second City** (⊠*1616 N. Wells St., Near North* ☎*312/337–3992*), an institution since 1959, has served as a launching pad for some of the hottest comedians around. Alumni include Dan Aykroyd and the late John Belushi. Funny, loony skit comedy is presented on two stages, with a free improv set after the show every night but Friday.

Zanies (⊠*1548 N. Wells St., Near North* ☎*312/337–4027*) books outstanding national talent and is Chicago's best stand-up comedy spot. Jay Leno, Jerry Seinfeld, and Jackie Mason have all performed at this intimate venue.

DANCE CLUBS

Most clubs don't get crowded until 11 or midnight, and they remain open into the early-morning hours. Cover charges range from $5 to $20. A few dance clubs have dress codes that don't allow jeans, gym shoes, or baseball caps.

To avoid the exhausting lines and cover charges at most nightclubs, chat with your hotel concierge or even your server at dinner. Admission into the VIP lounges of Chicago's hottest clubs is often a conversation-with-the-right-person away from becoming a reality.

Great news for those who like to club hop: most of Chicago's best dance clubs (Sound-Bar, Transit, and Le Passage, to name a few) are within the Near North and River North neighborhoods, just north of downtown. The close proximity makes it relatively easy (and cheap) to cab it from one club to another. Wicker Park and Lake View are also good 'hoods for when you feel like dancing.

Fodor's Choice **Berlin** (⊠*954 W. Belmont Ave., Lake View* ☎*773/348–4975*), a mul-
★ ticultural, pansexual dance club near the Belmont El station, has progressive electronic dance music and fun theme nights—Madonna and Prince are celebrated on the first and last Sunday of the month, and one Wednesday a month is devoted to disco. The crowd tends to be predominantly gay on weeknights, mixed on weekends.

Crobar—The Nightclub (⊠*1543 N. Kingsbury St., Near North* ☎*312/266–1900*) has scrapped its scruffy, Goth-like decor for a sprawling South Beach makeover complete with a glass-enclosed VIP lounge and booth-lined balcony. Top DJs spin house and techno over the enormous dance floor on Wednesday, Friday, and Saturday nights.

CLOSE UP

Looking for Laughs? Try Improv

Mike Myers, Tina Fey, Bill Murray, John Belushi, Dan Aykroyd, Alan Alda, Shelley Long, Ed Asner, John Candy, Andy Dick. These are just a few of the comic actors who, were they to attempt to trace their path to stardom, might credit nights spent improvising on Chicago stages.

Chicago was the birthplace of the improvisational comedy form some 50-odd years ago, and the city remains the country's primary breeding ground for this challenging art form. Performers, usually working in an ensemble, ask the audience for a suggestion, then launch into short, long, silly, serious, or surreal scenes loosely related to that original audience input.

Second City (☎ 312/337–3992) is the anchor of Chicago improv. The revues on the company's main stage and in its smaller e.t.c. space next door are actually sketch comedy shows, but the scripts in these pre-rehearsed scenes have been developed through improvisation and there's usually a little time set aside in each show for the performers to demonstrate their quick wit. Most nights there is a free improv set after the late show featuring cast members and invited guests (sometimes famous, sometimes not, never announced in advance). It's in Donny's Skybox upstairs that you're more likely to see one of Chicago's many fledgling improv comedy troupes making their first appearance working together on freshly penned material in public.

I.O. (☎ 773/880–0199) (formerly called ImprovOlympic) is the city's home of long-form improvisation. The signature piece is "The Harold," in which a team of improvisers explores a single audience suggestion throughout a series of stories and characters until they all eventually weave back together to fit with the original audience idea. At **ComedySportz Chicago** (☎ 773/549–8080), teams of professional improvisers perform songs and scenes all based on your suggestions in an audience-interactive competition. The itinerant group **Annoyance,** now settled into its new home in Uptown at 4840 North Broadway, is best known for past hits *Coed Prison Sluts* and *Splatter Theatre*.

Scope out the hordes of up-and-comers at neighborhood stages such as the **Playground Theater** (☎ 773/871–3793).

The springtime **Chicago Improv Festival** (☎ 773/935–9810), the nation's largest festival for improvisers, has stages devoted to group, pair, and single improv and sketch comedy and more.

6

Excalibur (✉ *632 N. Dearborn St., River North* ☎ *312/266–1944*) won't win any prizes for breaking new ground, but this River North nightclub complex, carved out of the Romanesque fortress that was the original home of the Chicago Historical Society, has been going strong for years with its mix of dancing, dining, and posing. At the same address and phone number but with a separate entrance is the smaller, alternative-dance club **Vision.** ■TIP➔ **Deejays and music styles change regularly (consequently, so does the club's vibe), so be sure to call ahead for information on the night's selections.**

Funky is the operative word for the **Funky Buddha Lounge** (⊠ *728 W. Grand Ave., Wicker Park* ☎ *312/666–1695*), with its diverse crowd, seductive dance music, and a big metal Buddha guarding the front door. It has an intimate bar and dark dance floor, where patrons groove as DJs spin dance hall, hip-hop, R&B, funk, and old-school house. The VIP room in back can be declared no-smoking upon request.

Le Passage (⊠ *937 N. Rush St., Near North* ☎ *312/255–0022*) is in the Gold Coast area, but it feels like an underground Parisian nightclub, complete with low ceilings, dim lighting, and French-colonial furniture. Stop in for an early-evening cocktail and plate of French-inspired cuisine and stay for late-night dancing. DJs spin house and hip-hop Thursday through Saturday.

Spy Bar (⊠ *646 N. Franklin St., River North* ☎ *312/587–8779*) pulls some smooth moves. Image is everything at this subterranean spot with a brushed stainless-steel bar and exposed brick walls. The slick, stylish crowd hits the tight dance floor for house, underground, and DJ remixes.

FodorśChoice ★ **Sound-Bar** (⊠ *226 W. Ontario St., River North* ☎ *312/787–4480*) reigns supreme as Chicago's trendiest and busiest dance club. Weave your way through a bi-level labyrinth of nine bars, each with a unique design and color scheme (some even serve matching colored cocktails), or nestle into one of four sleek boutique lounges. Feel like dancing? Join the pulse of Chicago's best-dressed on the huge dance floor.

Transit (⊠ *1431 W. Lake St., West Loop* ☎ *312/491–8600 or 312/491–9729*), despite being hidden away underneath the El tracks in a spooky stretch west of downtown, is wildly popular with young clubgoers. Inside, the multiroom space has a crisp design, earthy colors, and sumptuous VIP area.

GAY & LESBIAN NIGHTLIFE

Chicago's gay bars appeal to mixed crowds and tastes. Most are on North Halsted Street from Belmont Avenue to Irving Park Road, an area nicknamed Boys Town. Bars generally stay open until 2 AM weekends, but a few keep the lights on until 5 AM Sunday morning. The *Chicago Free Press, Windy City Times,* and *Gay Chicago* list nightspots, events, and gay and lesbian resources; all three are free and can be picked up at bookstores, bars, and some supermarkets, especially those in Boys Town.

Big Chicks (⊠ *5024 N. Sheridan Rd., Far North Side* ☎ *773/728–5511*), in the Uptown area of the Far North Side, is a striking alternative to the Halsted strip, with a funky crowd that appreciates the owner's art collection hanging on the walls. The fun-loving staff and their self-selected eclectic music are the payoffs for the hike to get here. Special attractions include weekend dancing and free Sunday-afternoon buffets.

Charlie's (⊠ *3726 N. Broadway, Lake View* ☎ *773/871–8887*), a country-and-western dance club, lets you two-step nightly to achy-breaky tunes, though dance music is played every night from 2 AM to 4 AM. It's mostly a boots-and-denim crowd on weekends.

Circuit (✉ *3641 N. Halsted St., Lake View* ☎ *773/325–2233*), the biggest dance club in Boys Town, is a stripped-down dance hall energized by flashing lights, booming sounds, and a partying crowd. Take a break in the up-front martini bar, Rehab.

The **Closet** (✉ *3325 N. Broadway, Lake View* ☎ *773/477–8533*) is a basic Chicago tavern with a gay twist. This compact bar—one of the few that caters to lesbians, though it draws gay men, too—can be especially lively after 2 AM when most other bars close. Stop by Sunday afternoons when bartenders serve up what are hailed as the best Bloody Marys in town.

Gentry (✉ *440 N. State St., River North* ☎ *312/836–0933*), one of the few gay bars downtown, is a premier piano bar/cabaret, featuring local and national talent. Sophisticates linger at the upscale piano bar; the video bar downstairs attracts a younger group. A smaller, Boys Town branch is at 3320 North Halsted Street.

Roscoe's Tavern (✉ *3356 N. Halsted St., Lake View* ☎ *773/281–3355*), in the heart of Boys Town, is a longtime favorite with a mix of amenities sure to please its peppy patrons, including a jam-packed front bar, a dance floor, a pool table, an outdoor garden, and lively music. The sidewalk café serves May through September.

The video bar **Sidetrack** (✉ *3349 N. Halsted St., Lake View* ☎ *773/477–9189*) is tuned into a different theme every night of the week, from show tunes on Monday to comedy on Thursday—all broadcast on TV screens that never leave your sight. The sprawling stand-and-pose bar and rooftop deck are always busy with a good-looking, professional crowd, and the vodka slushies are a house specialty.

At **Hydrate** (✉ *3458 N. Halsted St., Lake View* ☎ *773/975–9244*), sip a slushy in the blue-tinged front room, or head to the flashy mirror-banked dance floor, where an international roster of DJs spins nightly.

MUSIC

COUNTRY

There are slim pickin's for country-music clubs in Chicago, even though country radio continues to draw wide audiences.

Carol's Pub (✉ *4659 N. Clark St., Far North Side* ☎ *773/334–2402*), in the Uptown area of the Far North Side, showcased country before it was ever cool. The house band at this urban honky-tonk plays country and country-rock tunes on weekends, and the popular karaoke night on Thursday draws all walks of life, from preppie to punk.

★ **The Hideout** (⊠*1354 W. Wabansia, Bucktown* ☎*773/227–4433*), which is literally hidden away in a North Side industrial zone, has managed to make country music hip in Chicago. Players on the city's

alternative country scene have adopted the friendly hole-in-the-wall, and bands ranging from the obscure to the semi-famous take the stage. The bluegrass band Devil in a Woodpile plays on Tuesday.

ECLECTIC

Clubs in this category don't limit themselves to a single type of music. Call ahead to find out what's playing.

At **Baton Show Lounge** (⊠*436 N. Clark St., River North* ☎*312/644–5269*), boys will be girls. The lip-synching revues with female impersonators have catered to curious out-of-towners and bachelorette parties since 1969. Some of the regular performers, such as Chili Pepper and Mimi Marks, have become Chicago cult figures. The more the audience tips, the better the show gets, so bring your bills.

Beat Kitchen (⊠*2100 W. Belmont Ave., Lake View* ☎*773/281–4444*) brings in the crowds because of its good sound system and local and touring rock, alternative-rock, country, and rockabilly acts. It also serves soups, salads, sandwiches, pizzas, and desserts.

Elbo Room (⊠*2871 N. Lincoln Ave., Lincoln Park* ☎*773/549–5549*), a multilevel space in an elbow-shape corner building, has a basement rec-room feel. The bar plays host to talented live bands seven days a week, with a strong dose of nu-jazz, funk, soul, pop, and rock.

FitzGerald's (⊠*6615 W. Roosevelt Rd., Berwyn* ☎*708/788–2118*), though a 30-minute schlep west of Chicago, draws crowds from all over the city and suburbs with its mix of folk, jazz, blues, zydeco, and rock. This early 1900s roadhouse has great sound and sight lines for its roots music.

FodorsChoice **HotHouse** (⊠*31 E. Balbo Ave., South Loop* ☎*312/362–9707*) bills
★ itself as "the center for international performance and exhibition," and delivers globe-spanning musical offerings—Spanish guitar one night, mambo the next—in a spacious venue that can be counted on to draw an interesting crowd.

★ **House of Blues** (⊠*329 N. Dearborn St., River North* ☎*312/923–2000*), though its name implies otherwise, attracts big-name performers of all genres, from jazz, roots, blues, and gospel to alternative rock, hip-hop, world, and R&B. The interior is an elaborate cross between blues bar and ornate opera house. Its restaurant has live blues every night on a "second stage," as well as a satisfying Sunday gospel brunch. Part of the Marina City complex, the entrance is on State Street.

FOLK & ETHNIC

Old Town School of Folk Music (✉*4544 N. Lincoln Ave., Far North Side* ☎*773/728–6000*), Chicago's first and oldest folk-music school, has served as folk central in the city since 1957. This friendly spot in Lincoln Square hosts outstanding performances by national and local acts in a 420-seat concert hall.

Wild Hare (✉*3530 N. Clark St., Lake View* ☎*773/327–0868*), with a wide-open dance floor, is the place for infectious live reggae and world-beat music seven nights a week.

JAZZ

Jazz thrives all around town. For a recorded listing of upcoming live performances, call the **Jazz Institute Hot Line** (☎*312/427–3300*).

Andy's (✉*11 E. Hubbard St., River North* ☎*312/642–6805*), a favorite after-work watering hole with a substantial bar menu, has live, local jazz daily. In addition to the evening performances, there's a jazz program at noon on weekdays—a boon for music lovers who aren't night owls.

Green Dolphin Street (✉*2200 N. Ashland Ave., Lake View* ☎*773/395–0066*), a stylish, upscale club-restaurant with the glamour of the 1940s (in a converted auto-body shop, no less), attracts tight ensembles and smooth-voiced jazz divas for big band, bebop, Latin, and world jazz.

★ **Green Mill** (✉*4802 N. Broadway, Far North Side* ☎*773/878–5552*), a Chicago institution off the beaten track in not-so-trendy Uptown, has been around since 1907. Deep leather banquettes and ornate wood paneling line the walls, and a photo of Al Capone occupies a place of honor on the piano behind the bar. The jazz entertainment is both excellent and contemporary—the club launched the careers of Kurt Elling and Patricia Barber—and the Uptown Poetry Slam, a competitive poetry reading, takes center stage on Sunday.

After 24 years of living in Lake View, **Pops for Champagne** (✉*601 N. State St., River North* ☎*312/266–7677*) has up and moved to trendy River North. The new bi-level space is gloriously turned out with a champagne bar, raw bar, sidewalk café, and even a retail space called Pops Shop. Grab your (champagne) flute and head downstairs to the stylish jazz lounge for live music Tuesday through Saturday.

The owner of **Velvet Lounge** (✉*67 E. Cermak Rd., Near South* ☎*312/791–9050*), saxophonist Fred Anderson, has relocated his beloved institution to a cozy Near South locale, but the heart and soul of the place remains the same. Stop in for traditional and avant-garde jazz Tuesday through Saturday. Sunday is still Jam Session day.

ROCK

Chicago has an active rock scene with many local favorites, some of which—including Smashing Pumpkins, Wilco, and Liz Phair—have won national acclaim. Bone up on Chicago's rock scene by tuning into 91.5 Chicago Public Radio's Sound Opinions, a weekly radio show

OUR FAVORITE DIVE BARS

Matchbox (✉ *770 N. Milwaukee Ave., Wicker Park* ☎ *312/666–9292*), in West Town near Wicker Park, isn't much bigger than a you-know-what, but the hodgepodge of regulars don't seem to mind. In fact, many claim it's the dark, cramped quarters (and dirty martinis) that keep them coming back. The crowd spills outside in summer, when iron rod tables dot the sidewalk.

Rainbo Club (✉ *1150 N. Damen Ave., Wicker Park* ☎ *773/489–5999*) is the unofficial meeting place for Chicago hipsters and indie rockers. Apart from the working photo booth wedged into a corner, the stripped-down hangout is pretty barren, but drinks are dirt cheap and the bartenders are upbeat—and willing —conversationalists.

hosted by *Chicago Tribune* and *Chicago Sun-Times* rock critics, Greg Kot and Jim DeRogatis. The program airs Friday at 8 PM and Saturday at 11 AM.

The Abbey (✉ *3420 W. Grace St., Far North Side* ☎ *773/478–4408*), about 15 minutes northwest of downtown in the Irving Park neighborhood, showcases rock, as well as some Irish, Celtic, and country music, in a large concert hall with a separate, busy, smoky pub. By day, the hall is used to show soccer and rugby games from the United Kingdom and Ireland.

Double Door (✉ *1572 N. Milwaukee Ave., Wicker Park* ☎ *773/489–3160*) is a hotbed for music in hip Wicker Park. The large bar books up-and-coming local and national acts from rock to acid jazz. Unannounced Rolling Stones shows have been held here. The entrance is on Damen Avenue.

Empty Bottle (✉ *1035 N. Western Ave., Wicker Park* ☎ *773/276–3600*), in the Ukrainian Village near Wicker Park, may have toys and knick-knacks around the bar (including a case of macabre baby doll heads), but when it comes to booking rock, punk, and jazz bands from the indie scene, it's a serious place with no pretensions.

Martyrs' (✉ *3855 N. Lincoln Ave., Far North Side* ☎ *773/404–9869*) brings local and major-label rock bands to this small, North Side neighborhood sandwiched between Lincoln Square and Roscoe Village. Music fans can see the stage from just about any corner of the bar, while the more rhythmically inclined gyrate in the large standing-room area. A mural opposite the stage memorializes late rock greats.

Metro (✉ *3730 N. Clark St., Lake View* ☎ *773/549–0203*) brings in progressive, nationally known artists and the cream of the local crop. A former movie palace, it's an excellent place to see live bands, whether you're moshing on the main floor or above the fray in the balcony. In

Continued on page 221

CHICAGO STILL SINGS THE BLUES

The cool, electric, urban blues are the soundtrack of the Windy City. The blues traveled up the Mississippi River with the Delta sharecroppers during the Great Migration, settled down on Maxwell Street and South Side clubs, and gave birth to such big-name talent as Muddy Waters, Howlin' Wolf, Willie Dixon, and, later, Koko Taylor. Today, you can still hear the blues in a few South Side clubs where it all began, or check out the current scene on the North Side.

THE BIRTH OF THE CHICAGO BLUES

CHESS RECORDS

Founded by Philip and Leonard Chess, Polish immigrant brothers, in 1947. For the first two years, the label was called Aristocrat.

Its famous address, 2120 S. Michigan Avenue, was the nucleus of the blues scene. Up-and-comers performed on the sidewalk out front in hopes of being discovered. Even today, locals and visitors peek through the windows of the restored studio (now the Blues Heaven Foundation) looking for glimpses of past glory.

The label's first hit record was Muddy Waters' *I Can't Be Satisfied*.

The brothers were criticized for having a paternalistic relationship with their artists. They reportedly bought Muddy Waters a car off the lot when he wasn't able to finance it himself.

The label was sold in 1969 after Leonard's death.

Did you know? When the Rolling Stones recorded the track "2120 South Michigan Avenue" (off the *12 x 5* album) at the Chess Records studio in June 1964, the young Brits were reportedly so nervous about singing in front of Willie Dixon (Buddy Guy and Muddy Waters were also hanging around the studio that day) that they literally became tongue-tied. As a result, the song is purely instrumental.

WILLIE DIXON (7/1915–1/1992)

Chess Records' leading A & R (artist and repertoire) man, bass player, and composer. Founded the Blues Heaven Foundation, Chess Records' restored office and studio. *See Blues Heaven Foundation review next page.*

Famous compositions: "Hoochie Coochie Man" (recorded by Muddy Waters), "My Babe" (recorded by Little Walter), and "Wang Dang Doodle" (recorded by Koko Taylor)

MUDDY WATERS: KING OF ELECTRIC BLUES (4/1915–4/1983)

When Muddy Waters gave his guitar an electric jolt, he didn't just revolutionize the blues. His electric guitar became a magic wand: Its jive talk (and cry) turned country-blues into city-blues, and it gave birth to rock and roll. Waters' signature sound has been firmly imprinted on nearly all subsequent musical genres.

Best known for: Riveting vocals, a swooping pompadour, and, of course, plugging in the guitar

Biggest break: Leonard Chess, one of the Chess brothers of Chess Records, let Waters record two of his own songs. The record sold out in two days, and stores issued a dictum of "one per customer"

Biggest song: "Hoochie Coochie Man"

Lyrics: *Y'know I'm here / Everybody knows I'm here / And I'm the hoochie-coochie man*

Awards: 3 Grammies, Lifetime Achievement induction into the Rock and Roll Hall of Fame

Local honor: A strip of 43rd Street in Chicago is renamed Muddy Waters Drive

HOWLIN' WOLF (6/1910–1/1976)

In 1951, at the age of 41, Wolf recorded with Sun Studios in Memphis, TN. Shortly thereafter, Sun sold Wolf's only two songs, "Moanin' At Midnight" and "How Many More Years," to Chess Records, kicking off his prolific recording career with Chess.

Most popular songs: "Backdoor Man" and "Little Red Rooster"

Instruments: Electric guitar and harmonica

Dedication to his craft: Wolf was still taking guitar lessons even a year before his death, even though he was long recognized as one of the two greatest blues musicians in the world.

THE CHICAGO BLUES TODAY

KOKO TAYLOR:
Queen of the Blues

Blessed with neither Bessie Smith's beauty nor Billie Holiday's power of seduction, Taylor offers grit; a been-there-done-that wisdom that personified urban-blues by the 1970s.

Best known for: Slam-bang stage presence and powerhouse vocals

Big break: It wasn't until Chess Records blues producer Willie Dixon saw her singing at a South Side club one night in the early 1960s that her career really took off. Dixon reportedly said, "My God, I've never heard a woman sing the blues like you," and signed her up to record

Biggest song: "Wang Dang Doodle" sold a staggering one million copies in six weeks

Lyrics: *We gonna jump and shout 'til daylight / We gonna pitch a wang dang doodle / All night long*

Most significant hardship: Gettin' paid. Though Taylor was a star, she barely saw a penny of the profits while working with Chess Records and Willie Dixon

Awards: 25 W.C. Handy Awards (more than any other recording artist, male or female); a Grammy for *Blues Explosion*, 1984; Legend of the Year by Mayor Daley in 1993

Local honor: March 3rd is Koko Taylor Day in Chicago

Catch her act: Upcoming tour information is available at www.kokotaylor.com

BEST PLACES TO HEAR THE BLUES

Checkerboard Lounge (✉ 5201 S. Harper Ct., Hyde Park ☎ 773/684–1472) has reopened in Hyde Park! It was a sad day for blues fans when the world-famous Bronzeville location, owned by Buddy Guy in the 1970s and early 1980s, closed in 2003. Though the new location's in a shopping center—a far cry from its former gritty digs—it has the same diverse selection of local and big-name blues and jazz talent. Kudos on retaining some of the old picnic tables (used inside) from the first location. Note: Call ahead for information on the cover charge, which ranges from $3 to $20 depending on who's playing.

Chicago Blues Festival (☎ 312/744–3370) There's no doubt about it; Chicago still loves to sing the blues. Each June, the city pulses with sounds from the largest free blues festival in the world, which takes place over four days and on six stages in both Grant Park and Millennium Park. The always-packed open air festival has been headlined by blues legends such as B.B. King, Koko Taylor, and Buddy Guy.

Set in an upscale part of downtown, **Blue Chicago** (✉ 536 N. Clark St., River North ☎ 312/661–0100 ✉ 736 N. Clark St., River North ☎ 312/642–6261) has none of the trademark grit or edginess of the older South Side blues clubs. It does have two bars within two blocks of each other.

BUDDY GUY

Though he recorded his first album in 1958, Guy didn't really take off until he recorded with Vanguard in 1968 and was sent on tour with blues harmonica legend Junior Wells and the Rolling Stones.

Instrument: Electric guitar

Influenced: His stinging guitar playing had strong influences on Jimi Hendrix and Eric Clapton

Catch his act: Guy is still impressing fans with his sizzling guitar and vocals both on tour and in his Chicago-based club, Buddy Guy's Legends

Honors: 2005 inductee to the Rock and Roll Hall of Fame

DON'T MISS ACTS:

If these acts are playing when you're in town, don't miss them. For contact information for the venues mentioned below, see the club reviews on this page.

Classic slide-guitar and hard-driving blues beats mixed with jazz and even rock 'n' roll influences makes **Melvin Taylor & The Slack Band** a must-see. Call Rosa's Lounge for details. **Gloria Shannon Blues Band** plays everything from Delta blues to electric blues to Chicago blues. Catch their all-ages act every Saturday "Down in the Basement" at the Blue Chicago Store. **Billy Branch and the Sons Of Blues** frequently bring their forward-thinking sounds (steeped in blues tradition) to Rosa's Lounge and Kingston Mines, though they have been known to make rousing on-stage appearances at the Chicago Blues Festival.

Both have good sound systems, regularly book female vocalists, and attract a cosmopolitan audience that's a tad more diverse than some of the baseball-capped crowds at Lincoln Park blues clubs. We like that one cover gets you into both bars.

The **Blue Chicago Store** (✉ 534 N. Clark St., River North ☎ 312/661–1003) sells a variety of Blue Chicago–related souvenirs, from CDs and T-shirts to posters and books.

★ The best part about **B.L.U.E.S.** (✉ 2519 N. Halsted St., Lincoln Park ☎ 773/528–1012) is that there isn't a bad seat in the smoky joint. The worst part? The

smoke (stay away if you can't stand cigarettes). Narrow and intimate, the jam-packed North Side club has attracted the best in local talent since it opened in 1979. Big names such as Son Seals, Otis Rush, Jimmy Johnson, and Magic Slim have all played here.

★ Fodor's Choice **Buddy Guy's Legends** (✉ 754 S. Wabash Ave., South Loop ☎ 312/427–0333) serves up Louisiana-style barbecue along with the blues. The big club has good sound, good sight lines, and pool tables if you get restless in between sets. Look for local blues acts during the week and larger-scale touring acts on weekends. Don't miss Grammy

A MODERN HISTORY LESSON:

The Blues Heaven Foundation (✉ 2120 S. Michigan Ave., South Loop ☎ 312/808–1286)

Breathe the same rarefied air as blues (and rock 'n' roll) legends Muddy Waters, Howlin' Wolf, Chuck Berry, and the Rolling Stones, all of whom recorded here. Check out the Chess brothers' private offices, the recording studio, and the back stairway used only by signed musicians. Don't miss the eerie "Life Cast Portraits" wall showcasing the plaster heads of the Chess recording artists.

Note: Make a phone reservation before stopping by–the Foundation keeps irregular hours.

Award winning blues performer/owner Buddy Guy in January, when he performs a month-long home stand of shows (tickets go on sale one month in advance).

In 1968, **Kingston Mines** (✉ 2548 N. Halsted St., Lincoln Park ☎ 773/477–4646) went down in Chicago history as the first blues club to open on the North Side. Though it's since moved to bigger digs, it still offers the same traditional sounds and late-night hours as the original club. Swarms of blues lovers and par-

tying singles take in the good blues and tasty barbecue.

★ **Fodor's Choice** **Lee's Unleaded Blues** (✉ 7401 S. South Chicago Ave., Grand Crossing ☎ 773/493–3477) has been a South Side favorite since it opened in the early 1970's. Locals come decked out in their showiest threads and University of Chicago students often pop in for a round. The cramped, triangular bar may inhibit free movement, but that doesn't seem to bother the crowd that comes for powerhouse blues and jazz. Note: the club can be difficult to find if you don't know the area, so be sure to take a cab or study a map before making the trip.

★ **Fodor's Choice** On a given night at **Rosa's Lounge,** (✉ 3420 W. Armitage Ave., Bucktown in Logan Square ☎ 773/342–0452) near Bucktown, you'll find Tony, the owner, working the crowd, and his mother, Rosa, behind the bar. What makes the club extra special is that the duo moved here from Italy out of a pure love for the blues. Stop by and partake in Rosa's winning mixture of big-name and local talent, stiff drinks, and friendly service—the same since it opened in 1984.

the basement is **Smart Bar,** a late-night dance club that starts hopping after midnight.

Schubas Tavern (✉3159 N. Southport Ave., Lake View ☎773/525–2508) favors local and national power pop and indie rock bands. The wood-paneled back room has a laid-back atmosphere and good seating. The bar was built in 1900 by the Schlitz Brewing Company, and it still sells Schlitz beer—a bargain at about $2 a pop.

PIANO BARS

Coq d'Or (✉140 E. Walton St., Near North ☎312/932–4623) is a dark, wood-paneled room where Chicago legend Buddy Charles held court before retiring. Fine music and cocktails served in blown-glass goblets draw hotel guests as well as neighborhood regulars.

Davenport's (✉1383 N. Milwaukee Ave., Wicker Park ☎773/278–1830), a sophisticated cabaret booking both local and touring acts, brings a grown-up presence to the Wicker Park club scene. The piano lounge is set up for casual listening, while the cabaret room is a no-chat zone that requires your full attention—as well as reservations and a two-drink minimum.

The dueling pianists at **Howl at the Moon** (✉26 W. Hubbard St., Near North ☎312/863–7427) attract a rowdy crowd who delight in belting out popular tunes along with the pianos. Reservations aren't accepted, but party packages are available if you're willing to shell out beaucoup bucks (around $150) to avoid hassles like waiting in line and paying a cover charge.

★ **Pump Room** (✉Omni Ambassador East Hotel, 1301 N. State Pkwy., Near North ☎312/266–0360) shows off its storied past with photos of celebrities covering the walls. The bar at this restaurant has live piano music and a small dance floor that calls out for dancing cheek to cheek, especially on weekends.

Zebra Lounge (✉1220 N. State St., Near North ☎312/642–5140), small and funky with a striped motif, attracts a good crowd of dressed-up and dressed-down regulars who come to sing along to the pianist on duty.

SPORTS BARS

Gamekeepers (✉345 W. Armitage Ave., Lincoln Park ☎773/549–0400) is full of former frat boys and sports fans. With more than 40 TVs, three projection screens, and complete satellite sports coverage, there's barely a game Gamekeepers doesn't get.

Hi-Tops (✉3551 N. Sheffield Ave., Lake View ☎773/348–0009), within a ball's toss of Wrigley Field, may be the ultimate sports bar. Big-screen TVs, a lively crowd, and good bar food keep the Cubs fans coming. A dozen satellites and 65 TV monitors ensure that the place gets packed for a good game.

North Beach Chicago (⊠*1551 N. Sheffield Ave., Lincoln Park* ☎*312/266–7842*) is all about channeling your inner child. Multiple large-screen TVs plus two sand-filled indoor volleyball courts, pool tables, four bowling lanes, a mechanical bull, and even Sumo wrestling all contribute to generalized regression.

Sluggers (⊠*3540 N. Clark St., Lake View* ☎*773/248–0055*) is packed after Cubs games in the nearby stadium, and the ballplayers make occasional appearances in summer. Check out the fast- and slow-pitch batting cages on the second floor, as well as the pool tables, air hockey tables, and electronic basketball.

Where to Eat

WORD OF MOUTH

"For breakfast, Orange in Lincoln Park is not to be missed. I had eggs Benedict made with filet mignon (instead of Canadian bacon) over brioche, topped with hollandaise sauce and a drizzle of balsamic vinegar.

—sweet_polly

"Alinea is an amazing place. Some bites that you will always remember. I highly recommend that you go once."

—Lightspeed_Chick

THE SCENE

Updated by
Elaine Glusac
and Jay
Cheshes

Chicago is a city sans snobbery when it comes to food. The collective appetite champions both haute and street cuisine. Mediocrity, at any price level, just doesn't fly here, which makes Chicago a reliably tasty town to tour.

Down low, Chicago is famed for hot dogs, deep-dish pizza, and Italian beef sandwiches. On the high end, the city launched celebrity chef Charlie Trotter, cutting-edge molecular gastronomist Grant Achatz of Alinea, and Rick Bayless, who introduced the nation to authentic regional Mexican cuisine at Frontera Grill.

The city is home to over 7,000 restaurants, the most prominent of which cluster close to downtown expense accounts. But many of the most exciting restaurants that have opened in the past several years have been in residential neighborhoods, from Alinea in Lincoln Park to Spacca Napoli and Terragusto on the Far North Side to Spring in Wicker Park. The trend may reflect escalating downtown rents, which have nudged independents out of River North as chains take their places.

Sushi purveyors and small-plate specialists are now as ubiquitous as corner taverns once were. In the fight to keep their liquor licenses, many of these taverns are serving food, boosting bar fare by making burgers out of Kobe beef and serving fries with aioli. Chicago's steakhouse tradition dates to the days when the city was the railroad hub of the nation, sending meat in all directions from its near South Side stockyards. Lately the local steak house has been updated as big-name chefs, including Shawn McClain and David Burke, expand expectations and make the atmosphere less men's-club exclusive.

In coming years expect to see more outsiders in Chicago (Joël Robuchon is already on his way) eager to feed a populace that knows good food and isn't shy about eating it, at every level.

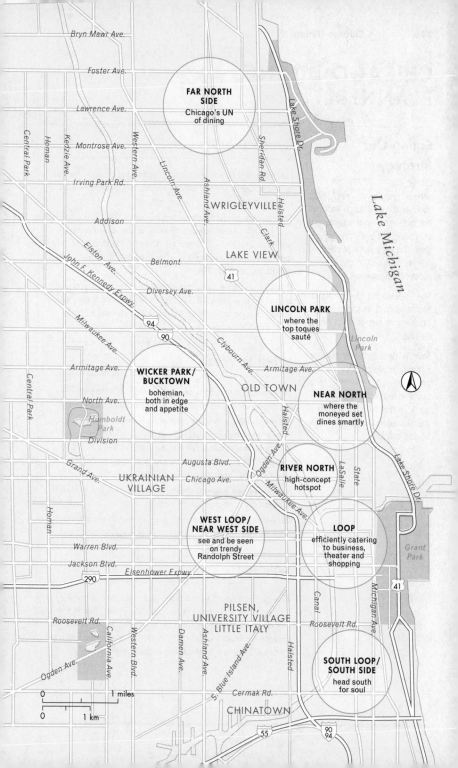

FAR NORTH SIDE
Chicago's UN
of dining

WRIGLEYVILLE

LAKE VIEW

LINCOLN PARK
where the
top toques
sauté

**WICKER PARK/
BUCKTOWN**
bohemian,
both in edge
and appetite

OLD TOWN

NEAR NORTH
where the
moneyed set
dines smartly

UKRAINIAN
VILLAGE

RIVER NORTH
high-concept
hotspot

**WEST LOOP/
NEAR WEST SIDE**
see and be seen
on trendy
Randolph Street

LOOP
efficiently catering
to business,
theater and
shopping

PILSEN,
UNIVERSITY VILLAGE
LITTLE ITALY

**SOUTH LOOP/
SOUTH SIDE**
head south
for soul

CHINATOWN

Lake Michigan

Lincoln
Park

Grant
Park

Humboldt
Park

Bryn Mawr Ave.
Foster Ave.
Lawrence Ave.
Montrose Ave.
Irving Park Rd.
Addison
Belmont
Diversey Ave.
Armitage Ave.
North Ave.
Division
Augusta Blvd.
Chicago Ave.
Grand Ave.
Warren Blvd.
Jackson Blvd.
Roosevelt Rd.
Cermak Rd.

Central Park
Homan
Kedzie Ave.
Western Ave.
Lincoln Ave.
Ashland Ave.
Sheridan Rd.
Halsted
Clark
Lake Shore Dr.

Elston Ave.
John F. Kennedy Expwy.
Milwaukee Ave.
Clybourn Ave.
Armitage Ave.
Ogden Ave.
Halsted
Milwaukee Ave.
LaSalle
State
Lake Shore Dr.

Central Park
Homan
California Ave.
Western Blvd.
Damen Ave.
Ashland Ave.
S. Blue Island Ave.
Halsted
Canal
Michigan Ave.
Roosevelt Rd.
Ogden Ave.

Eisenhower Expwy.
290
Roosevelt Rd.

41
94
90
94
90
55
41

0   1 miles
0   1 km

CHICAGO DINING PLANNER

Eating Out Strategy

Where should we eat? With thousands of Chicago eateries competing for your attention, it may seem like a daunting question. But fret not—our expert writers and editors have done most of the legwork.

The selections here represent the best this city has to offer—from hot dogs to haute cuisine.

Search "Best Bets" for top recommendations by price, cuisine, and experience. Sample local flavor in the neighborhood features. Or find a review quickly in the alphabetical listings. Delve in, and enjoy!

Reservations

Plan ahead if you're determined to snag a sought-after reservation. Some renowned restaurants are booked weeks or months in advance.

But you can get lucky at the last minute if you're flexible—and friendly. Most restaurants keep a few tables open for walk-ins and VIPs. Show up for dinner early (5:30 PM) or late (after 9 PM) and politely inquire about any last-minute vacancies or cancellations.

If you're calling a few days ahead of time, ask if you can be put on a waiting list. Occasionally, an eatery may ask you to call the day before your scheduled meal to reconfirm: don't forget or you could lose out.

What to Wear

In general, Chicagoans are neat but casual dressers; only at the top-notch dining rooms do you see a more formal style.

But the way you look can influence how you're treated—and where you're seated. Generally speaking, jeans will suffice at most table-service restaurants in the $ to $$ range. Moving up from there, many pricier restaurants require jackets, and some insist on ties.

In reviews, we mention dress only when men are required to wear a jacket or a jacket and tie.

Note that shorts, sweatpants, and sports jerseys are rarely appropriate. When in doubt, call the restaurant and ask.

Children

Though it's unusual to see children in the dining rooms of Chicago's elite restaurants, dining with youngsters in the city does not have to mean culinary exile. Many of the restaurants reviewed in this chapter are excellent chocies for families. They are marked with a duck symbol.

Wine

Although some of the city's top restaurants still include historic French vintages, most sommeliers are now focusing on small-production, lesser-known wineries. Some are even keeping their wine lists purposefully small, so that they can change them frequently to match the season and the menu. Half bottles are becoming more prevalent, and good wines by the glass are everywhere. Don't hesitate to ask for recommendations. Even restaurants without a sommelier on staff will appoint knowledgeable servers to lend a hand with wine selections.

Prices

If you're watching your budget, be sure to ask the price of daily specials recited by the waiter or captain. The charge for specials at some restaurants is noticeably out of line with the other prices on the menu. Beware of the $10 bottle of water; ask for tap water instead. And always review your bill.

If you eat early or late you may be able to take advantage of a prix-fixe deal not offered at peak hours. Most upscale restaurants offer great lunch deals with special menus at cut-rate prices designed to give customers a true taste of the place.

Credit cards are widely accepted, but many restaurants (particularly smaller ones downtown) accept only cash. If you plan to use a credit card it's a good idea to double-check its acceptability when making reservations or before sitting down to eat.

In This Chapter

7

What It Costs

	¢	$	$$	$$$	$$$$
For One Person	under $10	$10–$18	$19–$27	$28–$36	over $36

Prices are per person for a typical main course or equivalent combination of smaller dishes. Note: if a restaurant offers only prix-fixe (set-price) meals, it has been given the price category that reflects the full prix-fixe price.

BEST BETS FOR CHICAGO DINING

With thousands of restaurants to choose from, how will you decide where to eat? Fodor's writers and editors have selected their favorite restaurants by price, cuisine, and experience in the Best Bets lists below. In the first column, Fodor's Choice properties represent the "best of the best" in every price category. You can also search by neighborhood for excellent eats—just peruse the following pages. Or find specific details about a restaurant in the full reviews, listed alphabetically later in the chapter.

Fodor's Choice ★

Aigre Doux
Alinea
Avec
Bin 36
Green Zebra
Hopleaf Bar
Hot Doug's
Milk & Honey
North Pond
Spacca Napoli
Spring
West Town Tavern

¢

Billy Goat Tavern
Hot Doug's
Manny's Coffee Shop & Deli
Milk & Honey
Mr. Beef

$

Café Iberico
Hopleaf Bar
Lou Mitchell's
Piece
Spacca Napoli

$$

De Cero Taqueria
Green Zebra
Hot Chocolate
Terragusto
West Town Tavern

$$$

Aigre Doux
Bin 36
Frontera Grill
Park Grill
Spring

$$$$

Alinea
Blackbird
Charlie Trotter
North Pond
Spiaggia

Best by Cuisine

AMERICAN

Billy Goat Tavern
Hot Doug's
Ina's
Lou Mitchell's
RL

CHINESE

Lao Sze Chuan
Phoenix

FRENCH

Brasserie Jo
Everest
Le Bouchon
Les Nomades
Marché

FUSION

Aria
Le Lan
Sushi Samba Rio

ITALIAN

312 Chicago
Osteria via Stato
Spacca Napoli
Spiaggia
Terragusto

JAPANESE

Heat
Japonais
Kamehachi
Mirai Sushi

MEDITERRANEAN

Adobo Grill
Avec

MEXICAN

De Cero Taqueria
Frontera Grill
Salpicon
Topolobampo

PIZZA

Piece
Pompeii
Spacca Napoli
Uno Chicago Grill

LATIN

Coobah
DeLaCosta
Mas
Nacional 27

SPANISH

Café Ba-Ba-Reeba
Café Iberico

STEAKHOUSE

Custom House
Keefer's
Morton's
David Burke's
Primehouse

THAI

Arun's
Thai Classic
Vong's Thai Kitchen

VEGETARIAN

Charlie Trotter's
Green Zebra
Lula Cafe

Best by Experience

BAR FOOD

Hopleaf Bar
Rockit Bar & Grill
Twin Anchors Restaurant & Tavern
West Town Tavern

BUSINESS DINING

Custom House
NoMI
RL
Seasons Restaurant
Spiaggia

CAFÉ EATS

Bin 36
Café Selmarie
Julius Meinl Cafe
Milk & Honey
Pierrot Gourmet

CHICAGO CLASSICS

Billy Goat Tavern
Gene & Georgetti
Mr. Beef
Twin Anchors Restaurant & Tavern
Uno Chicago Grill

CHILD-FRIENDLY

Ann Sather
Café Selmarie
Ed Debevic's
Eleven City Diner
Maggiano's Little Italy
Piece
Scoozi!

GOOD FOR GROUPS

Fogo de Chao
Joe's Be-Bop Cafe and Jazz Emporium
Maggiano's Little Italy
Park Grill
The Parthenon

HOT SPOTS

Avec
Blackbird
DeLaCosta
Green Zebra
Primehouse

BEST HOTEL DINING

Avenues
Custom House
NoMI
Seasons Restaurant
Shanghai Terrace

MOST INNOVATIVE

Alinea
Avenues
Blackbird
Charlie Trotter's
Moto

LATE-NIGHT DINING

Avec
DeLaCosta
Nacional 27
Nine
Red Light

PRE-THEATER MEAL

312 Chicago
Atwood Café
Boka
Petterino's
Rhapsody

QUIET MEAL

Arun's
Avenues
Charlie Trotter's
Les Nomades
North Pond

SPECIAL OCCASION

Charlie Trotter's
Everest
North Pond
Park Grill
Spring

BEST VIEWS

NoMI
North Pond
Park Grill
Riva
Spiaggia

7

FAR NORTH SIDE

Some of Chicago's best ethnic food resides on the Far North Side, a vast catch-all district north of Irving Park Road running all the way to suburban Evanston.

Within its borders lie several food-happy neighborhoods, none more lively than Devon Avenue, traditional home to Chicago's Indian community and lined with Indian restaurants, Bollywood video stores and sari shops as well as Russian bakeries and Israeli eateries.

Two gentrifying neighborhoods, the Swede-settled Andersonville and the German enclave Lincoln Square, have lured a critical mass of retailers, delis, bars, and restaurants that warrant an afternoon or evening out. Both are pedestrian friendly; Lincoln Square lies on the Brown Line El, though Andersonville is better reached via cab.

To reach the other dining destinations in this area, such as **Arun's** (⌂4156 N. Kedzie Ave., ☎773/539–1909) and **Hot Doug's** (⌂3325 N. California Ave., ☎773/751–1500), you may want to consider renting a car, or expect a longish cab ride from downtown.

GASTROPUBBING

At **Hopleaf Bar** (⌂5148 N. Clark St., ☎773/334–9851), above, owner Michael Roper pairs food and beer, with sometimes surprising results. Here's what Roper recommends: Belgian-style mussels paired with Belgian blond ales like Leffe or Triple Karmeliet. Why: "Steamed with herbs and shallots, the mussels go great with blonds." For a snack, try a sandwich of ham, Gruyère cheese, and apple-tarragon slaw with a hoppy Lagunitas. Why: "Bigger, hoppier beers stand up to cured ham and bold cheese." On a cold night, dig into: Flemish beef stew with a pint of St. Bernardus Apt. 12. Why: "Rich, malty St. Bernardus matches the caramelized beef."

NOSHING UP NORTH

Decades ago, Germans settled Lincoln Square, and the Swedes populated Andersonville, two north-side neighborhoods not far apart. Do one, or make it a double header.

	Lincoln Square	Andersonville
Shop	Since 1875, Chicagoans have been shopping at **Merz Apothecary** (✉4716 N. Lincoln Ae., at Lawrence Ave., ☎773/989–0900), right, for homeopathic remedies, tonics and teas, and hard-to-find European candies.	Stop into **Wikstrom's Gourmet Foods** (✉5217 N. Clark St., at Foster Ave., ☎773/275–6100) for Swedish foodstuffs: sweet rye bread, pickled herring, and dry Vasterbotten cheese.
Sip	Try a stein of Spaten or a shot of the Goldwasser, a spiced citrus liqueur with flakes of 22k gold, at the Bavarian-themed **Huetten-bar** (✉4721 N. Lincoln Ave., at Lawrence Ave., ☎773/561–2507).	Drink free coffee at the stand-up bar while noshing on pastries at **Swedish Bakery** (✉5348 N. Clark St., ☎773-561-8919). Our favorites are the buttery spritz cookies and cinnamon streusel coffee cake.
Sup	The old-school **Chicago Brauhaus** (✉4732 N. Lincoln Ave., ☎773-784-4444) serves up mugs of suds, platters of brats, and jovial tunes by a live oom-pah band nightly.	Herring salad and smorgasar (open-faced sandwiches) are on the menu at **Svea Restaurant** (✉5236 N. Clark St., ☎773/275–7738). Fans rave about the Three Crown Special (Swedish meatballs, salt pork, and brown beans).

CHICAGO HOT DOGS

Two far-flung spots on the North Side warrant the trek for a dog. At **Superdawg Drive-In** car-hops deliver your chow (✉6363 N. Milwaukee Ave., at Devon Ave., ☎773/736–0660). Serving haut dogs, **Hot Doug's**, top right, does the classic Chicago all-beef as well as "encased meats" of kangaroo or rabbit (✉3324 N. California, at Henderson St., ☎773/279–9550). Check www.hotdougs.com for daily specials like bacon-jalapeño duck sausage and Chardonnay-infused rattlesnake sausage.

DINING BY CUISINE

Belgian
Hopleaf Bar, $
Bistro
La Tache, $$
Café
Café Selmarie, $
German
Chicago Brauhaus, $
Italian
La Donna, $
Spacca Napoli, $
Terragusto, $$
New American
Tomboy, $$
Scandinavian
Svea, ¢
Thai
Arun's, $$$$

LINCOLN PARK & LAKEVIEW

Of Chicago's 198 official neighborhoods, the North Side's popular Lincoln Park is definitely worth exploring. From a food lover's perspective, this neighborhood is host to several of Chicago's best restaurants, including Charlie Trotter's and Alinea.

Named for the lakefront park it borders, Lincoln Park is often a first stop for recent college grads moving to the city as well as the permanent residence of families inhabiting pricey brownstones. On commercial throughways such as Clark, Halsted, and Armitage, you can spend an afternoon bouncing back and forth from great restaurants and cafés to hip shops.

For more casual fare head north of Lincoln Park to Lake View, which includes the sub-districts of Wrigleyville and Boy's Town. Wrigleyville buffers Wrigley Field and hosts many bars serving beer and brats. Boy's Town refers to the gay district along Halsted between Belmont and Addison. Here the bars are equally raucous but the food is more refined.

URBAN GARDEN

Chef Bruce Sherman has an idyllic spot in **North Pond Café** (✉ *2610 N. Cannon Dr.,* ☎ *773/477–5845),* pictured above, is a restaurant lodged in a former skater's warming hut on the edge of a duck pond in the heart of Lincoln Park. To this greensward he has added a kitchen garden, growing almost all his own herbs and many of his own vegetables in the height of summer, resulting in urban-farm-to-table salads and sorbets. The only challenge is keeping the neighbors out of the garden. "Have people helped themselves? Of course, we're in a public park," Sherman says.

LINCOLN PARK—A TOP CHEF HUB

Restaurant name	Charlie Trotter (✉816 W. Armitage Ave., ☎773/248–6228), pictured below and right.	Alinea (✉1723 N. Halsted St., ☎312/867–0110)
What the name means	Eponymous (Don't you know who I am?).	A typographical symbol signifying the start of a new thought.
Culinary Style	Modern American; meticulous presentation; dedication to organic and free-range products.	Cutting-edge American; daring presentation; flavor is as important as form.
Menu	8-course degustation menus (grand and vegetarian) change daily.	12-course tasting menu or 22-course "tour;" menu changes often.
Wow Factor	Restrained. Sources luxury ingredients (Iranian pistachios, Spanish *percebes*, or barnacles) from around the world.	Unleashed. Custom service pieces reinvent fork and knife into spindles, tabletop pedestals.
Theater Analogy	Shakespearean drama	Performance art

EATING AROUND WRIGLEY FIELD

Hungry fans can find good eats in any direction: Go south on Sheffield Street three blocks to **Sheffield's** (✉3258 N. Sheffield St., at School St., ☎773/281–4989) for pulled-pork barbecue best consumed in the beer garden. Go west on Addison eight blocks to **Palmito** (✉3605 N. Ashland Ave., at Addison St., ☎773/248–3087, 🍷BYOB) for Costa Rican *arroz con pollo*. Go north on Sheffield three blocks, **Pizza Rustica** (✉3913 N. Sheridan Rd., at Byron St., ☎773/404–8955, 🍷BYOB) for pizza and pastas from an Italian owner.

DINING BY CUISINE

American
Green Dolphin Street, $$
Kitsch'n on Roscoe, $
Orange, ¢–$
North Pond, $$$
Asian Fusion
Yoshi's Cafe, $$
Bistro
Bistro Campagne, $$
Mon Ami Gabi, $–$$
Café
Julius Meinl Cafe, ¢
Cutting-Edge
Alinea, $$$$
French
Geja's, $$$$
Hot Dogs
Hot Doug's, ¢
Italian
Mia Francesca, $
Latin
Coobah, $
Mexican
Platiyo, $
New American
Brett's, $
Erwin, $$ '
Boka, $$$
Charlie Trotter's, $$$$
Sola, $$
Scandinavian
Ann Sather, $–$$
Southern
Heaven on Seven, $
Spanish
Café Ba-Ba-Reeba!, $
Thai
Thai Classic, ¢
Turkish
Turquoise Cafe, $–$$

7

THE LOOP

Business, theater, and shopping converge in the Loop, the downtown district south of the Chicago River so named for the elevated train that circles it.

Long the city's financial center, the Loop is commuter-central for inbound office workers. It is also Chicago's historic home of retail, where the flagship Marshall Field's (now Macy's) and Carson Pirie Scott (now defunct) made State Street a great shopping street. Newcomers like Old Navy and TJ Maxx update the mix, appealing to tourists as well as locals.

As a theater district, the Loop hosts the Tony-awarded Goodman Theater, which mounts its own productions, as well as the Chicago, Oriental, Palace and LaSalle theaters which generally run Broadway tours.

In feeding these diverse audiences, Loop restaurants run the gamut from quick service to high volume and special occasion as well as breakfast, lunch, and dinner. Beware noon-time and pre-curtain surges (you'll need a reservation for the latter).

NEW BAGEL?

Hannah's Bretzel (✉ *180 W. Washington Ave., at Wells St.,* ☎ *312/621-1111*), above, aims to replace the New World-popularized bagel with the Old World-ubiquitous pretzel. A soft pretzel, that is, made of organic wheat and cooked in imported German ovens by Stuttgart native and former ad exec Florian Pfahler who quit the corporate world to train in the art of baking pretzels. Get them spread with organic butter, stuffed with Gruyere and cucumbers, or slathered in Nutella. The results are lighter and tastier than a bagel sandwich, closer to a baguette with serious holes.

TOP PICKS FOR DINING IN THE LOOP

Whether you're looking for pre-theater eats, a quick bite on-the-go, or an intimate dining room for a special occasion, restaurants in the Loop deliver some of the city's best dining experiences.

■ *For pre-theater dining, try*: Italian pastas and chops at **Petterino's** (✉*150 N. Dearborn St., at Randolph St.,* ☎*312/422-0150)* adjacent to the Goodman Theater; **312 Chicago** (✉*136 N. LaSalle St., at Randolph St.,* ☎*312/696-2420)* for seasonal Italian adjacent to the Palace Theater; or **Rhapsody** (✉*65 E. Adams St., at Michigan Ave.,* ☎*312/786-9911)* for contemporary American adjacent to the Chicago Symphony Center.

■ *For a break while shopping, stop into*: **Atwood Café** (1 W. Washington Ave., at State St., 312/368-1900) for seasonal American comfort food, pictured below, and big-window views of the bustle; **Seven on State** (111 N. State St., 7th fl., at Randolph St., 312/781-3693) within Macy's for upscale food-court fare; or **Patty Burger** (72 E. Adams St., at Wabash Ave., 312/987-0900) for burgers and shakes in a retro diner setting.

■ *For a quiet dinner for two, try*: **Custom House** (✉*500 S. Dearborn St., at Congress,* ☎*312/523-0200)* for a steak house with chef flare and delightful desserts, pictured at top right; **Everest** (✉*440 S. LaSalle St., 40th fl., at Van Buren St.,* ☎*312/663-8920)* serving chef Jean Joho's refined French food and city views; or **Park Grill** (✉*11 N. Michigan Ave., at Randolph St.,* ☎*312/521-7275)* in thronged Millennium Park for contemporary fare.

FAST FOOD WITH A PEDIGREE

One of Chicago's most acclaimed chefs, Rick Bayless of Frontera Grill, has opened a fast-food outlet in the Loop. Bayless call his efforts "authentic Mexican street food" at **Frontera Fresco** in the Seven on State (✉*111 N. State St., 7th fl., at Randolph St.,* ☎*312/781-3693)* food court in Macy's serving *tortas* (Mexican sandwiches), tamales, and quesadillas with Bayless authentic regional flare.

DINING BY CUISINE

American
Atwood Café, $$
French
Everest, $$$$
International
Aria, $$$
Italian
312 Chicago, $$
Petterino's, $$
Trattoria No. 10, $$
Vivere, $$
New American
Park Grill, $$
Rhapsody, $$
Russian
Russian Tea Time, $$
Seafood
Catch 35, $$
Nick's Fishmarket, $$$
Steakhouse
The Grillroom, $$
Morton's, the Steakhouse, $$$–$$$$
The Palm, $$$$

7

NEAR NORTH

Chicago's tony Near North district, home to shopping's Magnificent Mile and the residential Gold Coast, specializes in upscale restaurants that suit the clientele like a bespoke suit.

It's the land of posh hotels (Peninsula, Ritz-Carlton, Four Seasons, Park Hyatt) and their posh dining rooms (Avenues, The Café, Seasons Restaurant and NoMI, respectively) as well as stand-alone stars like Tru, Spiaggia and Les Nomades. Even the Mag Mile's toniest retailers such as Polo/Ralph Lauren with the see-and-be-seen RL restaurant are in on the feed. If you're planning on dining on Michigan Avenue while you shop it, expect to spend like a platinum card holder (or read on for our budget-friendly advice below).

Just to the west of the Gold Coast lies the equally moneyed but more liberal Old Town district, home to Second City improv theater and a spate of restaurants that the actors can afford, at least once in a paycheck cycle.

EXPER-CHEESE

Contemporary Italian restaurant **Spiaggia** (✉ *980 N. Michigan Ave.,* ☎ *312/280–2750*) works hard to get things right, down to installing a *cava di stagionatura,* or cheese cave. Why? It ages the cheese properly, says chef Tony Montuano, by controlling the temperature and humidity of dozens of cheeses that the restaurant serves before or after dinner. Stocking those is Jose Flores, Chicago's first and perhaps only *formaggiaio*—or cheese guy. Don't expect an atmospheric, bat-dwelling cave; this one's a 7-by-3-foot cooler. Flores often gives tours of the "cave" to help guests choose their cheeses. A few of the many selections are pictured above.

CHICAGO'S CHICEST TABLES

If you want to rub elbows with Chicago's glitterati—real estate scions, ladies who lunch, and local media figures—head to:

✗ **RL** (✉115 E. Chicago Ave., ☎312/475–1100), especially at lunch when shoppers at Ralph Lauren/Polo rest their Amex cards and order the burger made of beef from the designer's own ranch in Colorado.

✗ **NoMI** (✉800 N. Michigan Ave., ☎312/239–4030), on the 7th floor of the Park Hyatt Chicago. Be sure to specify you want a table overlooking the landmark Water Tower under the Dale Chihuly chandeliers.

✗ **Gibsons Steakhouse** (✉1028 N. Rush St., ☎312/266–8999), a Chicago meat market popular with moneyed men, particularly those who play on and manage sports teams.

✗ **Bar at The Peninsula Chicago** (✉108 E. Superior St., at Michigan Ave., ☎312/573–6766), where local society types start their evenings with Champagne and end with privately blended bourbon in the leather-walled, art-filled barroom.

✗ **TRU** (✉676 N. St. Clair St., 312/202–0001), where there's an Andy Warhol silkscreen on the wall, a caviar course served on a table-top crystal staircase, and a multicourse dessert tasting for the truly indulgent.

BEST REFUELING STOPS FOR SHOPPERS

Around the corner from Tiffany & Co., **Pierrot Gourmet** (✉108 E. Superior St., ☎312/573–6749), below, run by The Peninsula Chicago hotel, serves savory soups and "tartines," open-face sandwiches. Three blocks from designer-lined Oak Street, **Big Bowl** (✉6 E. Cedar St., ☎312/640-8888) does a speedy job with Asian stir-fry and noodles (and tiki-inspired tropical drinks). At Nordstrom, look no farther than the **Nordstrom Café** (✉55 E. Grand Ave., at Michigan Ave., ☎312/464–1515) on the 4th floor for paninis and salads.

DINING BY CUISINE

American
Cru Café & Wine Bar, $$
Pump Room, $$
RL, $$
Signature Room at the 95th, $$$,
Viand, $$$
Barbecue
Twin Anchors Restaurant & Tavern, $$–$$$
Bistro
Bistro 110, $$
Bistrot Margot, $$
Branch
Heaven on Seven, $
Burger
Billy Goat Tavern, $
Café
Fox & Obel Food Market Cafe, ¢
Pierrot Gourmet, $
Chinese
Shanghai Terrace, $$–$$$
Cutting-Edge
Avenues, $$$$
French
Les Nomades, $$$$
Italian
The Caliterra Bar & Grille, $$
Spiaggia, $$$
Japanese
Kamehachi, $
Mexican
Salpicon, $$
New American
NoMI, $$$$
Seasons Restaurant, $$$$
TRU, $$$$
Pan Asian
Roy's, $$–$$$
Seafood
McCormick and Schmick's, $$$
Riva, $$$
Southern
Joe's Be-Bop Cafe and Jazz Emporium, $
Steakhouse
The Capital Grille, $$$
Gibsons Steakhouse, $$$$
Mike Ditka's Restaurant, $$$
Primehouse, $$$$

7

RIVER NORTH

The Chicago River bends around this 19th-century-factory district, which was reclaimed in the 1980s by art galleries, urban-living pioneers, and chef-owned eateries to become a crown jewel in the city's dining scene.

Today, the art and design trades—the mammoth Chicago Merchandise Mart anchors River North—patronize the area's trendy eateries, including Japonais, Sushi Samba Rio, and Nacional 27, as well its refined restaurants, such as mk, Naha, and Topolobampo. But while these notable restaurants have flourished, other independent eateries in the area have been forced out by soaring real-estate values and new high-rise developments. In the place of casual indie concepts, chains like Rainforest Café and ESPN Zone have taken root and gained market share.

In spite of all the change, down-home Chicago fare still thrives here, including the classic Italian beef sandwich and the famed deep-dish pizza, making River North the go-to district whether your tastes run high or low.

FOODIE DRINKS

Come cocktail hour grab a stool at the creative bar run by mad mixologist Adam Seger at **Nacional 27** (☎ *325 W. Huron St., at Wells,* ☎ *312/664-2727),* above. "I get most of my ideas from chefs and from food," says Seger, who was inspired by an arugula, warm goat cheese, and mango herb-dressed salad to create his signature mango-ginger-habañero daiquiri. On Thursday evenings he pours mini drinks ($3.95 each) so you can try several. The in-demand Seger also works as beverage director at **Osteria via Stato** (☎ *620 N. State St., at Ontario,* ☎ *312/642-8450)* where he creates seasonal "gastro-tails" as specials. Salut!

A STEAKHOUSE FOR ANY OCCASION

Steakhouses are a dime a dozen in River North, with its ample warehouse-sized buildings and proximity to the city center. With a meat market this robust, you can afford to be a little picky. Here are our top picks for various dining situations:

■ A festive atmosphere that's great for groups: **Fogo de Chao** (☎ 661 N. LaSalle St., ☎ 312/932-9330) is an all-you-can-eat Brazillian churrascaria. The restaurant's name, which means "fire on the ground," refers to a traditional gathering around the fire with good food, family, and friends. The celebratory mood is reproduced here with interactive elements: using a two-sided red and green chip, guests indicate when they're ready to have costumed gaucho cowboys come to their table to carve the skewered and grilled meats (you can stop and start as many times as you'd like). Guests also can watch their meat being roasted in dramatic fire pit while traveling back and forth to the lavish salad bar.

■ A Chicago classic with Italian-American flavor: **Gene & Georgetti** (☎ 500 N. Franklin St., ☎ 312/527-3718). Founded in 1941, this is Chicago's oldest steakhouse, and a current favorite of local politicians. On the walls you'll find autographed photos from Frank Sinatra and Lucille Ball, and on the menu you'll encounter Italian-American favorites like spaghetti and meatballs, along with classic favorites like creamed spinach. Don't miss the famed "garbage salad"—a kitchen-sink creation of greens with vegetables and meats.

■ A stylish setting that ladies will love: **Keefer's** (☎ 20 W. Kinzie St., ☎ 312/467-9525), below, boasts a sleek, modern bistro feel and has a broader menu than most steakhouses, with seafood, entrée salads and roasted chicken and chops. But don't mistake this award-winning venue for steakhouse-lite: its 22-oz. T-bone and 17-oz. corn-fed New York strip steak can compete with the manliest offerings in town. On the wine list you'll find more than 110 labels, with plenty of big reds.

DINING BY CUISINE

American
Bin 36, $$
Ed Debevic's, ¢
Mr. Beef, ¢
Rockit Bar & Grill, $$
Asian Fusion
Kevin, $$$
Le Lan, $$$
Bistro
Cyrano's Bistrot Wine Bar & Cabaret, $
Brasserie
Brasserie Jo, $$
Brazilian
Fogo de Chao, $$$$
Chinese
Ben Pao, $
Italian
Coco Pazzo, $$
Harry Caray's, $$
Maggiano's Little Italy, $$
Osteria via Stato, $$$
Pizzeria Due, ¢
Pizzeria Uno, $
Scoozi!, $$
Japanese
Japonais, $$$
SushiSamba Rio, $$
Latin
DeLaCosta, $$$
Nacional 27, $$
Mexican
Frontera Grill, $$
Topolobampo, $$$
New American
Crofton on Wells, $$$
mk, $$$
Naha, $$$
Aigre Doux, $$$
Allen's, $$$
Blue Water Grill, $$
Seafood
Joe's Seafood, Prime Steaks & Stone Crab, $$–$$$
Shaw's Crab House and Blue Crab Lounge, $$$
Spanish
Cafe Iberico, $
Steakhouse
Gene and Georgetti, $$$
Keefer's, $$$$
Ruth's Chris Steak House, $$$
Smith and Wollensky, $$$–$$$$

7

SOUTH LOOP & SOUTH SIDE

The South Side of Chicago is a vast district of largely undistinguished culinary reputation that makes its foodie islands—Chinatown and South Loop—shine all the brighter.

If you're planning on exploring the South Side, especially Chicago's soul foodie Army & Lou's and other stand-alone classics, plan to drive as distances are great and public transportation isn't, even to such hubs as the University of Chicago.

That said, you can actually spend time on foot at two rewarding South Side districts not far from the Loop. Begin at the South Loop adjacent to downtown which can easily feed Museum Campus-goers. The newly gentrifying district is home to a host of new condos and lofts which have drawn a range of interesting diners, restaurants and bars, primarily on Wabash Avenue. Farther south and easily accessed via the Red Line el, Chinatown is Chicago's colorful Chinese neighborhood where traditional dim sum specialists neighbor trendy bubble tea shops. Recently a new generation of Asian-Americans from Chicago and the suburbs have rediscovered Chinatown, energizing the scene.

CLASSIC SPOTS

Go out of your way to **Army & Lou's** (⊠ 422 E. 75th St., ☎ 312/483–3100), a soul food favorite since 1945, for catfish, chitterlings and smothered chicken served by bow-tied waiters on way-south 75th St.

Have the corned beef sandwich with a side of sass from the countermen at **Manny's Coffee Shop & Deli** (⊠ 1141 S. Jefferson St., ☎ 312/939–2855), pictured above, near the Maxwell Street Market, the city's best deli.

It's truly a no-frills place, but Hyde Parkers embrace the vintage cafeteria **Valois** (⊠ 1518 E. 53rd St., at S. Harper Ave., ☎ 773/667–0647) for breakfast (pancakes), lunch (mac-n-cheese) or dinner (barbecued ribs).

AFTERNOON IN CHINATOWN

Herbal-medicine shops, trinket sellers, candy specialists, dim-sum servers, bakeries, and noodle shops make Chinatown an entertaining day away within the city. Top stops include:

Herb shop: **Yin Wall City** (⌂2112 S. Archer Ave., at Wentworth Ave., ☎312/225–2888) for ginseng, Chinese teas, and Japanese mushrooms.

Candy shop: **Aji Ichiban** (⌂2117-A S. China Pl., at Cermak Rd., ☎312/328–9998) for dried-fruit and imported candy like lychee gummies and chocolate-covered sunflower seeds.

Bakery: **Tasty Place** (⌂2101 S. China Pl., at Cermak Rd., ☎312/842–2228) for coconut buns and chestnut cakes.

Dim Sum: **Phoenix** (⌂2131 S. Archer Ave., ☎312/328–0848) for barbecued pork buns and shrimp dumplings plucked from carts that wheel around the room.

Hot Pot: **Lao Sze Chuan** (2172 S. Archer Ave., ☎312/326–5040) for the all-you-can-eat Chinese fondue where diners cook their own veggies, noodles, and meat in boiling broth at the table. Also, don't miss the three chili chicken.

Noodles: **Joy Yee's Noodle** (⌂2159 S. China Pl., at Cermak Rd., ☎312/328–0001), pictured upper right, for standout sugarcane-shrimp-pork vermicelli and Korean beef chap chae.

Tea: **Ten Ren Tea** (⌂2247 S. Wentworth Ave., at Cermak Rd., ☎312/842–1171) for bubble tea and ceramic tea sets.

MUSEUM EATS

If you're making a trip to the Museum Campus, you don't have to eat in the pricey museum cafeterias. Nearby, there's a South Loop dish to satisfy every interest:

■ For visitors to the Ancient Americas exhibit at the Field Museum, try the chicken à la Azteca at **Zapatista** (⌂1307 S. Wabash Ave., at 13th St., ☎312/435–1307) to sate your craving for Latin American flavors.

■ For Shedd Aquarium goers whose visit gives them a hankering for fish, the albacore tuna sandwich and lox platter at **Eleven City Diner** (⌂1112 S. Wabash, at 11th St., ☎312/212–1112) can't be beat.

■ For show-goers in the Adler Planetarium's StarRider Theater, the very theatrical **Opera** (⌂1301 S. Wabash St., ☎312/461-0161), with its renowned "crisp eight immortal squid" appetizer, provides a dramatic setting for celestial conversations.

DINING BY CUISINE

American
Manny's Coffee Shop and Deli, ¢
Eleven City Diner, $
Bistro
Chez Joel, $$
Chinese
Opera, $$
Emperor's Choice, $
Lao Sze Chuan, ¢
Phoenix, $
Italian
Francesca's on Taylor, $
Gioco, $$
Pompei, ¢
Rosebud on Taylor, $
Tuscany, $$
Southern
Soul Queen, ¢
Army and Lou's, ¢
Steakhouse
Custom House, $$$$

7

WEST LOOP & NEAR WEST SIDE

Near enough to downtown to draw a critical mass of diners, but far enough away to keep the rents down, the West Loop—and particularly Randolph Street within it—has emerged as Chicago's restaurant row, lined with upscale eateries of every ethnic persuasion.

Most restaurants here warrant a full meal, but if you haven't the time or the attention span it's easy enough to stroll the street and feast on small bites.

The West Loop runs essentially from the south branch of the Chicago River to Ashland Avenue on the east and west, and Fulton Street and the Eisenhower Expressway (I–290) on the north and south, respectively.

Beyond it to the north lies the sketchy, unbounded but up-and-coming Near West Side. Its culinary contributions, including West Town Tavern and Green Zebra, are few but significant and require a cab to reach.

VA-VA-VEG

Chef Shawn McClain earned raves nationwide for giving veggies the gourmet treatment at **Green Zebra** *(1460 W. Chicago Ave., at Greenwood Ave., 312/243–7100)*, above. But don't call it vegetarian, McClain says. It's "flexitarian," mostly veggie but not strictly. "The restaurant is vegetable-focused," he says, "but we always have one fish and one chicken dish on the menu for guests who want some protein." The menu changes often, but may include dishes like a warm blue cheese cake with pea tendrils, almond "ice cream" and port reduction; parmesan gnocchi with Brussels sprouts, mustard, and chanterelle mushrooms.

EAT YOUR WAY DOWN RANDOLPH STREET

Foodies from around the city and beyond flock to Randolph Street, a.k.a. Chicago's Restaurant Row, for excellent eats. From pizza and pasta to curry and sushi, the flavors here are sure to satisfy any culinary craving. Here are our top recommendations, dish by dish, restaurant by restaurant. Choose your own food tour from the selections below. Bon appétit!

SOUTH SIDE OF RANDOLPH STREET (the numbers refer to street addresses)

■ No. 615: Marinated olives and truffle-scented focaccia at **Avec** (☎ 312/377–2002).

■ No. 609: Bouillabaisse-like West Coast mussel soup at **Blackbird** (☎ 312/715-0708).

■ No. 833: Rotisserie chicken and pomme frites at **Marché** (☎ 312/226-8399).

■ No. 847: Turtles and truffles and the Chicago Float at **Chicago Chocolate Café** (⊕ at Peoria St., 312/738–0888).

■ No. 945: "Fire Breather" sausage-pepperoni-hot-pepper pizza at **Tomatohead Pizza** (⊕ at Sangamon St., ☎ 312/226–1616).

■ No. 1235: Black bean-cheese-chorizo scrambled eggs called "scrapple" at **Ina's** (☎ 312/226-8227).

■ No. 1415: Global goat-cheese flight at **The Tasting Room** (⊕ at Ogden Ave., ☎ 312/942–1313).

NORTH SIDE OF RANDOLPH STREET:

■ No. 814: Chipotle chicken tacos **at De Cero Taqueria** (☎ 312/455-8114).

■ No. 820: Emerald jumbo prawn curry at **Red Light** (☎ 312/733-8880), pictured upper right.

■ No. 832: Dragonfly martini at **Dragonfly Mandarin** (⊕ at Green St., ☎ 312/455–1400).

■ No. 838: Squid ink linguine with crab meat at **Vivo** (☎ 312/733-3379).

■ No. 842: Dragon rolls (tempura shrimp, eel, and avocado) at **Sushi Wabi** (☎ 312/563-1224).

■ No. 1400: Kurobuta pork tenderloin with pork belly and dates at **one sixtyblue** (☎ 312/850-0303).

DINING BY CUISINE

American
Ina's, $
Lou Mitchell's, ¢
West Town Tavern, $$
Bistro
La Sardine, $$
Brasserie
Marché, $$
Cutting-Edge
Moto, $$$$
Greek
Costa's, $ $$
The Parthenon, $
Italian
Vivo, $$
Japanese
Sushi Wabi, $
Mexican
De Cero Taqueria, $$
New American
Blackbird, $$$
one sixtyblue, $$–$$$
Avec, $$
Pan Asian
Red Light, $$
Steakhouse
Carmichael's, $$
N9NE Steakhouse, $$$
Vegetarian
Green Zebra, $$$

7

WICKER PARK & BUCKTOWN

Chicago's edgiest bohemian 'hoods—neighbors Wicker Park and Bucktown—are a venturesome El stop away from downtown's deep pockets. Here you'll find hipsters and fashionistas aplenty.

Artists and musicians are responsible for its 1990s rise from blighted to trendy and residents prize the independent spirit here, from the local record labels and hole-in-the-wall bars to one-of-a-kind boutiques and funky eateries.

Though Starbucks is, as expected, already on the scene, the food landscape here is fittingly fun and diverse and surprisingly good at any hour, whether you want breakfast (ok, brunch, since no one gets up that early), lunch, or dinner.

A couple of Wicker Park's restaurants qualify as destinations themselves, but the best way to approach the area is to come out in the afternoon to nosh and troll the shops, stop into a bar for a drink then head to dinner, followed by a show at Double Door, a music club.

SWEET SPOTS

A trio of sweet spots puts the cherry on the Wicker Park neighborhood sundae. For south of the border palates, order soursop and tamarind milk shakes at the Costa Rican restaurant **Irazu** (1865 N. Milwaukee Ave., at Oakley Ave., 773/252-5687). Old-school fans from infants to seniors line up for ice cream sundaes at the family-owned **Margie's Candies** (1960 N. Western Ave., at Armitage Ave., 773/384-1035) dating to 1921. Progressive foodies rave for the cake and shake combo at **Hot Chocolate** (1747 N. Damen Ave., at Willow St., 773/489-1747), pictured above, a restaurant owned by acclaimed pastry chef Mindy Segal.

WICKER PARK TWO WAYS

	Save	Splurge
Foodie haunts	**Milk & Honey Café** (1920 W. Division St., at Damen Ave., 773/395–9434) distinguishes breakfast with house-made granola, and lunch with sandwiches like crab cake with chipotle mayo.	Acclaimed chef Shawn McClain runs **Spring** (2039 W. North Ave., at Damen Ave., 773/395–7100), serving gorgeous and savory Asian-inspired seafood in a former Russian bathhouse.
Music with your meal	**Smoke Daddy** (1804 W. Division St., at Wood St., 773/772–6656), pictured at upper right and below, serves up finger-lickin' barbecue like pulled-pork sandwiches and rib platters along with live R&B nightly.	Put yourself in the chef's hands at the sushi bar on the lower level of **Mirai Sushi** (2020 W. Division St., at Damen Ave., 773/862–8500), then head upstairs to check out the DJ vibe.
Unexpected flavors	Aficionados line up down the block on weekends for brunch at **Bongo Room** (1470 N. Milwaukee Ave., at Honore St., 773/427–9972) including stacks of chocolate mascarpone-stuffed French toast.	Wash down Latin braised rabbit and chimichurri tuna at **Mas** (1670 W. Division St., at Ashland Ave., 773/276–8700) with mojitos, caipirinhas, and prickly pear margaritas from the fun bar menu.

DINING BY CUISINE

Bistro
Le Bouchon, $$
Café
Hot Chocolate, $$
Milk & Honey Café, ¢
International
Feast, $
Japanese
Mirai Sushi, $$
Latin
Mas, $$
New American
Spring, $$
Café Absinthe, $$
Meritage Café and Wine Bar, $$–$$$
Pizza
Piece, $
Southern
Smoke Daddy, $

7

WHERE ROCKERS DINE

Come for the New Haven-style, free-form pizza and award-winning house-made brews at **Piece** (1927 W. North Ave., at Damen Ave., 773/772–4422). Stick around for the Saturday-night live-band karaoke. Co-owner Rick Nielsen is a former Cheap Trick band member. Between his rep and the pies, rockers from near (Billy Corgan of Smashing Pumpkins fame, Al Jourgensen of Ministry, producer Steve Albini) and far (Todd Rundgren) frequently dine here.

RESTAURANTS (in alphabetical order)

$$
ITALIAN
Loop
312 Chicago. Part handy hotel restaurant, part Loop power diner, and all Italian down to its second-generation chef, 312 Chicago earns its popularity with well-executed dishes that range from basic rigatoni with meatballs to grilled lamb chops with mascarpone and black-truffle polenta. We're tempted to carbo-load on the house-baked bread alone. Tables in the bi-level eatery are quieter aloft, though you still may see the occasional hotel guest wander through, looking for the elevator. ⊠*Hotel Allegro, 136 N. LaSalle St.* ☎*312/696–2420* ▤*AE, D, DC, MC, V* ⊘*No lunch Sat.*

$$$
NEW AMERICAN
River North
Fodor'sChoice
★
Aigre Doux. Tucked behind the mammoth Merchandise Mart, this stylish spot in an unsung locale warrants searching out for the considerable talents of its husband and wife chef-owners. He does the savories, she the sweets, which include stocking a café bakery case with to-go goodies and quick lunch bites. But come back for dinner when Aigre Doux (which means "sweet and sour") is at its best, serving deftly accented dishes like artichoke soup, slow-baked salmon with citrus, and maple-glazed duck. Attentive service, a selective wine list and modern decor including exposed light bulbs create a chameleon setting conducive, like the chefs' marriage, to both business and romance. ⊠*230 W. Kinzie St.* ☎*312/329–9400* ▤*AE, D, DC, MC, V* ⊘*No lunch weekends. Closed Sun.*

$$$$
CUTTING-EDGE
Lincoln Park
Fodor'sChoice
★
Alinea. Believe the hype and book well in advance. Chicago's most exciting restaurant—hidden in a bunker-like building on a residential block—demands an adventurous spirit, an ample appetite, and a serious commitment of time and money. If you have four hours and $300 to spare, the 23-course tasting menu is the best way to experience young whiz Grant Achatz's stunning cutting-edge food. The gastronomic roller coaster (there's also a less pricey 12-course version) takes you on a journey through intriguing aromas, visuals, flavors and textures. Buttery duck with extruded mango puree arrives perched on a pillow that emits juniper-scented air. A black truffle–bon bon explodes in your mouth when you bite. Brown butter turned into powder accompanies a skate fish fillet. Though some dishes—they range in size from one to four bites—may look like science projects, there's nothing gimmicky about the endless procession of bold and elegant tastes. The hours fly by in the windowless bi-level dining room, aided by the effortless service and muted decor. ⊠*1723 N. Halsted St.* ☎*312/867–0110* ⌂*Reservations essential* ▤*AE, D, DC, MC, V* ⊘*Closed Mon. and Tues. No lunch.*

$$$
NEW AMERICAN
River North
Allen's. Distinguishing himself from the pack of contemporary cooks, chef Allen Sternweiler goes boldly with wild game. Think roast rabbit stuffed with rabbit sausage and grilled quail stuffed with red Swiss chard and Serrano ham. If you're less adventurous, there are plenty of more familiar options in the meat and sea departments. The biggest treat here, though, is the massive collection of fine spirits, like Armagnacs, ports, and small-batch bourbons. Our favorite is the 16-year-old

Hirsch Reserve bourbon. ⊠*217 W. Huron St* ☎*312/587–9600* ▭*AE, D, DC, MC, V* ⊗*Closed Sun. No lunch Sat.*

$–$$
SCANDINAVIAN
Lake View
☖

Ann Sather. The aroma of fresh cinnamon rolls put this place on the map, and it still draws a mob that lines up down the block for weekend breakfasts. Lunches offer similar Scandinavian specialties as well as standard café sandwiches and salads. ⊠*929 W. Belmont Ave.* ☎*773/348–2378* ▭*AE, D, DC, MC, V* ⊗*No dinner.*

$$$
INTERNATIONAL
Loop

Aria. Can't decide between Moroccan, Asian, or Mediterranean? Take your globe-trotting taste buds to Aria, which roams the world larder with abandon: sashimi tuna salad from Japan, free-range chicken breast from Morocco, churrasco from Argentina, soy-glazed cod from Malaysia, Hong Kong barbecue duck and lobster chow mein, and the requisite American steaks. Among generous freebies, tandoori baked bread with Indian-inspired dipping sauces arrives before the meal and a trio of exotically spiced potatoes comes with the entrées. Art from the Far East visually reinforces Aria's Asian predilections. In the convivial lounge, a small-plate menu caters to abbreviated but equally adventurous appetites. ⊠*Fairmont Chicago, 200 N. Columbus Dr.* ☎*312/444–9494* ▭*AE, D, DC, MC, V.*

¢
SOUTHERN
South Side

Army and Lou's. First-rate home-cooked soul food banners this far South Side institution. The fried chicken is arguably the city's best, but leave room for outstanding corn bread, chicken gumbo, mustard greens, and sweet-potato pie. The setting is surprisingly genteel for such down-home fare: waiters in bow ties, tables with starched white cloths, and African and Haitian art on the walls. On Sunday dress up and join the after-church crowds. ⊠*422 E. 75th St.* ☎*773/483–3100* ▭*AE, D, DC, MC, V* ⊗*Closed Tues.*

$$$$
THAI
Irving Park

Arun's. The finest Thai restaurant in Chicago—some say in the country—is also the most expensive, featuring only 12-course tasting menus for a flat $85. That said, the kitchen readily adjusts its offerings to food preferences and, of course, distastes. The kitchen artfully composes six appetizers, four entrées, and two desserts using the freshest ingredients. Results might include shrimp-filled golden pastry baskets, whole tamarind snapper, and veal medallions with ginger-lemongrass sauce. Arun's out-of-the-way location in a residential neighborhood on the northwest side doesn't discourage a strong following among locals and visiting foodies. ⊠*4156 N. Kedzie Ave.* ☎*773/539–1909* ⊿*Reservations essential* ▭*AE, D, DC, MC, V* ⊗*Closed Mon. No lunch.*

$$
AMERICAN
Loop

Atwood Café. The Loop can be all business, even after-hours, but we found an enclave of personality at this spot in the Hotel Burnham. Mahogany columns, cherrywood floors, gold café curtains, and curvy banquettes provide color, and floor-to-ceiling windows provide light. The mostly American menu includes reliables like pan-roasted chicken breast and thick pork chops, peppered by contemporary fare such as crispy red lentil cakes and smoked paprika grilled salmon fillet. ⊠*Hotel Burnham, 1 W. Washington St.* ☎*312/368–1900* ▭*AE, D, DC, MC, V.*

7

$$
NEW AMERICAN
West Loop
Fodor'sChoice
★

Avec. Go to this Euro-style wine bar when you're feeling gregarious; the rather stark space only has seating for 55 people, and it's all at communal tables. The results are loud and lively, though happily the shareable fare—a mix of homemade charcuterie, Mediterranean, and American dishes from a wood-burning oven—is reasonably priced. It's as popular as its next-door neighbor Blackbird (and run by the same forces), and only early birds are guaranteed tables. The doors open at—yikes!—3:30 PM. ⊠615 W. Randolph St. ☎312/377–2002 ▤AE, D, DC, MC, V ☾No lunch.

$$$$
CUTTING-EDGE
Near North

Avenues. The least ostentatious of the city's cutting-edge restaurants, Avenues in the Peninsula Hotel lives a double life. The menu's most straightforward luxury items—butter-poached lobster, Kobe beef strip steak—aim to satisfy business travelers and other hotel guests, as does the sedate wood-paneled Prairie decor. But true culinary connoisseurs come here for something else altogether. Graham Elliot Bowles is one of Chicago's most creative young chefs. His lengthy tasting menus are the place to discover the sort of free-form pyrotechnics that landed him a challenger slot on TV's Iron Chef. Despite his experimental impulses, just about everything here looks and tastes like something you know. Caesar salad is deconstructed into its various parts while vichyssoise is expressed as both a soup and solid terrine. A classic steak frites becomes a remarkable dish, featuring hand-cut beef tartare, smoked gelato, and Béarnaise panna cotta. ⊠Peninsula Hotel, 108 E. Superior St. ☎312/573–6754 ▤AE, D, DC, MC, V ☾Closed Sun. and Mon. No lunch.

$
CHINESE
River North

Ben Pao. Snagging our award for the most Zen Chinese restaurant in town is this spot, with its minimalist black-and-gray decor and soothing water walls. The food livens up the scene, with spicy noodles, Cantonese roast duck, and plenty of the tried-and-true sesame chicken and kung pao chicken. A dozen or so small-plate starters and the Asian hot pot dish—a sort of fondue that uses bubbling broth to cook meat—encourage sharing, making this a good choice for the gang. ⊠52 W. Illinois St. ☎312/222–1888 ▤AE, D, DC, MC, V ☾No lunch weekends.

$
BURGER
Near North

Billy Goat Tavern. The late comedian John Belushi immortalized the Goat's short-order cooks on Saturday Night Live for barking, "No Coke! Pepsi!" and "No fries! Cheeps!" at customers. They still do the shtick at this subterranean hole-in-the-wall favored by reporters posted nearby at the Tribune and the Sun-Times. Griddle-fried "cheezborgers" are the featured chow, and people-watching the favored sport. ⊠430 N. Michigan Ave., lower level ☎312/222–1525 ▤No credit cards.

$$
AMERICAN
River North
Fodor'sChoice
★

Bin 36. This hip hybrid—fine-dining establishment, lively wine bar, and wineshop—serves wine any way you want it: by the bottle, glass, half glass, and as flights of multiple 1½-ounce tastings. The menu similarly encourages sampling, with lots of small-plate grazing choices. Contemporary entrées, such as braised lamb shank and peppercorn-crusted swordfish, are helpfully listed with wine recommendations. An all-glass west wall and 35-foot ceilings lend loft looks to the sprawling space, which can be noisy. Nonetheless, it's a good choice for group gatherings, and, since it's open all day, between-standard-mealtime nibbles. ⊠*339 N. Dearborn St.* ☎*312/755–9463* ⊟*AE, D, DC, MC, V.*

$$
BISTRO
Near North

Bistro 110. The knock against Bistro 110 is that it can be noisy and chaotic, but we consider that a testament to its popularity. Besides the lively bar scene and Water Tower views, the real draw is the food from the wood-burning oven. The kitchen consistently offers excellent renditions of French classics like roast chicken, and vegetarians praise the roasted-vegetable platter. The Sunday jazz brunch makes things more crowded—and louder—than usual. ⊠*110 E. Pearson St.* ☎*312/266– 3110* ⊟*AE, D, DC, MC, V.*

$$
BISTRO
Lake View

Bistro Campagne. This is the place to dine on the North Side for rustic French fare: crispy roast chicken, steak piled with frites, goat cheese salads, and ale-steamed mussels. The lovely, wood-trimmed Arts and Crafts interior provides instant attitude adjustment; in warmer weather, aim to get a table in the torch-lit garden. Prices are reasonable, including those for the French-centric wine list. ⊠*4518 N. Lincoln Ave.* ☎*773/271–6100* ⊟*AE, MC, V* ⊘*No lunch.*

$$
BISTRO
Near North

Bistrot Margot. We love this Old Town bistro for its faithfully executed menu, budget-friendly prices, and Parisian art-nouveau interior, even if we have to sit a little too close for comfort to our neighbors. Chef-owner Joe Doppes whips up silky chicken liver pâté, succulent *moules mariniere* (mussels in tomato sauce), and soul-satisfying coq au vin. Table spacing is tight and crowds abundant, warranting your best behavior. ⊠*1437 N. Wells St.* ☎*312/587–3660* ⊟*AE, D, DC, MC, V.*

$$$
NEW AMERICAN
West Loop

Blackbird. Being cramped next to your neighbor has never been as fun as it is at this hot spot run by foodie chef Paul Kahan. Celebs pepper the sleek see-and-be-seen crowd who delve into creative seasonal dishes, like seared Alaskan halibut and pickled bone marrow or crispy buckwheat crepes with hazelnut cassoulet. It all plays out against a minimalist backdrop of white walls, mohair banquettes, and aluminum chairs. Reservations aren't required, but they might as well be; the dining room is typically booked solid on weekends. ⊠*619 W. Randolph St.* ☎*312/715–0708* ⟁*Reservations essential* ⊟*AE, D, DC, MC, V* ⊘*Closed Sun. No lunch Sat.*

$$
SEAFOOD
River North

Blue Water Grill. This isn't your standard seafood restaurant. Nightcrawlers love this spot for its sleek design, chic amenities (like farewell chocolates in a small gift box), and a menu that fishes from Maine to Tokyo. The sexy L-shape interior spans a sushi bar, a cocktail lounge with low sofas, and two dining rooms with dark tables and throw pillows on the banquettes. There's the usual raw-bar oysters and steamed lobster, but the kitchen goes to work on creative maki rolls (try the spicy Baja), tempura calamari, and buttery bass. Upstairs the jazz lounge hosts pre- and postprandial entertainment. ⊠*520 N. Dearborn St.* ☎*312/777–1400* ⊟*AE, D, DC, MC, V* ⊘*No lunch Sat.*

$$$
NEW AMERICAN
Lincoln Park

Boka. If you're doing Steppenwolf pretheater dinner on North Halsted, this unpretentious spot gets foodies' stamp of approval. A seasonally driven menu includes standouts such as seared stuffed squid, beet salad, grilled hamachi with shrimp dumpling, and coriander-crusted venison. The slick lounge and bar, both serving food, draw a following independent of curtain time. ⊠*1729 N. Halsted St.* ☎*312/337–6070* ▤*AE, MC, V* ⊘*No lunch.*

$$
BRASSERIE
River North

Brasserie Jo. Come for the frites alone at Jean Joho's fun and more affordable brasserie (he of Everest fame). It's authentic down to its zinc-topped bar proffering complimentary hard-boiled eggs. Stay for the *choucroute garnie* (a crock full of pork cuts with Alsatian sauerkraut), fillet of trout, classic coq au vin, and steak tartare. It's most charming when it's bustling, though peak hours will force you to wait for a table. ⊠*59 W. Hubbard St.* ☎*312/595–0800* ▤*AE, D, DC, MC, V* ⊘*No lunch.*

$
NEW AMERICAN
Lake View

Brett's. This storefront charmer in Roscoe Village has soft lighting, classical music, and the kind of serious food you'd only expect downtown. Creative surprises spice the oft-changing menu: potato tacos with poblano chili sauce, Thai-style salmon, maple horseradish pork chops. Soups are a particular strength. Don't miss the homemade bread, fresh from the steam-injected oven. Neighborhood fans line the sidewalk for a seat at brunch, served both Saturday and Sunday. ⊠*2011 W. Roscoe St.* ☎*773/248–0999* ▤*AE, D, DC, MC, V* ⊘*Closed Mon. and Tues.*

$$
NEW AMERICAN
Bucktown

Café Absinthe. It's hip to be obscure. What else could explain Absinthe's move to put its sign out front but its entrance on an alley? Once you find the door, you'll enter a funky, theatrical restaurant well suited to the Bucktown neighborhood. Dishes like venison with cherries and butternut puree, asparagus-lobster risotto with mascarpone mousse, and horseradish-crusted salmon with a cabernet-tarragon-butter sauce play a starring role. ⊠*1954 W. North Ave.* ☎*773/278–4488* ▤*AE, D, DC, MC, V* ⊘*No lunch.*

$
SPANISH
Lincoln Park

Café Ba-Ba-Reeba! It has a kitschy name and is jammed with partying Lincoln Parkers, so at first you wouldn't expect much food-wise here, but expat Spaniards swear it's the best in town. Colorful interiors filled with folk art encourage the fiesta feel. The large assortment of cold and warm tapas ranges from toasted bread with Serrano ham to grilled squid. It's worth visiting the entrée menu for paella and skewered meats. In warm weather the sangria flows freely on the outdoor patio. ⊠*2024 N. Halsted St.* ☎*773/935–5000* ▤*AE, D, DC, MC, V* ⊘*No lunch weekdays.*

$
SPANISH
River North

Cafe Iberico. A Spanish expat from the province of Galicia runs this tapas place hailed by a range of fans from visiting Spaniards (including the national soccer team and guitarist Paco de Lucia) to family clans, dating couples, and cheap chowhounds. You can easily build a meal from the many $2–$7 small plates on offer like baked goat cheese, Spanish ham, grilled squid, and skewered beef. When busy, it's loud and boisterous, which is only annoying on weekends when the wait can stretch to hours. Only parties of six or more may make reservations for Sunday through Thursday. ⊠*739 N. LaSalle St.* ☎*312/573–1510* ▤*AE, D, DC, MC, V.*

$ | **Café Selmarie.** For a light meal in Lincoln Square, line up at this bakery-
CAFÉ | turned-café, a longstanding favorite among locals. Breakfast gets you
Far North Side | croissant French toast and corned-beef hash with eggs; lunch ranges
☾ | from goat cheese salads to smoked salmon baguettes; and dinner runs
to quiche and roast chicken. Don't miss the sink-your-teeth-in pastries
(you can also buy them to-go at the front counter). Pass summer waits
pleasantly in the neighboring plaza; during other seasons, you're out in
the cold. ✉ *4729 N. Lincoln Ave.* ☏ *773/989–5595* ▤ *MC, V.*

$$ | **The Caliterra Bar & Grille.** The seasonal orientation of the West Coast
ITALIAN | merges with old-world Italian recipes in dishes such as gnocchi Bolog-
Near North | nese, hazelnut-crusted sea bass, and braised veal shank. The wood-
trimmed dining room flows into a display kitchen and adjacent jazz
lounge, so wherever you sit, there's something to look at should the
conversation lag. ✉ *Wyndham Chicago Hotel, 633 N. St. Clair St.*
☏ *312/274–4444* ▤ *AE, D, DC, MC, V.*

$$$ | **The Capital Grille.** The Chicago outpost of this steak-house chain man-
STEAKHOUSE | ages to hold its own among the local players. You can see prime
Near North | steaks being dry aged in a glassed-in room. The menu also includes a
strong selection of fresh fish and shellfish. The decor avoids some of
the steak-house clichés by mixing mounted deer heads and portraits
in oil. ✉ *633 N. St. Clair St.* ☏ *312/337–9400* ▤ *AE, D, DC, MC, V*
☾ *No lunch weekends.*

$$ | **Carmichael's.** The look here is old-time Chicago—oak and brass, black-
STEAKHOUSE | and-white photographs, and waiters dressed in suspenders and shirt-
West Loop | sleeve garters—though the true vintage is late 1980s. We forgive them
the ruse for the well-priced (around $30) Angus steaks, which make
this one of the more reasonable top-tier steak houses in town. Planked
salmon is a good non-beef option. Live jazz lures prowling carnivores
to the lush garden in summer. ✉ *1052 W. Monroe St., West Loop*
☏ *312/433–0025* ▤ *AE, D, DC, MC, V* ☾ *No lunch weekends.*

$$ | **Catch 35.** Eavesdrop on advertising types who do the after-five mix-and-
SEAFOOD | mingle at this spot in the lobby of the Leo Burnett Building. When it
Loop | comes to food, have it your way: fish or shellfish comes grilled, seared,
or baked. The multilevel dining room provides plenty of eye candy,
plus glimpses of the Chicago River beyond. ✉ *35 W. Wacker Dr.*
☏ *312/346–3500* ▤ *AE, D, DC, MC, V* ☾ *No lunch weekends.*

$$$$ | **Charlie Trotter's.** Plan well in advance to dine at top toque Charlie Trotter's
NEW AMERICAN | namesake (or call the day of and hope for a cancellation). One of the
Lincoln Park | nation's most acclaimed chefs, Trotter prepares his menus daily from the
best of what's available globally. The results are daring, multi-ingredient
dishes that look like art on a dinner plate. Menus follow a multicourse,
$155 degustation format ($130 for the vegetarian version). For a worthwhile splurge, order the wines-to-match option. This temple of haute
cuisine occupies a stately Lincoln Park town house. ✉ *816 W. Armitage
Ave.* ☏ *773/248–6228* ☝ *Reservations essential* Jacket required ▤ *AE,
DC, MC, V* ☾ *Closed Sun and Mon. No lunch.*

7

$$ Chez Joel. Breaking Taylor Street's Italian allegiance, Chez Joel waves
BISTRO   the flag for France. The sunny bistro serves well-prepared classics like
South Loop   steak frites, coq au vin, and bouillabaisse. It's a good pasta-free date
choice, and a favorite of locals. ✉*1119 W. Taylor St.* ☎*312/226–6479*
⊟AE, D, DC, MC, V ⊘*Closed Mon. No lunch weekends.* .

$ Chicago Brauhaus. The German immigrants who settled in Lincoln
GERMAN   Square have mostly moved on, making room for a new generation of
Far North Side   urban hipsters. But they leave behind the Brauhaus, an Oktoberfest
of a restaurant featuring a *lederhosen*-clad duo playing nightly polkas
and waltzes that bring old-timers and new converts to the dance floor.
Though the atmosphere is the draw over the food, you can't go wrong
with the bratwurst and sauerkraut or the schnitzel. Large tables easily
accommodate groups. The spacious bar and a good selection of Ger-
man beers draws oompah-loving drinkers. ✉*4732 N. Lincoln Ave.*
☎*773/784–4444* *⊟AE, D, DC, MC, V* ⊘*Closed Tues.*

$$ Coco Pazzo. This restaurant focuses on Tuscan cuisine—lusty, aggres-
ITALIAN   sively seasoned fare, such as homemade pasta with rabbit ragu, herb-
River North   crusted half lamb rack, and wood-grilled Florentine steaks. Stop in at
lunch for pizzas fresh from the wood-fired oven. Swagged draperies
and discreet but professional service work hard to soften the open loft
setting of exposed brick walls and wood floors. ✉*300 W. Hubbard St.*
☎*312/836–0900* ⚱*Reservations essential* *⊟AE, DC, MC, V* ⊘*No
lunch weekends.*

$ Coobah. Loud and lively Coobah loves a good party and encourages
LATIN   reveling to the wee hours by serving dinner until 1 AM most nights,
Lake View   2 AM on Saturday. Unlike lots of lounge-restaurants, however, this
one doesn't rely on the mojitos and sangria to distract you from so-so
food. Indeed, dishes such as tamale-baked tilapia, mussels sautéed with
chili paste, and spicy pork tamales distinguish the kitchen. Weekend
brunches, held 10 AM to 3 PM, lend a Latin accent to eggs and sandwiches. ✉*3423 N. Southport Ave.* ☎*773/528–2220* *⊟AE, D, DC,
MC, V* ⊘*No lunch weekdays.*

$–$$ Costa's. Greektown is fairly labeled monotonous, cuisine-wise. But
GREEK   Costa's betters its many neighbors in both looks and taste. The multi-
West Loop   level Hellenic interior has terra-cotta tile work and rough-textured white
walls and archways. There's a generous assortment of *mezes* (tapas-like
Greek appetizers), traditional salt fish, kebobs, and roast leg of lamb.
Live piano and the enthusiasm of diners tend to send the decibels soaring.
✉*340 S. Halsted St.* ☎*312/263–9700* *⊟AE, D, DC, MC, V.*

$$$ Crofton on Wells. We like this place because it's really good and still
NEW AMERICAN   manages to be rather low-key. Chef–owner Suzy Crofton breaks a few
River North   contemporary-dining rules: she doesn't pack tables too closely together
in the small space, and she keeps the noise level down. Her food is
similarly short on clichés but gratifyingly long on flavor. Dig into gutsy
chipotle roasted Amish chicken or grilled venison with apricot jam.
✉*535 N. Wells St.* ☎*312/755–1790* ⚱*Reservations essential* *⊟AE,
D, DC, MC, V* ⊘*Closed Sun. No lunch Sat.*

$$ **Cru Café & Wine Bar.** After you've shopped Michigan Avenue and the
AMERICAN   Gold Coast and you're ready to drop, plant it at the well-located Cru
Near North   Café & Wine Bar for salve on a plate and in a glass. The 50-some by-
the-glass pours, in addition to several hundred more bottle selections,
pair well with elegant café fare such as the surf and turf lobster and beef
tenderloin club sandwich, Cobb salad, and steak frites with cabernet
jam. The gourmet take-out Goddess & The Grocer attached to Cru
sells wine and nibbles to go if you prefer picnicking in your hotel room.
✉ *25 E. Delaware Ave.* ☎ *312/337–4001* ☰ *AE, D, DC, MC, V.*

$$$$ **Custom House.** Chef Shawn McClain established his renown with Asian
STEAKHOUSE   seafood at Spring and vegetables at Green Zebra before giving the stan-
South Loop   dard Chicago steakhouse model a much needed update with Custom
House. The Printer's Row restaurant features sandstone block walls,
cozy leather booths and picture windows, a handsome but not overly
masculine setting that mirrors the food. You can get a New York Strip
or a flat iron steak, of course, but venturesome carnivores should try
the braised veal cheeks or roast quail. Outstanding sides include gratin
potatoes with sheep's milk cheese and desserts have a comforting qual-
ity in dishes like malted milk chocolate mousse. ✉ *500 S. Dearborn St.*
☎ *312/523–0200* ☰ *AE, D, DC, MC, V.*

$ **Cyrano's Bistrot Wine Bar & Cabaret.** Cyrano's flies under the radar in
BISTRO   restaurant-rich River North, which works to your advantage if you
River North   want a spontaneous meal. Chef and owner Didier Durand presents the
food of his birthplace, Bergerac, in this cheerful restaurant. Traditional
starters such as onion tart and bouillabaisse lead into mains of rotis-
serie chicken, rabbit, and duck. The wine list includes many vintages
from lesser-known producers in southern France. The basement caba-
ret doles out free nibbles with drinks at happy hour. ✉ *546 N. Wells
St.* ☎ *312/467–0546* ☰ *AE, D, DC, MC, V* ☉ *Closed Sun. and Mon.
No lunch weekends.*

$$$$ **David Burke's Primehouse.** New York celebrity chef David Burke runs
MEXICAN   Primehouse in the boutique James hotel and though local reception was
Near North   initially cautious—after all, what could a New Yorker teach a Chica-
goan about steak?—the restaurant has been roundly embraced for its
convivial setting and sense of playfulness, including identifying 207L,
the steer responsible for producing the menu's prime beef. Don't miss
Burke's innovative cuts including a 28-day-dry-aged rib eye and the
bone-in filet mignon. Interactive elements including table-side tossed
Caesar salads and fill-your-own doughnuts for dessert feed the consid-
erable energy in the generally packed room. The best seats are the red-
leather booths along the walls. ✉ *616 N. Rush St.* ☎ *312/660–6000*
☰ *AE, D, MC, V.*

$$ **De Cero Taqueria.** Sometimes you want celebrity chef-made regional
AMERICAN   Mexican, and sometimes you just want a really good taco. For the lat-
West Loop   ter, as well as zesty margaritas, a convivial setting, and lick-the-mor-
tar-clean guacamole, grab a table at De Cero, the Mexican standout
on Randolph Street's restaurant row. The highlight of the menu is the
taco list. Each of 16 tacos is priced individually and made to order for

7

a mix-and-match meal. Top choices include chipotle chicken, braised duck with corn salsa, and beef tenderloin tips braised with mushrooms. Though the spot is wood-tables-and-benches casual and very loud, beat the crowds by phoning ahead, especially on weekends. ⊠ *814 W. Randolph St.* ☏ *312/455–8114* ⊟ *AE, MC, V* ⊘ *Closed Sun. No lunch weekends.*

$$$
LATIN
River North

DeLaCosta. Hipster DeLaCosta imports the Nuevo Latino food of celebrity chef Douglas Rodriguez and amps up the club vibe for a see-and-be-seen spot that manages to do a credible job with the food. The décor is truly theatrical, down to placing menacing mannequins on the walls, renting private "cabanas" with bottle service and swathing the public lounge area in gauzy curtains. But foodies won't be disappointed by a seat at the stylish ceviche bar (don't miss the hamachi ceviche) or orders of marlin tacos and Uruguayan beef tenderloin. The later the hour, the louder and boozier this spot becomes; reserve accordingly. ⊠ *465 E. Illinois St.* ☏ *312/464–1700* ⊟ *AE, DC, MC, V* ⊘ *No lunch weekends.*

¢
AMERICAN
River North
⊘

Ed Debevic's. Gum-snapping waiters in garish costumes trade quips and snide remarks with customers at this tongue-in-cheek re-creation of a 1950s diner, but it's all good, clean fun (except perhaps when they dance on the counter without removing their shoes). The menu is deep and cheap with 10 different hamburgers, five chili preparations, four hot dogs, a large sandwich selection, and such "deluxe plates" as meat loaf, pot roast, and chicken-fried steak. The place is crawling with kids. Unlike a real 1950s diner, however, Ed's has a selection of cocktails and wines for their parents. ⊠ *640 N. Wells St.* ☏ *312/664–1707* ⊜ *Reservations not accepted* ⊟ *AE, D, DC, MC, V.*

$
AMERICAN
South Side
⊘

Eleven City Diner. For all its great food, Chicago is not a big deli town, which endears Eleven City Diner, an old-school deli and family restaurant in the South Loop, to the locals. You can get breakfast all day (bagel and lox, "hoppel poppel" scrambled eggs with salami, potatoes, onions and peppers), deli staples like matzoh-ball soup and pastrami and corned-beef sandwiches, diner options including burgers and soda-fountain floats and malts from the staff soda jerk. Breaking from the deli tradition, Eleven City sells beer and wine. In keeping with it there's an old-fashioned candy counter on your way out. ⊠ *1112 W. Wabash* ☏ *312/212–1112* ⊟ *AE, D, DC, MC, V.*

$
CHINESE
Chinatown

Emperor's Choice. This sophisticate sets out to prove that Chinese seafood specialties can go well beyond deep-fried prawns. It succeeds with dishes such as steamed oysters and Peking-style lobster. A separate menu includes such "delicacies" as shark's fin soup and pork bellies. Seating is cramped and not for serenity-seekers. Discounted parking (with validation) is available in the Cermak/Wentworth lot. ⊠ *2238 S. Wentworth Ave.* ☏ *312/225–8800* ⊟ *AE, D, MC, V.*

$$
NEW AMERICAN
Lake View

Erwin. Striking a pose between friendly and refined, this spot has comforting food, a cozy setting, and polished service. Chef Erwin Dreschsler often patrols the dining room of his namesake restaurant, greeting regulars. The straightforward, seasonal menu may look ordinary—roasted chicken with chili-pepper sauce and one of the city's best burgers—but the skillful cooking and vibrant flavors gives you new respect for simplicity. The booths by the front windows are the best for views of neighborhood comings and goings. ⊠*2925 N. Halsted St.* ☎*773/528–7200* ⊟*AE, D, DC, MC, V* ☾*Closed Mon. No lunch.*

$$$$ **Everest.** No one expects romance at the top of the Chicago Stock
FRENCH Exchange, but Everest does its best to throw you a curve wherever and
Loop whenever. Consider the trip: two separate elevators whisk you 40 stories up, where you have sweeping views of the city's sprawl westward. Then, there's the food. It's French, but with an Alsatian bent—a nod to Chef Jean Joho's roots. He might just bring edible gold leaf to his risotto (and you'll pay handsomely for it). The whole experience, from the tuxedoed waiters to the massive wine list, screams, "Special occasion!" ⊠*440 S. LaSalle St.* ☎*312/663–8920* ⚐*Reservations essential* Jacket required ⊟*AE, D, DC, MC, V* ☾*Closed Sun. and Mon. No lunch.*

$ **Feast.** The gregarious communal table, cozy fireplace, and sofa-filled
INTERNATIONAL lounge create a fittingly social setting for the arty Bucktown locals
Bucktown who dine here regularly. If you can't find something to eat here, you're not hungry. World cuisines from Cuba to India mingle freely on an expansive, bold menu; try the ancho chili and maple-glazed pork chop, barbecue salmon over corn buttermilk hot cakes, or chimichurri skirt steak. ⊠*1616 N. Damen Ave.* ☎*773/772–7100* ⊟*AE, DC, MC, V.*

$$$$ **Fogo de Chao.** Gaucho-clad servers parade through the dining room
BRAZILIAN brandishing carved-to-order skewered and grilled meats in this all-you-
River North can-eat Brazilian churrascaria. Diners warm up with a trip to the lavish salad bar. Then, using a plate-side chip, signal green for "go" to bring on lamb, pork loin, ribs, and several beef cuts, stopped only by flipping the chip to red. You can restart as often as you like. If that's not enough, there are starchy sides and dessert flans included in the $48.50 price as well; only drinks are extra. Compared to traditional steak houses, this carnivorous all-inclusive feast is a bargain. Go on a busy night (Thursday, Friday, or Saturday) to ensure the meat's tender—not dried out from reheating. ⊠*661 N. LaSalle St.* ☎*312/932–9330* ⊟*AE, D, DC, MC, V* ☾*No lunch weekends.*

¢ **Fox & Obel Food Market Cafe.** Skip the tourist trap funnel-cake fare at
CAFÉ Navy Pier. This riverside gourmet market a block away is a tooth-
Near North some escape. The prepared fine and organic foodstuffs are treated with reverence, and although service is cafeteria-style, selections are decidedly more sophisticated. We like the entrée southwestern chicken salad, chicken tomatillo soup, and roast beef–blue brie–caramelized onion sandwiches. ⊠*401 E. Illinois St., Near North* ☎*312/379–0112* ⊟*AE, D, MC, V.*

$ **Francesca's on Taylor.** Among the molto, molto Italianos on the block,
ITALIAN Francesca's one-ups 'em with good cooking and a modern menu. You
South Loop might find ravioli stuffed with spinach and a four-cheese sauce or tilapia with fresh oregano and roasted potatoes, and you won't break the bank. Early birds flock here before heading to the United Center for a Bulls game, Blackhawks game, or special event. ⊠*1400 W. Taylor St.* ☎*312/829–2828* ⊟*AE, DC, MC, V* ☾*No lunch weekends.*

7

$$ **Frontera Grill.** Devotees of chef-owner Rick Bayless queue up for his
MEXICAN distinct fare at this casual restaurant, brightly trimmed in Mexican folk
River North art. Bayless annually visits Mexico with the entire staff in tow. Servers,
consequently, are encyclopedic on the food, typified by trout in yellow
mole, red chili-marinated pork, and black-bean tamales filled with goat
cheese. The reservation policy is tricky: they're accepted for parties of five
or more, though smaller groups can phone in the same day. Otherwise,
make like most and endure the two-margarita wait. ✉*445 N. Clark St.*
☎*312/661–1434* ▭*AE, D, DC, MC, V* ☉*Closed Sun. and Mon.*

$$$$ **Geja's.** For every course there's a fondue at this Lincoln Park longtimer.
FRENCH Start with the cheese fondue, then progress to the sampler plate of
Lincoln Park shellfish, chicken, beef, and vegetables cooked in a kettle of hot oil (the
tables are riveted to the floor to avoid disaster). Finish by dunking fruits
and sweets in liquid chocolate, if you've got room. Candlelight, cozy
dining nooks, walls filled with empty wine bottles, and strumming gui-
tarists mean this place is packed on Valentine's Day. ✉*340 W. Armit-
age Ave.* ☎*773/281–9101* ▭*AE, D, DC, MC, V* ☉*No lunch.*

$$$ **Gene and Georgetti.** This old-school steak house thrives on the buddy
STEAKHOUSE network of high-powered regulars who pop into the historic River
River North North joint to carve up massive steaks, good chops, and the famed
"garbage salad"—a kitchen-sink creation of greens with vegetables and
meats. Service can be brusque if you're not connected, but the vibe is
Chicago to the core. ✉*500 N. Franklin St.* ☎*312/527–3718* ▭*AE,
DC, MC, V* ☉*Closed Sun.*

$$$$ **Gibsons Steakhouse.** Chicago movers and shakers mingle with conven-
STEAKHOUSE tioneers at Gibsons, a lively, homegrown, Gold Coast steak house
Near North renowned for overwhelming portions, good service, and celebrity spot-
ting. Generous steaks and chops center the menu, but there are plenty
of fish options including planked whitefish and massive Australian
lobster tails. One dessert will feed a table of four. Reservations aren't
required but are near essential given the hoards of fans. ✉*1028 N. Rush
St.* ☎*312/266–8999* ⚑*Reservations essential* ▭*AE, D, DC, MC, V.*

$$ **Gioco.** The name means "game" in Italian, and the restaurant fulfills the
ITALIAN promise not with venison, but in the spirit of playing a game. The decor is
South Loop distressed-urban, with plaster-spattered brick walls and well-worn hard-
wood floors, but the menu is comfort-Italian, with rustic fare like home-
made penne pasta with prosciutto, grilled lamb chops, and sausage with
beans. The Speakeasy Room, a private dining space with its own rear-alley
entrance, is homage to the building's notorious past under Prohibition.
✉*1312 S. Wabash Ave.* ☎*312/939–3870* ▭*AE, DC, MC, V.*

$$ **Green Dolphin Street.** It's hard to pass up this one-stop dinner-and-music
AMERICAN spot. There are globally influenced American dishes in the main din-
Lake View ing room, a sandwiches-and-salads bar menu in the jazz club, a cigar-
friendly bar, and a seasonal outdoor patio overlooking a relatively quiet
stretch of the Chicago River. Dinner in the main room gets you into
the handsome club, though you'll pay half the cover charge on weekends. ✉*2200 N. Ashland Ave.* ☎*773/395–0066* ▭*AE, D, DC, MC,
V* ☉*Closed Sun. and Mon. No lunch.*

Continued on page 261

CHICAGO'S HOLY TRINITY:
Pizza, Hot Dogs & Italian Beef Sandwiches

Long before Chicago's dining scene got all gussied up with boldface-named chefs and swanky hot spots, the City of Big Shoulders perfected hearty, gut-busting food for the Average Joe. Until you've pigged out on deep-dish pizza at Lou Malnati's or Gino's East, sunk your teeth into a loaded hot dog at Superdawg Drive-in, and wiped the grease off your face after devouring an Italian beef sandwich at Al's Italian Beef, you haven't done Chicago. So go on, leave your diet plans at home and get ready to sample the best of the big city.

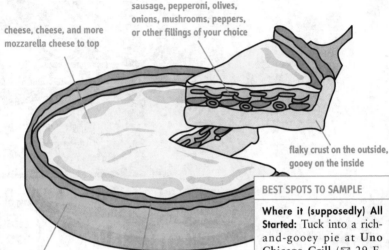

cheese, cheese, and more
mozzarella cheese to top

sausage, pepperoni, olives,
onions, mushrooms, peppers,
or other fillings of your choice

flaky crust on the outside,
gooey on the inside

two-inch-high
deep dish pan

spicy tomato sauce

TASTE 1 | DEEP-DISH PIZZA

A CALORIC HISTORY

Pizza—in one form or another—has been around since the sixth century B.C., but it only gained heft when it settled into this brash, entrepreneurial city. Pizzeria Uno founder Ike Sewell generally gets the credit for turning pizza inside out in 1943. His knife-and-fork creation started with a layer of cheese, followed by the toppings, and then the sauce, all tucked into a doughy crust that he yanked up the sides of a deep pan.

THE CRUST CONTROVERSY

The founders of Lou Malnati's pizzeria worked in Ike's kitchen at Pizzeria Uno and claim that *they* were the ones actually doing the cooking. They broke off and opened up Malnati's in 1971, and a classic Chicago rivalry was born.

BEST SPOTS TO SAMPLE

Where it (supposedly) All Started: Tuck into a rich-and-gooey pie at **Uno Chicago Grill** (⊠ 29 E. Ohio St. ☎ 312/321–1000 ⊕ www.unos.com), formerly the infamous Pizzeria Uno.

Most Authentic: Aficionados of **Lou Malnati's** (⊠ 439 N. Wells St. ☎ 312/828–9800 ⊕ www.loumalnatis.com) claim that their favorite pies have more flavor and like that there are fewer tourists to clog up the joint. If you're really feeling indulgent, order yours with a butter crust. Trust us.

Worth the Wait: Join the out-the-door line at **Gino's East** (⊠ 633 N. Wells St. ☎ 312/943–1124 ⊕ www.ginoseast.com) for caloric pies and a chance to add to the graffiti on the walls.

Easiest to Find: The ubiquitous **Giordano's** (⊠ 730 N. Rush St. ☎ 312/951–0747) has 13 locations throughout the city besides this one.

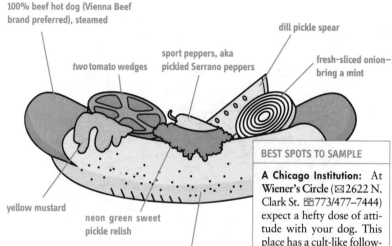

100% beef hot dog (Vienna Beef brand preferred), steamed

two tomato wedges

sport peppers, aka pickled Serrano peppers

dill pickle spear

fresh-sliced onion— bring a mint

yellow mustard

neon green sweet pickle relish

poppy seed bun

TASTE 2 | **HOT DOGS**

A DOG IS BORN

The iconic Chicago-style hot dog got its start at the 1893 World's Fair's Columbian Exposition. Two immigrants from Austria and Hungary hawked a beef frankfurter sandwich in a steamed bun piled with mustard, relish, onion, tomato, dill pickle, hot peppers, and celery salt. When the Fair moved on, the cravings persisted, launching an on-going affair with the Chicago-style hot dog.

HOW MUCH GARDEN CAN ONE BUN HOLD?

If you've walked a square block of Chicago, chances are you've passed a hot dog. Dog dealers lodge under El stops, on street corners, and at sports arenas. The one thing they all have in common? Their dogs get "dragged through the garden," or loaded with the aforementioned veggies, unless otherwise specified. Don't forget to grab a fistful of napkins—these dogs are messy.

BEST SPOTS TO SAMPLE

A Chicago Institution: At **Wiener's Circle** (✉2622 N. Clark St. ☎773/477–7444) expect a hefty dose of attitude with your dog. This place has a cult-like following of masochistic fans who line up for insults from the sassy, crass staffers. Get the Chicago dog, and don't ask for any substitutions. You've been warned.

Get 'em Retro Style: Look for the boy dog and girl dog on the roof of **Superdawg Drive-In** (✉6363 N. Milwaukee Ave. ☎773/763–0660 ⊕ www.superdawg. com), where car-hops deliver your chow.

Poshest Pick: For a weiner on a higher plane, check out **Hot Doug's** (✉ 3324 N. California ☎773/279–9550 ⊕ www.hotdougs. com). In addition to the classic Chicago beef, encased meats include kangaroo or rabbit on a rotating menu.

7

CHICAGO'S HOLY TRINITY

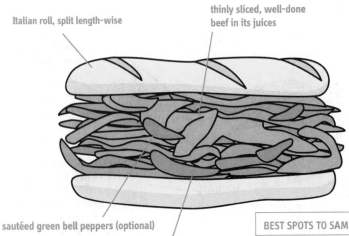

Italian roll, split length-wise

thinly sliced, well-done beef in its juices

sautéed green bell peppers (optional)

hot giardiniera peppers

TASTE 3 | ITALIAN BEEF SANDWICHES

IT'S ALL ABOUT THE BEEF

Italian immigrants in Chicago happily adapted to the locally abundant meat supply to produce the now-classic Italian beef sandwich. Hard hats and desk jockeys crowd beef stands at lunch, joined by the occasional visiting celebrity. Don't expect much in the way of atmosphere: Here it's Formica counters, fluorescent lights, and big shoulder–to–big shoulder intimacy.

GRAB YOUR NAPKINS

The two-fister, a popular lunchtime staple, stuffs an Italian roll, split length-wise, with thin slices of medium beef. Authentic Italian beef sandwiches use sirloin rump, top round, or bottom round that's wet-roasted and dripping in a broth that's spiked with garlic, oregano, and spices. The whole thing is topped with hot giardiniera, a spicy relish of Serrano peppers, diced carrots, cauliflower, celery, and olives in oil. If you've ordered it "wet," it comes with an extra ladle of juice and a stack of napkins; if you order a cheesy beef, they melt a slice or two of mozzarella over the whole mess.

BEST SPOTS TO SAMPLE

Roll up Your Sleeves: Plant your elbows at the window counter or a picnic table in the "elegant dining room" at **Mr. Beef** (✉ 666 N. Orleans St. ☎ 312/337–8500), where famous fans get their mugs on the wall.

Join the Masses: On Little Italy's Taylor Street, standing-room-only crowds of students and local business folk pack **Al's No. 1 Italian Beef** (✉ 1079 W. Taylor St., ☎ 312/226–4017, ⊕ www.alsbeef.com).

Soak Up Nostalgia: The cavernous space at **Portillo's** (✉ 100 W. Ontario St. ☎ 312/587–8910) is decked out with Capone-era gangster photos and an antique car that hangs from the ceiling. Fans rave about the sloppy sandwich, and you can buy souvenirs to commemorate the occasion.

$$$ **Green Zebra.** Chef Shawn McClain of Spring fame took the vegetable
NEW AMERICAN side dish and ran it up the marquee. The result gives good-for-you veg-
West Loop gies the star treatment in a sleek shop suave enough to attract the likes
Fodor'sChoice of Gwyneth Paltrow. All dishes are small and change seasonally. You
★ might see roast beets with horseradish foam or sunchoke raviolis with
melted goat cheese and hazelnuts. One chicken and one fish dish make
do for carnivores. ⊠*1460 W. Chicago Ave.* ☎*312/243–7100* ⊟*AE,
D, DC, MC, V* ⊘*Closed Mon.*

$$ **The Grillroom.** If you're going to a performance at the Shubert Theatre
STEAKHOUSE across the street, you're close enough to dash over here for a drink at
Loop intermission (we love the lengthy by-the-glass wine selections). Pre- and
post-curtain, the clubby confines fill with showgoers big on beef, though
there are also ample raw bar, seafood, and pasta choices. For the most
relaxing experience, come after Act I commences. ⊠*33 W. Monroe St.*
☎*312/960–0000* ⊟*AE, D, DC, MC, V* ⊘*No lunch weekends.*

$$ **Harry Caray's.** Famed Cubs announcer Harry Caray died in 1998, but
ITALIAN his legend lives on as fans continue to pour into the namesake res-
River North taurant where Harry frequently held court. Italian-American specialties
including pastas and chicken Vesuvio share menu space with top-qual-
ity prime steaks and chops. The wine list has won a number of national
awards. If you're looking for a classic Chicago spot to catch a game, the
generally thronged bar serves classic bar food and televised sports. Holy
cow! ⊠*33 W. Kinzie St.* ☎*312/828–0966* ⊟*AE, D, DC, MC, V.*

$ **Heaven on Seven.** Every day is Mardi Gras at Heaven on Seven, which
SOUTHERN pursues a good time all the time—and even more so during Cubs sea-
Lake View son. Tables are centered with a daring collection of hot sauces, and
the food, though it's well shy of ambrosia, is plentiful and filling. Ched-
dar-jalapeño biscuits and seven-layer cake are great menu book ends.
⊠*3478 N. Clark St.* ☎*773/477–7818* ⊟*AE, D, DC, MC, V* ⊠*600 N.
Michigan Ave., Near North* ☎*312/280–7774* ⊟*AE, D, DC, MC, V.*

$ **Hopleaf Bar.** True beer aficionados know beer is food. So when hops dev-
BELGIAN otee Michael Roper added a dining room onto the back of his beloved
Far North Side tavern, swillers thrilled to sop their suds with delectable specialties such
as Belgian-style mussels steamed in white ale with herbs, duck confit
crepes, and smoked pork belly with creamy white beans. Arrive early
to avoid waiting in the bar for a table. But don't bring the kids; Roper
is adamant that only those of legal drinking age can eat here. ⊠*5148
N. Clark St.* ☎*773/334–9851* ⊟*D, DC, MC, V.*

$$ **Hot Chocolate.** The city's most celebrated pastry chef, Mindy Segal,
CAFÉ strikes out solo at Hot Chocolate, a hit with, as you might expect,
Wicker Park a really great dessert selection. For the big finish, there's chocolate
mousse, baked pear, buttermilk cake, apple pot pie, and a myriad of
milk shakes and hot chocolate flavors with homemade marshmallows.
How sweet, and how swamped, it is. PS: the menu also has upscale café
fare like pork chops with spaetzle or a tuna melt with wild capers. But
who came here for the real food? ⊠*1747 N. Damen Ave., Wicker Park*
☎*773/489–1747* ⊟*AE, MC, V* ⊘*Closed Mon.*

7

¢ **Hot Doug's.** Don't tell the zealots who have made Hot Doug's famous
HOT DOGS that these are *just* hot dogs—these "encased meats" go beyond your
Lake View standard Vienna wiener. The gourmet purveyor wraps buns around
Fodor's Choice chipotle chicken sausage, smoked crawfish and pork sausage with spicy
★ remoulade, and even rabbit sausage. Make the trek on a Friday or
☾ Saturday, when the artery-clogging duck-fat fries are available. The
clientele is a curious mix of hungry hard-hats and serious foodies, neither of which care about the lack of frills. ⊠ *3325 N. California Ave.*
☎ *773/751–1500* ⊟ *No credit cards* ☾ *Closed Sun. No dinner.*

$ **Ina's.** It's so cozy you almost feel like you're at a diner—there's the lov-
AMERICAN ing presence of owner Ina Pinkney, reliable chow, and a regular follow-
West Loop ing. But dishes like vegetable hash and black bean–cheese-eggs-chorizo
"scrapple" (a loaded version of scrambled eggs) at breakfast and lamb
chops or seared tilapia at dinner food. Close to Oprah's studio and loft
dwellers up and down Randolph, Ina's regularly generates a queue,
especially on weekends. ⊠ *1235 W. Randolph St.* ☎ *312/226–8227*
⊟ *AE, D, DC, MC, V* ☾ *No dinner Sun. and Mon.*

$$$ **Japonais.** Style and substance come together at sleek and chic Japonais.
JAPANESE Don't be intimidated by the lengthy menu. Trust servers to direct you
River North to savories such as breaded oysters, sweet-vinegar-seaweed salad, and
a raft of winning maki-roll combinations including octopus with spicy
tuna. Traditional tables are supplemented by a couch-filled lounge
also serving the entire menu. Downstairs an indoor-outdoor bar pro-
vides seasonal seating along the Chicago River—don't attempt it on
weekends unless you have sharp elbows. ⊠ *606 W. Chicago Ave.*
☎ *312/822–9600* ⊟ *AE, D, DC, MC, V* ☾ *No lunch weekends.*

$ **Joe's Be-Bop Cafe and Jazz Emporium.** Joe's looks like a classic jazz club
SOUTHERN with a raised stage but plays like a family restaurant on raucous Navy
Near North Pier. Ribs and creole fare are clan-pleasing, and the jazz bands—booked
☾ most nights and during no more Sunday brunch—lift Joe's from merely
touristy to actually enjoyable. ⊠ *E. Grand Ave.* ☎ *312/595–5299*
⊟ *AE, D, DC, MC, V.*

$$–$$$ **Joe's Seafood, Prime Steaks & Stone Crab.** You might wonder what a South
SEAFOOD Floridian like Joe's is doing so far from the ocean. Apparently, raking
River North it in. Unlike its parent, Joe's Stone Crab in Miami Beach, this out-
let doesn't close when the Florida crabs are out of season in summer.
Which explains the extra emphasis on other denizens of the deep and
prime steaks. One thing this restaurant does share with the Miami
original is its popularity—people line up before the restaurant opens to
be sure they get a table. ⊠ *60 E. Grand Ave.* ☎ *312/379–5637* ⊟ *AE,
D, DC, MC, V* ☾ *No lunch Sun.*

¢ **Julius Meinl Cafe.** Viennese coffee roaster Julius Meinl operates this very
CAFÉ European café in an unexpected location at the intersection of Addi-
Lake View son and Southport, just a few blocks from Wrigley Field. Comfort-
able banquettes and a well-stocked supply of international newspapers
bid coffee sippers to stick around. Vegetable focaccia and pear and
brie sandwiches, hazelnut and blue-cheese salads, mushroom soup,
and loads of European pastries feed the peckish. We love the Austrian

breakfast of poached egg, ham, and Emmentaler cheese—this is the only place in the city that serves it. Classical and jazz combos entertain Friday and Saturday evenings. ✉*3601 N. Southport Ave.* ☎*773/868–1857* ⊟*AE, D, MC, V.*

$ **Kamehachi.** It seems like there's a sushi spot on practically every corner
JAPANESE
Near North
in Chicago, but when Kamehachi opened in Old Town in 1967, it was the first. Quality fish, updated decor, and eager-to-please hospitality keep fans returning. Behind the busy sushi bar, chefs manage both restaurant orders and the many take-out calls of neighbors. We find combinations, including maki rolls, nigiri sushi, and miso soup, are often a bargain, running from $13 to $30. Belly up to the sushi bar, or take a seat in the upstairs lounge, or the flowering garden (in season). The Streeterville spin-off offers semiprivate tatami rooms ideal for groups. ✉*1400 N. Wells St.* ☎*312/664–3663* ⊟*AE, D, DC, MC, V* ⊘*No lunch Sun.* ✉*240 E. Ontario, Near North* ☎*312/587–0600* ⊟*AE, D, DC, MC, V* ⊘*No lunch Sun. and Mon..*

$$$$ **Keefer's.** Few steak houses advertise their broiler men, but the barrier-
STEAKHOUSE
River North
busting Keefer's hired acclaimed chef John Hogan to run the kitchen. Hogan's definition of a steak-house menu breaks all conventions by including his signature bistro fare, inventive daily specials (pray for the seafood-rich bouillabaisse), and plenty of fish offerings as well as New York strips and hefty porterhouses. The circular room drops the he-man pose, too. All of which explains why Keefer's pulls the most diverse and gender-balanced crowd of the meat market. ✉*20 W. Kinzie St.* ☎*312/467–9525* ⊟*AE, D, DC, MC, V* ⊘*Closed Sun. No lunch Sat.*

$$$ **Kevin.** Harmony reigns at chef-owner Kevin Shikami's namesake, where
ASIAN FUSION
River North
an understated, soothing setting puts the focus squarely on the kitchen's French-Asian fusion. Fans come for Shikami's tuna tartare alone. The menu changes frequently but typical dishes might include roasted Alaskan halibut in olive oil–basil broth or duck breast in orange-star anise sauce. If price is a problem, try lunching here—entrées drop by almost half. ✉*9 W. Hubbard St.* ☎*312/595–0055* ⊟*AE, DC, MC, V* ⊘*Closed Sun. No lunch Sat.*

$ **Kitsch'n on Roscoe.** If you love all things seventies, you'll love Kitsch'n
AMERICAN
Lake View
like the regulars. It's a diner in retro garb, with lava lamps and vintage toasters–turned–table lamps. Dine, with tongue firmly in cheek, on pesto-dyed "green eggs and ham" and Twinkies tiramisu. Or play it straight with hefty tuna and grilled-cheese sandwiches. Weekends are jammed; midweek is better for relaxing. ✉*2005 W. Roscoe St.* ☎*773/248–7372* ⊟*AE, MC, V* ⊘*No dinner Sun. and Mon.*

$ **La Donna.** We deem this Andersonville's best Italian because of its excel-
ITALIAN
Far North Side
lent pastas—try the pumpkin ravioli in creamy balsamic sauce or the fine penne *arrabiata* (spicy tomato sauce)—and good, cracker-crust pizzas. The generally crowded storefront dining room either makes you feel like part of a very large party or just trapped. The wine list is well chosen and fairly priced, and there's a bargain-price Sunday brunch. ✉*5146 N. Clark St.* ☎*773/561–9400* ⊟*AE, D, DC, MC, V.*

7

$$ **La Sardine.** We don't know if the sardine reference was meant to tele-
BISTRO graph the seating arrangements, but, yes, it's snug here. Still, you'll find
West Loop it easier to tolerate your neighbors with a solid menu of traditional
bistro favorites including warm goat cheese salad, bouillabaisse, and
roasted chicken with mashed potatoes. Across the street from Harpo
Studios (where Oprah tapes her talk show), La Sardine seats audiences
close to producers. ⊠*111 N. Carpenter St.* ☎*312/421–2800* ▤*AE,
D, DC, MC, V* ⊘*Closed Sun. No lunch Sat.*

$$ **La Tache.** Warm, wood-paneled interiors, a classic bistro menu, and rea-
BISTRO sonable prices sum the charms of the 45-seat La Tache. You could make
Andersonville a meal of appetizers from charcuterie to egg-topped Lyonnaise salads.
But save room for steak frites, braised rabbit, and fish specials. The popular Sunday brunch features French toast, French-style eggs with leeks
and truffle oil, and savory salads. ⊠*1475 W. Balmoral Ave.* ☎*773/334–
7168* ⚘*Reservations not accepted* ▤*AE, D, DC, MC, V.*

¢ **Lao Sze Chuan.** If you're looking for spice, filling food, and great prices
CHINESE in Chinatown, check out this Szechuan kitchen. Chilies, garlic, and
Chinatown ginger seem to go into every dish, whether it's chicken, eggplant, or
dumplings. The digs are nothing to write a postcard home about, but
you'll feel smug for choosing it once the feast is finished. ⊠*2172 S.
Archer Ave.* ☎*312/326–5040* ▤*AE, D, DC, MC, V.*

$$ **Le Bouchon.** The French comfort food at this charming-but-cramped
BISTRO bistro in Bucktown is in a league of its own. Onion tart has been a
Bucktown signature dish of owner Jean-Claude Poilevey for years; he also does
a succulent sautéed rabbit and a definitive *salade Lyonnaise* (mixed
greens topped with a creamy vinaigrette and a poached egg). Save room
for the fruit tarts. Don't attempt Le Bouchon on weekends without a
reservation. ⊠*1958 N. Damen Ave.* ☎*773/862–6600* ▤*AE, D, DC,
MC, V* ⊘*Closed Sun. No lunch.*

$$$ **Le Lan.** Top toques Roland Liccioni of Le Francais and Arun Sampan-
ASIAN FUSION thavivat of Arun's teamed up to create this elegant French-Vietnamese
River North boîte. We like the sophisticated-without-being-stuffy vibe—sharply
dressed (yes, don your black to fit in here) foodies fill the exposed
brick room that has green accents and orchids on the tables. The menu
manages the same balance: the rich flavors of France are piqued by
Asian notes. Look for the Asian squash dumplings and the tea-smoked
duck breast ⊠*749 N. Clark St.* ☎*312/280–9100* ▤*AE, D, DC, MC,
V* ⊘*Closed Sun. No lunch.*

$$$$ **Les Nomades.** Intimate and elegant don't make headlines, but Les
FRENCH Nomades holds a torch for tender refinements. Wood-burning fireplaces
Near North and original art warm the dining rooms of the Streeterville brownstone.
A carefully composed menu of contemporary French food includes the
usual suspects, such as duck consommé and warm asparagus with
crispy poached egg, plus earthy indulgences like roasted squab breast
with crispy sweetbreads. Compose your own prix-fixe dinner from the
menu; four courses cost $100, five go for $112. ⊠*222 E. Ontario St.*
☎*312/649–9010* ⚘*Reservations essential* Jacket required ▤*AE, D,
DC, MC, V* ⊘*Closed Sun. and Mon. No lunch.*

¢
AMERICAN
West Loop
☺
Lou Mitchell's. Shelve your calorie and cholesterol concerns; Lou Mitchell's heeds no modern health concerns. The diner, a destination close to Union Station since 1923, specializes in high-fat breakfasts and comfort food lunches. Start the day with double-yolk eggs and homemade hash browns by the skillet (BYO Lipitor). Later break for meat loaf and mashed potatoes. Though you have to deal with out-the-door waits, staffers dole out doughnut holes and Milk Duds to pacify pangs. ✉*565 W. Jackson Blvd.* ☎*312/939–3111* ▭*AE, V* ☾*No dinner.*

$$
AMERICAN
Logan Square
Lula Café. For the kind of modern cooking made from locally sourced ingredients that distinguishes downtown chefs—but at half the price and with zero attitude—locals throng Lula Café in Logan Square. This bohemian storefront of closely set wooden tables and chairs serves stellar cuisine such as wild bass with blood orange and olives, and maple-scented rabbit with rosemary sweet potatoes. Menus are seasonal, change frequently and champion farm sources; in fact the restaurant holds prix-fixe farm dinners each Monday. Open for breakfast and lunch too, Lula is a neighborhood hangout for arty neighbors during the day, drawing from far and wide for dinner, when weekend waits are common. ✉*2537 N. Kedzie Blvd.* ☎*773/489–9554* ▭*AE, MC, V* ☾*Closed Tues.*

$$
ITALIAN
River North
☺
Maggiano's Little Italy. Large portions generate large followings. Maggiano's has followed this mantra, dishing up enormous servings of red-sauced Italian food in this homage to Little Italy and doggie bags. Expect hearty, stereotypical Italian-American fare—brick-size lasagna, chicken Vesuvio, and veal scaloppini. Order two entrées for every three diners in your party and you'll be as happy as the other cheerfully loud patrons in the wide-open dining room. ✉*516 N. Clark St.* ☎*312/644–7700* ▭*AE, D, DC, MC, V.*

¢
AMERICAN
Sotuh Loop
Manny's Coffee Shop and Deli. Kibitzing counter cooks provide commentary as they sling the chow—thick pastrami sandwiches, soul-nurturing matzo-ball soup, and piping-hot potato pancakes—at this classic South Side cafeteria. Though they occasionally bark at dawdlers, it's all in good fun; looking for seating in two teaming, fluorescent-lit rooms is not. Don't try to pay the hash-slingers; settle up as you leave. ✉*1141 S. Jefferson St.* ☎*312/939–2855* ⌨*Reservations not accepted* ▭*AE, MC, V* ☾*Closed Sun. No dinner.*

$$
BRASSERIE
West Loop
Marché. If all the world's a stage, everyone from the waiters to the patrons are players at this theatrical West Loop brasserie. The set: a lively, loftlike room trimmed in collage and paint and furnished with curvaceous metal chairs. The program: classic French onion soup and housemade pâté, braised lamb, and an excellent steak tartare. The finale: one of the largest sweets lists in town. Ovations at your discretion. ✉*833 W. Randolph St.* ☎*312/226–8399* ▭*AE, DC, MC, V* ☾*No lunch.*

$$
LATIN
Wicker Park
Mas. Inventive nuevo Latino fare, creative pan-Latin cocktails, and intimate 74-seat confines generate a significant buzz (and, some complain, noise) at Mas. We love perusing the menu over Chilean pisco sours or Cuban mojitos. The flavors here are nothing if not bold: Hondu-

ran seafood stew, sautéed tilapia with olive salsa, chili-cured pork loin, and tuna-and-papaya tacos. Phone ahead for a table on weekends. ✉ *1670 W. Division St.* ☎ *773/276–8700* ☐ *AE, MC, V* ☉ *No lunch.*

$$$ **McCormick and Schmick's.** If you're
SEAFOOD the indecisive type, don't even
Near North think about dining here. This link in the Oregon-based chain updates its massive menu twice daily to list the freshest fish available. Expect six varieties of oysters, regional specialties like Louisiana crab cakes and Wisconsin rainbow trout, and several dozen fish, like Barcelona anchovies and Hawaiian marlin. Wood paneling, cozy booths, and high ceilings generate a clubby setting. We love the bar not just for the cheap happy hour nibbles, but because the bartenders squeeze all the juices that go into the fresh and zesty cocktails. ✉ *41 E. Chestnut St.* ☎ *312/397–9500* ☐ *AE, D, DC, MC, V.*

$$–$$$ **Meritage Café and Wine Bar.** Locals come here for downtown caliber
NEW AMERICAN fare in the neighborhood. The menu dabbles in French (duck breast
Bucktown with fennel and pancetta risotto) and Pacific Northwest (seared diver scallops with braised oxtails) flavors. The digs are warmly lighted and romantic, but in season opt for the lovely outdoor dining patio. Meritage's namesake blended wines and other American vintages center the wine list. ✉ *2118 N. Damen Ave.* ☎ *773/235–6434* ☐ *AE, MC, V* ☉ *No lunch.*

$ **Mia Francesca.** Moderate prices and a smart, urbane style drive ceaseless
ITALIAN crowds to this Wrigleyville storefront. Enlightened Italian dishes like
Lake View classic bruschetta, *quattro formaggi* (four-cheese) pizza, sausage and wild-mushroom pasta, and roast chicken are made with fresh ingredients and avoid stereotypical heaviness. With the exception of one pricey veal dish, the limited meat options keep the prices low here. While you wait for one of the small, tightly spaced tables—and you *will* wait— you can have a drink at the bar. ✉ *3311 N. Clark St.* ☎ *773/281–3310* ☐ *AE, D, DC, MC, V* ☉ *No lunch weekdays.*

$$$ **Mike Ditka's Restaurant.** NFL Hall-of-Famer Mike Ditka was the only
JAPANESE coach to take the Bears to the Super Bowl. Sure, it was in 1985, but
Near North Bears fans have long memories, and they still love "Da Coach" as well as his clubby, sports-themed restaurant. The dark-wood interior, upstairs cigar lounge, and sports memorabilia are predictable, but the menu clearly aims to please large and diverse audiences. Café staples (salads, fish) and bar food (burgers, meat loaf) join steak-house fare (steaks, chops) and a few unexpected indulgences (crab and Parmesan-crusted halibut). ✉ *Tremont Hotel, 100 E. Chestnut St.* ☎ *312/587– 8989* ☐ *AE, D, DC, MC, V.*

Milk & Honey Café. Wicker Park's Division Street has long been a prowl of night owls. But with the advent of spas and boutiques in the area, not to mention the many work-from-home locals, the boho neighborhood needed a good breakfast and lunch spot. Milk & Honey exceeds expectations with hearty (eggs) and healthful (granola) breakfasts, and creative sandwiches (avocado with smoked Gouda) at lunch. Choice seats change with the season: out on the sidewalk café in warm weather, in near the fireplace in cooler temps. ✉*1920 W. Division St., Wicker Park* ☎*773/395–9434* ▭*AE, MC, V* ☾*No dinner.*

¢
CAFÉ
Wicker Park
Fodor's Choice
★

Mirai Sushi. This Japanese hipster helped turn Wicker Park's Division Street into a foodie destination. Make the trek for top-quality classic sushi and sashimi dishes, as well as lesser-known varieties, such as monkfish, horse mackerel, and rockfish. Display tanks keep a fresh supply of fish on hand. Don't know your toro from your hirame? Knowledgeable servers can guide you through the menu. For the full monty, sit at the sushi bar and put yourself into the hands of the inventive sushi chefs. The upstairs sake lounge is more about the scene and less about cuisine. ✉*2020 W. Division St.* ☎*773/862–8500* ▭*AE, D, DC, MC, V* ☾*No lunch.*

$$
NEW AMERICAN
Wicker Park

mk. Foodies and fashionistas favor owner-chef Michael Kornick's ultra-hip spot for its sleek look and elegant menu. Occupying a renovated warehouse, mk weights brick walls and soaring ceilings with fine linens, expensive flatware, and designer wine stems. Menus change with the season and hew to two or three dominant flavors à la halibut with braised baby fennel and kalamata olives, and rack of pork with mustard greens. It's not cheap, but it is special. ✉*868 N. Franklin St.* ☎*312/482–9179* ⌨*Reservations essential* ▭*AE, DC, MC, V* ☾*No lunch.*

$$$
STEAKHOUSE
River North

Mon Ami Gabi. This little piece of Paris recreates a classic bistro with views of Lincoln Park that could pass—with the help of a couple of glasses of *vin* from the rolling wine cart—for the Tuileries. Park-front windows let in ample natural light, warming the wood-trimmed interior. Best bites include several versions of steak frites, as well as such bistro essentials as mussels and *skate* with crispy garlic chips. ✉*2300 N. Lincoln Park W* ☎*773/348–8886* ▭*AE, D, DC, MC, V* ☾*No lunch.*

$–$$
BISTRO
Lincoln Park

Morton's, The Steakhouse. Morton's on the Gold Coast is more fun, but this is Chicago's best steak house, a spin-off of the Gold Coast original. Excellent service and a good wine list add to the principal attraction: beautiful, hefty steaks cooked to perfection. A kitschy tradition mandates that everything you order, from gargantuan Idahos to massive slabs of beef, is brought to the table for your approval before the chef gets started. White tablecloths and chandeliers create a classy feel. It's

$$$–$$$$
STEAKHOUSE
Loop

7

no place for the budget conscious, but for steak lovers it's a 16-ounce (or more) taste of heaven. ⊠ *65 E. Wacker Pl.* ☎ *312/201–0410* ▭ *AE, D, DC, MC, V* ⊘ *No lunch weekends.*

$$$$
CUTTING-EDGE
West Loop

Moto. Mad-scientist chef Homaru Cantu has become a cult figure in the Windy City. His restaurant-cum-laboratory is sequestered in the city's still working meatpacking district. Look for the well-dressed couples handing their keys to valets (it's the only restaurant on the block). Many of the techniques perfected in the basement kitchen are later put to use in the chef's work with NASA and corporate America. Inside the minimalist dining room patrons pay for the privilege of being literal guinea pigs. The daily changing multicourse menus—available in 5-, 10-, and 16-course options—are printed on edible paper. Flavors are seared into wine glasses by an industrial laser, rigatoni is fashioned from lychee puree, and frozen flapjacks are "cooked" table-side on a liquid-nitrogen-filled box. The spectacle is big but the portions are small. ⊠ *945 W. Fulton Market, at N. Sangamon St.* ☎ *312/491–0058* ⌕ *Reservations essential* ▭ *AE, D, MC, V.*

¢
AMERICAN
River North

Mr. Beef. A Chicago institution for two-fisted Italian beef sandwiches piled with red peppers and provolone cheese *(see Chicago's Holy Trinity, for more information on these sandwiches)*, Mr. Beef garners citywide fans from area hard-hats to restaurateurs and TV personalities. Service and setting—two indoor picnic tables and a dining rail—are fast-food no-nonsense. This workingman's favorite is, go figure, located near River North's art galleries. ⊠ *666 N. Orleans St.* ☎ *312/337–8500* ▭ *No credit cards* ⊘ *Closed Sun. No dinner.*

$$$
STEAKHOUSE
West Loop

N9NE Steakhouse. Nightclub meets steak house in N9NE, replete with mirrored columns, futuristic plasma-TV screens, and a dramatic, circular champagne-and-caviar bar set smack in the middle of the dining room. Scenesters and business folk find common ground in the menu: prime steaks and chops complemented by fresh fish and shellfish. If you crave caviar choose from beluga and sevruga by the ounce or cute crispy cones layered with caviar and egg salad. On weekends, dress to thrill—most of the trendy patrons do. ⊠ *440 W. Randolph St.* ☎ *312/575–9900* ▭ *AE, DC, MC, V* ⊘ *Closed Sun. No lunch Sat.*

$$
LATIN
River North

Nacional 27. Here's a bit of trivia to spring on fellow diners: there are 27 nations south of the U.S. border, and it's the cuisine of those 27 that supposedly comprise the pan-Latin menu here. That may be an exaggeration, but the menu does offer variety. Try the barbecued lamb tiny tacos appetizer and follow with the pork tenderloin smeared with corn-mushroom flan. The circular bar draws a following independent of the food. After 11 PM on weekend nights, the floor in the middle of the dining room is cleared for salsa and merengue dancing. ⊠ *325 W. Huron St.* ☎ *312/664–2727* ▭ *AE, D, DC, MC, V* ⊘ *Closed Sun. No lunch.*

$$$
NEW AMERICAN
River North

Naha. Carrie Nahabedian lends her name (well, the first two syllables, anyway) and considerable culinary skills to this upscale venture. In a clean space done in shades of cream and sage, Nahabedian presents eye-catching dishes such as wood-grilled Spanish sausage with Italian frisee, honey-lacquered duck breast, or wild bass in yellow-pepper broth. Wine is treated with reverence, from the well-chosen selection of vintages to the high-quality stemware. Solos and social-seekers can sit at the convivial bar and order from the main menu. ✉*500 N. Clark St.* ☎*312/321–6242* ▤*AE, D, DC, MC, V* ✆*Closed Sun. No lunch Sat.*

$$$
SEAFOOD
Loop
Nick's Fishmarket. The bold and pricey menu matches the well-paid power lunchers who get down to business over Pacific fish, California abalone, and Maine lobster. If your purse strings are tight, angle for a spot at the Grill, where the lobster comes in bisque and windows frame the Marc Chagall mosaic on the plaza outdoors. ✉*51 S. Clark St.* ☎*312/621–0200* ⚘*Reservations essential* ▤*AE, D, DC, MC, V* ✆*Closed Sun. No lunch Sat.*

$$$$
NEW AMERICAN
Near North
NoMI. The expensive linens, Limoges china, and Isamu Noguchi sculpture make NoMI completely luxurious, but the vibe here is casual, as if all this elegance were everyday and not special occasion. This is the place to call if you're celebrating the latter or traveling on a generous expense account—you'll have one of the city's best tables, overlooking the historic Water Tower from a seven-story perch. The menu leans French, with strong Asian and Mediterranean accents. ✉*Park Hyatt Hotel, 800 N. Michigan Ave.* ☎*312/239–4030* ▤*AE, D, DC, MC, V.*

$$$
AMERICAN
Lincoln Park
Fodor'sChoice
★
North Pond. A former Arts and Crafts–style warming house for ice-skaters at Lincoln Park's North Pond, this gem-in-the-woods fittingly champions an uncluttered culinary style. Talented chef Bruce Sherman emphasizes organic ingredients, wild-caught fish, and artisanal farm products. Menus change seasonally, but order the Midwestern favorite walleye pike if available. Like the food, the wine list seeks out small American craft producers. The food remains top-notch at lunch but the scene, dense with strollers and high chairs, is far from serene. ✉*2610 N. Cannon Dr.* ☎*773/477–5845* ▤*AE, D, DC, MC, V* ✆*Closed Mon. No lunch Oct.–May.*

$
MEXICAN
Pilsen
Nuevo Leon. Fill up on the exotic (tripe soup) or the familiar (tacos) at this bustling, family-run restaurant in the heart of Pilsen, Chicago's Mexican neighborhood. Big tables accommodate big families, lending a fiesta feel to the scene. Meals run from breakfast chilaquiles (eggs scrambled with tortillas) to dinners of shrimp fajitas. Brush up your Spanglish; not all servers are fluent in English. ✉*1515 W. 18th St.* ☎*312/421–1517* ⚘*Reservations not accepted* ▤*No credit cards.*

$$–$$$
NEW AMERICAN
West Loop
one sixtyblue. Never mind that former Chicago Bulls superstar Michael Jordan owns a piece of this place or that the private, cigar-friendly room has entertained its share of celebs. The real reason to come here is chef Martial Noguier. His graceful but approachable food balances challenge-me tastes, like Kurobuta pork tenderloin, with standbys

7

like Delmonico steak with caramelized shallots (Jordan's fave). The leather-sofa lounge makes a sexy site for nibbles and drinks. ✉ *1400 W. Randolph St.* ☎ *312/850–0303* ▭ *AE, D, DC, MC, V* ⊗ *Closed Sun. No lunch Sat.*

$$
CHINESE
South Loop

Opera. Creative Chinese fare and theatrical design share the stage at Opera. Only top-flight ingredients and sparing sauces go into the cooking, distinguishing the five-spice squid, say, or lobster spring roll or roasted Scottish salmon from more familiar take-out fare. Former film-storage vaults—the building was once used by Paramount Studios—now hold a series of tables for two, providing intimacy for those who want it. Everyone else revels in the eye candy that includes Asian newspaper collages, oversize suspended lamps, and a multicolor-glass-wrapped wine cellar. ✉ *1301 S. Wabash St.* ☎ *312/461–0161* ▭ *AE, DC, MC, V* ⊗ *No lunch.*

¢–$
AMERICAN
Lake View

Orange. Follow Wrigleyville's weekend crowds to the cheerful Orange for inventive, and thronged, breakfasts. If you think breakfast has to be dull, try the fruit sushi, kebab-style skewered French toast, or jam-filled pancakes. Standard stuff is done right, too: the fruit's juiced on-site and the omelets are big enough to take you through lunch. Arrive early or prepare to wait for tables, especially on game days. ✉ *3231 N. Clark St.* ☎ *773/549–4400* ▭ *D, MC, V* ⊗ *No dinner Mon.*

$$$
ITALIAN
River North

Osteria via Stato. It's no-brainer Italian here, where the shtick is to feed you without asking too many questions. You pick an entrée from the $35.95 prix fixe, and waiters do the rest, working the room with several rounds of communal platters of antipasti, then pasta, followed by your entrée, and dessert. There's even a "just bring me wine" program that delivers preselected vino to your table throughout your meal. The results are savory enough, but Osteria shines brightest at making you feel comfortable. If conversation is important, make a reservation here. You won't spend but a precious minute reading the menu. ✉ *620 N. State St.* ☎ *312/642–8450* ▭ *AE, D, DC, MC, V* ⊗ *No lunch Sun.*

$$$$
STEAKHOUSE
Loop

The Palm. If you're somebody in this town, your caricatured mug is hung here on the wood-paneled wall, a practice that feeds the egos of the Palm's power-player regulars. Sizeable steaks and even bigger lobsters sate their appetites. Chicago's soaring skyscrapers and Disney-esque Navy Pier provide distraction on the outdoor patio, making this an all-together handsome link in a national chain. ✉ *Swissôtel, 323 E. Wacker Dr.* ☎ *312/616–1000* ⌦ *Reservations essential* ▭ *AE, D, DC, MC, V.*

$$
NEW AMERICAN
Loop

Park Grill. Location trumps service at Park Grill, where a seat on the patio in summer, in full view of Millennium Park, is among the best in the city. Sadly, the waitstaff lapses—grin and bear it with another drink from the outdoor bar. The burgers are first rate, as is the more ambitious seasonal fare. A grab-and-go window supplies park picnics. In winter the scene moves indoors as indulgent calorie consumers watch ice-skating athletes through picture windows. ✉ *Millennium Park, 11 N. Michigan Ave.* ☎ *312/521–7275* ▭ *AE, D, DC, MC, V.*

Continued on page 275

CULINARY MAVERICKS STORM WINDY CITY

Step into the kitchen, but don't forget your protective goggles. Whether "negative grilling" at minus 30 degrees Celsius or serving you an edible menu (literally—it's printed on soy paper), this trio of young chefs in Chicago is redefining haute cuisine.

Just three years ago, three young chefs, each a veteran of local icon Charlie Trotter's kitchen, took a simultaneous gamble on the sophistication and daring of Chicago diners, unveiling cutting-edge menus the likes of which the Windy City had never seen before. Though a visit to their restaurants—Alinea, Moto, and Avenues—demands an adventurous palate and serious commitment of time and money, all three places instantly thrived.

The chefs leading these restaurants—Grant Achatz, Homaru Cantu, and Graham Elliot Bowles—have brought an American touch to techniques and ideas first explored and popularized in Europe, toying with devices and chemicals more suited to a lab than a kitchen. This marriage of science and cooking is known as molecular gastronomy. Though follow-ing in the footsteps of chefs like Heston Blumenthal in Britain and Ferran Adrià in Spain, the Chicago pack prided themselves on being trailblazers, not imitators. "For Picasso to do something that looked like a Dalí would've been a sham," says Cantu. "It's the same thing in these restaurants. There's a certain amount of pride in originality."

Before long the national press began to take notice. "One chef is unique," says Bowles. "Two could be a fluke, but three guys doing this stuff in the same city, maybe something is going on." Writers from *GQ, Gourmet, The New York Times,* and *Vogue* gushed over Chicago's new "sci-fi" cuisine. The city, they wrote, had become the capital of avant-garde food in America.

by Jay Cheshes

GRANT ACHATZ

(previous page) From Alinea, a spiral of quince wrapped in prosciutto. (clockwise from top left) Grant Achatz; bacon with butterscotch, apple, and thyme; inside the Alinea kitchen; mango disc with sesame oil, soy, and bonito flakes.

Born into a restaurant family in Michigan, Achatz, who turned 30 two years before his colleagues, is the triumvirate's senior statesman. After working at Charlie Trotter and at Thomas Keller's French Laundry in Napa, he began experimenting with molecular gastronomy at Trio in the Chicago suburbs. In 2005 he launched Alinea, his first solo project, just up the block from the Steppenwolf Theatre. The restaurant was named the best in the country by *Gourmet* barely a year after it opened.

Techniques & Trademarks

There are two dining options at Alinea—long and longer. "When we first opened we were serving 28 courses," says the chef. "People were fatiguing. When you cross over four hours you're getting into dangerous territory." Tiny one- to four-bite courses flow one into the next, with sweet dishes not just ending the meal but also interrupting it midway. "It breaks the monotony," Achatz says.

Though ingredients are as likely to be flash-frozen on a stainless steel "negative grill" (at minus 30 degrees Celsius) as seared on an old-fashioned Japanese charcoal barbecue, not much of this food (served on pedestals and prongs) will look familiar. In the kitchen you'll also find an immersion circulator (for cooking vacuum-sealed food "sous-vide") and containers of calcium lactate and sodium alginate (for encasing liquids in a yolk-like skin so they explode when you bite them).

HOMARU CANTU

Cantu, the most wildly experimental and scientifically minded of the Chicago chefs, worked in kitchens up and down the West Coast before landing at Charlie Trotter, where he eventually rose to the position of sous chef. Moto, opened in 2005 in a desolate stretch of the city's meatpacking district, is equal parts restaurant and mad-scientist workshop. The chef, who holds some two-dozen food patents, sells innovations perfected in the restaurant's basement kitchen to corporate and government clients (including NASA).

Techniques & Trademarks

The kitchen at Moto resembles a James Bond villain's lair. When the industrial laser is turned on, protective-goggle-clad chefs work in near darkness on orders transmitted by a computer-generated voice. The daily changing prix-fixe menus (in 5-, 10-, or 20-course options) are printed to order in edible ink on

(clockwise from top left) Homaru Cantu; steamed sea bass; deconstructed mac-and-cheese; edible menu made of soybeans with food-based inks.

soy-based paper (one of the chef's many patents). Here theatricality and trompe l'oeil presentations rule. "When you order a tasting menu it's like going out for a night at the opera," Cantu says. "You don't get to choose Act One, Scene Five; you get the entire production as the composer intended you to see it." You might encounter chemically treated lychee puree, mimicking pasta dough, molded into translucent rigatoni. Or a new wave "nitro" sushi roll made with liquid nitrogen—treated tofu skin that emits cool smoke through your mouth and nose.

GRAHAM ELLIOT BOWLES

(clockwise from top left) Graham Elliot Bowles; lamb with crushed Altoids; the kitchen at Avenues; butter-poached lobster with toasted curry.

After making his professional debut at the pastoral Jackson House Inn in rural Vermont, Bowles worked alongside Cantu at Charlie Trotter. The chefs, who started two weeks apart, became good friends. Later Bowles returned to the Jackson House, where he first experimented with molecular gastronomy (and where *Food & Wine* named him one of America's best new chefs). Just as his colleagues were launching their own places, he landed his current perch at the flagship restaurant of Chicago's Peninsula Hotel.

Techniques & Trademarks

Since taking over Avenues, an understated stage in a luxury hotel, Bowles says, his wildest impulses have been reined in considerably. "I used to be much more about being different for different's sake," he says. "Not pushing the envelope but tearing it up." Though his food is recognizable, it remains thought-provoking—and delicious. Avant-garde techniques are added as one ingredient among many. You might find, for example, an Altoids jus served with rare tender lamb ("It's whimsical but still makes sense," Bowles says), almond soup poured over sage marshmallows, or smoked ice cream (the sugar and eggs are smoked beforehand) served atop hand-cut steak tartare (it makes the whole dish taste like bacon).

$ **The Parthenon.** The claim to fame here is the *saganaki*, the Greek flam-
GREEK ing-cheese dish, which the Parthenon says it invented in the late 1960s,
West Loop thereby introducing "opa!" to the American vocabulary. They also
take credit for being the first to serve gyros stateside. True or not,
indulge the legends and stick to these classics. The food is cheap and
the atmosphere festive, generating happy campers. ⊠*314 S. Halsted
St.* ☏*312/726–2407* ▭*AE, D, DC, MC, V.*

$$ **Petterino's.** Goodman, Palace, and Oriental theatergoers pack Petterino's
ITALIAN (next door to the Goodman lobby) nightly. Not that the Italian supper
Loop club with framed caricatures of celebs past and present couldn't stand
on its own merits. The deep, red-leather booths make a cozy stage for
old-school classics like shrimp *de jonghe* (covered in garlicky bread
crumbs then baked) and Bookbinder soup, plus prime steaks, seafood,
and the ever-present pasta. ⊠*150 N. Dearborn St.* ☏*312/422–0150*
▭*AE, D, DC, MC, V* ⊗*No lunch Sun.*

$ **Phoenix.** Phoenix softens you up with second-floor picture-window
CHINESE views that frame the Loop skyline. Just when you're most vulnerable, it
Chinatown develops the food punch—and it's a pretty good one, too. The dim sum,
dispensed from rolling carts daily from 8 AM to 3 PM, is a big draw (serv-
ers often don't speak English; just smile and point at what you want).
Arrive before noon on the weekends or stew as you wait … and wait.
⊠*2131 S. Archer Ave.* ☏*312/328–0848* ▭*AE, D, DC, MC, V.*

$ **Piece.** The antithesis of Chicago-style deep-dish pizza, Piece's flat pies
PIZZA mimic those made famous in New Haven, Connecticut. The some-
Wicker Park what free-form, eat-off-the-baking-sheet pizzas come in plain (tomato
☾ sauce, Parmesan, and garlic), white (olive oil, garlic, and mozzarella)
or traditional red, with lots of topping options. Salads like the greens
with Gorgonzola and pears are more stylish than expected, and house-
brewed beers pair perfectly with the chow. It's good enough that mul-
tipierced Wicker Parkers are willing to risk dining alongside local
families (with kids in tow) in this former garage space. ⊠*1927 W.
North Ave.* ☏*773/772–4422* ▭*AE, D, DC, MC, V.*

$ **Pierrot Gourmet.** Despite the legions of shoppers on Michigan Avenue
CAFÉ there are few casual cafés to quell their collective hunger, making this
Near North bakery-patisserie-café a welcome neighbor. Lunches center on upscale
greens like herb salad with olives and Parmesan, along with open-
face *tartine* sandwiches on crusty, house-made sourdough. Break mid-
afternoon for a *tarte flambé,* an Alsatian flat bread with cheese and
cream, and a glass of Riesling. Solos are accommodated at the maga-
zine-strewn communal table. Meals are served 7 AM to 7 PM daily. The
upscale Peninsula hotel runs Pierrot, accounting for both the high qual-
ity and the high cost. ⊠*108 E. Superior St.* ☏*312/573–6749* ▭*AE,
D, DC, MC, V.*

¢ **Pizzeria Due.** This is where everyone goes when they've found out that
ITALIAN Uno, the original home of Chicago's deep-dish pizza up the street, has
River North an hour-plus wait. The caveat is that Due quickly builds its own wait-
☾ ing list. The best strategy for dining out at either spot is to arrive early
or opt to come at lunch. ⊠*619 N. Wabash Ave.* ☏*312/943–2400*
▭*AE, D, DC, MC, V.*

$ **Pizzeria Uno.** Chicago deep-dish pizza got its start here in 1943, and
ITALIAN both local and out-of-town fans continue to pack in for filling pies.
River North Housed in a Victorian brownstone, Uno offers a slice of old Chicago
in dim paneled rooms with reproduction light fixtures. Spin-off Due
down the street handles the overflow. Plan on two thick, cheesy slices
or less as a full meal. This is no quick-to-your-table pie, so do order
salads and be prepared to entertain the kids during the inevitable wait.
⊠*29 E. Ohio St.* ☎*312/321–1000.*

$ **Platiyo.** The folks behind the wildly successful Mia Francesca next door
MEXICAN run Platiyo, another Wrigleyville hit, this time for Mexican food. Col-
Lake View orful artwork, Mexican tiles, and piñatalike sculptures conjure a fiesta-
ready setting for marlin ceviche, *carne asada* (marinated strip steak),
and double-cut pork chops in pineapple mole. A selection of tacos and
enchiladas placate Tex-Mex fans. ⊠*3313 N. Clark St.* ☎*773/477–
6700* ⊟*AE, D, DC, MC, V.*

¢ **Pompei.** Cheap, cheerful, and fast—what's not to love about Pompeii?
ITALIAN Little Italy's only casual café with a strong kitchen specializes in square
Sotuh Loop slices of pizza, each under $3, with toppings ranging from shredded
onions and sausage to bread crumbs and tomato. One to two easily makes a meal. Between University of Illinois Chicago students and
Rush-Presbyterian hospital workers, Pompeii is jammed at lunch. If
you can tolerate the self-serve system at dinner, the evening hours are
more relaxing. If pizza's not your thing, salad, generous sandwiches,
and homemade pastas are also on the menu. ⊠*1531 W. Taylor St.*
☎*312/421–5179* ⊟*AE, D, DC, MC, V.*

$$ **Pump Room.** The Pump Room clings to its 1930s Chicago fame, when
STEAKHOUSE celebrities passing through town via rail beat it to the restaurant to see
Near North and be seen. The likes of Frank Sinatra, Bette Davis, and Humphrey
Bogart held court in the storied Booth One, and publicity photos taken
there line the entrance to the restaurant. In keeping with tradition, the
booth is off-limits to all but A-list celebs who, truthfully, don't show
like they used to. Now the regulars are wealthy Gold Coasters, but
new management is working hard to lure the next generation, mean-
ing there's European sea bass alongside filet mignon. ⊠*1301 N. State
Pkwy.* ☎*312/266–0360* ⊟*AE, D, DC, MC, V.*

$$ **Red Light.** Sultry, all-red decor and a club sound track stoke the high-
PAN ASIAN energy vibe (read: loud) at Red Light. Chinese, Thai, Vietnamese, and
West Loop Indonesian dishes commingle on the pan-Asian menu, which is heavily weighted with appetizers to encourage nibbling. Standout dishes
include foie gras and pork dumplings, jumbo shrimp curry, a miso-lob-
ster seafood stew, and the signature "chocolate bag" dessert filled with
white-chocolate mousse. ⊠*820 W. Randolph St.* ☎*312/733–8880*
⊟*AE, D, DC, MC, V* ☉*No lunch weekends.*

$$ **Rhapsody.** Attached to the Symphony Center, home of the Chicago
NEW AMERICAN Symphony, Rhapsody is more than a handy spot for a preconcert din-
Loop ner. This restaurant combines fine-dining ambitions with a pleasant
urban greenhouse setting graced by potted palms and picture windows.
Despite a few chef changes in recent years, the food is consistently

solid. Rhapsody's handsome bar, pouring an expansive wine-by-the-glass selection, is a perfect post-performance hangout. ✉*65 E. Adams St.* ☎*312/786–9911* ▭*AE, D, DC, MC, V* ⊘*Closed Sun. mid-June– mid-Sept. No lunch weekends.*

$$$
SEAFOOD
Near North

Riva. Riva's got the lock on upscale dining in the middle of junk-food–central Navy Pier. The restaurant relies a bit too much on the views—which, gazing southward over Lake Michigan, are admittedly fantastic—when it should concentrate on better cooking. Opt for simpler preparations, such as grilled salmon or various pastas, over the menu's more ambitious efforts. Grilled fish, shellfish, and steaks are pricey, though the hordes that crowd the place, especially in summer, don't seem to mind (good service helps). A casual grill downstairs, which spills onto the pier's promenade in summer, is kinder to your wallet. ✉*700 E. Grand Ave.* ☎*312/644–7482* ▭*AE, D, DC, MC, V.*

$$
AMERICAN
Near North

RL. Power brokers, moneyed locals, and Michigan Avenue shoppers keep the revolving doors spinning at RL, the initials of designer Ralph Lauren who lent his name and signature soignée style to the eatery that adjoins his Polo/Ralph Lauren store. The cozy confines cluster leather banquettes under hunt-club-style art hung on wood-paneled walls. The menu of American classics, including steak tartare, Dover sole in butter, and steak Diane flamed table-side, suits the country-club-in-the-city setting. ✉*115 E. Chicago Ave.* ☎*312/475–1100* ▭*AE, DC, MC, V.*

$$
AMERICAN
River North

Rockit Bar & Grill. A classic tavern for the club set, Rockit Bar & Grill serves upscale bar food, pours creative cocktails, and aims to please everyone from celebrity visitors (given wide berth in the barroom upstairs) to kids (served Lincoln Log-like stacks of brioche French toast for brunch). The extensive menu spans salads, sandwiches, and burgers (try the Kobe version) as well as comfort food entrées like Thanksgiving turkey and pesto-cream pasta with salmon. Oprah-famed-designer Nate Berkus did the rustic-chic interiors including tree-stump cocktail tables and antler chandeliers. After dinner head upstairs to shoot some pool and check out the singles scene. ✉*22 W. Hubbard St.* ☎*312/645– 6000* ▭*AE, MC, V.*

$
ITALIAN
South Loop

The Rosebud on Taylor. For *Sopranos*-style food and scene, crowd in here with half of Chicago. What's all the fuss about? Truthfully, the food breaks no new ground: there's the typical roasted peppers, homemade sausage, and pastas, and most of them are red-sauced. But the old neighborhood vibe is authentic—and extremely loud. Come prepared for a three-cocktail wait. ✉*1500 W. Taylor St.* ☎*312/942–1117* ▭*AE, D, DC, MC, V.*

$$–$$$
PAN ASIAN
Near North

Roy's. Hawaii's most exported chef, Roy Yamaguchi, raids the island pantry, refining the goods with Asian flourishes. The results are busy, multi-ingredient dishes that seduce with the ease of a trade wind. Roy's signatures include many seafood dishes like blackened ahi in soy mustard and butterfish in ginger-wasabi sauce. But honey-mustard short ribs please heartier palates. Though the cozy and warm dining room says contemporary chic, the waiters' greetings and flower-print ties spread a little aloha around the place. ✉ *720 N. State St.* ☎ *312/787–7599* 🍴 *AE, D, DC, MC, V* ⊘ *No lunch.*

$$ **Russian Tea Time.** Exotica is on the
RUSSIAN   menu and in the air at this spot
Loop   that's favored by visitors to the nearby Art Institute and Symphony Center. Mahogany trim, samovars, and balalaika music set the stage for dishes from Russia and neighboring republics (the owners hail from Uzbekistan), including Ukrainian borscht, *blinis* (small, savory pancakes) with salmon caviar, Maldovian meatballs, and game sausages. Chilled vodka flights (three shots) help the herring go down. ✉ *77 E. Adams St.* ☎ *312/360–0000* 🍴 *Reservations essential* 🍴 *AE, D, DC, MC, V.*

$$$ **Ruth's Chris Steak House.** With excellent steaks and outstanding service,
STEAKHOUSE   the Chicago outpost of this fine-dining chain holds its own in this defin-
River North   itive steak town. The lobster is good, although expensive, and there are more appetizer and side-dish options than at most other steak houses. Woody surrounds and low lighting lend a masculine character and draw a clientele of business diners. ✉ *431 N. Dearborn St.* ☎ *312/321–2725* 🍴 *AE, D, DC, MC, V* ⊘ *No lunch weekends.*

$$ **Salpicon.** Anyone who does authentic Mexican in Chicago operates in
MEXICAN   the shadow of Frontera Grill's Rick Bayless, which makes it easier for
Near North   those in the know to snag a table at Salpicon. Chef Priscila Satkoff grew up in Mexico City and her renditions of Oaxacan mole pork and grilled fish with salsa fresca have unforced flare. Wash 'em down with a belt of one of 100 tequilas or 800 vintage wines. Once you try the Mexican-style Sunday brunch, with dishes like skirt steak and eggs, you'll never go back to eggs Benedict. ✉ *1252 N. Wells St.* ☎ *312/988–7811* 🍴 *AE, D, DC, MC, V* ⊘ *No lunch.*

$$ **Scoozi!** This ever-popular trattoria continues to attract a yuppie crowd
ITALIAN   after five and plenty of wandering suburbanites on the weekend.
River North   You'll recognize it by the gigantic tomato over the front door; inside,
☺   a sprawling, two-level dining room sports loft-chic looks of exposed brick walls, open truss ceiling, and steel garage doors. This place is nothing if not chameleon; groups love the shareable antipasti and pizzas, families with kids meld right into the cacophony, and couples find the energy relieves the focus on a boring date. ✉ *410 W. Huron St.* ☎ *312/943–5900* 🍴 *AE, D, DC, MC, V* ⊘ *No lunch.*

$$$$ **Seasons Restaurant.** How the Four Seasons's boîte manages to please
NEW AMERICAN   business diners and traveling families is a mystery worthy of a hotel-
Near North   school case study. Service is suave, the room elegant, and the seasonal food refined; altogether, it's an ideal spot for power-dining appointments. At the same time, the hotel makes a big deal about being family friendly, which, if you read between the lines a bit, means there's a children's menu for better behaved clans (it *is* still the Four Seasons). Fixing

for a good deal and a quick lunch? There's an affordable three-course daily lunch menu that's served within an hour. Dinner menus include five- and eight-course tasting options. Reservations are essential for Chicago's best (and most expensive) Sunday brunch. ⊠ *Four Seasons Hotel, 120 E. Delaware Pl.* ☎ *312/280–8800* 🖃 *AE, D, DC, MC, V.*

$$–$$$
CHINESE
Near North

Shanghai Terrace. As precious as a jewel box, and as pricey, this red, lacquer-trimmed 40-seater hidden away in the Peninsula Hotel reveals the hotelier's Asian roots. Come for upscale dim sum, stylishly presented, and luxury-laden entrées such as steamed fish, Szechuan beef, and wok-fried lobster. A summer patio lets you revel in the skyline, seven stories above the madding crowds of Michigan Avenue. ⊠ *Peninsula Hotel, 108 E. Superior St.* ☎ *312/573–6744* 🖃 *AE, D, DC, MC, V* ☉ *Closed Sun.*

$$$
SEAFOOD
River North

Shaw's Crab House and Blue Crab Lounge. Hands down, this is the city's best seafood spot. Though it's held the position a long time, it doesn't rest on its laurels. The kitchen stays on track, turning out famed classics like silky crab cakes and rich halibut while updating the menu with sushi, maki, and fresh tartare selections. The seafood salad served at lunch is loaded and big enough for two. (Lunch, by the way, is a good bargain, with well-priced entrées and $1 desserts.) The city's chief specialist in bivalves nurtures a split personality, spanning a clubby main dining room in nautically themed loft digs and a lively exposed-brick bar where shell shuckers work harder than the barkeeps. ⊠ *21 E. Hubbard St.* ☎ *312/527–2722* 🖃 *AE, D, DC, MC, V.*

$$$
AMERICAN
Near North

Signature Room at the 95th. When you've got the best view in town and a lock on the prom business, do you need to be daring with the food? Signature Room isn't, making a formal affair of dishes such as rack of lamb and salmon in puffed pastry while couples ogle the skyline views from the John Hancock's 95th floor. Avoid the clichés by calling here at lunch: the $18 buffet gets you good and stuffed and the daytime light lets you see Lake Michigan. The appeal of the lavish and pricey Sunday brunch? The abundance of food. Brunch reservations essential. ⊠ *John Hancock Center, 875 N. Michigan Ave.* ☎ *312/787–9596* 🖃 *AE, D, DC, MC, V.*

$$$–$$$$
STEAKHOUSE
River North

Smith and Wollensky. Aged-on-the-premises prime beef and an extensive wine cellar are hallmarks of this riverfront steak house, part of a New York–based chain. United by remarkable river views, the dining area is divided into several spaces, one of which is Wollensky's Grill, a more casual room with a compact menu and later serving hours. Steaks and chops are the big draw, but deep-fried pork shank and pepper-dusted "angry lobster" are customer favorites, too. ⊠ *318 N. State St.* ☎ *312/670–9900* 🖃 *AE, D, DC, MC, V.*

$
SOUTHERN
Wicker Park

Smoke Daddy. A rib and blues emporium in a funky Wicker Park corner bar, Smoke Daddy serves tangy barbecued ribs with generously supplied paper towels for swabbing stray sauce. Fans pack bar stools and booths for the chow, which includes richly flavored smoked pork and homemade fries, as well as for the no-cover R&B and jazz bands that play nightly after 9:30. ⊠ *1804 W. Division St.* ☎ *773/772–6656* 🖃 *AE, D, MC, V.*

$$
NEW AMERICAN
Lincoln Park

Sola. While you can dine very well in Chicago's neighborhoods, most local joints aren't as ambitious as Sola, which would be right at home downtown and probably far more expensive there. Now North Side visitors don't have to travel far for miso-glazed black cod, bacon-wrapped venison, and wasabi-crusted scallops. Chef-owner-surfer Carol Wallack's affinity for Hawaii shows in Pacific Rim fare like seaweed salad and salmon carpaccio. Proving its affection for the neighborhood, the restaurant is fronted by a wall of windows and warm within, thanks to a gas fireplace. A five-minute cab ride from Wrigley Field, this is a good option for beyond-ballpark fare. ⊠*3868 N. Lincoln Ave.* ☎*773/327–3868* ⊟*AE, D, DC, MC, V* ☺*No lunch Mon.–Wed.*

¢
SOUTHERN
South Shore

Soul Queen. Since 1971, Soul Queen has been sating the famished with one of the most generous buffets in town. For $7.75, help yourself to fried chicken, chicken and dumplings, ham hocks, turkey wings, black-eyed peas, succotash, peach cobbler, and more. The spread gets even more elaborate on Sunday when the price goes up $2. ⊠*9031 S. Stony Island Ave.* ☎*773/731–3366* ⚐*Reservations not accepted* ⊟*No credit cards.*

$
ITALIAN
Far North Side
Fodor'sChoice
★

Spacca Napoli. Despite Chicago's renown for deep-dish pizza, locals are lately swept away by Neapolitan pies bested by this bright, 50-seat Ravenswood gem. Finely ground Italian flour, imported buffalo mozzarella, hand-tossed dough and a brick, wood-fired oven built by Italian craftsmen are credited for producing bubbling, chewy crusts that edge savory, uncut, thin pies which diners eat with a fork. Antipasti and desserts like tiramisu round out the short menu. The proprietors shun take-out and turn up the lights a little too high, but the food wins out, accounting for out-the-door waits, even on weekdays. In summer, angle for a table on the pleasant sidewalk patio. ⊠*1769 W. Sunnyside* ☎*773/878–2420* ⊟*AE, MC, V* ☺*Closed Mon. and Tues.*

$$$
ITALIAN
Near North

Spiaggia. Refined Italian cooking dished alongside three-story picture-window views of Lake Michigan make Spiaggia one of the city's top eateries. The tiered dining room guarantees good sight lines from each table. Chef Tony Mantuano prepares elegant, seasonal dishes such as veal-filled pasta with fennel pollen, roast guinea hen with truffle sauce, or Mediterranean bass with saffron potato puree. Oenophiles consider the wine list scholarly. For Spiaggia fare, minus the luxury ingredients, try lunch or dinner at the casual Cafe Spiaggia next door. ⊠*980 N. Michigan Ave.* ☎*312/280–2750* ⚐*Reservations essential* Jacket required ⊟*AE, D, DC, MC, V* ☺*No lunch.*

$$
NEW AMERICAN
Wicker Park
Fodor'sChoice
★

Spring. Leave pretense downtown. Chef Shawn McClain's artistic but unfussy fish preparations—from Kumomoto oysters with grated fresh wasabi root to Atlantic skate wing, white polenta, and roasted cauliflower—distinguish the sophisticated Spring from the seasonal restaurant. Like McClain's cooking, the restaurant's interior design faces east for inspiration, beginning with a rock garden in the foyer. Original white glazed-tile walls hearken back to the space's former life as a bathhouse. ⊠*2039 W. North Ave.* ☎*773/395–7100* ⊟*AE, DC, MC, V* ☺*Closed Mon. No lunch.*

$$ **SushiSamba Rio.** *Sex and the City* made SushiSamba a star in New York,
JAPANESE and look-alike hotties make the Chicago version a scene. The trendy
River North Brazilian–Japanese hot spot combines a nightclub vibe—dramatic mul-
tilevel design, freely flowing cocktails, male servers in eye makeup—
with an inventive menu. All the usual sushi suspects are here, as well
as offbeat sashimi choices, Brazilian-style marinated fish, and fusion
rolls that don't always work. For best results sample the menu with an
adventurous, party-hardy crowd on Wednesday when there's a band
and samba dancers. An all-weather rooftop lounge, popular with the
late-night crowd, serves cocktails (try the sparkling sake) and some
sushi. ⊠ *504 N. Wells St.* ☎ *312/595–2300* ⊟ *AE, D, DC, MC, V.*

$ **Sushi Wabi.** This funky, West Loop sushi restaurant dances to an
JAPANESE industrial-pop beat—on weekend evenings, at least, when it employs
West Loop a DJ (club attitude suffices on weekdays). The urban-chic brick-and-
exposed-steel interior draws a young, martini-swilling crowd. Superior
sushi and maki rolls along with straightforward entrées such as grilled
peppercorn-crusted tuna with soy and lemon, bring substance to the
style haunt. ⊠ *842 W. Randolph St.* ☎ *312/563–1224* ⊟ *AE, D, DC,
MC, V* ⊘ *No lunch weekends.*

¢ **Svea.** The North Side's Andersonville neighborhood, once a haven for
SCANDINAVIAN Swedes, plays host to the humble Svea, a Swedish version of an Ameri-
Far North Side can diner. There are Swedish pancakes with lingonberries and Swedish
rye *limpa* bread with eggs in the morning, Swedish meatball heroes and
open-face roast beef sandwiches at lunch. The digs are no-frill, but the
service is friendly. ⊠ *5236 N. Clark St.* ☎ *773/275–7738* ⊟ *No credit
cards* ⊘ *No dinner.*

$$ **Terragusto.** Chicago storefront dining doesn't get any better than this
ITALIAN Italian haunt in Roscoe Village. Bring your own wine and sit down in
Far North Side the exposed-brick dining room for dishes comprised mainly of organic
and sustainable ingredients and pastas made that day by your chef-cum-
waiter. The house specializes in family-style service, enabling diners to
choose an antipasti, salad, a couple of pastas and entrées to split, making it a nice choice for groups who like to graze. Though it occupies an
unlikely corner of Addison Street in Roscoe Village, it's only about a mile
from Wrigley Field and neighbors the Brown Line El stop. ⊠ *Addison St.*
☎ *773/248–2777* ⊟ *AE, D, DC, MC, V* ⊘ *No lunch. Closed Mon.*

¢ **Thai Classic.** With apologies to Chinatown, Chicago is really a Thai
THAI town when it comes to outstanding Asian food. The assets here include
Lake View a prime location three blocks south of Wrigley Field, good service, and
even better dishes. Not only are prices low, but there is no liquor license
(pick up a six-pack of Singha beer from the liquor store down the
street), saving you the mark-up. Bargain hunters should hit the $11.75
buffet, available Saturday afternoon and all day Sunday. Come on foot
during Cubs games when parking is near impossible. ⊠ *3332 N. Clark
St.* ☎ *773/404–2000* ⊟ *AE, D, DC, MC, V* ⊠ *BYOB.*

$$ **Tomboy.** Here's your spot for great people-watching. A bohemian crowd
NEW AMERICAN mingles in this funky, brick-walled storefront that plates food with
Far North Side a playful presentation. There's a fanciful "porcupine" shrimp coated

with splayed-out spikes of phyllo dough and a crème brûlée served in a cookie cone inside a martini glass. ⊠*5402 N. Clark St.* ☎*773/907–0636* ☰*AE, D, DC, MC, V* ⊘*Closed Sun.*

$$$
MEXICAN
River North

Topolobampo. The name is a mouthful; do like a local and call it "Topolo." Chef-owner Rick Bayless wrote the book on regional Mexican cuisine—several books, actually—and here he takes his faithfully regional food upscale. Next door to the more casual Frontera Grill *(see review above)*, Topolo is the higher-end room, with a more subdued mood and luxury menu, though it shares Frontera's address, phone, and dedication to quality. The ever-changing offerings showcase game, seasonal fruits and vegetables, and exotic preparations: adobo-marinated lamb and rock hen in a sauce of almonds and tomatoes are two examples. ⊠*445 N. Clark St.* ☎*312/661–1434* ♦*Reservations essential* ☰*AE, D, DC, MC, V* ⊘*Closed Sun. and Mon. No lunch Sat.*

$$
ITALIAN
Loop

Trattoria No. 10. It's hard to camouflage a basement location, but Trattoria No. 10 gives it a good go with terra-cotta colors, arched entryways, and quarry-tile floors, all of which evoke Italy. Pretheater diners crowd in for the house specialty ravioli filled with seasonal stuffings, classic antipasti selections like caprese salad with vine-ripened tomatoes and bufala mozzarella, and substantial *secondi piatti* like fillet of beef with roasted Parmesan potatoes. Cheap chowsters, meanwhile, elbow into the bar for the $12 nibbles buffet served from 5 to 8 PM weekdays with a $6 drink minimum. ⊠*10 N. Dearborn St.* ☎*312/984–1718* ☰*AE, D, DC, MC, V* ⊘*Closed Sun. No lunch Sat.*

$$$$
NEW AMERICAN
Near North

TRU. Chefs Rick Tramonto and, on pastries, Gale Gand do fine dining with a sense of humor. The quite-serious food is leavened by the presentations: caviar atop a tabletop crystal staircase, between-course sorbets in cones, or dishes served over a mini fishbowl occupied by a live fighting fish. The dining room resembles a gallery, with white walls and carefully chosen art, including an Andy Warhol. The menu starts with a basic three-course prix fixe, priced at $95, and escalates to nine courses. Several of those are dessert, so save space. ⊠*676 N. St. Clair St.* ☎*312/202–0001* ♦*Reservations essential* Jacket required ☰*AE, D, DC, MC, V* ⊘*Closed Sun. No lunch.*

$–$$
TURKISH
Lake View

Turquoise Cafe. The bustling Turkish-owned café attempts to please every palate with a mixed menu of continental and Turkish foods, but it's the latter that stars here. Don't-miss items include lamb kebabs, *sogurme* (a smoked eggplant, yogurt, and walnut dip), and homemade noodles with feta and dill. Vested waiters, a martini menu, and wood-trimmed surroundings outclass the neighborhood lot. ⊠*2147 W. Roscoe St.* ☎*773/549–3523* ☰*AE, D, DC, MC, V.*

$$
ITALIAN
South Loop

Tuscany. *Under the Tuscan Sun* fans, Italo-philes, and University of Illinois at Chicago staffers beat it to Tuscany for the rustic but celebrated fare of the Tuscan countryside. Recommended: rotisserie-grilled chicken, thin-crust pizzas, and, for splurgers, the Black Angus New York strip steak. Not recommended: carbo-loading at lunch. ⊠*1014 W. Taylor St.* ☎*312/829–1990* ☰*AE, D, DC, MC, V* ⊘*No lunch weekends.*

$$–$$$
BARBECUE
Old Town

Twin Anchors Restaurant & Tavern. For a taste of classic Chicago, stop into Twin Anchors, which has been dishing babyback ribs since 1932. The nautically-themed brick tavern was a favorite of Frank Sinatra who still croons nightly on the jukebox. If you're not in the mood for a messy slab of ribs, which come mild or zesty, order the battered cod fish fry or the fried chicken. In truth, dinner here is really less about cuisine than scene—local and touring celebs often visit and many locals are loyal regulars—but lovers of barrooms with personality don't mind the typically long waits during prime time. ⊠ *1655 N. Sedgwick St.* ☏ *312/266–1616* ⚓ *Reservations not accepted* ▤ *AE, D, DC, MC, V* ⊘ *No lunch weekdays.*

$$
INDIAN
River North

Vermilion. Vermilion touts itself as a Latin–Indian fusion restaurant, but its best dishes are strictly Eastern. Skip the Latin-salute ceviche and empanadas in favor of the Coca-Cola–marinated . Lots of small-plate options—led by the lamb chops and scallops—encourage sampling. Despite cool fashion photography on the walls and techno music in the air, the welcome here is warm. Late-night dining hours draw a club-going crowd. ⊠ *10 W. Hubbard St.* ☏ *312/527–4060* ▤ *AE, D, DC, MC, V* ⊘ *No lunch Sat.*

$$$
AMERICAN
Near North

Viand. Ebullient chef-owner Steve Chiappetti's personality is written all over Viand, a lively restaurant and bar that's a breath of fresh air from the seriously designer-centric Michigan Avenue a half block away. "Dining should be fun," says the chef, and so it is here where Oscar-style statuettes deliver chopsticks and the Junk Food Cart dessert option packs homemade Oreos, marshmallows, and brownies in a mini shopping cart. Don't miss the braised short ribs, the four-cheese ravioli with truffle sauce, and a chat with the friendly chef. Adjacent to a Courtyard by Marriott the restaurant serves breakfast, lunch, and dinner and has a steady bar trade. ⊠ *155 E. Ontario St.* ☏ *312/255–8505* ▤ *AE, MC, V.*

$$
ITALIAN
Loop

Vivere. There's no resting on old world looks at Vivere: think Italian baroque on acid. Cones, swirls, and bright colors guarantee an—ahem—interesting view, should conversation lag. The regional Italian menu includes excellent, beyond-the-norm dishes such as pheasant *agnolotti* (half-moon-shape ravioli) and grilled venison loin with polenta. We love the extensive Italian wine list. ⊠ *71 W. Monroe St.* ☏ *312/332–4040* ▤ *AE, D, DC, MC, V* ⊘ *Closed Sun. No lunch Sat.*

$$
ITALIAN
West Loop

Vivo. Vivo was trendy on this west-of-the-Loop stretch long before Randolph Street's restaurant row got hot. Slightly more about scene—brick walls, black ceiling, open wine racks, and lots of pretty people—than cuisine, Vivo manages reliable Italian fare. You can't go wrong with carpaccio, grilled portobello mushroom salad, seafood linguine, and a thin-sliced veal chop. ⊠ *838 W. Randolph St.* ☏ *312/733–3379* ▤ *AE, DC, MC, V* ⊘ *No lunch weekends.*

$$
THAI
River North

Vong's Thai Kitchen. This casual spin-off of chef Jean-Georges Vongerichten's New York Thai–French fusion Vong concentrates solely on Thai fare with upmarket accents and pretty presentations. Look for tuna sashimi rolls, beef tenderloin over noodles, and a laundry list of curries ranging from mild to "jungle" hot. Candles and palms boost the romance quotient by night, but this is also a strong candidate for a working lunch. ⊠6 *W. Hubbard St.* ☎*312/644–8664* ⊟*AE, D, DC, MC, V* ⊘*No lunch weekends.*

$$$
AMERICAN
River North

Weber Grill Restaurant. How cheesy is it to dine at a brand extension of a popular backyard grill? Okay, a little, but get over yourself and look for the red kettle cooker outside Weber Grill where commercial versions of the namesake appliance demonstrate its versatility. Suburban Chicago-based Weber takes on the range of grill cookery at its River North restaurant, offering burgers, ribs, steaks, chops, veggie sides, and novelties like "beer-can chicken" on the extensive menu. Adjacent to the Hilton Garden Inn, the restaurant also serves standard breakfast fare. Spacious booths line the State Street windows and make for the best views of the opening cooking line. ⊠*539 N. State St.* ☎*312/467–9696* ⊟*AE, D, DC, MC, V.*

$$
AMERICAN
West Loop
FodorśChoice
★

West Town Tavern. It's not easy to find this find in a neighborhood bereft of many restaurants, but trust your cabbie to get you here. The handsome wood bar and brick walls may be tavern staples, but the open kitchen and oversize dining room mirror promise more than cheeseburgers. The menu delivers with a mix of upscale comfort foods (try the beer cheese—a cheese ball made with cheddar cheese and spices—and pizza-style flat breads) and gussied-up American classics like peppercrusted beef tenderloin in a zinfandel sauce. The focused wine list globe trots for value. ⊠*1329 W. Chicago Ave.* ☎*312/666–6175* ⊟*AE, MC, V* ⊘*Closed Sun. No lunch.*

$$
AMERICAN
River North

Wildfire. This is as close as you can get to the grill without staying home and firing up the barbie. A triple hearth of roaring fires runs along the back wall of the supper club–style joint that plays a soundtrack of vintage jazz. No culinary innovations here, just exceptional aged prime rib, barbecued ribs, and roasted fish, along with wood-fired pizzas and skillet-roasted mussels. Top taste: the horseradish-crusted filet mignon. ⊠*159 W. Erie St.* ☎*312/787–9000* ⊟*AE, D, DC, MC, V* ⊘*No lunch.*

$$
ASIAN FUSION
Lake View

Yoshi's Cafe. Decades ago Yoshi's launched as a pricey fine-dining restaurant in the 'hood. We offer this history lesson to say that while the atmosphere went jeans-casual and the prices south, the cooking quality remained, and remains, high. Yoshi Katsumura turns out informal French-Asian, like duck breast with baked quail egg in brioche or roasted Japanese pumpkin filled with tofu (it's good enough to convert a carnivore). Sunday brunch includes the expected eggs along with a Japanese-inspired breakfast (rice, tofu, and seaweed). ⊠*3257 N. Halsted St.* ☎*773/248–6160* ⊟*AE, DC, MC, V* ⊘*Closed Mon. Sun. brunch.*

Chicago Dining & Lodging Atlas

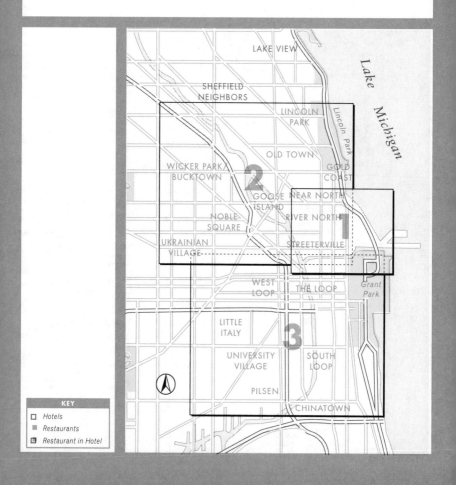

KEY
- ☐ Hotels
- ■ Restaurants
- ▣ Restaurant in Hotel

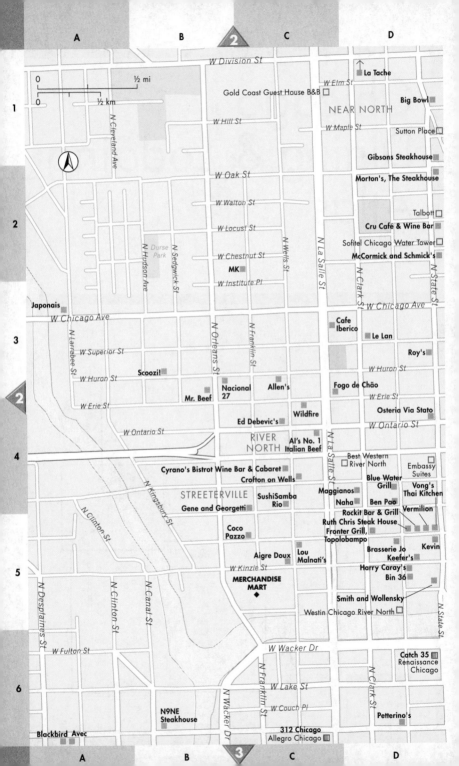

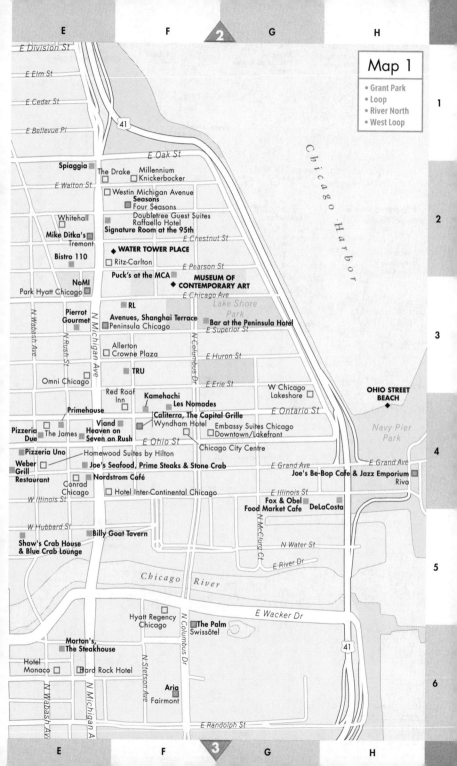

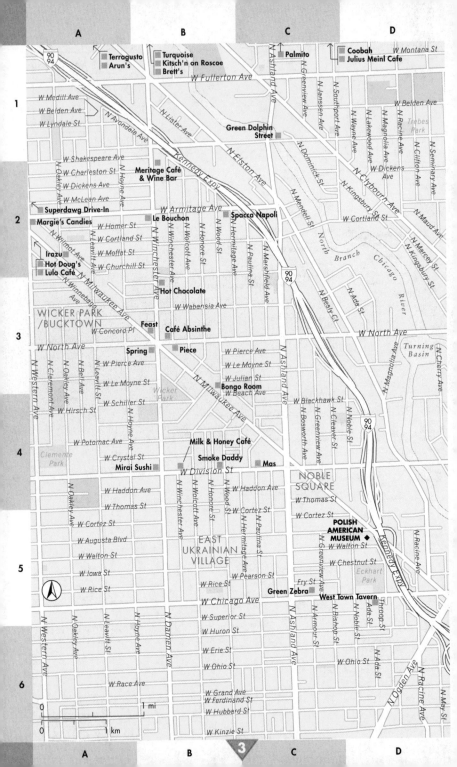

A

B

C

D

1

90 94

Terragusto
Arun's

Turquoise
Kitsch'n on Roscoe
Brett's

Palmito

Coobah
Julius Meinl Cafe

W Montana St

W Medill Ave
W Belden Ave
W Lyndale St

N Avondale Ave

N Lister Ave

W Fullerton Ave

N Ashland Ave

N Greenview Ave

N Janssen Ave

N Southport Ave

N Wayne Ave

N Lakewood Ave

N Magnolia Ave

N Racine Ave

N Clifton Ave

N Seminary Ave

W Belden Ave

Thebes
Park

Green Dolphin
Street

2

W Shakespeare Ave
W Charleston St
W Dickens Ave
W McLean Ave

N Oakley Ave

N Hoyne Ave

Meritage Café
& Wine Bar

Kennedy Expy

N Elston Ave

N Dominick St

N Clybourn Ave

W Dickens
Ave

W Cortland St

N Kingsbury St

N Maud Ave

N Marcey St

N Kingsbury St

Superdawg Drive-In

Margie's Candies

W Homer St
W Cortland St
W Moffat St
W Churchill St

Le Bouchon

N Winchester Ave

N Wolcott Ave

N Honore St

Spacca Napoli

N Hermitage Ave

N Paulina St

N Marshfield Ave

W Cortland St

North

Branch

Chicago

River

N Leavitt St

N Wilmot Ave

Irazu
Hot Doug's
Lula Café

N Milwaukee Ave

N Winnebago Ave

N Winchester Ave

Hot Chocolate

90 94

N Besly Ct

N Ada St

3

WICKER PARK
/BUCKTOWN

Feast

W Concord Pl

Café Absinthe

W Wabansia Ave

W North Ave

Turning
Basin

N Cherry Ave

W North Ave

Spring

Piece

W Pierce Ave
W Le Moyne St
W Julian St

N Milwaukee Ave

Bongo Room

N Ashland Ave

N Magnolia Ave

4

N Western Ave

N Claremont Ave

N Oakley Ave

N Bell Ave

N Leavitt St

W Pierce Ave
W Le Moyne St
W Schiller St
W Hirsch St

N Hoyne Ave

Wicker
Park

W Beach Ave

W Blackhawk St

N Bosworth Ave

N Greenview Ave

N Cleaver St

N Noble St

90 94

Clemente
Park

W Potomac Ave
W Crystal St

Mirai Sushi

Milk & Honey Café

Smoke Daddy

W Division St

Mas

N Winchester Ave

N Wolcott Ave

N Honore St

N Wood St

W Haddon Ave

W Thomas St
W Cortez St

NOBLE
SQUARE

5

N Oakley Ave

W Haddon Ave
W Thomas St
W Cortez St
W Augusta Blvd
W Walton St
W Iowa St
W Rice St

N Leavitt St

N Hoyne Ave

N Damen Ave

EAST
UKRAINIAN
VILLAGE

N Hermitage Ave

N Paulina St

W Rice St

W Pearson St

W Chicago Ave

Green Zebra

Fry St

N Greenview Ave

N Armour Ave

N Bishop St

N Noble St

POLISH
AMERICAN
MUSEUM ◆

W Walton St
W Chestnut St

Eckhart
Park

West Town Tavern

Kennedy Expy

N Racine Ave

6

N Western Ave

W Race Ave

N Oakley Ave

N Leavitt St

N Hoyne Ave

N Damen Ave

W Superior St
W Huron St
W Erie St
W Ohio St

W Grand Ave
W Ferdinand St
W Hubbard St

W Kinzie St

N Ashland Ave

N Armour St

W Ohio St

N Ada St

Throop St

N Ogden Ave

N May St

N Racine Ave

0   1 mi
0   1 km

3

A

B

C

D

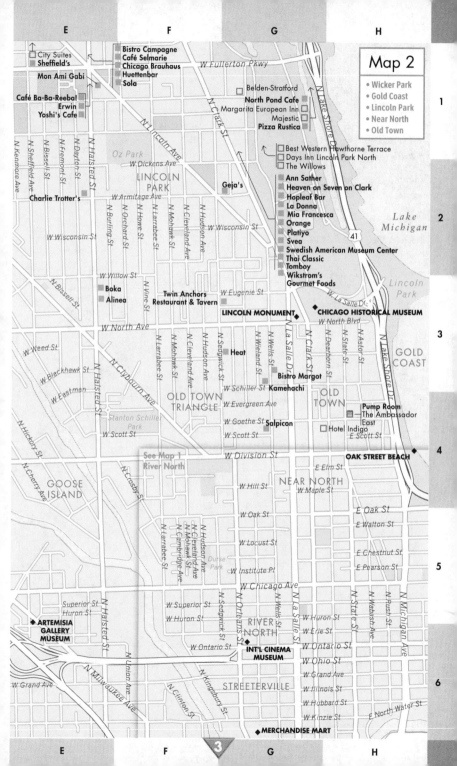

Map 2

- Wicker Park
- Gold Coast
- Lincoln Park
- Near North
- Old Town

City Suites
Sheffield's
Mon Ami Gabi
Café Ba-Ba-Reebal
Erwin
Yoshi's Cafe
Charlie Trotter's
Bistro Campagne
Café Selmarie
Chicago Brauhaus
Huettenbar
Sola

W Fullerton Pkwy

Belden-Stratford
North Pond Cafe
Margarita European Inn
Majestic
Pizza Rustica

Best Western Hawthorne Terrace
Days Inn Lincoln Park North
The Willows

Ann Sather
Heaven on Seven on Clark
Hopleaf Bar
La Donna
Mia Francesca
Orange
Platiyo
Svea
Swedish American Museum Center
Thai Classic
Tomboy
Wikstrom's
Gourmet Foods

Lake
Michigan

Lincoln
Park

Geja's

Boka
Alinea

Twin Anchors
Restaurant & Tavern

LINCOLN MONUMENT

CHICAGO HISTORICAL MUSEUM

GOLD
COAST

Heat

Bistro Margot

Kamehachi

Salpican

OLD TOWN
TRIANGLE

OLD
TOWN

Pump Room
The Ambassador
East
Hotel Indigo

OAK STREET BEACH

See Map 1
River North

NEAR NORTH

GOOSE
ISLAND

ARTEMISIA
GALLERY
MUSEUM

RIVER
NORTH

INT'L CINEMA
MUSEUM

STREETERVILLE

MERCHANDISE MART

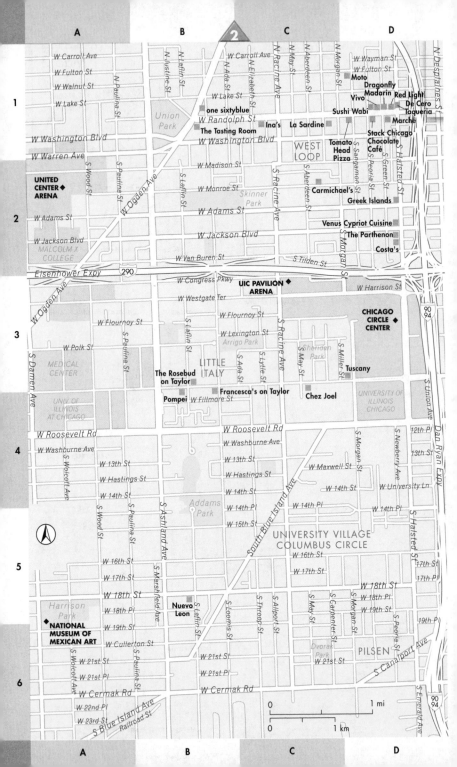

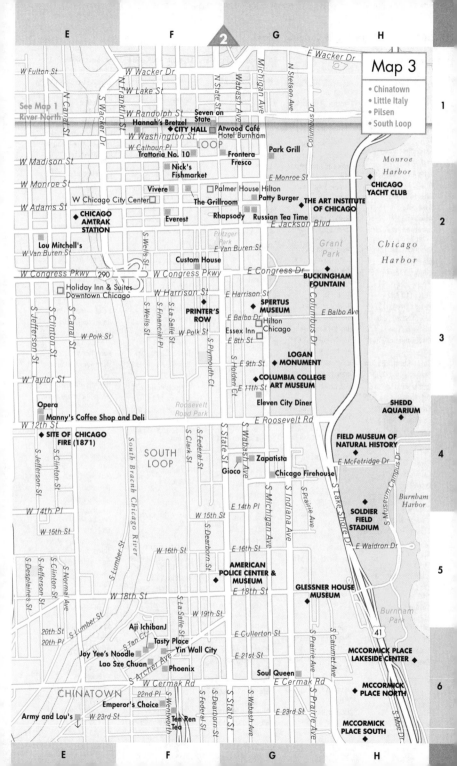

Restaurants

312 Chicago, 1:C6
Aigre Doux, 1:C5
Aji Ichiban, 3:F6
Alinea, 2:F3
Allen's, 1:C3
Al's No. 1 Italian Beef, 1:C4
Ann Sather, 2:G2
Aria, 1:F6
Army and Lou's, 3:E6
Arun's, 2:A1
Atwood Café, 3:F1
Avec, 1:A6
Avenues, 1:E3
Bar at The Peninsula Hotel, 1:F3
Ben Pao, 1:D4
Big Bowl, 1:D1
Billy Goat Tavern, 1:E5
Bin 36, 1:D5
Bistro 110, 1:E2
Bistro Campagne, 2:F1
Bistrot Margot, 2:G3
Blackbird, 1:A6
Blue Water Grill, 1:D4
Boka, 2:F3
Bongo Room, 2:B3
Brasserie Jo, 1:D5
Brett's, 2:B1
Cafe Iberico, 1:D3
Café Absinthe, 2:B3
Café Ba-Ba-Reeba!, 2:E1
Café Selmarie, 2:F1
Caliterra Bar & Grille, The, 1:F4
Capital Grille, The, 1:F4
Carmichael's, 3:C2
Catch 35, 1:D6
Charlie Trotter's, 2:E2
Chez Joel, 3:C3
Chicago Brauhaus, 2:F1
Chicago Firehouse, 3:G4
Coco Pazzo, 1:C5
Coobah, 2:D1
Costa's, 3:D2
Crofton on Wells, 1:C4
Cru Café & Wine Bar, 1:D2
Custom House, 3:F2
Cyrano's Bistrot Wine Bar & Cabaret, 1:C4
De Cero Taqueria, 3:D1
DeLaCosta, 1:H4
Dragonfly Mandarin, 3:D1
Ed Debevic's, 1:C4
Eleven City Diner, 3:G3
Emperor's Choice, 3:F6
Erwin, 2:E1
Everest, 3:F2

Feast, 2:B3
Fogo de Chao, 1:D3
Fox & Obel Food Market Cafe, 1:G4
Francesca's on Taylor, 3:B3
Frontera Fresco in Seven on State, 3:G1
Frontera Grill, 1:D5
Geja's, 2:G2
Gene and Georgetti, 1:C4
Gibsons Steakhouse, 1:D2
Gioco, 3:G4
Greek Islands, 3:D2
Green Dolphin Street, 2:C1
Green Zebra, 2:C5
Grillroom, The, 3:F2
Hannah's Bretzel, 3:F1
Harry Caray's, 1:D5
Heat, 2:F3
Heaven on Seven, 2:G2
Heaven on Seven, 1:E4
Hopleaf Bar, 2:G2
Hot Chocolate, 2:B3
Hot Doug's, 2:A2
Huettenbar, 2:F1
Ina's, 3:C1
Irazu, 2:A2
Japonais, 1:A3
Joe's Be-Bop Cafe and Jazz Emporium, 1:H4
Joe's Seafood, Prime Steaks & Stone Crab, 1:E4
Joy Yee's Noodle, 3:F6
Julius Meinl Cafe, 2:D1
Kamehachi, 2:G3; 1:F3
Keefer's, 1:D5
Kevin, 1:D5
Kitsch'n on Roscoe, 2:B1
La Donna, 2:G2
La Sardine, 3:C1
La Tache, 1:D1
Lao Sze Chuan, 3:F6
Le Bouchon, 2:B2
Le Lan, 1:D3
Les Nomades, 1:F4
Lou Malnati's, 1:C5
Lou Mitchell's, 3:E2
Lula Café, 2:A2
Maggiano's Little Italy, 1:D4
Manny's Coffee Shop and Deli, 3:E4
Marché, 3:D1
Margie's Candies, 2:A2
Mas, 2:C4
McCormick and Schmick's, 1:D2

Meritage Café and Wine Bar, 2:B2
Mia Francesca, 2:G2
Mike Ditka's Restaurant, 1:E2
Milk & Honey Café, 2:B4
Mirai Sushi, 2:B4
mk, 1:C2
Mon Ami Gabi, 2:E1
Morton's, The Steak-house, 1:D2
Moto, 3:D1
Mr. Beef, 1:B3
N9NE Steakhouse, 1:B6
Nacional 27, 1:C3
Naha, 1:D4
Nick's Fishmarket, 3:F2
NoMI, 1:E3
Nordstrom Café, 1:E4
North Pond Café, 2:G1
Nuevo Leon, 3:B5
one sixtyblue, 3:B1
Opera, 3:E3
Orange, 2:G2
Osteria via Stato, 1:D4
Palm, The, 1:F6
Palmito, 2:C1
Park Grill, 3:G1
Parthenon, The, 3:D2
Patty Burger, 3:G2
Petterino's, 1:D6
Phoenix, 3:F6
Piece, 2:B3
Pierrot Gourmet, 1:E3
Pizza Rustica, 2:G1
Pizzeria Due, 1:E4
Pizzeria Uno, 1:E4
Platiyo, 2:G2
Pompei, 3:B4
Primehouse, 1:E4
Puck's at the MCA, 1:F2
Pump Room, 2:H4
Red Light, 3:D1
Rhapsody, 3:G2
RL, 1:F3
Rockit Bar & Grill, 1:D5
Rosebud on Taylor, The, 3:B3
Roy's, 1:D5
Russian Tea Time, 3:G2
Ruth's Chris Steak House, 1:D5
Salpicon, 2:G4
Scoozi!, 1:B3
Seasons Restaurant, 1:F2
Seven on State, 3:F1
Shanghai Terrace, 1:F3
Shaw's Crab House and Blue Crab Lounge, 1:E5
Sheffield's, 1:E1

Signature Room at the 95th, 1:F2
Smith and Wollensky, 1:D5
Smoke Daddy, 2:B4
Sola, 2:F1
Soul Queen, 3:G6
Spacca Napoli, 2:B2
Spiaggia, 1:E2
Spring, 2:B3
Stack Chicago Chocolate Café, 3:D1
Superdawg Drive-In, 2:A2
Sushi Wabi, 3:D1
SushiSamba Rio, 1:C4
Sutton Place Hotel, 1:D1
Svea, 2:G2
Swedish American Museum Center, 2:H2
Tasting Room, The, 3:B1
Tasty Place, 3:F6
Ten Ren Tea, 3:F6
Terragusto, 2:A1
Thai Classic, 2:G2
Tomato Head Pizza, 3:D1
Tomboy, 2:G2
Topolobampo, 1:D5
Trattoria No. 10, 3:F1
TRU, 1:F3
Turquoise Cafe, 2:B1
Tuscany, 3:C3
Twin Anchors Restaurant & Tavern, 2:G3
Valois, address not on map
Venus Cypriot Cuisine, 3:D2
Vermilion, 1:D5
Viand, 1:F4
Vivere, 3:F2
Vivo, 3:D1
Vong's Thai Kitchen, 1:D5
Weber Grill, 1:E4
West Town Tavern, 2:D5
Wikstrom's Gourmet Foods, 2:H2
Wildfire, 1:C4
Yin Wall City, 3:F6
Yoshi's Cafe, 2:E1
Zapatista, 3:G4
Zealous, 1:B3

Hotels

Allerton Hotel, 1:E3
Ambassador East, The, 2:H4
Belden-Stratford, 2:G1
Best Western Haw-thorne Terrace, 2:G1
Best Western River North, 1:D4

City Suites Hotel, 2:E1
Conrad Chicago, 1:E4
Days Inn Lincoln Park North, 2:G2
Doubletree Guest Suites, 1:F2
Drake Hotel, The, 1:E2
Embassy Suites, 1:D4
Embassy Suites Chicago Downtown/Lakefront, 1:F4
Essex Inn, 3:G3
Fairmont, 1:F6
Four Seasons, 1:F2
Gold Coast Guest House Bed & Breakfast, 1:C1
Hard Rock Hotel, 1:E6
Hilton Chicago, 3:G3
Holiday Inn & Suites Downtown Chicago, 3:E3
Homewood Suites by Hilton, 1:E4
Hotel Allegro Chicago, 1:C6
Hotel Burnham, 3:F1
Hotel Indigo, 1:G4
Hotel Inter-Continental Chicago, 1:E4
Hotel Monaco, 1:E6
Hyatt Regency Chicago, 1:F6
Majestic Hotel, 2:G1
Margarita European Inn, Evanston, 2:G1
Millennium Knickerbock-er Hotel, 1:F2
Omni Chicago Hotel, 1:E3
Palmer House Hilton, 3:F2
Park Hyatt, 1:E3
Peninsula Chicago, 1:E3
Raffaello Hotel, 1:F2
Renaissance Chicago Hotel, 1:D6
Ritz-Carlton, 1:F2
Sofitel Chicago Water Tower, 1:D2
Sutton Place Hotel, 1:D1
SwissÔtel, 1:F6
Talbott, 1:D2
Tremont, 1:E2
W Chicago City Center, 1:F4
W Chicago Lakeshore, 1:G4
Westin Chicago River North, 1:D5
Westin Michigan Avenue, 1:E2
Whitehall Hotel, 1:E2
Willows, The, 2:G1
Wyndham Hotel, 1:F4

Where to Stay

WORD OF MOUTH

"Chicago has a fantastic mass transit system, so you can stay just about anywhere and have fairly rapid access to both Wrigley Field and O'Hare Airport."

—Paul Rabe

"Chicago can be very hot in July and August. The city also gets crowded in the summer, and there are festivals all summer long, so plan ahead on hotels. The 4th of July is always busy."

—Kris

Updated by
Kelly Aiglon

THE SCENE

Chicago hotel rates are as temperamental as the city's climate. And, just as snow in April and 70-degree weather in November is not uncommon, it is widely accepted that a hotel's room rates may drop $50 to $100 overnight—and rise again the next day. It all depends on the season (summers are most pricey, unsurprisingly) and what's happening in town (big conventions at McCormick Place, like February's annual Chicago Auto Show, throw a wrench in the system, kicking up rates citywide).

Even so, it's wise to shop around. Focus on a neighborhood of interest, such as the Michigan Avenue area, also called Near North, and you'll find budget chains like Red Roof Inn, where prices start at $95, and luxury properties like The Four Seasons Hotel Chicago, within a few blocks of each other.

On the lower end, expect well-maintained yet boxy and sparsely decorated rooms. The good news is that free Wi-Fi is now a feature of most budget-friendly hotels, like the Best Western and Holiday Inn chains, or local outfits like the Essex Inn.

Top-tier hotels have no problem filling their rooms: In some cases, this has little to do with amenities. Instead, they're vibrant bar scenes are the draw, as is the case at the W Chicago Lakeshore, W Chicago City Center, and The James Hotel. Rooms at these hotspots usually don't go for under $300, but the "it" factor is huge, with attractive crowds queuing at the bar and lounging in the restaurants.

Looking forward, there are a few high-profile projects on the horizon, with a Shangri-La Hotel and a Mandarin Oriental Hotel set to open in 2009 near Millennium Park.

WHERE SHOULD I STAY?

	Neighborhood Vibe	Pros	Cons
The Loop	Mostly historic hotels of architectural interest in an area trolled by businesspeople during weekdays and shoppers on weekends	Accessible public transportation and abundant cabs; sidewalk panels point out important buildings; several major theaters	El train noise; construction common; streets are bare after 8 PM.
South Loop & West Loop	Mixed residential and business neighborhoods that are gentrifying, although empty buildings and storefronts are prevalent.	Hotels are cheaper; streets are quieter; Museum Campus and McCormick Place are within easy reach.	Long walks to public transportation; minimal shopping.
Near North	The pulse of the city, on and around North Michigan Avenue, has ritzy high-rise hotels, attractive boutiques, and restaurants; the further north you go, streets become residential.	Many lodging options; lively streets abuzz until late night; safe.	Some hotels on the pricey side; crowded sidewalks.
River North	Lots of chains, from hotels to restaurants to shops, patronized mostly by travelers	Affordable lodging; easy access to public transportation; attractions nearby are family-friendly.	Area might be too touristy for some; noisy construction is common.
Lincoln Park	Small, boutique hotels tucked on quiet, tree-lined streets with pockets of independent shops and restaurants.	Low crime; great paths for walks; lots of parkland.	Limited hotel selection; difficult parking; long walks to El train.
Lake View & North of the City	Especially lively around Wrigley Field, where both Chicagoans and travelers congregate in summertime, the area's lodging is midsized boutique hotels and B&Bs.	Low crime; moderately priced hotels; shopping and dining options at all price ranges, including many vintage-clothing boutiques.	Congested traffic; difficult parking; panhandlers common, especially around El stations and Wrigley Field.

8

LODGING PLANNER

Strategy

Where should we stay? With hundreds of Chicago hotels, it may seem like a daunting question. But fret not—our expert writers and editors have done most of the legwork.

The 50 selections here represent the best this city has to offer—from the best budget motels to the sleekest designer hotels.

Scan "Best Bets" on the following pages for top recommendations by price and experience. Or find a review quickly in the listings. Search by neighborhood, then alphabetically. Happy hunting!

Facilities

Unless otherwise noted in the individual descriptions, all the hotels listed have private baths, central heating, air-conditioning, and private phones. Almost all hotels have data ports and phones with voice mail, as well as valet service. Many now have wireless Internet (Wi-Fi) available, although it's not always free. Most large hotels have video or high-speed checkout capability, and many can arrange babysitting. Pools are rare, but most properties have gyms or health clubs, and some have full-scale spas; hotels without facilities usually have arrangements for guests at nearby gyms, sometimes for a fee.

Need a Reservation?

Yes. Hotel reservations are an absolute necessity when planning your trip to Chicago—hotels often fill up with convention traffic, so book your room in advance.

Prices

The price categories we've printed are based on standard double rooms at high season, excluding holidays. Although we list all of the facilities that are available at a property, we don't specify what is included and what costs extra as those policies are subject to change without notice.

What It Costs

¢	$	$$	$$$	$$$$
under $110	$110–$219	$220–$319	$320–$419	over $420

Prices exclude service charges and Chicago's 15.4% room tax.

BEST BETS FOR CHICAGO LODGING

Fodor's offers a selective listing of quality lodging experiences at every price range, from the city's best budget motel to its most sophisticated luxury hotel. Here, we've compiled our top recommendations by price and experience. The very best properties—in other words, those that provide a particularly remarkable experience in their price range—are designated in the listings with the Fodor's Choice logo.

Fodor'sChoice ★

Essex Inn, p. 313
Four Seasons, p. 305
Hotel Burnham, p. 301
Park Hyatt, p. 309
Peninsula Chicago, p. 309
Ritz-Carlton, p. 310
Sofitel Chicago Water Tower, p. 310
The James Hotel, p. 307
W Chicago Lakeshore, p. 311

Best by Price

BEST ¢

Days Inn Lincoln Park North, p. 300
Red Roof Inn, p. TK

BEST $

Best Western Hawthorne Terrace, p. 298
Essex Inn, p. 313
Margarita European Inn, p. 298

W Chicago Lakeshore, p. 311

BEST $$

Hilton Chicago, p. 314
Hyatt Regency Chicago, p. 302
Millennium Knickerbocker Hotel, p. 309
Westin Chicago River North, p. 313

BEST $$$

Hard Rock Hotel, p. 300
Hotel Burnham, p. 301
Sofitel Chicago Water Tower, p. 310
W Chicago City Center, p. 304

BEST $$$$

Four Seasons, p. 305
Lynfred Winery Bed & Breakfast, p. 314
Park Hyatt, p. 309
Peninsula Chicago, p. 309
Ritz-Carlton, p. 310

Best by Experience

BEST SPA

Four Seasons, p. 305
The James Hotel, p. 307
W Chicago Lakeshore, p. 311

BEST CONCIERGE

Doubletree Guest Suites, p. TK
Fairmont, p. 300
Hotel Monaco, p. 301
Renaissance Chicago Hotel, p. 302
Ritz-Carlton, p. 310

GREAT POOLS

Essex Inn, p. 313
Hilton Chicago, p. 314
Hotel Inter-Continental Chicago, p. 307
Peninsula Chicago, p. 309

MOST KID-FRIENDLY

Best Western River North, p. 312
Holiday Inn & Suites Downtown Chicago, p. 314
Hotel Allegro Chicago, p. 301

MOST ROMANTIC

Belden-Stratford, p. 299
Drake Hotel, p. 305
Four Seasons, p. 305
Majestic Hotel, p. 299
Sutton Place Hotel, p. 311

BUSINESS TRAVEL

Embassy Suites, p. 313
Hotel Burnham, p. 301
Palmer House Hilton, p. 302
Park Hyatt, p. 309
Talbott, p. 311

HOT SCENE

Hard Rock Hotel, p. 300
Hyatt Regency Chicago, p. 302
The James Hotel, p. 307
Peninsula Chicago, p. 309
W Chicago City Center, p. 304

BEST DESIGN

Hotel Indigo, p. 307
Hyatt Regency Chicago, p. 302
Sofitel Chicago Water Tower, p. 310
Swissôtel, p. 302

8

LISTINGS (alphabetical within neighborhood)

EVANSTON

$ **Margarita European Inn.** While the tiny rooms, shared bathrooms, and narrow corridors recall a college dormitory, you won't find a more charming place to stay in Chicago's near north suburbs. The inn was formerly an all-girls residence club built in the late 1920s and a lot of its original features, including the iron-girded elevator shaft and antiques-laden parlor, remain intact. The staff is small, but helpful. The best feature is the "borrowing" library, where guests can swap their rare and used books for those of others. If you're in no rush to go downtown, eat at the lower-level Va Pensiero restaurant, a fancy Italian spot that serves more than 10 kinds of grappa and dishes like pancetta-wrapped pork tenderloin. ⊠*1566 Oak Ave., Evanston, 60201* ☎*847/869–2273* 🖷*847/869–2353* ⊕*www.margaritainn.com* ☞*42 rooms, 22 with bath* &In-room: dial-up. In-hotel: restaurant, public Internet, public Wi-Fi, parking (fee) ⊟AE, D, DC, MC, V ❦CP.

LAKE VIEW

Seemingly light years away from the downtown buzz, Lake View hotels entice with their proximity to Wrigley Field and the summertime street festivals for which the neighborhood is known. As you venture farther north, accommodations tend to be quainter; spaces more intimate; and guests much quieter.

$ **Best Western Hawthorne Terrace.** The hotel's front terrace becomes a place to see and be seen in the summer months, especially when street festivals roar into town. There's little room to relax in the American colonial–style lobby, but rooms are inviting enough; deluxe rooms come with whirlpool tubs. △**Proximity to Wrigley Field is a plus.** ⊠*3434 N. Broadway, Lake View, 60657* ☎*773/244–3434 or 888/675–2378* 🖷*773/244–3435* ⊕*www.hawthorneterrace.com* ☞*46 rooms, 13 suites* &*In-room: refrigerator (some), dial-up, Wi-Fi. In-hotel: gym, laundry facilities, laundry service, parking (fee)* ⊟*AE, D, DC, MC, V* ❦*CP.*

$ **City Suites Hotel.** The neighborhood is a little dicey, being the stomping grounds for the city's goth and punk kids, but it's safe and pretty appealing if you want to escape the sometimes stiff downtown scene. European travelers love the hotel for its cozy, residential feel (it's a mostly suites property and two-thirds of rooms have separate sitting areas and pull-out couches). Its proximity to the El train is both a blessing and a curse; you'll have easy access to downtown and the North Side, but the rumbling noise into the wee hours might not make for the most restful night. Amenities include complimentary Continental breakfast, afternoon cookies, free wireless Internet access, luxury robes, and access to a health club nearby. ⊠*933 W. Belmont Ave., Lake View, 60657* ☎*773/404–3400 or 800/248–9108* 🖶*773/404–3405* ⊕*www.cityinns.com* ⤵*16 rooms, 29 suites* ⌂*In-room: refrigerator (some), Wi-Fi. In-hotel: concierge, parking (fee)* ⊟*AE, D, DC, MC, V* ⎮⎰⎮*CP.*

$$ **Majestic Hotel.** It's no wonder lovey-dovey couples are a big part of this hotel's clientele; everything here—from the roaring fireplace in the lobby to wood-laden, cozy rooms with Prairie-style furnishings, poster beds, and dried flowers—says romance. Rely on the friendly concierge for just about anything, including reservations at the many restaurants in the lively Boystown and Wrigleyville neighborhoods, found just outside the door. Transportation can be tricky; because the hotel is on a quiet side street, you'll have to walk a block to flag a cab and the El train is at least five minutes away on foot. ⊠*528 W. Brompton Ave., Lake View, 60657* ☎*773/404–3499 or 800/727–5108* 🖶*773/404–3495* ⊕*www.cityinns.com* ⤵*28 rooms, 23 suites* ⌂*In-room: refrigerator (some), dial-up, Wi-Fi. In-hotel: concierge, laundry facilities, laundry service, parking (fee)* ⊟*AE, D, DC, MC, V* ⎮⎰⎮*CP.*

$ **The Willows.** The lobby of this 1920s boutique hotel, designed in 19th-century French Provincial style, opens onto a tree-lined street in Lake View, a lively area three blocks from the lake and central to stores, restaurants, and movie theaters. The complimentary Continental breakfast makes it an inviting alternative to area bed-and-breakfasts. ⊠*555 W. Surf St., Lake View, 60657* ☎*773/528–8400 or 800/787–3108* 🖶*773/528–8483* ⊕*www.cityinns.com* ⤵*51 rooms, 4 suites* ⌂*In-room: dial-up, Wi-Fi. In-hotel: concierge, laundry facilities, laundry service, parking (fee)* ⊟*AE, D, DC, MC, V* ⎮⎰⎮*CP.*

LINCOLN PARK

Three miles of lakefront parkland draw people to this neighborhood—and most hotels here are just blocks away. Room rates are decidedly lower than those downtown, with the downside being that you'll invest more in transportation to hit top sites. Parking is easier, but never a snap; plan on using the valet.

$$ **Belden-Stratford.** The 60 rooms—all with full kitchens or kitchenettes—are apartments for long-term rental, but, on any given night, there are plenty available for overnight stays at very reasonable rates. Don't be fooled; the feel is not that of a generic, extended-stay hotel. Its lobby, in fact, looks palatial, thanks to the polished gold chandelier, grand piano, and handwoven tapestries. The lobby and hallways are praised for being quiet, so families should prepare to clam up their kids. The biggest treat is the on-site dining at French restaurant Mon Ami Gabi. Another on-site eatery is scheduled to open in 2008. Another highlight?

The Lincoln Park Zoo is across the street. And the lakefront is just a few blocks further. ⊠*2300 N. Lincoln Park W, Lincoln Park, 60614* ☎*773/281–2900 or 800/800–8301* 🖷*773/880–2039* ⊕*www.belden-stratford.com* ➲*30 rooms, 30 suites* ♿*In-room: kitchen, Ethernet, Wi-Fi. In-hotel: 2 restaurants, gym, laundry facilities, laundry service, parking (fee)* ▤*AE, D, DC, MC, V.*

$ **Days Inn Lincoln Park North.** This award-winning Days Inn is one of the
Fodor's Choice more luxurious in the sometimes so-so chain, featuring a lobby with a
★ pressed-tin ceiling and brass chandeliers. The updated look of its guest rooms is one of cheery mixed patterns and dark-wood furniture. All guests have free use of a nearby health club. ⊠*644 W. Diversey Pkwy., Lincoln Park, 60614* ☎*773/525–7010 or 888/576–3297* 🖷*773/525–6998* ⊕*www.lpndaysinn.com* ➲*129 rooms, 4 suites* ♿*In-room: safe, refrigerator (some), dial-up, Wi-Fi. In-hotel: laundry facilities, laundry service, parking (fee), no-smoking rooms* ▤*AE, D, DC, MC, V* ⫟|*CP.*

THE LOOP

Chicago's business district, laced with overhead train tracks, is a desirable—if slightly noisy—place to stay. Hotels here tend to be moderately priced; many are housed in historic buildings, giving them a charm you won't find along glitzier North Michigan Avenue. Easy access to the Art Institute and Millennium Park is a plus.

$$–$$$ **Fairmont.** On a quiet block near the Loop, this 45-story pink-granite tower fluctuates between the understated and the opulent, with a huge, glistening chandelier in the foyer and guest rooms bedecked in less-than-brilliant shades of beige. Good thing that it caters to the chatty; there are three telephones per room (including one hanging conspicuously on the bathroom wall). Suites offer stunning views of Lake Michigan and feature dining rooms. Coveted whirlpools are only available in grand suites, which, housed on the top floor also boast fireplaces, libraries, and kitchenettes. Aria, an upscale restaurant within the Fairmont, attracts plenty of locals; it's a global-cuisine gem, featuring American food with Indian, Greek, Asian, and Turkish influences. ⊠*200 N. Columbus Dr., Loop, 60601* ☎*312/565–8000 or 800/526–2008* 🖷*312/856–1032* ⊕*www.fairmont.com* ➲*628 rooms, 53 suites* ♿*In-room: Ethernet, dial-up. In-hotel: restaurant, room service, bars, concierge, laundry service, public Wi-Fi, parking (fee), no-smoking rooms, some pets allowed* ▤*AE, D, DC, MC, V.*

$$–$$$ **Hard Rock Hotel.** We're not huge fans of the ubiquitous restaurant chain, but the hotel—flashy, loud, and packed with plasma TVs—has our approval. Set within the 40-story Carbide and Carbon Building, it touts modern rooms adorned with rock-and-roll paraphernalia and a brilliant dining concept called China Grill. Ask for a tower room, which offers striking views of Michigan Avenue, Millennium Park, and the Chicago River. ⊠*230 N. Michigan Ave., Loop, 60601* ☎*312/345–1000 or 800/966–5166* 🖷*312/345–1012* ⊕*www.hardrockhotelchicago.com* ➲*381 rooms, 20 suites* ♿*In-room: DVD, Ethernet, dial-up.*

In-hotel: restaurant, room service, bar, gym, concierge, public Wi-Fi, parking (fee), no-smoking rooms ⊟AE, D, DC, MC, V.

$$$ **Hotel Allegro Chicago.** The Cadillac Palace Theater is an appropriate neighbor for this music-themed hotel: witness the clefs on the shower curtains, a music room off the lobby, and the *High Society*–inspired watercolor mural by the lobby stairs at the entrance. While the standard rooms—lusciously decorated with chocolate browns and grapefruit pinks—are charming, they're outshined by premium rooms, which have whirlpool tubs, and complimentary bottles of Mr. Bubble. Suites have themes; the surprisingly unkitschy Lion King suite, for example, emits an African wilderness vibe, with wicker furniture and netting hanging over the bed. ✉*171 W. Randolph St., Loop, 60601* 🕿*312/236–0123 or 800/643–1500* 🖷*312/236–0917* ⊕*www.allegrochicago.com* 🛏*451 rooms, 32 suites* ♿*In-room: Wi-Fi, refrigerator. In-hotel: 2 restaurants, room service, bar, gym, concierge, parking (fee), no-smoking rooms, some pets allowed* ⊟*AE, D, DC, MC, V.*

$$$ **Hotel Burnham.** Making creative use of a city landmark, this hotel is housed in the famed 13-story Reliance Building, which D.H. Burnham & Company built in 1895. The refurbished interior retains such original details as Carrara marble wainscoting and ceilings, terrazzo floors, and mahogany trim. Guest rooms, which were once the building's offices, are compact. But we'll overlook the lack of wiggle room thanks to perks like the "pillow library," which offers anything from firm to hypoallergenic pillows. On the ground floor, the intimate Atwood Cafe has a stylish mahogany bar and serves contemporary American fare, including its popular potpies. ✉*1 W. Washington St., Loop, 60602* 🕿*312/782–1111 or 877/294–9712* 🖷*312/782–0899* ⊕*www.burnhamhotel.com* 🛏*103 rooms, 19 suites* ♿*In-room: Wi-Fi, refrigerator. In-hotel: restaurant, room service, bar, gym, concierge, laundry service, public Wi-Fi, parking (fee), some pets allowed* ⊟*AE, D, DC, MC, V.*

FodorsChoice
★

8

$$$ **Hotel Monaco.** A registration desk, fashioned after a classic steamer trunk, and meeting rooms named for international destinations such as Tokyo and Paris inspire wanderlust here. Besides the bellhops dressed in safari gear, we love each room's bay windows (the Monaco is the only hotel in the city with 'em) and the pet-goldfish-in-a-bowl, provided on request. It's clear this hotel has humor: look to the honor bars stocked with wax lips, Etch-A-Sketches, and hand buzzers. ✉*225 N. Wabash Ave., Loop, 60601* 🕿*312/960–8500 or 800/397–7661* 🖷*312/960–1883* ⊕*www.monaco-chicago.com* 🛏*170 rooms, 22*

suites ⌖*In-room: safe, dial-up, Wi-Fi, refrigerator. In-hotel: restaurant, room service, bar, gym, concierge, laundry service, parking (fee), some pets allowed* ▭*AE, D, DC, MC, V.*

$$ **Hyatt Regency Chicago.** Ficus trees, palms, and gushing fountains fill the two-story greenhouse lobby. This is one of the largest hotels in the world, with illuminated signs that guide you through the labyrinth of halls. In the comfortably sized guest rooms, black-and-white photographs of Chicago landmarks give things an authentic spin. ✉*151 E. Wacker Dr., Loop, 60601* ☎*312/565–1234 or 800/233–1234* 🖶*312/239–4414* ⊕*www.chicagohyatt.com* ⥲*2,000 rooms, 119 suites* ⌖*In-room: safe, Ethernet, refrigerator (some). In-hotel: 5 restaurants, room service, gym, spa, concierge, laundry service, parking (fee), no-smoking rooms* ▭*AE, D, DC, MC, V.*

$$$ **Palmer House Hilton.** The *grand palais* feel of this historic property is conveyed through the huge lobby ceiling mural, which gets touched up every four years by the same Florentine gentleman who restores the art in the Sistine Chapel. Rooms—reached via a winding maze of corridors—are adequately sized. With more than 1,600 rooms, the property can seem overwhelming; luckily one executive level, nabbed for $80 above standard rates, has its own lobby and concierge, providing a hotel-within-a-hotel feel. Note: The property is scheduled to undergo renovations to its rooms and its restaurant throughout 2008. Call to find out how this might impact your stay. ✉*17 E. Monroe St., Loop, 60603* ☎*312/726–7500 or 800/445–8667* 🖶*312/263–2556* ⊕*www.hilton.com* ⥲*1,639 rooms, 88 suites* ⌖*In-room: Ethernet, dial-up. In-hotel: restaurant, room service, bar, pool, gym, concierge, laundry service, public Wi-Fi, parking (fee), no-smoking rooms, some pets allowed* ▭*AE, D, DC, MC, V.*

$$–$$$ **Renaissance Chicago Hotel.** The cosmopolitan Renaissance Chicago, situated on the south bank of the Chicago River, puts a premium on a good night's sleep: there's no missing the seven—yep, seven—fluffy white pillows on each bed. Cushiness carries through to the lobby, where guests are treated to live music Thursday through Sunday. Stay on the hotel's slightly pricier "club levels" for a more exclusive feel and access to a private business center. ✉*1 W. Wacker Dr., Loop, 60601* ☎*312/372–7200 or 800/468–3571* 🖶*312/372–0093* ⊕*www.renaissancehotels.com* ⥲*513 rooms, 40 suites* ⌖*In-room: refrigerator, Ethernet, Wi-Fi. In-hotel: 2 restaurants, room service, bar, pool, gym, spa, concierge, laundry service, public Internet, public Wi-Fi, parking (fee), no-smoking rooms, some pets allowed* ▭*AE, D, DC, MC, V.*

$$ **Swissôtel.** The Swissôtel's triangular Harry Weese design allows for panoramic vistas of the city, lake, or river. The comfortable, contemporary rooms have a condo feel, with two-line phones and marble bathrooms. A 42nd-floor fitness center, pool, and spa manage to draw even the most exercise-reticent, thanks to the bird's-eye views. ✉*323 E. Wacker Dr., Loop, 60601* ☎*312/565–0565 or 888/737–9477* 🖶*312/565–0540* ⊕*www.swissotel.com* ⥲*596 rooms, 36 suites* ⌖*In-room: VCR (some), Wi-Fi. In-hotel: 2 restaurants, room service, bars,*

CLOSE UP

A Beautiful Stay in the Neighborhood

Chicago is, famously, a city of neighborhoods. Chicagoans like to define themselves by where they hang their hat, with attendant pride, snobbery, or aspirations to street cred (of all kinds). For visitors, setting up a temporary base in one of the neighborhoods offers many advantages. This is especially true for leisure travelers. Without an expense account to ease downtown's hotel bills and menu shock, staying right downtown can get very costly very quickly.

When choosing accommodations, it pays to look beyond the Loop and the Magnificent Mile.

A walk up Clark Street or Lincoln Avenue in Lincoln Park opens up miles of reasonably priced dining possibilities. Along one short stretch of the former you'll pass an excellent fusion restaurant, a take-out crepes place, a grocery store, and a couple of diners where the waitress might call you "hon." Remember that the next time you're called something else in the Loop.

There's also better and cheaper parking. Downtown you'll usually pay at least $30 a day. Rates at garages in outlying neighborhoods run less. There's even a chance, albeit rather remote, of finding street parking. Some days that's like saying there's a chance of a Republican mayor, but it happens.

The best reason to stay in a neighborhood is the chance to immerse yourself in the rhythms of the city. You get a chance to live as most Chicagoans live. In the neighborhoods you'll see the sky. You'll have countless independently owned shops and restaurants to browse.

If you'd like to be somewhat near downtown, the happening Lincoln Park and Lake View neighborhoods offer a handful of hotels. As a bonus, accommodations are relatively near the lakefront. Most also have relatively easy access to public transportation or routes well traveled by cabs. A determined walker can even get from Lincoln Park to the Magnificent Mile in a half hour.

Getting to downtown sights from farther afield may sound like too much trouble. But keep in mind thousands upon thousands of Chicagoans make the trip every day. And, like them, you'll come home to something vital and intriguing at night. Much of the Loop, on the other hand, turns into a ghost town after rush hour. In places like Lake View, the starting gun goes off at 7pm.

The neighborhood experience isn't for everyone. Those determined to "see it all" may find the journey in from such outposts takes too much time. And small hotels and B&Bs cannot offer the same pampering and facilities typical at the luxury digs downtown.

It's a search for small moments, for random encounters, for something indefinable—the vibe, you might say—that most appeals to visitors who stay in outer neighborhoods. Each district's rhythm is different. And it's easier to hear the city's songs away from the bustle and tall buildings.

–by Kevin Cunningham

8

pool, gym, spa, concierge, laundry service, parking (fee), no-smoking rooms ⊟*AE, DC, MC, V.*

$$-$$$$ **W Chicago City Center.** Bellhops in slick black pants and T-shirts, plus a welcome mat imprinted with "Well, Hello There," are early indicators that this hotel is hip. The couch-filled lobby (nicknamed the Living Room) is seemingly always dark (during our visit, candles were flickering at noon), and kaleidoscopic-looking film projections on walls complemented ambient music. Rooms cater to the business traveler, with desks, WebTV, and cordless phones. **Whiskey Blue,** the hotel bar, is frequented by celebs passing through town. ✉*172 W. Adams St., Loop, 60603* ☎*312/332–1200 or 800/621–2360* ⎙*312/917–5771* ⊕*www.starwood.com* ⌨*358 rooms, 11 suites* ⚑*In-room: safe, Ethernet, Wi-Fi. In-hotel: restaurant, room service, bar, gym, spa, concierge, laundry service, public Wi-Fi, parking (fee), no-smoking rooms, some pets allowed* ⊟*AE, D, DC, MC, V.*

NEAR NORTH

With a cluster of accommodations around North Michigan Avenue (the "Magnificent Mile"), this area is where new hotels are springing up—or reinventing themselves, thanks to multimillion-dollar renovations. Prices hover at the high end, but there are a few deals to be found if you're willing to forego a pool or concierge service. Consider the wealth of shopping in easy reach part of the bargain.

$$$ **Allerton Hotel.** Named a national historic landmark in 1998, this limestone building was a residential "club hotel" for men when it opened in 1924. A welcome 1999 renovation restored the limestone facade and overhauled the interior. The small rooms each have a unique layout, with classic wood furnishings, dramatic floral bedspreads, and marble baths. The bar adjoining the second-floor restaurant **Taps on Two**— Parisian in setting with its tiny tables and piped-in jazz music—will make you want to linger over cappuccino on blustery days. ✉*701 N. Michigan Ave., Near North, 60611* ☎*312/440–1500* ⎙*312/440–1819* ⊕*www.theallertonhotel.com* ⌨*383 rooms, 60 suites* ⚑*In-room: safe, refrigerator, Ethernet, dial-up. In-hotel: restaurant, room service, bar, gym, concierge, laundry facilities, laundry service, parking (fee), no-smoking rooms* ⊟*AE, D, DC, MC, V.*

$$ **The Ambassador East.** One of the few hotels tucked in the residential Gold Coast neighborhood, this small 1920s property is a 10- to 15-minute cab ride from the Loop. The secluded setting makes it popular with celebs and literary figures, and the world-famous **Pump Room** still attracts a loyal following (Humphrey Bogart and Lauren Bacall celebrated their wedding in Booth One). Rooms have a certain amount of glitz, with jewel tones and cherrywood furniture. Bookworms, take heed: the "author" suite has held book signings by the likes of John Grisham and Maya Angelou. ✉*1301 N. State Pkwy., Near North, 60610* ☎*312/787–7200 or 800/843–6664* ⎙*312/787–4760* ⊕*www. theambassadoreasthotel.com* ⌨*239 rooms, 46 suites* ⚑*In-room: refrigerator, Ethernet, Wi-Fi. In-hotel: restaurant, room service, bar,*

gym, concierge, laundry service, parking (fee), no-smoking rooms, some pets allowed ▤*AE, D, DC, MC, V.*

$$$$ **Conrad Chicago.** Formerly Le Meridien hotel, this hotel's art-deco-inspired lobby has a residential feel, with clean-lined furniture and a large mural. Rooms—featuring European duvets, oversize pillows, plush bathrobes, and slippers—aim to pamper. Don't leave without checking out the building's limestone facade, cut from the same quarries as the Empire State Building and Tribune Tower, and depicting figures from ancient mythology and the zodiac. ✉*521 N. Rush St., Near North, 60611* ☎*312/645-1500* 🖷*312/645-1550* ⊕*www.conradhotels.com* ⤳*278 rooms, 33 suites* ⏃*In-room: safe, Ethernet, Wi-Fi. In-hotel: 2 restaurants, room service, bar, gym, concierge, laundry service, public Wi-Fi, parking (fee), no-smoking rooms, some pets allowed* ▤*AE, D, DC, MC, V.*

$$$$ **Drake Hotel.** Built in 1920, the grande dame of Chicago hotels presides over the northernmost end of Michigan Avenue. The lobby, inspired by an Italian Renaissance palace, is all deep-red walls and glimmering crystal. The sounds of a fountain and harpist beckon at Palm Court, a traditional setting for afternoon tea. There's live jazz in the **Coq d'Or** most nights and the **Cape Cod Room** serves to-die-for crab cakes. The downsides? No swimming pool (a bummer for the price you're paying) and some rooms are tiny. ✉*140 E. Walton Pl., Near North, 60611* ☎*312/787-2200 or 800/553-7253* 🖷*312/787-1431* ⊕*www.thedrakehotel.com* ⤳*535 rooms, 55 suites* ⏃*In-room: safe, Ethernet, dial-up, refrigerator. In-hotel: 4 restaurants, room service, bar, gym, concierge, laundry service, public Wi-Fi, parking (fee), no-smoking rooms* ▤*AE, D, DC, MC, V.*

$$$$ **Embassy Suites Chicago Downtown/Lakefront.** Every guest in this all-suites hotel has views of either Lake Michigan or the Chicago skyscrapers. And they also have room to roam, thanks to the spacious layout of each suite (rooms have separate bedrooms and living rooms). The sleek glass atrium bustles in the morning for complimentary breakfast buffet and in the evening for complimentary manager's reception; happy hour is illegal in Chicago. A bonus for families on vacation is the location: within walking distance of Navy Pier and North Michigan Avenue. Note: Rooms are set to be renovated in early 2008. Call to find out how renovations might impact your stay. ✉*511 N. Columbus Dr., Near North, 60611* ☎*312/836-5900 or 800/362-2779* 🖷*312/836-5901* ⊕*www.chicagoembassy.com* ⤳*455 suites* ⏃*In-room: refrigerator, Ethernet, dial-up. In-hotel: restaurant, room service, bar, pool, gym, concierge, laundry facilities, laundry service, airport shuttle, parking (fee), no-smoking rooms* ▤*AE, D, DC, MC, V* ⏺*BP.*

$$$ **Four Seasons.** At the ultra-refined Four Seasons, guest rooms begin on Fodor'sChoice the 30th floor (the hotel sits atop the tony 900 North Michigan Shops), ★ so there's a distinct feeling of seclusion—and great views, to boot. The rooms look elegant, 1940's French decor and spa-like baths with honed Chinese marble. The property recently underwent a massive renovation. To get the most out of the experience, buy a package, like "Girls

8

When Not To Go To Chicago

Here are some considerations if you're looking for headache-free travel.

■ Many leisure travelers are fazed by Chicago's frigid winters and the somewhat rough conditions they can cause (slippery roads, delayed traffic, the very thought of schlepping around in big boots). So, while museums and performances are at their max during winter, it might not be the opportune time to travel stress-free.

■ Also be aware of the more than 1,000 conventions and trade shows scheduled throughout the year. The National Restaurant Association show in May; the manufacturing technology show in September; the Radiological Society of American show in late November; and the National Housewares Manufacturing show in January are among the biggest. Hotel rooms may be hard to come by—and tables at popular restaurants even harder.

■ Contact the Chicago Convention and Tourism Bureau at 877/CHICAGO (877/244-2246) for information on conventions, trade shows, and other travel concerns before you book your trip.

■ Proximity to McCormick Place, where most of Chicago's huge trade shows hunker down, is often a conventioneer's top priority, so most wind up staying in the Loop or South Loop, where hotels are just a five-minute cab ride away from the mammoth venue. In these neighborhoods, accommodations tend to be older and somewhat less expensive—although there are certainly a few exceptions. Expect somewhat quiet nights in these parts; while the Loop boasts a revitalized theater district, come sundown, there's a lot more revelry north of the Chicago River in the neighborhoods surrounding the Mag Mile. Vibrant Rush Street is the site of many bars, while River North has a high concentration of restaurants and nightclubs.

■ A meeting or convention in Rosemont or a tight flight schedule should be the only reasons to consider an airport hotel. Prices at these properties are a bit lower, but the O'Hare area is drab. Plus, trips from there to downtown may take an hour during rush hour, bad weather, or periods of heavy construction on the Kennedy Expressway.

Just Wanna Have Fun," in which a handsome gent who makes custom martinis shows up at your room door. ✉ *120 E. Delaware Pl., Near North, 60611* ☎ *312/280–8800 or 800/332–3442* 🖷 *312/280–9184* 🖳 *www.fourseasons.com* ⇥ *174 rooms, 169 suites* ⌂ *In-room: refrigerator, safe, Ethernet, Wi-Fi. In-hotel: 3 restaurants, room service, bar, pool, gym, spa, concierge, laundry service, public Wi-Fi, parking (fee), no-smoking rooms* ☰ *AE, D, DC, MC, V.*

$$ **Gold Coast Guest House Bed & Breakfast.** Set an enviable three blocks north of the Magnificent Mile, this 1873 brick town home is the ideal place to get a feel for Chicago's chichi side. It's set on a tree-lined street dappled with preserved Queen Anne homes from which well-coiffed women wearing Prada drift in and out with their terriers in tow. Sunny but cramped, the inn's biggest draw is its backyard patio that spills into a private, statuary-splayed garden. Ask the owner, Sally Baker,

for discounted tickets to Chicago's First Lady, worthwhile architecture-focused boat tours along the Chicago River (spring, summer, and fall only). ✉*113 W. Elm St., Near North, 60610* ☎*312/337–0361* ⊕*bbchicago.com* ➶*4 rooms* △ *In room: VCR. In hotel: no elevator, laundry facilities, parking (fee), no-smoking rooms* ▤*AE, D, MC, V.*

$$ **Homewood Suites by Hilton.** Suites here seem custom designed for families, with sleeper sofas, separate bedrooms, and fully equipped kitchens with dishwashers. Free food isn't lacking; indulge in a complimentary breakfast buffet seven days a week, and an evening reception with drinks and a light meal Monday through Thursday. Another bonus? Work out for free at the Gorilla Sports facility in the basement. ✉*40 E. Grand Ave., Near North, 60611* ☎*312/644–2222 or 800/225–5466* ☎*312/644–7777* ⊕*www.homewoodsuiteschicago.com* ➶*233 suites* △*In-room: kitchen, refrigerator, Ethernet, dial-up. In-hotel: room service, pool, gym, laundry facilities, parking (fee), no-smoking rooms* ▤*AE, D, DC, MC, V* ⏉*BP.*

$ **Hotel Indigo.** Even though this hotel caters to business travelers, there is something refreshingly noncorporate about its guest rooms and lobby dressed in plucky blues and greens and smattered with beachy Adirondack chairs. The airy guest rooms have wall-to-wall photo murals (for a real vacation feel, ask for one featuring colorful sea glass). Furthering the summer-in-Cape Cod feel are the rooms' white wooden lounge chairs and hardwood floors. It's located just on the fringe of downtown activity—expect a 10-minute cab ride to the Loop—but, on the flip side, you'll walk to Oak Street Beach, located a few blocks southeast, in no time. ✉*1244 N. Dearborn Pkwy., Near North, 60610* ☎*312/787–4980* ⊕*www.goldcoastchicagohotel.com* ➶*165 rooms* △*In room: Wi-Fi. In hotel: restaurant, room service, bar, gym, spa, laundry facilities, laundry service, concierge, public Wi-Fi, parking (fee), no-smoking rooms* ▤*AE, D, DC, MC, V.*

$$$ **Hotel Inter-Continental Chicago.** The Shriner greeting "Es Salamu Aleikum" ("Peace Be To God") that's etched on foyer columns and the marble lions throughout remind us of the building's past as the Medinah Health Club, a private men's club. Lodging is found in two adjoining buildings. We love the contemporary air of the main building's guest rooms, featuring mahogany furniture and rich red-and-gold fabrics. The historic tower rooms, however, are more matronly, with floral bedspreads and russet colors. The pinnacle of the whole place is the junior Olympic swimming pool, and a newly renovated fitness center. And be sure to check out Eno, a wine, cheese, and chocolate bar that opened in 2007. ✉*505 N. Michigan Ave., Near North, 60611* ☎*312/944–4100 or 800/628–2112* ☎*312/944–1320* ⊕*www.chicago.intercontinental.com* ➶*735 rooms, 72 suites* △*In-room: refrigerator, safe, Wi-Fi. In-hotel: 2 restaurants, room service, bar, pool, gym, spa, concierge, laundry service, public Internet, public Wi-Fi, parking (fee), no-smoking rooms, some pets allowed* ▤*AE, D, DC, MC, V.*

Fodor'sChoice **The James Hotel.** If you don't get the hint from the bustling bar scene
★ spilling into the lobby or the antique suitcases stacked as an art piece
$$$ near the elevator, the James further announces its hipster pedigree when

LODGING ALTERNATIVES

APARTMENT RENTALS

Furnished rentals can save you money, especially if you're traveling with a group. Home-exchange directories sometimes list rentals as well as exchanges.

Rental apartments are available in the Loop for temporary business lodging.

Hideaways International ✉ 767 Islington St., Portsmouth, NH 03801 ☎603/430–4433 or 800/843–4433 🖷 603/430–4444 ⊕www.hideaways.com; annual membership $145.

BED-AND-BREAKFASTS

Chicago Bed & Breakfast Association ✉ Box 14088, 6061 ☎ 773/394–2000 or 800/375–7084 🖷773/394–2002 ⊕www.chicago-bed-breakfast.com

HOME EXCHANGES

HomeLink International ✉ Box 47747, Tampa, FL 33647 ☎ 813/975–9825 or 800/638–3841 🖷 813/910–8144 ⊕www.homelink.org; $110 yearly for a listing, online access, and catalog; $70 without catalog. **Intervac U.S.** ✉ 30 Corte San Fernando Tiburon, CA 94920 ☎ 800/756–4663 🖷415/435–7440 ⊕www.intervacus.com; $125 yearly

for a listing, online access, and a catalog; $65 without catalog.

HOSTELS

No matter what your age, you can save on lodging costs by staying at hostels. In some 4,500 locations in more than 70 countries around the world, **Hostelling International (HI)**, the umbrella group for a number of national youth-hostel associations, offers single-sex, dorm-style beds and, at many hostels, rooms for couples and family accommodations. Membership in any HI national hostel association, open to travelers of all ages, allows you to stay in HI-affiliated hostels at member rates; one-year membership is about $28 for adults (C$35 for a two-year minimum membership in Canada, @14 in the United Kingdom, A$52 in Australia, and NZ$40 in New Zealand); hostels charge about $10–$30 per night. Members have priority if the hostel is full; they're also eligible for discounts around the world, even on rail and bus travel in some countries.

ORGANIZATIONS

Hostelling International—USA, ✉ 8401 Colesville Rd., Suite 600, Silver Spring, MD 20910 ☎301/495–1240 🖷301/495–6697 ⊕www.hiusa.org.

---

near the elevator, the James further announces its hipster pedigree when you enter your room. Pre-programmed alt-rock plays on the iPod-ready stereo system perched on the bar beneath the ready-to-party bottles (not minis) of vodka, whiskey, and rum. Some rooms feature not one but two flat-screen TVs, not to mention Kiehl's bath products and design-conscious furnishings like platform beds and full-length lean-to mirrors. The relatively hands-off service is fitting enough—for a party hotel. ✉55 E. Ontario St., at Rush St., Near North, 60611 ☎312/337–1000 ⊕www.jameshotels.com/chicago/ ⤢297 rooms ⌂In-room: refrigerator, safe, Wi-Fi. In-hotel: restaurant, room service, bar, gym, spa, concierge, laundry service, public Wi-Fi, parking (fee), no-smoking rooms, some pets allowed ▤AE, D, DC, MC, V.

$ **Millennium Knickerbocker Hotel.** This 1927 hotel has had a number of identities in its time—including a 1970s stint as the Playboy Hotel and Towers under owner Hugh Hefner. Chinoiserie wallpaper and dark-wood armoires lend an Asian feel to guest rooms. We love the complimentary shoeshine service; hang your kicks on the door at night and they'll be spiffed up by morning. Your downtime is well spent in the Lobby Bar, which features 50 different kinds of martinis. ⊠ *163 E. Walton St., Near North, 60611* 🕾*312/751–8100 or 866/866–8086* 🖷*312/751–9205* ⊕*www.millenniumhotels.com* ⤶*279 rooms, 26 suites* ⚒*In-room: Ethernet, dial-up. In-hotel: restaurant, room service, bar, gym, concierge, laundry service, public Wi-Fi, parking (fee), no-smoking rooms* ☰*AE, D, DC, MC, V* ⧉*CP.*

$$$$ **Omni Chicago Hotel.** The only all-suites hotel on Michigan Avenue has another thing going for it: every room has a plasma TV. Large suites with French doors separate the parlor from the bedroom, giving it a residential atmosphere. Its new restaurant is 676 Restaurant & Bar featuring Northern Italian and American cuisine with views overlooking Michigan Avenue. Good choice for extended stays or traveling with kids—young travelers receive a suitcase filled with games and books to borrow, and a goodie bag upon check-in. ⊠*676 N. Michigan Ave., Near North, 60611* 🕾*312/944–6664 or 800/843–6664* 🖷*312/266–3015* ⊕*www.omnihotels.com* ⤶*347 suites* ⚒*In-room: safe, Ethernet, Wi-Fi. In-hotel: restaurant, room service, bar, pool, gym, concierge, laundry service, parking (fee), no-smoking rooms, some pets allowed* ☰*AE, D, DC, MC, V.*

$$$$ **Park Hyatt.** The 67-story Park Hyatt, which dominates the skyline high
Fodor'sChoice above the old water tower, outdoes its grand hotel neighbors by going
★ all out with extras. Splash out on one of their enormous suites and you'll discover Art of Shaving amenities in the bathrooms, TVs over the bathtubs, and motion-sensor lights in the closets. Not much here has been overlooked. For a price there are plenty more extravagances to be had, including a butler-drawn candlelit bath. The beautifully designed public spaces feature a world-class collection of sculpture and painting, including works by Gerhardt Richter and Isamu Noguchi. The sweeping views from the pool and spa look out to the horizon over Lake Michigan. ⊠*800 N. Michigan Ave., Near North, 60611* 🕾*312/335–1234 or 800/778–7477* 🖷*312/239–4000* ⊕*www.parkchicago.hyatt.com* ⤶*183 rooms, 13 suites* ⚒*In-room: safe, refrigerator, DVD, Ethernet, Wi-Fi. In-hotel: restaurant, room service, bar, pool, gym, spa, concierge, laundry service, parking (fee), no-smoking rooms* ☰*AE, D, DC, MC, V.*

$$$$ **Peninsula Chicago.** On weekend nights the Peninsula's soaring lobby
Fodor'sChoice lounge becomes a chocolate fantasia, centered on an overflowing choc-
★ olate buffet. The hotel, committed to keeping its guests well fed and well rested, is also home to one of the city's most creative restaurants (Avenues) along with a lavish and popular afternoon tea. One of only three branches in the United States of the venerable Hong Kong–based Peninsula chain, its comfortable rooms feature plush pillow-top beds, Wi-Fi, and state-of-the-art bedside consoles that control both the TV

8

and "do not disturb" light. The rooftop lap pool is enclosed in a Zen aerie offering stunning views over the city. Make time to enjoy the property's award-winning spa. ⊠*108 E. Superior St., Near North, 60611* ☎*312/337–2888 or 866/288–8889* 🖷*312/751–2888* ⊕*www. chicago.peninsula.com* ⟿*339 rooms, 83 suites* ⌂*In-room: refrigerator, safe, DVD, Ethernet, Wi-Fi. In-hotel: 4 restaurants, room service, bar, pool, gym, spa, concierge, laundry service, parking (fee), no-smoking rooms, some pets allowed* ▤*AE, D, DC, MC, V.*

$$$ **Raffaello Hotel.** It's hard to tell what kind of crowd this hotel will attract, given its complete renovation and name change (it was formerly the Raphael Hotel)—but its steps-from-Michigan Avenue location is in its favor. Don't dither in the lobby; it's small and—with just a small check-in desk, a few chairs, and little else—there's not much excitement there. Guest rooms are spacious and comfortable, however. Dressed in varying shades of a neutral hay color, they have modern-looking bathrooms with rain showers, and excellent city views (ask for a room facing north for a close-up look at the John Hancock Building). Visit the library on the top floor, which has floor-to-ceiling bookshelves that you are free to browse. ⊠*201 E. Delaware Pl., Near North, 60611* ☎*888/560–4977* ⊕*chicagoraffaello.com* ⟿*174 rooms* ⌂*In room: kitchen, refrigerator, DVD, Wi-Fi. In hotel: restaurant, room service, gym, laundry service, concierge, public Wi-Fi, airport shuttle, parking (fee), no-smoking rooms* ▤*AE, D, DC, MC, V.*

$$$$ **Ritz-Carlton.** Perched over Water Tower Place, Michigan Avenue's best-
Fodor'sChoice known shopping mall, the Ritz-Carlton specializes in showering guests
★ with attention. Amenities aren't for wont: rooms are spacious, with walk-in closets and separate dressing areas, plus little luxuries like Anichini bed throws. The two-story, flower-filled greenhouse lobby serves afternoon tea, and the **Café**'s chef, Mark Payne, has earned a top-notch reputation. ⊠*160 E. Pearson St., Near North, 60611* ☎*312/266–1000, 800/621–6906 outside Illinois* 🖷*312/266–1194* ⊕*www.fourseasons.com* ⟿*435 rooms, 91 suites* ⌂*In-room: refrigerator, safe, Wi-Fi. In-hotel: 2 restaurants, room service, bar, pool, gym, spa, concierge, laundry service, public Internet, public Wi-Fi, parking (fee), no-smoking rooms, some pets allowed* ▤*AE, D, DC, MC, V.*

$$$$ **Sofitel Chicago Water Tower.** A wonder of modern architecture, this
Fodor'sChoice French-owned gem is a prism-shaped structure that juts over the street
★ and widens as it rises. Design sensibility shines in guest rooms, too, with beechwood furnishings, Barcelona chairs, and marble bathrooms bedecked with bamboos (think feng shui). The sophisticated **Cafe des Architectes** is notable for its 30-minute executive lunch, while **Le Bar** is a homey den of sorts, replete with books about architecture and a rack of international newspapers. The hotel's on-site boutique, Petit Bijou, is a far cry from the typical souvenir shop, carrying handcrafted jewelry, paper goods, and more. ⊠*20 E. Chestnut St., Near North, 60611* ☎*312/324–4000 or 877/813–7700* 🖷*312/324–4026* ⊕*www. sofitel.com* ⟿*383 rooms, 32 suites* ⌂*In-room: safe, Ethernet, dial-up, Wi-Fi. In-hotel: restaurant, room service, bars, gym, concierge, laundry*

service, parking (fee), no-smoking rooms, some pets allowed ⊟AE, D, DC, MC, V.

$$$ **Sutton Place Hotel.** Talk about art in unexpected places: the largest single collection of original Robert Mapplethorpe floral photographs grace the walls in rooms and common spaces at this hotel. Rooms—decorated in calming sage and periwinkle tones—have sound-resistant walls, down duvets, and three phones. Splurge for a loft suite, with terraces overlooking bustling Rush Street. Rande Gerber (Cindy Crawford's husband) owns the Whiskey Bar and Grill, serving seasonal selections for breakfast, lunch, and dinner. ⊠*21 E. Bellevue Pl., Near North, 60611* ☎*312/266–2100 or 800/606–8188* ☐*312/266–2141* ⊕*www.suttonplace.com* ⊅*206 rooms, 40 suites* �*In-room: refrigerator, safe (some), dial-up, Wi-Fi. In-hotel: restaurant, room service, bar, gym, concierge, laundry service, public Internet, parking (fee), no-smoking rooms, some pets allowed* ⊟AE, D, DC, MC, V.

$$$$ **Talbott.** The Talbott has a large European following, thanks to its intimacy and multilingual staff. In 2006 guest rooms were renovated with new carpets, drapes, and custom furniture, making the moderate-size lodgings even more appealing. Coffee and tea are served fireside in the lobby on winter nights—a lovely touch. Another bonus? Guests get free admission to the nearby gym. ⊠*20 E. Delaware Pl., Near North, 60611* ☎*312/944–4970 or 800/825–2688* ☐*312/944–7241* ⊕*www. talbotthotel.com* ⊅*120 rooms, 29 suites* �*In-room: safe, dial-up, Wi-Fi. In-hotel: restaurant, room service, bar, concierge, laundry service, parking (fee), no-smoking rooms, some pets allowed* ⊟AE, D, DC, MC, V.

$$ **Tremont.** Just off North Michigan Avenue, this hotel's restaurant, **Mike Ditka's,** gets infinitely more attention than the rooms do (we love Ditka's "Da Pork Chop" dish). Standard guest rooms—with yellow walls and white molding—are on the small side. Need more space? Book a suite, which are equipped with kitchens. ⊠*100 E. Chestnut St., Near North, 60611* ☎*312/751–1900 or 800/621–8133* ☐*312/751–8691* ⊕*www.tremontchicago.com* ⊅*118 rooms, 12 suites* �*In-room: refrigerators (some), safe, dial-up. In-hotel: restaurant, bar, concierge, laundry service, public Internet, parking (fee), no-smoking rooms* ⊟AE, D, DC, MC, V.

$ **W Chicago Lakeshore.** Once a dreary Days Inn, a complete renovation transformed this space into a sleek, high-energy hotel—and the only in Chicago directly overlooking Lake Michigan. The lobby is part lounge, part club scene, with velvety couches and DJs on weekends. The hotel's "whatever, whenever" desk—its version of a concierge service—is on call 24 hours a day. ⊠*644 N. Lake Shore Dr., Near North, 60611* ☎*312/943–9200 or 888/627–9034* 🖷*312/255–4411* ⊕*www.who-tels.com* 🗗*525 rooms, 27 suites* ⚬*In-room: safe, DVD, Ethernet, Wi-Fi. In-hotel: restaurant, room service, bar, pool, gym, spa, concierge, laundry service, public Wi-Fi, airport shuttle, parking (fee), no-smoking rooms, some pets allowed* ⊟*AE, D, DC, MC, V.*

$$$$ **Westin Michigan Avenue.** The lobby of the Westin reminds us of an airport hangar—long, narrow, and full of folks tapping away on laptops. Location-wise, the hotel scores big, as major malls and flagship shops are within steps of the hotel's front door. Rooms are furnished with specially designed Simmons Heavenly Beds with quilted mattresses—which guests have raved about and even purchased—as well as foam, feather, and rolled pillows. The lobby restaurant, the Grill on the Alley, is a steak house with a clubby atmosphere. ⊠*909 N. Michigan Ave., Near North, 60611* ☎*312/943–7200 or 800/937–8461* 🖷*312/397–5580* ⊕*www.westin.com/michiganave* 🗗*728 rooms, 23 suites* ⚬*In-room: Ethernet, Wi-Fi. In-hotel: restaurant, room service, bar, gym, spa, concierge, laundry service, public Wi-Fi, parking (fee), some pets allowed* ⊟*AE, D, DC, MC, V.*

$$ **Whitehall Hotel.** There's a woodland-lodge feel in this hotel's lobby, where oil paintings of hunting dogs and horses hang in gilt frames. The old-world-style rooms, many with four-poster beds, include modern luxuries such as Anichini bedding, marble bathrooms, and broadband. Fornetto Mei is a Pan-Italian dining concept that deserves more attention than it gets. ⊠*105 E. Delaware Pl., Near North, 60611* ☎*312/944–6300 or 800/948–4255* 🖷*312/944–8552* ⊕*www.thewhitehallhotel.com* 🗗*213 rooms, 8 suites* ⚬*In-room: safe, Ethernet, dial-up. In-hotel: restaurant, room service, bar, gym, concierge, laundry service, public Wi-Fi, parking (fee), no-smoking rooms* ⊟*AE, D, DC, MC, V.*

RIVER NORTH

Besides the concentration of independently owned galleries, commerce around these parts tends to be of a national-chain nature (note the Hard Rock Cafe and Red Lobster). The same can be said of the hotels. But while boutique-lodging charm is harder to find, good prices are not; you'll find plenty of competitive rates from familiar names.

$ **Best Western River North.** Partially housed in a turn-of-the-last-century freezer building, this hotel retains a loft-like air. The somewhat forgettable lobby decor is offset by large and reasonably priced guest rooms featuring black-and-

> **WORD OF MOUTH**
>
> "The huge advantage to Best Western River North is the free parking during your stay. Ordinarily parking is close to $40 a night. But it's about a 5 block walk to Michigan Avenue, which can get tiring, if you are walking all day then trudging back to the hotel a couple of times."
>
> –eileenleft

white tiled bathrooms. Parking is free, a cost-saving rarity downtown. Families convene at the on-site Pizzeria Ora for Chicago-style deep-dish pies. ⊠*125 W. Ohio St., River North, 60610* ☎*312/467–0800 or 800/727–0800* 🖷*312/467–1665* ⊕*www.rivernorthhotel.com* ↩*125 rooms, 25 suites* ♿*In-room: safe, refrigerator (some), dial-up, Wi-Fi. In-hotel: restaurant, room service, bar, pool, gym, laundry service, parking (no fee), no-smoking rooms* ▤*AE, D, DC, MC, V.*

\$\$\$ Embassy Suites. Too misleading suites are arranged around an 11-story, plant-filled atrium lobby, where bubbling fountains and birds keep noise levels relatively high. Bright rooms use space efficiently, with sensible separate living rooms with a pullout sofa, four-person dining table, and extra television. A complimentary full breakfast each morning and cocktails each evening are especially appealing to business travelers. ⊠*600 N. State St., River North, 60610* ☎*312/943–3800 or 800/362–2779* 🖷*312/943–7629* ⊕*www.embassysuites.com* ↩*367 suites* ♿*In-room: refrigerator, Ethernet, dial-up. In-hotel: restaurant, room service, bar, pool, gym, concierge, laundry facilities, laundry service, parking (fee), no-smoking rooms* ▤*AE, D, DC, MC, V* ��|*BP.*

\$\$\$ Westin Chicago River North. Gym rats don't need to hoof it to the on-site fitness center, thanks to four Westin Workout Guest Rooms that come equipped with either a bicycle or a treadmill. Standard rooms—some with views of the Chicago River—have all the basics, including high-speed Internet. Nab a Deluxe Room for more square footage. ⊠*320 N. Dearborn St., River North, 60610* ☎*312/744–1900 or 800/937–8461* 🖷*312/527–2650* ⊕*www.westinchicago.com* ↩*407 rooms, 17 suites* ♿*In-room: Ethernet, dial-up. In-hotel: 3 restaurants, room service, bar, gym, spa, concierge, laundry service, parking (fee), some pets allowed* ▤*AE, D, DC, MC, V.*

SOUTH LOOP

Rapid gentrification, most apparent in the new restaurants popping up along South Michigan Avenue, has made this area increasingly popular. A hotel boom has not occurred here yet, so lodging choices are limited to a few old and reliable standards. Many hotels offer package deals with the nearby Museum Campus.

Fodor'sChoice   **Essex Inn.** Don't judge this hotel on appearance alone: the nondescript,
★   plain-brick tower containing small, boxlike guest rooms is actually
\$ one of the city's most accessible and family-friendly. Along with being a five-minute walk from the Museum Campus, it offers package deals with popular attractions such as the John G. Shedd Aquarium and Sears Tower. That said, you might not want to leave the hotel; its huge rooftop swimming pool is open year-round (note to anxious parents: a lifeguard is always on duty) and is surrounded by sliding-glass doors that open to views of Grant Park and Lake Michigan. ⊠*800 S. Michigan Ave., South Loop, 60605* ☎*800/621–6909* ⊕*essexinn.com* ↩*254 rooms* ♿*In room: kitchen (some), refrigerator (some), Wi-Fi. In hotel: restaurant, room service, pool, gym, laundry service, public Wi-Fi, parking (fee), no-smoking rooms* ▤*AE, D, DC, MC, V.*

8

$$$ **Hilton Chicago.** On a busy day the lobby of this Hilton might be mistaken for a terminal at O'Hare Airport; it's a bustling convention hotel, but one that retains its distinguished 1920s heritage in a Renaissance-inspired entrance hall and gold-and-gilt Grand Ballroom. We're fans of its gym, which, at 28,000 square feet, includes an indoor track and swimming pool. Tip for families: ask for a room with two double beds and two baths (if you nab one with a view of Lake Michigan and the Museum Campus, all the better). ✉ *720 S. Michigan Ave., South Loop, 60605* ☎ *312/922–4400 or 800/445–8667* 🖷 *312/922–5240* ⊕ *www.hiltonchicagosales.com* ⮒ *1,544 rooms, 67 suites* ♿ *In-room: refrigerator, Ethernet. In-hotel: 3 restaurants, room service, bar, pool, gym, spa, concierge, laundry service, parking (fee), no-smoking rooms, some pets allowed* ⊟ *AE, D, DC, MC, V.*

> **WORD OF MOUTH**
>
> "My family loves tea time. We have tried almost all of the places in Chicago. The Ritz-Carlton and Peninsula have the best selection for tea sandwiches and pastries, although the Ritz is nicer about refills. Sometimes, in the winter, the Ritz has chocolate fondue—you should call and check. The Four Seasons has the best atmosphere, especially if you get a spot by the fireplace. You must make a reservation, no matter where you choose. All of these places fill up quickly."
>
> —Rine1967

$$$ **Holiday Inn & Suites Downtown Chicago.** Thanks to its proximity to the financial district, this hotel welcomes hordes of business travelers. But leisure seekers have an added incentive to visit in the summer months: the rooftop pool. The on-site **Aurelio's,** part of a popular pizza chain, serves breakfast, lunch, and dinner. ✉ *506 W. Harrison St., South Loop, 60607* ☎ *312/957–9100* 🖷 *312/957–0474* ⊕ *www.hidowntown.com* ⮒ *145 rooms, 27 suites* ♿ *In-room: refrigerator (some), Wi-Fi. In-hotel: restaurant, room service, bar, pool, gym, laundry facilities, laundry service, parking (fee), no-smoking rooms* ⊟ *AE, D, DC, MC, V.*

WESTERN SUBURBS

$$$$ **Lynfred Winery Bed & Breakfast.** Something of an anomaly amid the strip malls and big restaurant chains in nearby Schaumberg, located 45 minutes northwest of downtown Chicago, this B&B feels like a quaint country farmhouse—one with surprising gourmet leanings. Each of its four generously sized suites has heated bathroom floors and is decorated in the style of a different country (the French Suite has a gilded mirror and Louis IV–style chairs). The adjoining wine cellar and tasting room is where you'll try inexpensive yet tasty cabernets, aged in barrels on-site. All stays include a cellar tour and a full breakfast cooked by a Culinary Institute of America grad. ✉ *15 S. Roselle Rd., Western Suburbs, 60172* ☎ *630/529–9463* ⊕ *lynfredwinery.com* ⮒ *4 rooms* ♿ *In-room: refrigerator, DVD, Wi-Fi. In-hotel: room service, laundry facilities, laundry service, parking (no fee), no guests under 21, no-smoking rooms* ⊟ *AE, D, MC, V.*

UNDERSTANDING CHICAGO

CHICAGO SLANG

Like New Yorkers and New Englanders, Chicagoans put their own *unique* twist on the English language. Here's a quick primer to help you talk like a native while you're visiting.

Beef—Short for Italian beef sandwiches, a Chicago staple made of thinly sliced roast beef served on a long crusty Italian roll. Beefs are ordered "wet" (dipped in the meat juices), "hot" (with *giardiniera*, an Italian relish containing jalapeños), and/or "sweet" (with roasted sweet peppers).

Bleacher Bums—Regulars who sit in the bleachers at the "Friendly Confines" *(see below)*.

The Blizzard of Oz—Nickname for Ozzie Guillen, the charismatic and often foul-mouthed manager of the 2005 World Champion Chicago White Sox.

The Boot—Short for the Denver Boot, a contraption the city uses to lock the wheels of cars with unpaid traffic and parking tickets. Often heard around town: "My car just got booted."

Brat—Short for bratwurst, a staple at sporting events and tailgating parties (pronounced "braht").

The Cell—What White Sox fans affectionately call U.S. Cellular Field, formerly known as Comiskey Park.

Cheesehead—What the locals call people from Wisconsin.

Chicagoland—Chicago and the surrounding suburbs.

The Curse—A local legend which says that a Chicago barkeep whose pet goat was denied entry into the 1945 Chicago Cubs–Detroit Tigers World Series put a curse on the team. The Cubs lost, and have not been to a World Series since. Their last championship was in 1908.

Da Mare—"The Mayor," pronounced like a dyed-in-the-wool native.

The El—The nickname for the city's public train system, short for "elevated." Even though most of the system is aboveground, the term is used even when the train goes underground.

Friendly Confines—This means Wrigley Field, home of the Chicago Cubs. A sign inside the ballpark says WELCOME TO THE FRIENDLY CONFINES OF WRIGLEY FIELD.

Gapers—Drivers who slow down traffic to look at an accident. You'll hear about "gapers blocks" or "gapers delays" on traffic reports.

Pop—A soft drink, like Coca-Cola. Don't use the word "soda" here.

Reversibles—The express lanes on the Kennedy Expressway, which reverse direction depending upon the time of day.

Sammitch—A sandwich, of course!

Trixies—A jabbing nickname for the young, ex-sorority types who live in and around the Lincoln Park neighborhood.

CHICAGO AT A GLANCE

FAST FACTS

Nickname: Second City, Windy City, City of the Big Shoulders, Gem of the Prairie, Hog Butcher to the World, "I Will" City, Packingtown, City in a Garden (the city's motto)

Type of government: Mayor elected every four years; 50 aldermen, one from each of the city's wards; city clerk and treasurer also elected to citywide positions

Population: 2.8 million (city); 9.6 million (metro)

Population Density: 12,750 people per square mi

Median age: 32

Crime: Violent crimes were down 2.5% in 2006

Literacy: 37% have trouble with basic reading; 35% speak a language other than English at home, usually Spanish

Ethnic groups: White 57%; Latino 19%; black 18%; Asian 5%; other 1%

Chicago seems a big city instead of merely a large place.
–A.J. Liebling

Things are so tough in Chicago that at Easter time, for bunnies the little kids use porcupines.
–Fred Allen

Chicago is not the most corrupt American city, it's the most theatrically corrupt.
–Studs Terkel

Chicago is a city of contradictions, of private visions haphazardly overlaid and linked together.
–Pat Colander

GEOGRAPHY & ENVIRONMENT

Latitude: 41° N (same as Barcelona, Spain; Istanbul, Turkey)

Longitude: 87° W (same as San Salvador, El Salvador)

Elevation: 579 feet

Land area: 228 square mi

Parkland: 7,337 acres

Terrain: Flat lakefront, extending inland to the west

Natural hazards: Extreme winter storms, tornadoes

Environmental issues: Toxic pollution, invasive species, habitat destruction, and contamination on Lake Michigan; air pollution from coal-fired power plants and diesel engines; wastewater treatment plants have exceeded pollution limits for effluents often

I miss everything about Chicago, except January and February.
–Gary Cole

ECONOMY

Per capita income: $38,439

Unemployment: 3.9%

Workforce: 4.2 million; trade, transportation, and utilities 21%; professional and business services 15%; other 14%; government 13%; manufacturing 12%; educational and health services 12%; leisure and hospitality 8%; construction 5%

Major industries: Aircraft, business services, chemicals, electronics, food processing, insurance, iron, machinery, manufacturing, meatpacking, retail, shipping, steel fabricators, trade

DID YOU KNOW?

- The nickname "the Windy City" doesn't come from Chicago's bitter winter conditions. Promoters of the city went to the East Coast boasting of Chicago's greatness, in hopes of securing the World's Fair of 1893. *New York Sun* editor Charles Dana tired of the bragging and bestowed the "windy" nickname.

- Chicago's name comes from a Potawatomi Indian word meaning "wild onion" or "skunk." When Indians first arrived, the future home of America's third-largest city was a patch of rotting marshland onions.

- The Chicago Post Office at 433 W. Van Buren is the only postal facility in the world that you can drive through.

- Chicago's sports teams hold many distinctions, among them: the highest points-scoring average in NBA playoff games (Michael Jordan, 33.4 points), the most home runs hit in one month (Sammy Sosa, 20), and the most touchdowns in an NFL game (Ernie Nevers, 6).

- Chicago produced the first roller skates (1884), steel-framed skyscraper (1885), elevated railway (1892), pinball game (1930), and blood bank (1937), among other things.

- The last concert that the perennial tour band the Grateful Dead ever played was at Soldier Field in Chicago, on July 9, 1995.

- The world's longest street is Chicago's Western Avenue.

- In April 2000, the northwest corner of Walton Street and Michigan Avenue was named Hugh Hefner Way. The Chicago native, raised as a strict Methodist, went on to found *Playboy*, a magazine some credited with helping Americans talk about sex and others said popularized demeaning pornography.

- Chicago counts the world's largest sewage tunnel among its many architectural and engineering distinctions. The Chicago Tunnels and Reservoir Plan (TARP) has 93 mi of machine-bored sewer tunnels 9 to 33 feet in diameter.

- Rudolph the Red-Nosed Reindeer is a Chicago native. A copywriter for Montgomery Ward department store created the character as part of a Christmas promotion in 1939.

- O'Hare Airport used to be a military airport named Orchard Place. That's the reason your luggage tags read ORD today.

With costs so high, restaurateurs demand formulaic, steak-and-potatoes formats. Except for Wylie Dufresne, there are no experimental chefs in New York these days. Where are they? Chicago.
–Grub Street (www.nymag.com)

BOOKS & MOVIES

Books

For the flavor of the city a century ago, pick up a copy of Theodore Dreiser's *Sister Carrie,* the story of a country innocent who falls from grace in Chicago. Upton Sinclair's portrayal in *The Jungle* of the meatpacking industry's squalor and employee exploitation raised a public outcry. *The Pit,* Frank Norris's 1903 muckraking novel, captures the frenzy (yes, even then) of future speculation on the Board of Trade.

Native Chicagoan Saul Bellow set many novels in the city, most notably *Humboldt's Gift* and *The Adventures of Augie March.* Richard Wright's explosive *Native Son* and James T. Farrell's *Studs Lonigan* depict racial clashes in Chicago. The works of longtime resident Nelson Algren—*The Man with the Golden Arm, A Walk on the Wild Side,* and *Chicago: City on the Make*—show the city at its grittiest, as does playwright David Mamet's *American Buffalo.* Two series of detective novels use a current-day Chicago backdrop: Sara Paretsky's excellent V.I. Warshawski novels and the Monsignor Ryan mysteries of Andrew Greeley. Greeley has set other novels in Chicago as well, including *Lord of the Dance.* Local author Marcus Sakey set *The Blade Itself,* his debut novel about reunited crime partners, on Chicago's North and South sides. Sakey—with Paretsky and Chicago crime writers Sean Chercover, Barbara D'Amato, Michael Allen Dymmoch, Kevin Guilfoile, and Libby Hellman—are known collectively as "The Outfit" (check out their blog at www.theoutfitcollective.com).

Chicago was once the quintessential newspaper town; the play *The Front Page,* by Ben Hecht and Charles MacArthur, is set here. Local reporters have penned some excellent chronicles, including *Fabulous Chicago,* by Emmett Dedmon; and *Boss,* a portrait of the late mayor Richard J. Daley, by the late Mike Royko. For a selection of Royko's award-winning columns, check out *One More Time: The Best of Mike Royko.*

Lois Wille's *Forever Open, Clear and Free* is a superb history of the fight to save Chicago's lakefront parks. Books by Studs Terkel, a great chronicler of Chicago, include *Division Street: America* and *Chicago.* Erik Larson traces two men, architect Daniel Burnham and serial killer Henry H. Holmes, through the Chicago World's Fair of 1893 in *The Devil in the White City. Never a City So Real* is a collection of essays by Alex Kotlowitz. Even graphic novelists have a soft spot for Chicago; one of Chicago's better known, Chris Ware, juxtaposes lovable-looking characters with disparaging dialogue in his graphic novel *Jimmy Corrigan: The Smartest Kid on Earth.*

Architecture buffs can choose from a number of excellent guidebooks. James Cornelius revised *Chicago on Foot,* by Ira J. Bach and Susan Wolfson; the book contains dozens of architecture-driven walking tours. Franz Schulze and Kevin Harrington edited the fourth edition of *Chicago's Famous Buildings,* a pocket guide to the city's most important landmarks and buildings. The *A.I.A. Guide to Chicago,* edited by Alice Sinkevitch, is an exhaustive source of information about local architecture. The pocket-size *Chicago: A Guide to Recent Architecture,* by Susanna Sirefman, covers everything from office buildings to the new airport terminal. For thought-provoking critique of Chicago's major buildings, pick up *Why Architecture Matters: Lessons From Chicago,* a compilation of articles written by Chicago Tribune architecture critic Blair Kamin. Finally, David Garrad Lowe's *Lost Chicago* is a fascinating, heartbreaking history of vanished buildings.

Movies

Chicago has been the setting for films about everything from gangsters to restless suburbanites. Classic early gangster flicks include *Little Caesar* (1930), with Edward G. Robinson, and *Scarface* (1932), starring Paul Muni and George Raft. The theme is carried out on a lighter note in *The Sting* (1973), George Roy Hill's charming Scott

Joplin–scored movie that stars Paul Newman and Robert Redford as suave con men. *Carrie* is the 1952 adaptation of Dreiser's novel about a country girl who loses her innocence in the city; Laurence Olivier and Jennifer Jones are the stars. Lorraine Hansberry's drama about a black Chicago family, *A Raisin in the Sun*, became a film with Sidney Poitier in 1961.

As Elwood and Jake, respectively, Dan Aykroyd and the late John Belushi brought wild energy and cool music to the screen in *The Blues Brothers* (1980). *Ordinary People,* the Oscar-winning 1980 film, starred Mary Tyler Moore in a drama about an affluent and agonized North Shore family. John Hughes directed 1986's *Ferris Bueller's Day Off,* in which Matthew Broderick and a couple of his high-school friends play hooky and tour Chicago for a day. In *About Last Night* (1986), which is based on the David Mamet play *Sexual Perversity in Chicago,* Demi Moore and Rob Lowe go through realistic modern dating games with the help (and hindrance) of hilarious friends played by Elizabeth Perkins and Jim Belushi. Brian De Palma's *The Untouchables* (1987) stars Kevin Costner as Eliot Ness and Robert De Niro as Al Capone in a gangster tale with a 1920s Chicago background. *Eight Men Out* (1988)—with John Cusack, John Mahoney, and Charlie Sheen—depicts baseball's infamous Black Sox scandal, when members of the Chicago White Sox took bribes to throw the 1919 World Series against the Cincinnati Reds.

Kurt Russell and William Baldwin play firefighter brothers in *Backdraft* (1991). In the action thriller *The Fugitive* (1993), Harrison Ford pulls off one narrow escape in Chicago's St. Patrick's Day parade. Steve James's *Hoop Dreams* (1994) is a powerful documentary about a couple of inner-city teens who dream that basketball will be their ticket out. In the romantic comedy *While You Were Sleeping* (1995), Sandra Bullock plays a CTA clerk who saves a man from death on the El. *My Best Friend's Wedding* (1997) is a romantic comedy starring Julia Roberts, who tries to break up the wedding of Dermot Mulroney and Cameron Diaz. Roberts and Mulroney dance on a boat tour in the Loop.

In *High Fidelity* (2000), John Cusack is a record-store owner struggling with his past and present romantic life. In *Save the Last Dance* (2001), suburban ballerina Julia Stiles learns hip-hop from Sean Patrick Thomas on Chicago's South Side. Second City alum Nia Vardalos adapted the screenplay for the wildly popular *My Big Fat Greek Wedding* (2002) from her one-woman play. *Chicago* (2002) razzle-dazzled its way to six Oscars, helping to bring back the movie musical. *The Road to Perdition* (2002) stars Tom Hanks and Paul Newman in a 1930s gangster drama. *Barbershop* (2002) chronicles a day in the life of a South Side barbershop. Director Robert Altman and star Neve Campbell go behind the scenes with the Joffrey Ballet of Chicago in *The Company* (2003). Will Smith visits the Lake Michigan Landfill in the 2035 Chicago created in the sci-fi thriller *I, Robot* (2004). Josh Hartnett plays a young ad exec in Chicago in *Wicker Park* (2004). As a down-on-his-luck divorcé in *The Weather Man* (2004), Nicolas Cage filmed scenes in both north suburban Evanston and downtown. In *Batman Begins* (2004) Christian Bale, as Batman, is seen racing through Chicago's Lower Wacker Drive in the Batmobile. Jennifer Aniston spent some quality time in the Windy City while filming *Derailed* (2005; co-starring Clive Owen); then she was rumored to have fallen in love with Vince Vaughn while filming *The Break Up* (2006). Will Ferrell got a Golden Globe nomination for Best Actor in a Musical or Comedy for his portrayal of a regular guy whose fate is controlled by a neurotic writer in *Stranger Than Fiction* (2006), which was filmed in Chicago.

Chicago
Essentials

PLANNING TOOLS, EXPERT INSIGHT,
GREAT CONTACTS

There are planners and there are those who, excuse the pun, fly by the seat of their pants. We happily place ourselves among the planners. Our writers and editors try to anticipate all the issues you may face before and during any journey, and then they do their research. This section is the product of their efforts. Use it to get excited about your trip to Chicago, to inform your travel planning, or to guide you on the road should the seat of your pants start to feel threadbare.

GETTING STARTED

We're really proud of our Web site: Fodors.com is a great place to begin any journey. Scan Travel Wire for suggested itineraries, travel deals, restaurant and hotel openings, and other up-to-the-minute info. Check out Booking to research prices and book plane tickets, hotel rooms, rental cars, and vacation packages. Head to Talk for on-the-ground pointers from travelers who frequent our message boards. You can also link to loads of other travel-related resources.

▌ RESOURCES

ONLINE TRAVEL TOOLS

ALL ABOUT CHICAGO

The Chicago Convention and Tourism Bureau's site, ⊕*www.choosechicago.com*, has plenty of general tips on the city and local events, plus helpful information on convention facilities. There's also plenty of information on the City of Chicago Web site, ⊕*egov.cityofchicago.org*, from festival details to neighborhood overviews and services for visitors from the Chicago Office of Tourism. For a user-friendly introduction to the city, log on to ⊕*www.chicago.com*.

NEWSPAPERS & MAGAZINES

The Web sites of the city's daily newspapers, the *Tribune* (⊕*www.chicagotribune. com*) and the *Sun-Times* (⊕*www.suntimes. com/index*) are great sources for reviews and events listings. The *Chicago Reader*'s site, ⊕*www.chireader.com*, is rich in arts, entertainment, and dining reviews. *Chicago* magazine's site, ⊕*www.chicagomag.com*, carries a few Web-exclusive features along

with articles from the monthly. Metromix's ⊕*www.metromix.com* thoroughly covers Chicago's entertainment scene. Another good online entertainment reference is ⊕*www.timeout.com/chicago*, which gives an irreverent, in-depth look at Chicago diversions.

PUBLIC TRANSIT

To sort out the public-transit system, log on to the CTA's site at ⊕*www.transit chicago.com*.

Safety **Transportation Security Administration** (TSA; ⊕www.tsa.gov).

Time Zones **Timeanddate.com** (⊕www.timeanddate.com/worldclock) can help you figure out the correct time anywhere in the world.

Weather **Accuweather.com** (⊕www.accuweather.com) is an independent weather-forecasting service with especially good coverage of hurricanes. **Weather.com** (⊕www.weather. com) is the Web site for the Weather Channel.

VISITOR INFORMATION

The Chicago Convention and Tourism Bureau is a great place to start planning your visit to the Windy City. The organization's Web site (⊕ www.choosechicago.com) is a veritable goldmine of information, from hotel packages, sample itineraries, event calendars, and maps. You can also call the toll-free number (☎ 877/CHICAGO) to speak with a travel consultant. The Mayor's Office of Special Events Web site will give you detailed instructions about getting around the city, neighborhood tours, and city-sponsored initiatives. The Illinois Bureau of Tourism offers much of the same Chicago information and is especially helpful if your travel plans will bring you outside of the downtown area. Once you're here, you can count on the visitor centers at the Chicago Cultural Center, Chicago Water Works, and Navy Pier. They are stocked with free maps, local publications, and knowledgeable staff to help you out.

WORD OF MOUTH

After your trip, be sure to rate the places you visited and share your experiences and travel tips with us and other Fodorites in Travel Ratings and Talk on www.fodors.com.

Contacts Chicago Convention and Tourism Bureau (✉ 2301 S. Lake Shore Dr., 60616 ☎ 312/567–8500 or 877/CHICAGO [877/244–2246] ⊕ www.choosechicago.com). **Chicago Cultural Center** (✉ 78 E. Randolph St., 60602 ☎ 312/744–6630 ⊕ egov.cityofchicago.org). **Chicago Water Works** (✉ 163 E. Pearson, 60610 ☎ 312/742–8811 ⊕ www.choosechicago.com). **Illinois Bureau of Tourism** (✉ James R. Thompson Center, 100 W. Randolph St., Suite 3-400, 60601 ☎ 800/2CONNECT [800/226–6632] ⊕ www.enjoyillinois.com). **Mayor's Office of Special Events, General Information, and Activities** (✉ 121 N. LaSalle St., Room 806, 60602 ☎ 312/744–3315 ⊕ egov.cityofchicago.org). **Navy Pier Welcome Center** (✉ 600 E. Grand Ave. ☎ 800/595–7437 or 312/595–7437 ⊕ www.navypier.com).

❚ THINGS TO CONSIDER

GEAR

In general, Chicago's out-and-about look is casual—jeans, a polished top, and comfortable shoes should be fine for touring around the city. The weather can change abruptly, so it's a good idea to dress in layers. Summers can be very hot and winters very cold and windy—hat, gloves, a scarf, and a warm coat are vital. Don't forget an umbrella.

For dining out, most elegant restaurants in the city require a shirt and tie for men and a dressy look for women. For mass, church, or synagogue services, people usually dress in nice slacks or skirts or dresses. Men do not always wear a suit or a sport jacket, but rarely wear jeans.

SHIPPING LUGGAGE AHEAD

Imagine globe-trotting with only a carry-on in tow. Shipping your luggage in advance via an air-freight service is a great way to cut down on backaches, hassles, and stress—especially if your packing list includes strollers, car seats, etc. There are some things to be aware of, though. First, research carry-on restrictions; if you absolutely need something that isn't practical to ship and isn't allowed in carry-

---

---

ons, this strategy isn't for you. Second, plan to send your bags several days in advance to U.S. destinations and as much as two weeks in advance to some international destinations. Third, plan to spend some money: it will cost least $100 to send a small piece of luggage, a golf bag, or a pair of skis to a domestic destination, much more to places overseas. Some people use Federal Express to ship their bags, but this can cost even more than air-freight services. All these services insure your bag (for most, the limit is $1,000, but you should verify that amount); you can, however, purchase additional insurance for about $1 per $100 of value.

Contacts Luggage Concierge (☎ 800/288–9818 ⊕ www.luggageconcierge.com). **Luggage Express** (☎ 866/744–7224 ⊕ www.usxpluggageexpress.com). **Luggage Free** (☎ 800/361–6871 ⊕ www.luggagefree.com). **Sports Express** (☎ 800/357–4174 ⊕ www.sportsexpress.com) specializes in shipping golf clubs and other sports equipment. **Virtual Bellhop** (☎ 877/235–5467 ⊕ www.virtualbellhop.com).

TRIP INSURANCE

What kind of coverage do you honestly need? Do you even need trip insurance at all? Take a deep breath and read on.

Trip Insurance Resources

INSURANCE COMPARISON SITES		
Insure My Trip.com	800/487-4722	www.insuremytrip.com
Square Mouth.com	800/240-0369	www.quotetravelinsurance.com
COMPREHENSIVE TRAVEL INSURERS		
Access America	866/807-3982	www.accessamerica.com
CSA Travel Protection	800/873-9855	www.csatravelprotection.com
HTH Worldwide	610/254-8700 or 888/243-2358	www.hthworldwide.com
Travelex Insurance	888/457-4602	www.travelex-insurance.com
Travel Guard International	715/345-0505 or 800/826-4919	www.travelguard.com
Travel Insured International	800/243-3174	www.travelinsured.com
MEDICAL-ONLY INSURERS		
International Medical Group	800/628-4664	www.imglobal.com
International SOS	215/942-8000 or 713/521-7611	www.internationalsos.com
Wallach & Company	800/237-6615 or 504/687-3166	www.wallach.com

We believe that comprehensive trip insurance is especially valuable if you're booking a very expensive or complicated trip (particularly to an isolated region) or if you're booking far in advance. Who knows what could happen six months down the road? But whether or not you get insurance has more to do with how comfortable you are assuming all that risk yourself.

Comprehensive travel policies typically cover trip-cancellation and interruption, letting you cancel or cut your trip short because of a personal emergency, illness, or, in some cases, acts of terrorism in your destination. Such policies also cover evacuation and medical care. Some also cover you for trip delays because of bad weather or mechanical problems as well as for lost or delayed baggage. Another type of coverage to look for is financial default—that is, when your trip is disrupted because a tour operator, airline, or cruise line goes out of business. Generally you must buy this when you book your trip or shortly thereafter, and it's only available to you if your operator isn't on a list of excluded companies.

Expect comprehensive travel-insurance policies to cost about 4% to 7% or 8% of the total price of your trip (it's more like 8%–12% if you're over age 70). A medical-only policy may or may not be cheaper than a comprehensive policy. Always read the fine print of your policy to make sure that you are covered for the risks that are of most concern to you. Compare several policies to make sure you're getting the best price and range of coverage available.

■ TIP→ There's always a chance that a severe storm will disrupt your plans. The solution? Look for hotels and resorts that offer storm/hurricane guarantees. Although they rarely allow refunds, most guarantees do let you rebook later if a storm strikes.

PACKING 101

Why do some people travel with a convoy of huge suitcases yet never have a thing to wear? How do others pack a duffle with a week's worth of outfits *and* supplies for every contingency? We realize that packing is a matter of style, but there's a lot to be said for traveling light. These tips help fight the battle of the bulging bag.

Make a list. In a recent Fodor's survey, 29% of respondents said they make lists (and often pack) a week before a trip. You can use your list to pack and to repack at the end of your trip. It can also serve as record of the contents of your suitcase—in case it disappears in transit.

Think it through. What's the weather like? Is this a business trip? A cruise? Going abroad? In some places dress may be more or less conservative than you're used to. As you create your itinerary, note outfits next to each activity (don't forget accessories).

Edit your wardrobe. Plan to wear everything twice (better yet, thrice) and to do laundry along the way. Stick to one basic look—urban chic, sporty casual, etc. Build around one or two neutrals and an accent (e.g., black, white, and olive green). Women can freshen looks by changing scarves or jewelry. For a week's trip, you can look smashing with three bottoms, four or five tops, a sweater, and a jacket.

Be practical. Put comfortable shoes atop your list. (Did we need to say this?) Pack lightweight, wrinkle-resistant, compact, washable items. (Or this?) Stack and roll clothes, so they'll wrinkle less. Unless you're on a guided tour or a cruise, select luggage you can readily carry. Porters, like good butlers, are hard to find these days.

Check weight and size limitations. In the United States you may be charged extra for checked bags weighing more than 50 pounds. Abroad some airlines don't allow you to check bags over 60 to 70 pounds, or they charge outrageous fees for every excess pound—or bag. Carry-on size limitations can be stringent, too.

Check carry-on restrictions. Research restrictions with the TSA. Rules vary abroad, so check them with your airline if you're traveling overseas on a foreign carrier. Consider packing all but essentials (travel documents, prescription meds, wallet) in checked luggage. This leads to a "pack only what you can afford to lose" approach that might help you streamline.

Rethink valuables. On U.S. flights, airlines are liable for only about $2,800 per person for bags. On international flights, the liability limit is around $635 per bag. But items like computers, cameras, and jewelry aren't covered, and as gadgetry can go on and of the list of carry-on no-no's, you can't count on keeping things safe by keeping them close. Although comprehensive travel policies may cover luggage, the liability limit is often a pittance. Your home-owner's policy may cover you sufficiently when you travel—or not.

Lock it up. If you must pack valuables, use TSA-approved locks (about $10) that can be unlocked by all U.S. security personnel.

Tag it. Always tag your luggage; use your business address if you don't want people to know your home address. Put the same information (and a copy of your itinerary) inside your luggage, too.

Report problems immediately. If your bags—or things inside them—are damaged or go astray, file a written claim with your airline *before leaving the airport.* If the airline is at fault, it may give you money for essentials until your luggage arrives. Most lost bags are found within 48 hours, so alert the airline to your whereabouts for two or three days. If your bag was opened for security reasons in the United States and something is missing, file a claim with the TSA.

BOOKING YOUR TRIP

Unless your cousin is a travel agent, you're probably among the millions of people who make most of their travel arrangements online. But have you ever wondered just what the differences are between an online travel agent (a Web site through which you make reservations instead of going directly to the airline, hotel, or car-rental company), a discounter (a firm that does a high volume of business with a hotel chain or airline and accordingly gets good prices), a wholesaler (one that makes cheap reservations in bulk and then re-sells them to people like you), and an aggregator (one that compares all the offerings so you don't have to)? Is it truly better to book directly on an airline or hotel Web site? And when does a real live travel agent come in handy?

ONLINE

You really have to shop around. A travel wholesaler such as Hotels.com or Hotel-Club.net can be a source of good rates, as can discounters such as Hotwire or Priceline, particularly if you can bid for your hotel room or airfare. Indeed, such sites sometimes have deals that are unavailable elsewhere. They do, however, tend to work only with hotel chains (which makes them just plain useless for getting hotel reservations outside of major cities) or big airlines (so that often leaves out upstarts like jetBlue and some foreign carriers like Air India). Also, with discounters and wholesalers you must generally prepay, and everything is nonrefundable. And before you fork over the dough, be sure to check the terms and conditions, so you know what a given company will do for you if there's a problem and what you'll have to deal with on your own.

■ TIP→ **To be absolutely sure everything was processed correctly, confirm reservations made through online travel agents, discounters, and wholesalers directly with your hotel before leaving home.**

Booking engines like Expedia, Travelocity, and Orbitz are actually travel agents, albeit high-volume, online ones. And airline travel packagers like American Airlines Vacations and Virgin Vacations—well, they're travel agents, too. But they may still not work with all the world's hotels.

An aggregator site will search many sites and pull the best prices for airfares, hotels, and rental cars from them. Most aggregators compare the major travel-booking sites such as Expedia, Travelocity, and Orbitz; some also look at airline Web sites, though rarely the sites of smaller budget airlines. Some aggregators also compare other travel products, including complex packages—a good thing, as you can sometimes get the best overall deal by booking an air-and-hotel package.

TRANSPORTATION

Chicago is famously known as a city of neighborhoods. The Loop is Chicago's epicenter of business, finance, and government. Neighborhoods surrounding the Loop include River North (an area populated by art galleries and high-end boutiques), Streeterville (bordered by Lake Michigan and Navy Pier), and West Loop and South Loop, both up-and-coming areas with trendy residential areas and hip dining and shopping options.

Moving north, you'll encounter the Magnificent Mile (North Michigan Avenue), which gives way to the Gold Coast, so named for its luxurious mansions, stately museums, and deluxe entertainment venues. Lincoln Park, Lake View, Wrigleyville, Lincoln Square, and Andersonville all lie north of these areas, and each has considerable charms to explore.

Neighborhoods west of the Loop include River West, West Town, Wicker Park, and Bucktown, where of-the-moment art, shopping, dining, and nightlife venues line the streets.

Beyond South Loop lies Hyde Park, home to the University of Chicago and the Museum of Science and Industry.

Traveling between neighborhoods is a relatively sane experience, thanks to the matrix of bus and train routes managed by the Chicago Transit Authority. Driving can be harried, but taxis are normally plentiful in most parts of town.

Chicago streets generally follow a grid pattern, running north–south or east–west and radiating from a center point at State and Madison streets in the Loop. East and west street numbers go up as you move away from State Street; north and south street numbers rise as you move away from Madison Street. Each block is represented by a hundred number.

■ TIP➔ Ask the local tourist board about hotel and local transportation packages that include tickets to major museum exhibits or other special events.

▌ BY AIR

To Chicago: From New York, 2 hours; from San Francisco, 4 hours; from Los Angeles, 4 hours; from Dallas, 2½ hours; from London, 7 hours; from Sydney, 17 hours.

In Chicago, the general rule is to arrive at the airport two hours before an international flight; for a domestic flight, plan to arrive 90 minutes early if you're checking luggage and 60 minutes if you're not.

There are no direct flights from Chicago to Australia or New Zealand. There are several daily direct flights to the United Kingdom by British Midland, United, and American.

Smoking policies vary from carrier to carrier. U.S. airlines prohibit smoking on all flights.

Airlines & Airports **Airline and Airport Links.com** (⊕www.airlineandairportlinks.com) has links to many of the world's airlines and airports.

Airline Security Issues **Transportation Security Administration** (⊕www.tsa.gov) has answers for almost every question that might come up.

AIRPORTS

The major gateway to Chicago is **O'Hare International Airport** (ORD). As one of the world's busiest airports, all major airlines pass through O'Hare. The sprawling structure is situated 19 mi from downtown, in the far northwest corner of the city. It can take anywhere from 30 to 90 minutes to travel between downtown and O'Hare, based on time of day, weather conditions, and construction on the Kennedy Expressway (Interstate 90). The Blue Line El train offers a reliable 40-minute trip between the Loop and O'Hare.

Got some time to spend before your flight? Plenty of dining and shopping options are scattered throughout O'Hare's four terminals. Chicago favorites such as the Billy Goat Tavern, Goose Island Brewing Company, Pizzeria Uno, and Gold Coast Dogs can be found amongst the usual chain restaurants. Grab that last-minute souvenir or in-flight necessity at an array of shops, including the Chicago Historical Society Gift Shop, the Field Museum Gift Shop, and Landau Jewelers. Or spring for a mini-massage from the Back Rub Hub. Wi-Fi is also available throughout the building.

■TIP➡ If you're stuck at O'Hare longer than you expected, the Hilton Chicago O'Hare (773/686–8000) is located within walking distance of all terminals.

Midway Airport (MDW) is situated about 11 mi southwest from downtown. Midway Airport serves American, Continental, and Delta airlines along with budget carriers like Southwest, Airtran, and United Express. Driving between Midway and downtown can take 30 to 60 minutes, depending on traffic conditions on the Stevenson Expressway (Interstate 55). The Orange Line El train runs from the Loop to Midway in about 30 minutes.

Some say the recently renovated Midway has better dining options than O'Hare. With downtown standouts such as Harry Caray's, Tuscany, Manny's Deli, and Superdawg all on-site, it's a good point. The Midway Boulevard area in the center of the building features cute shops such as Chicago Treasures and Kid's Corner. Wi-Fi is available throughout the airport.

An extended stay near Midway Airport can be spent at a number of nearby hotels, including Chicago Marriott Midway (800/671–9207), Hampton Inn (800/671–9207) and Hilton Garden Inn (800/671–9207).

Security screenings at both airports are fairly quick (it takes about 15 to 30 minutes or less to get through security lines);

> ### SCI-FI, INDEED
>
> If you travel frequently, look into the TSA's Registered Traveler program. The program, which is still being tested in several U.S. airports, is designed to cut down on gridlock at security checkpoints by allowing prescreened travelers to pass quickly through kiosks that scan an iris and/or a fingerprint. How sci-fi is that?

however, during peak holiday travel, you should arrive about two hours before your flight.

■TIP➡ Long layovers don't have to be only about sitting around or shopping. These days they can be about burning off vacation calories. Check out www.airportgyms. com for lists of health clubs that are in or near many U.S. and Canadian airports.

Airport Information **Midway Airport** (☎773/686–2200 or 800/832–6352 ⊕www. chicago-mdw.com or www.flychicago.com). **O'Hare International Airport** (☎773/686–2200 or 800/832–6352 ⊕www.ohare.com or www.flychicago.com).

GROUND TRANSPORTATION

If you're traveling to or from the airport by bus or car during morning or afternoon rush hours, factor in some extra time—ground transport to or from both O'Hare and Midway airports can be slow.

BY BUS:

Shuttle buses run between O'Hare and Midway airports and to and from either airport and various points in the city. When taking an airport shuttle bus to O'Hare or Midway to catch a departing flight, be sure to allow at least 1½ hours. When going to either airport, it's a good idea to make a reservation 24 hours in advance. Though some shuttles make regular stops at the major hotels and don't require reservations, it's best to check. Reservations are not necessary from the airports. Omega Airport Shuttle runs an hourly shuttle between the two airports for approximately $16 per person. Travel time is approximately one hour. Omega Airport Shuttle also provides an hourly service from the two airports and Hyde Park. The fare is $30 from O'Hare to Hyde Park and $17 from Midway to Hyde Park. Continental Airport Express coaches provide service from both airports to major downtown and Near North locations and the northern suburbs. The trip downtown from O'Hare takes at least 45 minutes, depending on traffic conditions; the fare is $25, $45 round-trip. The trip downtown from Midway takes at least a half hour; the fare is $20, $35 round-trip. Call to find out times and prices for other destinations.

BY CAR:
Depending on traffic and the time of day, driving to and from O'Hare takes about an hour, and driving to and from Midway takes at least 45 minutes. From O'Hare, follow the signs to Interstate 90 east (Kennedy Expressway), which merges with Interstate 94 (Edens Expressway). Take the eastbound exit at Ohio Street for Near North locations, the Washington or Monroe Street exit for downtown. After you exit, continue east about a mile to get to Michigan Avenue. From Midway, follow the signs to Interstate 55 east, which leads to Interstate 90.

BY TAXI:
Metered taxicab service is available at both O'Hare and Midway airports. Trips to and from O'Hare may incur a $1 surcharge to compensate for changing fuel costs. Expect to pay about $40 to $45 plus tip from O'Hare to Near North and downtown locations, about $30 to $35 plus tip from Midway. Some cabs, such as Checker Taxi and Yellow Cab, participate in a share-a-ride program in which each cab carries up to four individual passengers going from the airport to downtown. The cost per person is substantially lower than the full rate, which is approximately $50.

BY TRAIN:
Chicago Transit Authority (CTA) trains are the cheapest way to and from the airports; they can also be the most convenient transfer. TRAINS TO CITY signs will guide you to the subway or elevated train line. In O'Hare Airport the Blue Line station is in the underground concourse between terminals. Travel time to the city is about 45 minutes. Get off at the station closest to your hotel, or from the first stop in the Loop (Washington and Dearborn streets) you can take a taxi to your hotel or change to other transit lines. At Midway Airport the Orange Line El runs to the Loop. The stop at Adams Street and Wabash Avenue is the closest to the hotels on South Michigan Avenue; for others, the simplest strategy is to get off anywhere in the Loop and hail a cab to your final destination. Train fare is $2, which you'll need in dollar bills (turnstiles don't give change) and/or coins. A fare card is another option. Pick up brochures outside the entrances to the platforms that detail the stops of the train lines; the "Downtown Transit Sightseeing Guide" is also helpful.

TRANSFERS BETWEEN AIRPORTS
O'Hare and Midway airports are located on opposite ends of the city, so moving between them can be a time-consuming and arduous task. Your best and cheapest move is hopping on the El. You will travel the Blue Line to the Orange Line, transferring at the Clark Street stop to get from O'Hare to Midway, reversing the trip to go from Midway to O'Hare. The entire journey should take you under 2 hours. If time is an issue, you may want to consider Coach USA Wisconsin, a shuttle bus that makes the trip between the two airports several times a day from 6:30 AM to 10:30 PM. The fare is $14 per person, one way; $25 round-trip. You can purchase tickets from the driver or in advance from the company's Web site. The trip should take you about 1 hour, depending on traffic conditions.

Taxis & Shuttles **American United Cab Co.** (☎773/248–7600). **Coach USA Wisconsin** (☎800/236–2028 ⊕www.coachusa.com/wisconsincoach). **Continental Airport Express** (☎888/2THEVAN ⊕www.airportexpress.com). **Checker Taxi** (☎312/243–2537). **Flash Cab** (☎773/561–1444). **Omega Airport Shuttle** (☎773/734–6688 ⊕www.omegashuttle.com). **Yellow Cab Co.** (☎312/829–4222 ⊕www.yellowcabchicago.com).

Public Transit Information **CTA** (☎312/836–7000 ⊕www.transitchicago.com).

FLIGHTS

Airline Contacts **Alaska Airlines** (☎800/252–7522 ⊕www.alaskaair.com). **American Airlines** (☎800/433–7300 ⊕www.aa.com). **ATA** (☎800/435–9282 or 317/282–8308 ⊕www.ata.com). **Continental Airlines** (☎800/523—3273 for U.S. and Mexico reservations, 800/231–0856 for international reservations ⊕www.continental.com). **Delta Airlines** (☎800/221–1212 for U.S. reservations, 800/241–4141 for international reservations ⊕www.delta.com). **jetBlue** (☎800/538–2583 ⊕www.jetblue.com). **Northwest Airlines** (☎800/225–2525 ⊕www.nwa.com). **Southwest Airlines** (☎800/435–9792 ⊕www.southwest.com). **Spirit Airlines** (☎800/772–7117 or 586/791–7300 ⊕www.spiritair.com). **United Airlines** (☎800/864–8331 for U.S. reservations, 800/538–2929 for international reservations ⊕www.united.com). **USAirways** (☎800/428–4322 for U.S. and Canada reservations, 800/622–1015 for international reservations ⊕www.usairways.com).

▌ BIKE TRAVEL

Mayor Daley's goal is to make Chicago the most bike-friendly city in the United States, and he's well on his way. One-hundred-twenty miles of designated bike routes run throughout the city, through historic areas, beautiful parks, and along city streets (look for the words BIKE LANE). Bicycling on busy city streets can be a challenge and is not for the faint of heart—cars come within inches of riders, and the doors of parked cars can swing open at any time. The best bet for a scenic ride is the lakefront, which has a traffic-free 18-mi asphalt trail affording scenic views of the skyline. When your bike is unattended, always lock it; there are bike racks throughout the city. In Millennium Park at Michigan Avenue and Randolph Street (⊕*www.chicagobikestation.com*), there are 300 free indoor bike spaces plus showers, lockers, and bike-rental facilities offering beach cruisers, mountain and road bikes, hybrid/comfort models, tandem styles, and add-ons for kids (wagon, baby seat, etc.). Bike rentals are also readily available at Bike Chicago, which has four locations, one at Millennium Park, one at Navy Pier and two along the lakefront (⊕*www.bikechicago.com*). Bike Chicago carries a good selection of mountain and cross bikes. Rates start at $8.75 per hour. The Chicago Department of Tourism publishes free route maps. Chicagoland Bicycle Federation maps cost $6.95 plus a membership fee of $5. Maps are updated every few years. From April through October, Bobby's Bike Hike takes guests on cycling tours of Chicago. The three-hour tours begin at the Water Tower on the Magnificent Mile and cycle through historic neighborhoods, shopping areas, and the lakefront. A $30 to $35 fee includes bikes, helmets, and guides.

Information **Bobby's Bike Hike** (☎312/915–0995 ⊕www.bobbysbikehike.com). **Chicago Department of Tourism (CDOT)** (☎312/742–2453 ⊕www.cityofchicago.org/Transportation) publishes free route maps. **Chicagoland Bicycle Federation** (☎312/427–3325 ⊕www.biketraffic.org).

▌ BY BOAT

Water taxis are an economical and in-the-know way to cruise parts of the Chicago River and Lake Michigan. A combination of working stiffs and tourists board these boats daily. You won't get the in-depth narrative of an architecture tour, but the views of Chicago's waterways are just as good.

FLYING 101

Flying may not be as carefree as it once was, but there are some things you can do to make your trip smoother.

Minimize the time spent standing in line. Buy an e-ticket, check in at an electronic kiosk, or—even better—check in on your airline's Web site before leaving home. Pack light and limit carry-on items to only the essentials.

Arrive when you need to. Research your airline's policy. It's usually at least an hour before domestic flights and two to three hours before international flights. But airlines at some busy airports have more stringent requirements. Check the TSA Web site for estimated security waiting times at major airports.

Get to the gate. If you aren't at the gate at least 10 minutes before your flight is scheduled to take off (sometimes earlier), you won't be allowed to board.

Double-check your flight times. Do this especially if you reserved far in advance. Schedules change, and alerts may not reach you.

Don't go hungry. Ask whether your airline offers anything to eat; even when it does, be prepared to pay.

Get the seat you want. Often, you can pick a seat when you buy your ticket on an airline Web site. But it's not guaranteed; the airline could change the plane after you book, so double-check. You can also select a seat if you check in electronically. Avoid seats on the aisle directly across from the lavatories. Frequent fliers say those are even worse than back-row seats that don't recline.

Got kids? Get info. Ask the airline about its children's menus, activities, and fares. Sometimes infants and toddlers fly free if they sit on a parent's lap, and older children fly for half price in their own seats. Also inquire about policies involving car seats; having one may limit seating options. Also ask about seat-belt extenders for car seats. And note that you can't count on a flight attendant to produce an extender; you may have to ask for one when you board.

Check your scheduling. Don't buy a ticket if there's less than an hour between connecting flights. Although schedules are padded, if anything goes wrong you might miss your connection. If you're traveling to an important function, depart a day early.

Bring paper. Even when using an e-ticket, always carry a hard copy of your receipt; you may need it to get your boarding pass, which most airports require to get past security.

Complain at the airport. If your baggage goes astray or your flight goes awry, complain before leaving the airport. Most carriers require this.

Beware of overbooked flights. If a flight is oversold, the gate agent will usually ask for volunteers and offer some sort of compensation for taking a different flight. If you're bumped from a flight *involuntarily*, the airline must give you some kind of compensation if an alternate flight can't be found within one hour.

Know your rights. If your flight is delayed because of something within the airline's control (bad weather doesn't count), the airline must get you to your destination on the same day, even if they have to book you on another airline and in an upgraded class. Read the Contract of Carriage, which is usually buried on the airline's Web site.

Be prepared. The Boy Scout motto is especially important if you're traveling during a stormy season. To quickly adjust your plans, program a few numbers into your cell: your airline, an airport hotel or two, your destination hotel, your car service, and/or your travel agent.

Wendella Boats operates Chicago Water Taxis, which use four downtown docks (Madison Street, LaSalle Street, Michigan Avenue, and River East Plaza) along the Chicago River. The entire ride takes about a half hour, and you'll get to see a good portion of the downtown part of the Chicago River. The boats operate seven days a week, May through October. You can purchase tickets at any dock or on the company's Web site.

Shoreline Water Taxis run two routes: the River Taxi cruises between the Sears Tower and Navy Pier, and the Harbor Taxi navigates Lake Michigan between Navy Pier and the Museum Campus. Water Taxis run 10 AM to 6 PM late May to early September. You can purchase tickets at any dock or in advance on the company's Web site.

Information Shoreline Sightseeing (⊠474 N. Lake Shore Dr., Suite 3511 ☎312/222–9328 ⊕www.shorelinesightseeing.com). **Wendella Boats** (⊠400 N. Michigan Ave. [main dock] ☎312/337–1446 ⊕www.wendellaboats.com).

BY BUS

Greyhound has nationwide service to its main terminal in the Loop and to neighborhood stations, at the 95th Street and Dan Ryan Expressway CTA station and at the Cumberland CTA station, near O'Hare Airport. The Harrison Street terminal is far from most hotels, so plan on another bus or a cab to your hotel.

For information on bus travel within Chicago, see By Public Transportation.

Bus Information Chicago Transit Authority (☎888/968–7282 ⊕www.transitchicago.com). **Greyhound Lines** (☎800/231–2222 ⊕www.greyhound.com). **Main Depot** (⊠630 W. Harrison St. ☎312/408–5800). **South Depot** (⊠14 W. 95th St. ☎312/408–5999). **Northwest Depot (O'Hare)** (⊠CTA Transit Building, 5800 N. Cumberland Ave. ☎773/693–2474).

BY CAR

Chicago's network of buses and rapid-transit rail is extensive, and taxis and limousines are readily available (the latter often priced competitively with metered cabs), so rent a car *only* to visit the outlying suburbs that are not accessible by public transportation. Chicago traffic is often heavy, on-street parking is nearly impossible to find, parking lots are expensive, congestion creates frustrating delays, and other drivers may be impatient with those who are unfamiliar with the city and its roads. Expect snarled traffic during rush hours. In these circumstances you may find a car to be a liability rather than an asset. The Illinois Department of Transportation gives information on expressway congestion, travel times, and lane closures and directions on state roadways.

The Illinois tollways snake around the outskirts of the city. Interstate 294 runs north and south between Wisconsin and Indiana. Interstate 90 runs northwest to western Wisconsin, including Madison and Wisconsin Dells. Interstate 88 runs east–west and goes from Eisenhower to Interstate 55. Traffic on all is sometimes just as congested as on the regular expressways. Most toll gates are unmanned, so bring lots of change if you don't have an I-Pass, which are sometimes included with rental cars. Even though tolls are double without the I-Pass, it's not cost effective to purchase one for a couple of days.

GASOLINE

Gas stations are less prevalent in downtown Chicago than in the outlying neighborhoods and suburbs. Filling up is about 50 cents higher per gallon downtown when you can find a station. Expect to pay anywhere between $3 and $4 per gallon of gas (per prices at time of writing). Major credit cards are accepted at all gas stations, and the majority of stations are completely self-serve.

PARKING

Most of Chicago's streets have metered parking, but during peak hours it's hard to find a spot. Most meters take quarters, buying as little as 5 minutes in high-traffic areas, up to an hour in less crowded neighborhoods. Parking lots and garages are plentiful downtown, but they're expensive. You could pay anywhere from $13 for the day in a municipal lot to $24 for three hours in a private lot. Some neighborhoods, such as the area of Lake View known as Wrigleyville, enforce restricted parking and will tow cars without permits. You won't really find parking lots in the neighborhoods. Many major thoroughfares restrict parking during peak travel hours, generally 9 to 11 AM heading toward downtown and 4 to 6 PM heading away. Read street signs carefully to determine whether a parking spot is legal. During the winter snow days, cars parked in designated "snow route areas" will be towed. There's a $30 fine plus the cost of towing the car. In sum, Chicago isn't the most car-friendly place for visitors. Unless it's a necessity, it's best to forget renting a car and use public transportation.

ROAD CONDITIONS

Chicago drivers can be reckless, zipping through red lights and breaking posted speed limits. The Loop and some residential neighborhoods such as Lincoln Park, Lake View, and Bucktown are made up of mostly one-way streets, so be sure to read signs carefully. Check both ways after a light turns green to make sure that the cross traffic has stopped.

Rush hours are 6:30 to 9:30 AM and 4 to 7 PM, but don't be surprised if the rush starts earlier or ends later, depending on weather conditions, big events, and holiday weekends. There are always bottlenecks on the expressways, particularly where the Edens and Kennedy merge, and downtown on the Dan Ryan from 22nd Street into the Loop. Sometimes anything around the airport is rough. There are electronic signs on the express-

NAVIGATING CHICAGO

Chicago is a surprisingly well-ordered and manageable city. A few city-planning quirks do exist, however. Streets that run on a diagonal, such as Milwaukee, Elston, and Lincoln avenues, jut and hurtle drunkenly through the city. These passageways are actually old Indian trails that followed the Chicago River (but make it a bit difficult for modern-day travelers to follow). Chicago also has a proliferation of double- and even triple-decker streets, Wacker Drive being the best-known example. The uppermost level is generally used for street traffic, while the lower levels serve as thoroughfares for cutting through the city rather quickly.

The most helpful landmark to help you navigate Chicago is Lake Michigan. Seriously, you can't miss it. It will always lie on the east, as it serves as the city's only eastern border. Also, look for the Sears Tower and John Hancock Center; these skyscrapers reach up far enough into the sky to serve as beacons. The Sears Tower in situated in the Loop, and the John Hancock Center lives in the northern reaches of Michigan Avenue.

Chicago's public transit system blankets the city well and is fairly intuitive. Major bus lines include the 151-Sheridan, which runs along the Lakefront, the 36-Broadway, which cuts through the Gold Coast, Lincoln Park, and Lakeview, and the 125-Water Tower Express, which takes a meandering route from Union Station to Water Tower. The train system (referred to as the El, short for "elevated"), is an even more comprehensive network with eight train lines criss-crossing through the city and nearby suburbs. The most popular routes are the Blue Line, which runs from O'Hare International Airport into the city through Bucktown, and back out again through the Loop. The Red Line cuts a north–south swath through the city, crossing through Andersonville, Wrigleyville, Lake View, Lincoln Park, Old Town, the Gold Coast, the Loop, and the South Side along the way.

ways that post updates on the congestion. Additionally, summertime is high time for construction on highways and inner-city roads. Drive with patience.

■ TIP→ **For more information about Chicago's roadways, including up-to-the-minute road conditions, check out the Illinois Department of Transportation's Web site at www.dot.state.il.us.**

ROADSIDE EMERGENCIES

Dial 911 in an emergency to reach police, fire, or ambulance services. AAA Chicago provides roadside assistance to members. Mr. Locks Emergency Locksmith & Security Service will unlock your vehicle 24 hours a day.

Emergency Services AAA Chicago (☎800/222–4357 [AAA–HELP)] ⊕ www.auto-clubgroup.com). **Mr. Locks Emergency Locksmith & Security Service** (☎866/675–6257 ⊕ www.mr-locks.com).

RULES OF THE ROAD

Speed limits in Chicago vary, but on most city roads it's 35 mph. Most interstate highways, except in congested areas, have a speed limit of 55 mph. In Chicago, you may turn right at a red light after stopping if there's no oncoming traffic and no posted restrictions. When in doubt, wait for the green. Cameras have been installed at certain intersections in the city to catch drivers who run red lights. There are many one-way streets in Chicago, particularly in and around the Loop, so be alert to signs and other cars. Illinois drunk-driving laws are quite strict. Anyone caught driving with a blood-alcohol content of .08 will automatically have his or her license seized and be issued a ticket, and authorities in home states will be notified. Those with Illinois drivers' licenses can have their licenses suspended for three months on the very first offense.

Passengers are required to wear seat belts. Always strap children under age eight into approved child-safety seats.

It's illegal to use hand-held cellular phones in the city, but there aren't any restrictions in the suburbs. Headlights are compulsory if you're using windshield wipers. Radar detectors are legal in Illinois.

■ BY PUBLIC TRANSPORTATION

Chicago's extensive public transportation network includes rapid-transit trains, buses, and a commuter-rail network. The Chicago Transit Authority, or CTA, operates the rapid-transit trains (the El), city buses, and suburban buses (PACE). Metra runs the commuter rail.

The Regional Transportation Authority (RTA) for northeastern Illinois oversees and coordinates the activities of the CTA and Metra. The RTA's Web site can be a useful first stop if you are planning to combine suburban and city public transit while in Chicago.

Information RTA Travel Information Center (☎312/836–7000 ⊕ www.rtachicago.com).

CTA: THE EL & BUSES

The Chicago Transit Authority (CTA) operates rapid-transit trains and buses. Chicago's rapid-transit train system is known as the El. Each of the eight lines has a color name as well as a route name: Blue (O'Hare–Congress–Douglas), Brown (Ravenswood), Green (Lake–Englewood–Jackson Park), Orange (Midway), Purple (Evanston), Red (Howard–Dan Ryan), Yellow (Skokie–Swift), and Pink (Cermak). In general, the route names indicate the first and last stop on the train. Chicagoans refer to trains both by the color and the route name. Most, but not all, rapid-transit lines operate 24 hours; some stations are closed at night. The El, though very crowded during rush hours, is the quickest way to get around (unless you're coming from the suburbs, in which case the Metra is quicker but doesn't run as often). Trains run every 15 minutes, though during rush hour they run about every 10 minutes and on weekends, every 30 minutes. Pick up the brochure "Downtown Transit Sightseeing Guide" for hours, fares, and other pertinent information. In general, late-night CTA travel is not recommended. Note that the Red and Blue lines are subways; the rest are elevated. This means if you're heading to O'Hare and looking for the Blue Line, look for a stairway down, not up.

Exact fares must be paid in cash (dollar bills or coins; no change given by turnstiles on train platforms or fare boxes on buses) or by transit card. Transit cards are flimsy plastic and credit-card size and can be purchased from machines at CTA train stations as well as at Jewel and Dominicks grocery stores and currency exchanges. These easy-to-use cards are inserted into the turnstiles at CTA train stations and into machines as you board CTA buses; directions are clearly posted. Use them to transfer between CTA vehicles. To transfer between the Loop's elevated lines and the subway or between rapid-transit trains and buses, you must either use a transit card with at least 30¢ stored on it, or, if you're not using a transit card, buy a transfer when you first board. If two CTA train lines meet, you can transfer for free. You can also obtain free train-to-train transfers from specially marked turnstiles at the Washington/State subway station or the State/Lake El station, or ask for a transfer card, good on downtown trains, at the ticket booth.

Buses generally stop on every other corner northbound and southbound (on State Street they stop at every corner). Eastbound and westbound buses generally stop on every corner. Buses from the Loop generally run north–south. Principal transfer points are on Michigan Avenue at the north side of Randolph Street for northbound buses, Adams Street and Wabash Avenue for westbound buses and the El, and State and Lake streets for southbound buses.

Buses are crowded during rush hour. Schedules vary depending on the time of day and route, and run every eight to 15 minutes, though service is less frequent on weekends, very early in the morning, and late at night. Schedules are available online at www.transitchicago.com.

Pace runs suburban buses in a six-county region; these connect with the CTA and use CTA transit cards, transfers, and passes.

CTA FARES:
The CTA fare structure is as follows: the basic fare for rapid-transit trains is $2 when paying cash or using a transit card. The basic fare for buses is $2 when paying cash and $1.75 when using a transit card. Transfers are 25¢ when using a transit card; no transfers are issued when paying cash. Transit cards can be purchased in preset denominations of $10 ($11 worth of rides) or $20 ($22 worth of rides) at many local grocery stores, currency exchanges, and stations. You can also purchase a transit card of any denomination over $2 at any CTA stop. Transfers can be used twice within a two-hour time period. Transfers between CTA train lines are free—no transfer card is needed. Transit cards may be shared.

For $5, a one-day Visitor Pass offers 24 hours of unlimited CTA riding from the time you first use it. Visitor Passes are sold at hotels, museums, and other places tourists frequent, plus all transit-card booths. A two-day pass is $9, a three-day pass is $12, and a five-day pass is $18.

Information CTA (✉ Merchandise Mart, 350 N. Wells St., 60654 ☎ 888/968–7282 ⊕ www. transitchicago.com).

METRA: COMMUTER TRAINS
Metra commuter trains serve the city and surrounding suburbs. The Metra Electric railroad has a line close to Lake Michigan; its trains stop in Hyde Park. The Metra commuter rail system has 11 lines to suburbs and surrounding cities including Aurora, Elgin, Joliet, and Waukegan;

one line serves the North Shore suburbs, and another has a stop at McCormick Place. Trains leave from a number of downtown terminals.

Metra trains use a fare structure based on the distance you ride. A Metra weekend pass costs $5 and is valid for rides on any of the eight operating lines all day on weekends, except for the South Shore line.

Information **Metra information line** (☎312/322–6777 ⊕www.metrarail.com).

TICKET/PASS	PRICE
Single Fare	$2
Weekly Pass	$20
Monthly Unlimited Pass	$75

ZONE	PRICE
A	$1.50
B	$3.00
C	$4.50

▌ BY TAXI

You can hail a cab on just about any busy street in Chicago. Hotel doormen will hail a cab for you as well. Cabs aren't all yellow anymore, but look for standard-size sedans or, in some cases, minivans. Available taxis are sometimes indicated by an illuminated rooftop light. Chicago taxis are metered, with fares beginning at $2.25 upon entering the cab and $1.90 for each additional mile. A charge of $1 for the first additional passenger and 50¢ is made for each additional passenger. There's no extra baggage or credit-card charge. Taxi drivers expect a 15% tip.

Taxi Companies **American United Cab Co.** (☎773/248–7600). **Checker Taxi** (☎312/243–2537). **Flash Cab** (☎773/561–1444). **Yellow Cab Co.** (☎312/829–4222 ⊕www.yellowcabchicago.com).

▌ BY TRAIN

Amtrak offers nationwide service to Chicago's Union Station, located at 225 South Canal Street. Some trains travel overnight, and you can sleep in your seat or book a sleeper car at an additional cost. Train schedules and payment options are available by calling Amtrak directly or consulting its Web site. Amtrak trains tend to fill up, so if you don't purchase a ticket in advance at least make a reservation.

Information **Amtrak** (☎800/872–7245 ⊕www.amtrak.com).

ON THE GROUND

▪ BUSINESS SERVICES & FACILITIES

Another one of Chicago's many nicknames is the City That Works. Numerous travelers come to Chicago for conventions taking place at the massive McCormick Place or to do business in the Loop. Various local companies are at your service to facilitate business trips; FedEx Kinko's business service centers can be found throughout the city, and various translation and interpreting services can help make your transactions seamless.

Contacts FedEx Kinko's (☎312/670–4460 ⊕www.fedexkinkos.com for more locations). **McCormick Place** (✉2301 S. Lake Shore Dr. ☎312/791–7000 ⊕www.mccormickplace. com). **TransPerfect Translations Chicago** (✉150 N. Michigan Ave., Suite 2935 ☎312/578–0887).

▪ COMMUNICATIONS

INTERNET

Chicago is more and more a wireless city, with many hotels and restaurants offering high-speed wireless access. Some hotels have a nominal fee (usually less than $10) that gets you online for 24 hours. You can also duck into places like FedEx Kinko's to check your e-mail, either on your own laptop or the available computers, but charges there can run high if you're online longer than a few minutes.

Contacts Cybercafes (⊕www.cybercafes. com) lists over 4,000 Internet cafés worldwide. **FedEx Kinko's** (✉444 N. Wells St. ☎312/670–4460 ⊕www.fedexkinkos.com). **Filter** (✉1585 N. Milwaukee Ave. ☎773/227–4850). **Intelligentsia Coffee & Tea** (✉3123 N. Broadway St. ☎773/348–8058). **Swim Cafe** (✉1357 W. Chicago Ave. ☎312/492–8600).

▪ DAY TOURS & GUIDES

A comprehensive collection of Chicago tours by air, water, and land can be found through **Chicago Tours** (☎888/881–3284 ⊕*www.chicagotours.us*), a travel-reservation company offering more than 75 tours, cruises, events, and activities.

BOAT TOURS

Get a fresh perspective on Chicago by taking a water tour or cruise. Boat tour schedules vary by season; be sure to call for exact times and fares. The season usually runs from May 1 through October 1. One cruise in particular stands out, though it's a bit more expensive than the rest: the Chicago Architecture Foundation river cruise aboard *Chicago's First Lady*. The CAF tour highlights more than 50 architecturally significant sights. The cost is $26 Monday through Friday, $28 on weekends and holidays; reservations are recommended.

If you're looking for a maritime adventure, you can get a blast from the past on the *Windy*, a 148-foot ship modeled on old-time commercial vessels. Passengers may help the crew or take a turn at the wheel during sailing cruises of Lake Michigan. The cost is $27.

Boat Tours Chicago Architecture Foundation river cruise (☎312/922–3432 information, 312/902–1500 tickets ⊕www. architecture.org). **Mercury Chicago Skyline Cruiseline** (☎312/332–1353 recorded information ⊕www.mercuryskylinecruiseline. com/). **Shoreline Marine** (☎312/222–9328 ⊕www.shorelinesightseeing.com). **Wendella Sightseeing Boats** (✉400 N. Michigan Ave. ☎312/337–1446 ⊕www.wendellaboats.com). **Windy of Chicago Ltd.** (☎312/595–5555 ⊕www.tallshipwindy.com).

BUS & TROLLEY TOURS

A narrated bus or trolley tour can be a good way to orient yourself among Chicago's main sights. Tours cost roughly $20 and normally last two hours. American Sightseeing offers two routes; combined, they cover the city quite thoroughly. The double-decker buses of Chicago Motor Coach Company tour downtown Chicago and the lakefront.

Chicago Trolley Charters schedules stops at all the downtown attractions. You can get on and off the open-air trolleys as you like; these tours vary in price, so call for details. The Chicago Architecture Foundation's bus tours often go farther afield, exploring everything from cemeteries to movie palaces.

Bus & Trolley Tours American Sightseeing (☎800/621–4153 ⊕www.grayline.com). **Chicago Architecture Foundation** (Tour Center ✉Santa Fe Bldg., 224 S. Michigan Ave. ☎312/922–3432 ⊕www.architecture.org). **Chicago Trolley Charters** (☎773/648–5000 ⊕www.chicagotrolley.com).

FOREIGN-LANGUAGE TOURS

Foreign-Language Tours Chicago Tour Guides Institute, Inc. (☎773/276–6683 ⊕www.chicagoguide.net).

SPECIAL-INTEREST TOURS

African-American Black Coutours (☎773/233–8907 ⊕www.blackcoutours.com). **Tour Black Chicago** (☎773/684–9034 ⊕www.tourblackchicago.com).

Architecture ⇨ Walking Tours.

Chocolate Accenting Chicago (☎312/819–5363 ⊕www.accentingchicago.com). **Chicago Chocolate Tours** (☎312/925–5377 ⊕www.chicagochocolatetours.com).

Gangsters Untouchable Tours (☎773/881–1195 ⊕www.gangstertour.com).

Ghosts Chicago Supernatural Ghost Tours (☎708/499–0300 ⊕www.ghosttours.com).

Historic Neighborhoods Black Metropolis Convention and Tourism Council (☎773/373–2842 ⊕www.bronzevilleonline.com/bvic.htm). **Chicago Neighborhood Tours** (☎312/742–1190 ⊕www.chicagoneighborhoodtours.com).

Horse & Carriage Rides Antique Coach and Carriage (☎773/735–9400 ⊕www.antiquecoach-carriage.com). **Chicago Horse & Carriage Ltd.** (☎312/953–9530 ⊕www.chicagocarriage.com). **Noble Horse** (☎312/266–7878 ⊕www.noblehorsechicago.com).

WALKING TOURS

The Chicago Architecture Foundation has by far the largest selection of guided tours, with more than 50 itineraries covering everything from department stores to Frank Lloyd Wright's Oak Park buildings. Especially popular walking tours of the Loop are given daily throughout the year. Chicago Greeter and InstaGreeter (for last-minute weekend visits) are two free city services that match knowledgeable Chicagoans with visitors for tours of various sights and neighborhoods. Friends of the Chicago River has Saturday-morning walking tours along the river. The organization also has maps of the walking routes, available for a small donation.

Information Chicago Architecture Foundation (Tour Centers ✉Santa Fe Bldg., 224 S. Michigan Ave. ☎312/922–3432 ⊕www.architecture.org). **Chicago Greeter and InstaGreeter** (✉Chicago Office of Tourism, 78 E. Washington St. ☎312/744–2400 ⊕www.chicagogreeter.com). **Friends of the Chicago River** (✉407 S. Dearborn St., Suite 1580 ☎312/939–0490 ⊕www.chicagoriver.org).

▌EATING OUT

Chicago is a big city with a big appetite. Known for such delicacies as the Chicago-style hot dog and deep-dish pizza, this is not a "light bites" kind of town. But you'll also find a thriving, constantly evolving restaurant scene, filled with anything from casual cafés to the most haute of cuisine. Traveling with kids? Not a problem, as there are plenty of places to keep them entertained.

MEALS & MEALTIMES

Unless otherwise noted, the restaurants listed in this guide are open daily for lunch and dinner.

Generally, breakfast is served in cafés, diners, and certain establishments that specialize in breakfast and lunch that are open until late afternoon. Restaurants that serve lunch and dinner generally open around 11 AM. Restaurants that are dinner-only open around 5 PM. Serving times are usually until 10 PM weeknights and 11 PM Friday and Saturday. There is a proliferation of late-night dining venues, where you can get a full menu or an edited version into the wee hours. Credit cards are widely accepted at all restaurants.

RESERVATIONS & DRESS

Regardless of where you are, it's a good idea to make a reservation if you can. In some places (Hong Kong, for example), it's expected. We only mention them specifically when reservations are essential (there's no other way you'll ever get a table) or when they are not accepted. For popular restaurants, book as far ahead as you can (often 30 days), and reconfirm as soon as you arrive. (Large parties should always call ahead to check the reservations policy.) We mention dress only when men are required to wear a jacket or a jacket and tie.

Online reservation services make it easy to book a table before you even leave home. OpenTable covers most states, including 20 major cities, and has limited listings in Canada, Mexico, the United Kingdom, and elsewhere. DinnerBroker has restaurants throughout the United States as well as a few in Canada.

Contacts **OpenTable** (⊕ www.opentable. com). **DinnerBroker** (⊕ www.dinnerbroker. com).

WINES, BEER & SPIRITS

Get a taste of Chicago at Goose Island Brewpub, a beloved local microbrewery. Named for a historic part of the Lincoln Park neighborhood, Goose Island crafts

CON OR CONCIERGE?

Good hotel concierges are invaluable—for arranging transportation, getting reservations at the hottest restaurant, and scoring tickets for a sold-out show or entrance to an exclusive nightclub. They're in the know and well connected. That said, sometimes you have to take their advice with a grain of salt.

It's not uncommon for restaurants to ply concierges with free food and drink in exchange for steering diners their way. Indeed, European concierges often receive referral *fees*. Hotel chains usually have guidelines about what their concierges can accept. The best concierges, however, are above reproach. This is particularly true of those who belong to the prestigious international society of Les Clefs d'Or.

What can you expect of a concierge? At a typical tourist-class hotel you can expect him or her to give you the basics: to show you something on a map, make a standard restaurant reservation (particularly if you don't speak the language), or help you book a tour or airport transportation. In Asia concierges perform the vital service of writing out the name or address of your destination for you to give to a cab driver.

Savvy concierges at the finest hotels and resorts can arrange for just about any good or service imaginable—and do so quickly. You should compensate them appropriately. A $10 tip is enough to show appreciation for a table at a hot restaurant. But the reward should really be much greater for tickets to that U2 concert that's been sold out for months or for those last-minute sixth-row-center seats for *The Lion King*.

award-winning stouts, lagers, and ales that are available at its Lincoln Park and Wrigleyville brewpubs, as well as at bars, restaurants, and stores throughout the area.

Most restaurants serve alcohol during business hours, but some have licensing that allows you to "bring your own bottle" (BYOB). At these establishments, you can bring in beer, wine, or liquor to consume during your meal.

Goose Island Brewpubs (⊠1800 N. Clybourn Ave. ☎312/915–0071 ⊠3535 N. Clark St. ☎773/832–9040 ⊕www.gooseisland.com).

▌HOURS OF OPERATION

Neighborhood business hours are generally 9 to 6 Friday through Wednesday, and 9 to 9 on Thursday. When holidays fall on a weekend, businesses usually close around four on the preceding Friday. On a Monday following a weekend holiday, retail businesses are rarely closed but regular businesses often are. Most stores close for Christmas, New Year's, and Easter Sunday.

Chicagoland museums are generally open daily 9 to 5, closing only on major holidays; some larger attractions keep later hours (until about 8 PM) one weeknight per week. A number of smaller museums keep limited hours; it's always advisable to phone ahead for details.

Most pharmacies are open regular business hours, starting as early as 8 AM. Some close as early as 5 PM, but many stay open later, anywhere from 6 to 10 PM.

Most businesses in Chicago are open 9 to 5 Monday through Saturday; many are open Sunday, too, but often with shorter hours (for example, noon to 4 or 5).

▌MONEY

Costs in Chicago are quite reasonable compared to other large cities such as San Francisco and New York. Restaurants, events, and parking costs are markedly higher in the Loop than in any other area of the city.

ATMs are plentiful. You can find them in banks, grocery stores, and hotels, as well as at some drug stores, gas stations, and convenience stores.

Prices throughout this guide are given for adults. Substantially reduced fees are almost always available for children, students, and senior citizens.

CREDIT CARDS

Throughout this guide, the following abbreviations are used: **AE**, American Express; **D**, Discover; **DC**, Diners Club; **MC**, MasterCard; and **V**, Visa.

It's a good idea to inform your credit-card company before you travel, especially if you're going abroad and don't travel internationally very often. Otherwise, the credit-card company might put a hold on your card owing to unusual activity—not a good thing halfway through your trip. Record all your credit-card numbers—as well as the phone numbers to call if your cards are lost or stolen—in a safe place, so you're prepared should something go wrong. Both MasterCard and Visa have general numbers you can call (collect if you're abroad) if your card is lost, but you're better off calling the number of your issuing bank, since MasterCard and Visa usually just transfer you to your bank; your bank's number is usually printed on your card.

Reporting Lost Cards American Express (☎800/528–4800 in the U.S. or 336/393–1111 collect from abroad ⊕www.american-express.com). **Diners Club** (☎800/234–6377 in the U.S. or 303/799–1504 collect from abroad ⊕www.dinersclub.com). **Discover** (☎800/347–2683 in the U.S. or 801/902–3100 collect from abroad ⊕www.discovercard.com). **MasterCard** (☎800/627–8372 in the U.S. or 636/722–7111 collect from abroad ⊕www.mastercard.com). **Visa** (☎800/847–2911 in the U.S. or 410/581–9994 collect from abroad ⊕www.visa.com).

TRAVELER'S CHECKS & CARDS

Some consider this the currency of the cave man, and it's true that fewer establishments accept traveler's checks these days. Nevertheless, they're a cheap and secure way to carry extra money, particularly on trips to urban areas. Both Citibank (under the Visa brand) and American Express issue traveler's checks in the United States, but Amex is better known and more widely accepted; you can also avoid hefty surcharges by cashing Amex checks at Amex offices. Whatever you do, keep track of all the serial numbers in case the checks are lost or stolen.

American Express now offers a stored-value card called a Travelers Cheque Card, which you can use wherever American Express credit cards are accepted, including ATMs. The card can carry a minimum of $300 and a maximum of $2,700, and it's a very safe way to carry your funds. Although you can get replacement funds in 24 hours if your card is lost or stolen, it doesn't really strike us as a very good deal. In addition to a high initial cost ($14.95 to set up the card, plus $5 each time you "reload"), you still have to pay a 2% fee for each purchase in a foreign currency (similar to that of any credit card). Further, each time you use the card in an ATM you pay a transaction fee of $2.50 on top of the 2% transaction fee for the conversion—add it all up and it can be considerably more than you would pay when simply using your own ATM card. Regular traveler's checks are just as secure and cost less.

Contacts American Express (☎888/412–6945 in the U.S., 801/945–9450 collect outside of the U.S. to add value or speak to customer service ⊕www.americanexpress.com).

▌ RESTROOMS

Facilities are readily available in tourist areas and throughout the downtown malls, Navy Pier, North Pier, and in many larger department stores. For the most part, restrooms are quite clean. Along the lakefront and in the park districts, public facilities close in wintertime. Most gas stations have restrooms, though sanitation standards vary.

Find a Loo The Bathroom Diaries (⊕www. thebathroomdiaries.com) is flush with unsanitized info on restrooms the world over—each one located, reviewed, and rated.

▌ SAFETY

The most common crimes in public places are pickpocketing, purse snatching, jewelry theft, and gambling scams. Men: keep your wallet in a front coat or pants pocket. Women: close your purse securely and keep it close to you. Also beware of someone jostling you and of loud arguments; these could be ploys to distract your attention while another person grabs your wallet. Leave unnecessary credit cards at home and hide valuables and jewelry from view.

Although crime on CTA buses and trains has declined, several precautions can reduce the chance of your becoming a victim: look alert and purposeful; know your route ahead of time; have your fare ready before boarding; and keep an eye on your purse or packages during the ride. Avoid taking public transit late at night.

▌TIP➔ **Distribute your cash, credit cards, I.D.s, and other valuables between a deep front pocket, an inside jacket or vest pocket, and a hidden money pouch. Don't reach for the money pouch once you're in public.**

▌ TAXES

At restaurants, you'll pay approximately 10% meal tax (thanks to special taxing initiatives, some parts of town are higher than others).

The hotel tax in Chicago is 15.39%, and slightly less in suburban hotels.

FOR INTERNATIONAL TRAVELERS

CURRENCY

The dollar is the basic unit of U.S. currency. It has 100 cents. Coins are the penny (1¢); the nickel (5¢), dime (10¢), quarter (25¢), half-dollar (50¢), and the very rare golden $1 coin and even rarer silver $1. Bills are denominated $1, $5, $10, $20, $50, and $100, all mostly green and identical in size; designs and background tints vary. You may come across a $2 bill, but the chances are slim.

CUSTOMS

Information **U.S. Customs and Border Protection** (⊕www.cbp.gov).

DRIVING

Driving in the United States is on the right. Speed limits are posted in miles per hour (usually between 55 mph and 70 mph). Watch for lower limits in small towns and on back roads (usually 30 mph to 40 mph). Most states require front-seat passengers to wear seat belts; many states require children to sit in the back seat and to wear seat belts. In major cities rush hour is between 7 and 10 AM; afternoon rush hour is between 4 and 7 PM. To encourage carpooling, some freeways have special lanes, ordinarily marked with a diamond, for high-occupancy vehicles (HOV)—cars carrying two people or more.

Gas stations are plentiful. Most stay open late (24 hours along major highways and in big cities) except in rural areas, where Sunday hours are limited and where you may drive for long stretches without a refueling opportunity. Along larger highways, roadside stops with restrooms, fast-food restaurants, and sundries stores are well spaced. State police and tow trucks patrol major highways. If your car breaks down on an interstate, pull onto the shoulder and wait for help.

ELECTRICITY

The U.S. standard is AC, 110 volts/60 cycles. Plugs have two flat pins set parallel to each other.

EMBASSIES

Contacts **Australia** (☏202/797–3000 ⊕www.austemb.org). **Canada** (☏202/682–1740 ⊕www.canadianembassy.org). **United Kingdom** (☏202/588–7800 ⊕www.britainusa.com).

EMERGENCIES

For police, fire, or ambulance, dial 911 (0 in rural areas).

HOLIDAYS

New Year's Day (Jan. 1); Martin Luther King Day (3rd Mon. in Jan.); Presidents' Day (3rd Mon. in Feb.); Memorial Day (last Mon. in May); Independence Day (July 4); Labor Day (1st Mon. in Sept.); Columbus Day (2nd Mon. in Oct.); Thanksgiving Day (4th Thurs. in Nov.); Christmas Eve and Christmas Day (Dec. 24 and 25); and New Year's Eve (Dec. 31).

MAIL

You can buy stamps and aerograms and send letters and parcels in post offices. Stamp-dispensing machines can occasionally be found in airports, bus and train stations, office buildings, drugstores, and convenience stores. U.S. mail boxes are stout, dark blue steel bins; pickup schedules are posted inside the bin (pull down the handle to see them). Parcels weighing more than a pound must be mailed at a post office or at a private mailing center.

Within the United States a first-class letter weighing 1 ounce or less costs 41¢; each additional ounce costs 17¢. Postcards cost 26¢. Postcards or 1-ounce airmail letters to most countries costs 90¢; postcards or 1-ounce letters to Canada or Mexico cost 69¢.

To receive mail on the road, have it sent c/o General Delivery at your destination's main post office (use the correct five-digit ZIP code). You must pick up mail in person within 30 days, with a driver's license or passport for identification.

Contacts **DHL** (☏800/225–5345 ⊕www.dhl.com). **Federal Express** (☏800/463–

3339 ⊕www.fedex.com). **Mail Boxes, Etc./ The UPS Store** (☎800/789-4623 ⊕www. mbe.com). **United States Postal Service** (⊕www.usps.com).

PASSPORTS & VISAS

Visitor visas aren't necessary for citizens of Australia, Canada, the United Kingdom, or most citizens of European Union countries coming for tourism and staying for fewer than 90 days. If you require a visa, the cost is $100, and waiting time can be substantial, depending on where you live. Apply for a visa at the U.S. consulate in your place of residence; also check the U.S. State Department's special Visa Web site.

Visa Information **Destination USA** (⊕www.unitedstatesvisas.gov).

PHONES

Chicago has six local area codes: 312 covers the downtown vicinity; 773 blankets the surrounding city neighborhoods. In the near west and south suburbs of Cook and Will counties, 708 fits the bill. The vast expanse of northern and northwestern suburbs in Cook, Lake, and Kane counties get the 847 area code, while the suburbs due west of the city have 630 before their phone numbers. Far outlying areas northwest and south of Chicago in McHenry, Will, and Kendall counties are outfitted with the prefix 815.

Numbers consist of a three-digit area code and a seven-digit local number. Within many local calling areas you dial only the seven digits; in others you dial "1" first and all 10 digits—just as you would for calls between area-code regions. The same is true for calls to numbers prefixed by "800," "888," "866," and "877"—all toll free. For calls to numbers prefixed by "900" you must pay—usually dearly.

For international calls, dial "011" followed by the country code and the local number. For help, dial "0" and ask for an overseas operator. Most phone books list country codes and U.S. area codes. The country code for Australia is 61, for New Zealand 64, for the United Kingdom 44. Calling Canada is the same as calling within the United States, whose country code, by the way, is 1.

For operator assistance, dial "0." For directory assistance, call 555-1212 or occasionally 411 (free at many public phones). You can reverse long-distance charges by calling "collect"; dial "0" instead of "1" before the 10-digit number.

Instructions are generally posted on pay phones. Usually you insert coins in a slot (usually 25¢ to 50¢ for local calls) and wait for a steady tone before dialing. On long-distance calls the operator tells you how much to insert; prepaid phone cards, widely available in various denominations, can be used from any phone. Follow the directions to activate the card (there's usually an access number, then an activation code), then dial your number.

Cell Phones The United States has several GSM (Global System for Mobile Communications) networks, so multiband mobiles from most countries (except for Japan) work here. Unfortunately, it's almost impossible to buy a pay-as-you-go mobile SIM card in the U.S.—which allows you to avoid roaming charges—without also buying a phone. That said, cell phones with pay-as-you-go plans are available for well under $100. The cheapest ones with decent national coverage are the GoPhone from Cingular and Virgin Mobile, which only offers pay-as-you-go service.

Contacts **Cingular** (☎888/333-6651 ⊕www.cingular.com). **Virgin Mobile** (☎888/322-1122 ⊕www.virginmobileusa. com).

In Chicago a 9% state and county sales tax is added to all purchases except groceries, which have a 2% tax. Sales tax is already added into the initial price of prescription drugs.

▌ TIME

Chicago is in the central standard time zone. It's 1 hour behind New York, 2 hours ahead of Los Angeles, 6 hours behind London, and 16 hours behind Sydney.

▌ TIPPING

You should tip 15% for adequate service in restaurants and up to 20% if you feel you've been treated well. At higher-end restaurants, where there are more service personnel per table who must divide the tip, up these measures by a few percentage points. An especially helpful wine steward should be acknowledged with $2 or $3. It's not necessary to tip the maître d' unless you've been done a very special favor and you intend to visit again. Tip $1 per checked coat.

Taxi drivers, bartenders, and hairdressers expect about 15%. Bellhops and porters should get about $1 per bag; valet-parking attendants $1 or $2 (but only after they bring your car to you, not when they park it), and hotel maids about $1 to $2 per room per day of your stay. On package tours, conductors and drivers usually get about $2 to $3 per day from each group member. Concierges should get tips of $5 to $10 for special service.

TIPPING GUIDELINES FOR CHICAGO	
Bartender	$1 to $5 per round of drinks, depending on the number of drinks
Bellhop	$1 to $5 per bag, depending on the level of the hotel
Hotel Concierge	$5 or more, if he or she performs a service for you
Hotel Doorman	$1 to $2 if he helps you get a cab
Hotel Maid	1$ to $3 a day (either daily or at the end of your stay, in cash)
Hotel Room-Service Waiter	$1 to $2 per delivery, even if a service charge has been added
Porter at Airport or Train Station	$1 per bag
Skycap at Airport	$1 to $3 per bag checked
Taxi Driver	15% to 20%, but round up the fare to the next dollar amount
Tour Guide	10% of the cost of the tour
Valet-Parking Attendant	$1 to $2, but only when you get your car
Waiter	15% to 20%, with 20% being the norm at high-end restaurants; nothing additional if a service charge is added to the bill
Restaurant Employees	Restroom attendants in more expensive restaurants expect some small change or $1. Tip coat-check personnel at least $1 to $2 per item checked unless there is a fee, then nothing.

INDEX

ABOUT OUR WRITERS

Kelly Aiglon is a Chicago-based freelance writer who enjoys sleeping in hotels—even if they're just blocks from her home. The former editor of *Where Chicago Magazine*, she is a frequent contributor to *The Chicago Tribune*, *Midwest Living*, and *Modern Luxury Magazines*.

Jay Cheshes, a New York–based food and travel writer, tackled 46 cutting-edge courses (along with a pizza, hot dog, and Italian beef sandwich) over a three-day Fodor's eating excursion in the Windy City. When he's not recovering from a food coma, he writes for *Saveur* and the *New York Daily News*, among other publications.

Elaine Glusac, author of the dining chapter, is a pizza aficionado who writes about travel and food from an office near landmark Wrigley Field. Her work regularly appears in the *New York Times*, *Bon Appetit*, and *National Geographic Traveler*.

Wendy Kasper writes about Chicago's thriving entertainment, dining, fashion, and art scenes for *Chicago Tribune* publications *RedEye* and Metromix.com, as well as StyleChicago.com.

Roberta Sotonoff, a confessed travel junkie, writes to support her habit. Over 30 domestic and international newspapers, magazines, online sites, and guidebooks have published her work. One of her favorite destinations is her hometown, Chicago.

Perpetually in search of the newest, most exciting things Chicago has to offer, freelance writer **Judy Sutton Taylor** has spent the last 14 years scouring the shops and neighborhoods of her adopted hometown. A mother of twin toddlers, Judy is also the kids editor for *Time Out Chicago*.

Jessica Volpe is a Chicago-based freelance writer whose writing credits include *Chicago Tribune's* publication *RedEye* and Metromix.com.